VULGAR

FAVORS

WANTED BY THE FBI

UNLAWFUL FLIGHT TO AVOID PROSECUTION - MURDER

ANDREW PHILLIP CUNANAN

Alias: Andrew Phillip DeSilva

DESCRIPTION

Date of Birth: August 31, 1969; Place of Birth: San Diego, California;
Race: White; Sex: Male; Height: 5' 9"-5' 10"; Weight: 160 - 180 pounds;
Eyes: Brown; Hair: Dark Brown.

If you have any information concerning this person, please contact
the San Diego FBI
or
the San Diego Police Department

San Diego FBI (619)565-1255
FBI Toll Free Hotline 1-888-324-9800
San Diego Police Department (619)531-2000

ARMED AND EXTREMELY DANGEROUS

ADDITIONAL INFORMATION MAY BE FOUND ON THE FBI INTERNET PAGE:
http://www.fbi.gov

FBI Ten Most Wanted Fugitive: June,1997.   FBI/DOJ

VULGAR FAVORS

ANDREW CUNANAN,
GIANNI VERSACE, AND THE
LARGEST FAILED MANHUNT
IN U.S. HISTORY

Maureen Orth

DELACORTE PRESS

Published by
Delacorte Press
Random House, Inc.
1540 Broadway
New York, New York 10036

Library of Congress Cataloging in Publication Data
Orth, Maureen
    Vulgar favors : Andrew Cunanan, Gianni Versace, and the largest
failed manhunt in U.S. history / by Maureen Orth.
        p.   cm.
    ISBN 0-385-33286-6
    1. Cunanan, Andrew, 1969–1997. 2. Versace, Gianni. 3. Serial
murders—United States. 4. Serial murderers—United States.
5. Serial murder investigation—United States. 6. Gay men—
Crimes against—United States. 7. Fashion designers—Crimes
against—United States. I. Title.
HV6529.O77   1999
364.15′23′0973—dc21   98-54318
                                                                          CIP

Book design by Virginia Norey

Manufactured in the United States of America
Published simultaneously in Canada

March 1999

10   9   8   7   6   5   4   3   2

BVG

For Tim and for Luke and
for my mother, who told me
"Any damn fool can write a book."

Contents

Just look at the vulgar favors that give the crowds of the capital such delight. . . . Its amusements are insolent, obscene, clumsy and boorish. . . . You despise these lewd doings and yet you suffer them.

—from the Richard Strauss opera *Capriccio*

VULGAR
FAVORS

Prologue

THE PHONE RANG ABOUT ONE A.M., and my husband sleepily caught the receiver.

"Is Maureen Orth there? Is this Maureen Orth, the writer?" The male voice was insistent.

"Who's this?"

"I want to discuss the article." A pause, then a click.

"It sounds like him," my husband told me.

"Who?"

"The guy you're writing about."

"What? You mean Andrew Cunanan?"

"Weird," my husband said. Then he flopped over and went back to sleep. But by then I was wide awake.

About ten days later, hours after Gianni Versace, the famed fashion designer and gay icon, was murdered, the phone rang again a little after one A.M. I was already booked on a morning plane to Miami to report the breaking story of Versace's murder, because the number-one suspect was Andrew Cunanan. By then I had been reporting on Cunanan for nearly two months for *Vanity Fair* magazine—his favorite publication. I also had learned that he had met Versace several years earlier and that he was suspected of killing four other people, including his best friend and the only man he ever said he loved.

"Hello. Is Maureen Orth there?" My husband recognized the same gay male voice. "Who's calling?" But the person on the other end thought better of it. The long-distance background sound cut off abruptly. I will never know if I thereby lost the scoop of my life.

Under any other circumstances, appearing in *Vanity Fair* would have been Andrew Cunanan's dream come true. By then, however, in early July 1997, he was about to become the subject of one of the largest manhunts in FBI history. Thousands of people would be looking for him, yet nobody knew where he was.

Nine days later, Andrew Cunanan's body was found on what would become an infamous Miami Beach houseboat. Moreover, the aftermath of his crimes and his cruel and tragic journey through America would reverberate for months. What began in the media misleadingly as a "gay lover's quarrel," confined to a closed but "out" gay world, built as Cunanan's murders became more heinous and bold into a story that catapulted him to the forefront of the mainstream press—leading the evening news, on the cover of both *Time* and *Newsweek*. But before Andrew Cunanan killed Gianni Versace and gained worldwide notoriety, he had already traversed a gay parallel universe in America today—traveling from the seamy, drug-addled underbelly of the demimonde to the cultured and privileged world of the rich and the closeted.

Andrew fit in anywhere. He could discourse about art and architecture, and he was a walking encyclopedia of labels and status. As a kept boy, he got all the way to the Gritti Palace in Venice and a house on Cap-Ferrat. But then he fell in love with a hardworking young architect and—ostensibly because the rich older man who paid his way wouldn't give him the model Mercedes he wanted—he walked out of the pampered world to which he'd always aspired.

No matter how much Andrew Cunanan got, he always wanted more—more drugs, kinkier sex, better wine. Somehow he had come to believe that they were his due. And why not? He was always the life of the party, the smartest boy at the table. But at twenty-seven he was also a narcissistic nightmare of vainglorious self-absorption, a practiced pathological liar who created alternate realities for himself and was clever enough to pull off his deceptions. In the trusting or superficial circles in which he traveled, Andrew made himself indispensable. Lurking just beneath the charm, however, a sinister psychosis was brewing, aided by Andrew's habits of watching violent pornography and ingesting crystal meth, cocaine, and various other drugs so prevalent in some circles of gay life today—but not spoken of. "Anyone who has done crystal and been on a bad streak can look at this whole thing [and understand]," says Joe Sullivan, a former crystal meth user who knew Andrew in San Diego. "I cannot believe not one person has associated a crystal freakout with this."

As I reported Andrew Cunanan's story, it was up to me to try to unravel the lies and untangle the contradictions—he did not yield his secrets easily. He began life as a beautiful child of mixed Filipino and Italian heritage with an IQ of 147. But his parents had a desperately unhappy marriage, and they counted on their youngest child to save and validate them. Under tremendous pressure from them, the gifted little boy was never able to form a coherent adult personality. The more I learned about him, the sadder it was to see how drugs and illicit sex increasingly coarsened his instincts, how prostitution on many levels eventually left him lazy and unprepared. When the jig was up, he had no professional or moral resources to fall back on. He had been seduced himself by a greedy, callous, and pornographic world that proffered the superficial values of youth, beauty, and money as the maximum attainments of a happy life. In the end Andrew Cunanan, so witty and quick, the product of a fanatically Catholic mother and a just as fanatically materialistic father, gave in to his mean darkness and inflicted incalculable pain on others.

In following the skewed path of Andrew Cunanan, I became fascinated with the idea that I was not merely reporting about a warped young man and his bloody violence. I, too, was making an offbeat odyssey through end-of-the-century America, where new communities had formed in the last two decades, where political correctness in the melt-resistant melting pot paralyzed many aspects of law enforcement and the media, where money papered over a lot of lapses. Some things, of course, are eternal, such as the ability of powerful families to block exposition of the truth and to keep their secrets hidden.

Throughout my travels I found that gays as a cohesive group are in dynamic, alternating stages of political formation. Their ability to organize locally directly affects their influence with law enforcement. In San Francisco and New York, Andrew would have been hard put to hide. In South Beach, a mecca created for tourist escape, on the other hand, the large gay community demands little in the way of protection. In fact, it often appears that they are in complete denial about needing protection of any kind, including sexual.

Beyond South Beach, I found denial throughout the country of widespread drug use as well as of structures designed to foster such use, both in the gay community and on the part of law enforcement, which seems uncomfortable with the idea of broaching certain subjects for fear it will be perceived as harassing gays. If the FBI were more familiar with the gay world of South Florida, for example, Andrew Cunanan, a Top Ten Wanted criminal, would never have been able to live freely at the Normandy Plaza hotel for nearly two months or to leave a stolen red truck in a parking garage for weeks on end. As it was, a nationwide manhunt that cost millions yielded little result. Kevin Rickett, the intense young FBI agent in charge of the Minnesota Fugitive Task Force for the Bureau, which led the national investigation, told me, "There were not many successful moments of the investigation, because we never were really close to him. We never did catch up with him."

The story, which leapt from coast to coast, kept taking me into areas I could not have imagined at the onset. I had no idea of the profound affect the O. J. Simpson trial has had on local and state prosecutors, who now are extremely reluctant to charge suspected killers on less than airtight circumstantial evidence. "O.J.'s tainted everything," Paul Scrimshaw, Miami Beach's lead detective in the Versace investigation, told me. "Everybody's afraid; nobody wants to look bad. Every investigation is now tainted because of O.J. Barry Scheck should be drawn and quartered."

It was heartening by the end to see the FBI, at least on the national level, make a real effort to redress its previous weaknesses. Andrew Cunanan's evil crimes turned out to be a positive catalyst for putting new practices into effect and for helping foster cooperation among police agencies as well as between the police and the gay community. To this day, however, although there is a national mechanism to trace a missing car, there is none that can find a missing person.

Andrew Cunanan also fueled a tabloid era of saturation coverage of sensational crime stories that O.J. had revived. *Hard Copy* producer Santina Leuci says, "Cunanan had all the elements—sex, violence, a serial killer. And he's on the run, a whole police force looking for him, a whole country waiting for him to be caught." What happens when a story becomes the number-one story in America today? I was suddenly in the middle of the tidal wave. The tabloid media are the modern day equivalent of the circus sideshows of the early part of the century. We now have around-the-clock televised freaks we can all watch together every day and every night, and each year certain individuals are exalted to Exhibit Number One. Andrew Cunanan—"He's Gay! He's Sick! He Kills the Rich and Famous!"—occupied that space for a short while, only to be displaced by a princess.

I was amazed by how much and how fast money changes hands when a story such as this one explodes. A conventional print journalist is at a total disadvantage. A kind of frenzy takes hold in which the media coverage drives the police investigation and the political response, and anyone who wants to can participate through broadcast and print and the Internet with the grieving families at the funerals, with the beleaguered police, with the entire cast of characters. It's an all-day, all-night global soap opera. The overwhelmed families of victims are forced to feed the hungry beast. So are the cops and politicians.

I will never forget the day I was sitting in a mixed bar—one for both gays and lesbians—in the heart of the Castro district of San Francisco with a witty denizen, Doug Conaway, who directed my attention to a metal grille beside a bank building across the street. It was covered with dead bouquets, which had been placed there to commemorate Princess Diana's funeral. The bouquets, he said, were a way for the neighborhood to get in on the act. The neighborhood, it seemed, felt similarly proprietary toward Andrew.

"When I came home to hear that Versace had been shot and they think it's Cunanan, I thought, my God, he once lived in our neighborhood," Conaway confided. "If it weren't for Cunanan, we wouldn't have seen Diana at Versace's funeral, so someone from our neighborhood caused that. But then, when Cunanan's body was found, I was so disappointed. What am I supposed to go back to? Campaign finance reform?

"Thank God for Diana's death—it's been like a miniseries. Her death gave our street so much to do." He regarded me dryly, decided he was on a roll, and continued: "Now, if Elton John gets AIDS, and Liz Taylor goes to his bedside, and Liz Taylor has a stroke and she dies, and Michael Jackson goes to her funeral and his face falls off—it makes everyone feel the connection."

By the time I finished my reporting, I realized that I had been on a long, strange trip, from the United States Naval Academy at Annapolis to FBI headquarters in Washington, from the cornfields of the Midwest to the skyscrapers of Chicago, from Mr. S Leather in San Francisco to the San Francisco Opera. I walked the beaches of tony, closeted La Jolla and frolicked in the gay abandon of South Beach. I met important law-enforcement officials, crystal-meth dealers, homicide detectives, dungeon masters, and personal trainers. Some of my sources were in jail. I got to know police chiefs and $10,000-a-weekend male prostitutes—even the piano player in the whorehouse. Andrew Cunanan shook all of those worlds.

After he died, I tried to pick up the pieces.

PART

ONE

1

Mother

THE LAST REMAINS OF Andrew Cunanan have been interred behind a marble slab in a sunny mausoleum at the Holy Cross Cemetery in San Diego, paid for with money his mother received for doing an interview on Paramount television's *Hard Copy.* In order to keep the media out that day, the security was ironclad. Only one car, with a previously cleared license number, was allowed to approach the site. The FBI was on alert. By then it had been six weeks since the twenty-seven-year-old Cunanan had calmly walked up and shot Gianni Versace at point-blank range on the steps of the Italian fashion designer's Miami Beach mansion, touching off the largest failed manhunt in U.S. history.

Now, several days later, on August 29, 1997, two days before what would have been Andrew's twenty-eighth birthday, a Mass for the Souls is being offered in the cemetery chapel for all those put to rest during the previous week. On this occasion, neither the FBI nor the news media is anywhere in sight. Andrew's mother, MaryAnn Schillaci Cunanan, has invited to attend old friends and acquaintances who knew Andrew as a bright schoolboy, not as the psychotic "gay gigolo" of the headlines. About fifteen people show up, including Andrew's Filipino godfather, eighty-six-year-old Delfin Labao. None of his three siblings, who live at some distance and have already attended a family memorial, is here; nor is his father, who fled in disgrace to his native Philippines in

1988, leaving his family behind. Modesto "Pete" Cunanan has not been in the United States since.

MaryAnn has arrived early to light candles at the as yet uncarved tombstone commemorating her son. She chooses to believe—in the face of overwhelming evidence to the contrary—that the youngest of her four children was not a sexually sadistic spree killer. She refuses to believe that he killed five innocent people before turning a stolen .40 caliber weapon on himself. MaryAnn is obviously very fragile, by turns garrulous and stupefied, teetering on the brink of total emotional meltdown. Mainly, she seems to be all sweetness and light, but her mood can swing at any time.

She is wearing a yellow shirt of Andrew's and blue rayon printed pants. She goes up the aisle to a front-row pew, clutching a large plastic mug filled with ice water with which to wash down her medications. From her pocket she takes out printed mass cards in Andrew's honor and distributes them. On the front is a picture of either Jesus or Mary. On the back is written:

> *In memory of Andrew P. Cunanan,*
> *August 31, 1969–July 23, 1997.*
>
> *I'd like the memory of me*
> *to be a happy one . . .*
> *I'd like to leave an echo*
> *of happy times and laughing times*

Andrew Cunanan's name does not appear on the handwritten list posted at the back of the church to indicate the individuals for whom the Mass is being celebrated. Indeed, when the priest reads his name, he reads it as MaryAnn has submitted it to him: Andrew Cunanan Schillaci. The other worshipers, who have also lost loved ones, have no idea that one infamous soul is being prayed for here today.

By coincidence the Gospel, from St. Mark, is the story of the beheading of John the Baptist. "Now, nobody's going to cut off anybody's head," Monsignor Francis Pattison says calmly from the pulpit. Maybe he doesn't know that Andrew's third victim, Chicago real-estate magnate Lee Miglin, had his throat brutally slit with a garden bow saw. "And why do people do such things?" the priest asks. "Saying there is evil in the world, or the devil made me do it, is the biggest cop-out there is. You have to take responsibility for your actions." MaryAnn Cunanan stares straight ahead.

And why did Andrew kill those five people before killing himself on a boarded-up houseboat in Miami Beach? The FBI conducted more than a thousand interviews, but still the Bureau professes to know very little. Andrew's old schoolmates and the hundreds of people he interacted with in his short life appear perplexed. His mother believes that whatever happened, her son was set up and is now a saint in heaven.

MaryAnn's dark eyes burn as she hugs those who have come to the service. One well-dressed woman presses money into her palm. "Closure," whispers Sister Dolores, Andrew's old catechism teacher from Saint Rose of Lima Parish in nearby Chula Vista, when she comes up to MaryAnn. She urges her to think about other things and rest. "You need closure."

But there is too much pain for that.

2

Childhood

MARYANN CUNANAN GIVES AWAY whatever money she gets—to cab drivers, to the church, to whomever. On the dusty street where she lives alone in a small, run-down, one-bedroom bungalow in National City, far from her other three children, she has sunk several thousand dollars into landscaping a small plot next to her house as a memorial garden to Andrew.

Following Andrew's Mass for the Souls at Holy Cross, MaryAnn returns home and shows visitors the plot, which contains a few sad cacti and a wilted basil plant. Then she goes inside, puts her false teeth in her pocket, and begins chain-smoking and talking nonstop—demanding constant attention, changing her mind repeatedly about what she wants for lunch, telling one visitor to look for forks "in the drawer with the brooches."

It is one of the grotesqueries of the tabloid culture we live in that no matter what heinous crimes an individual commits, a temptation of the individual's family is to make money off the tragedy. And so it was with the Cunanans. Even MaryAnn. Dazed and confused, they were besieged to go public, wooed with bouquets and limousines by TV networks, hounded by tabloid reporters offering money, by producers ready to offer deals for putative books and TV movies, and by lawyers only too happy to act as their agents and to draft contracts signing over the family's exclusive "life rights." In this case those rights would be for stories of a son and a brother they no longer knew, the more sensational and sordid the better, from the media's standpoint.

Although they had no communication with Andrew for nearly a decade, Elena and Christopher Cunanan, Andrew's older sister and brother, had made a book deal and attempted to include their unpredictable mother in it. They will not speak for publication unless they are paid, and thus would not participate in this book. Shortly after Andrew's death, MaryAnn began traveling with a lawyer, who could monitor her remarks. Her daughter Gina alone refused to sell her memories.

MaryAnn's living room is furnished with four old wooden folding chairs, a worn metal desk chair, a sixties bamboo barrel chair with a faded pillow on it, a broken electric fan, and a new television set and tape deck. But the dominant feature is a shrine to Andrew, an altar on which she keeps a burning candle, family photos from happier times, cards people have sent her, pictures of saints, and a rosary blessed by the pope.

Despite being heavily medicated and having a tenuous hold on lucidity in conversations about her youngest child, MaryAnn has an alarming fierceness about her. And a defiance. She is Sicilian, she says, and proud to be "a peasant." She went on *Larry King Live* to describe Andrew as "beautiful, intelligent, handsome, bright . . . gifted . . . I just want to remember the good things." She has been under a psychiatrist's care for years and receives medical disability payments from the government. More than once since Andrew's death, she has attempted suicide. One minute she can be kind and accommodating, almost cloyingly so, the next she is snarling and bitter, giving a visitor the evil eye. Do you know what *mal occhio* means? I'm giving it to you right now." She contorts her face into a satanic mask. It's scary. Her son Christopher described it to the *San Diego Union-Tribune* by saying, "She is very vulnerable and emotionally frail. Mentally she's just not right."

MaryAnn Schillaci was the child of immigrants. Her parents had come to Ohio from Palermo in 1928 and she boasts that her father was in the Mob. She calls herself a "menopause baby," born late to her mother. Her father, she says, owned a barber shop and part of a bar. As a child she was doted on and overprotected, and she was happiest when her parents would put her up on a table to dance and perform. MaryAnn has come to believe that her parents' age at her birth contributed to her being born with a "defect" and a "dark side" that she has to struggle to control. Like many children of immigrants, she did not speak English until she went to school, but once she starts talking she has few natural brakes. "Am I talking too much?" she will ask. "Should I take a pill? My husband used to hit me to get me to stop. He said he couldn't think."

Today, her life is full of strangers—FBI agents, lawyers promising deals, TV bookers, and friends of "Andrew DeSilva," as Andrew called himself in local gay bars, which his mother sometimes visits. To all who will listen, MaryAnn Cunanan insists that her son was not responsible for the death of Gianni Versace. She declares that his murder spree was all a Mafia setup: "Andrew met Versace through S&M sex," she says. But then the details get vague.

In her grief, MaryAnn has become Andrew's protector and archivist. She has collected his clothes and his property and she gives his shirts away to people she likes. She excitedly declares that "Vanity Fair was Andrew's favorite magazine," then darts into her bedroom and emerges with the latest Vogue, a startling item given her surroundings. "I bought this because this is where Andrew purchased all his clothes from." She means that he wore designer labels. In a curious way she is proud of his notoriety and wonders who should play Andrew in the movie. She says she had hoped her son Christopher would, "but he can't act." She is also thinking of former Olympic diver Greg Louganis.

Asked when she first realized Andrew was gay, she snaps, "From the time he was born, stupid." A few minutes later she corrects herself, saying that she knew on his sixteenth birthday, by "the way he put on a pink sweater." In fact, his homosexuality could never be broached at home. MaryAnn seems to acknowledge this chasm when she says, "You can pray all you want and say all the rosaries you want, but they all have free will. Just wait until your son is sixteen. As soon as they can drive, they no longer belong to you."

For years, MaryAnn and her absent husband lived through their two youngest children, particularly Andrew, because they had "no emotional life together," according to a neighbor. MaryAnn says, "Andrew was my marriage counselor. We would take walks around the block together and he would explain things to me." Andrew became his parents' confidant. Despite the bleakness of the union, MaryAnn emphasizes she has never divorced her husband. After giving unflattering portraits of several people close to her—always excluding Andrew— MaryAnn begins to tire. She disappears into the bedroom and returns wearing white pantyhose and a *Sesame Street* T-shirt with the puppet characters Bert and Ernie on the front. She is carrying a Bert doll.

Her medication is making her sleepy. She closes her eyes, but not before revealing, "I'm a Scorpio. I have a dark side, which I try to overcome with the good. I have a bad and a good, and the good overcomes the bad—if I wear my glasses. Where are my glasses?" She impatiently searches for a pair of iridescent blue sunglasses, finds them, and pops them on. "If I wear my glasses, then I'm good, because nobody can see me."

Before her visitors go, MaryAnn wants snapshots taken. She imitates movie stars, posing with her hand on her hip, turning for a three-quarter view, throwing her head back over her shoulder. She demands, "Who am I? Don't you remember Silvana Mangano? Don't you remember Anna Magnani?" As she recalls these fifties and sixties Italian actresses, MaryAnn suddenly smolders with hostility. "I'm ugly but I'm the actress, *right?*" she implores. *"Right?"*

Then she announces that we must stand up, join hands with her in a circle, and sing along to "Everybody sing praise to the Lord, for He is wonderful." MaryAnn makes everyone swing their arms up and down and step into the middle of the circle and back. "You're not singing right," she growls impatiently, asserting her control. "You're moving your arms too fast!" With her cigarette clenched between her gums, MaryAnn dances in and out, in and out, and when she looks at a visitor her eyes are filled with hatred.

Andrew Phillip, the spoiled baby, was meant to fulfill the dreams of his mismatched parents. MaryAnn's own mother had died when Mary-Ann was nineteen, and the young girl moved to southern California to live with her older brother. She claims that his wife did not appreciate the affectionate hugs and kisses that the brother and sister, who had grown up in a warm, demonstrative family, bestowed on each other. She knew she was not really welcome. She worked as a telephone operator and waitressed at a bar in Long Beach, a sailor's town then, twenty-five miles southeast of Los Angeles. One night at the bar, in 1961, she looked up and her heart stopped. Pete Cunanan, eleven years older than her, had just swaggered in. "He was dressed in a white tuxedo, and I thought he looked like a Filipino Errol Flynn."

Pete Cunanan knew he had a way with the ladies, and he and Mary-Ann danced the night away. Pete was a career enlisted man who had joined the U.S. Navy "fresh off the banana boat" from his village of Baliuag, twenty-five miles from Manila, nearly a decade before. He had a booming voice and a knowing manner. He was a navy hospital corpsman and a striver, acutely aware of rank and gradations of status. To fortify his big dreams and limitless ambition, he was taking courses in financial management and later would go to school at night and eventually earn two master's degrees, in business administration and health finance. He was proud of his military record. Pete believed in spit and polish—he wanted to be a big shot.

Short and powerfully built, he had a pencil-thin mustache and, later, a nail two inches long on one pinky finger. There were rumors that he was descended from a fierce warrior tribe and that he had been a fearless guerrilla fighter in World War II. Fun-loving MaryAnn, with dark hair, large eyes, and a piercing laugh, would stuff socks in her bra to make herself more sexy to him. Although she was promised to someone back home, and sent money to Ohio every week for her wedding, she was instantly attracted to Pete.

MaryAnn was six months pregnant when she and Pete got married. Their first child, Christopher, was born in August 1961. Pete was soon transferred to the U.S. Naval Hospital in St. Albans, New York, where MaryAnn gave birth to blond, blue-eyed Elena in 1963. In 1966 the family moved to Newport, Rhode Island, and when the Vietnam War began heating up, Pete became part of the First Hospital Company, First Marine Division. The Fleet Marines, who hit the beaches from naval ships, counted on the hospital to tend to their wounded. Mary-

Ann stayed behind with the two babies, but even before Pete left, their marriage was awash in acrimony.

Pete had become convinced that his wife was unfaithful to him. Today, he flat-out declares that "she is the mother of four; I am the father of three." Andrew's godfather, Delfin Labao, who comes from Pete's town in the Philippines and is called Uncle Del by the Cunanan children, has known the couple from the beginning. He confirms Pete's belief that Elena is not his daughter. Pete soon adopted an attitude of total disgust toward his wife. "He abused her so much," says Labao. "It was a very sad marriage."

Pete Cunanan denies that he was ever physically abusive but Mary-Ann insists that he struck her and pulled her hair. Pete's strong belief in her infidelity fueled an anger that convinced him he had license to behave as he wished. MaryAnn, never very stable, eventually became fragile and dependent, yet at the same time passive-aggressive and manipulative. Money was a constant source of friction.

MaryAnn would spend freely, and she was not above withholding sex as a way to get things out of her husband. "I used sex to get him to buy me dining room furniture," she says. She indulged the kids with music lessons and toys. "She spent money like crazy," Pete says. "I had three bank accounts, but only one with my home address. If she thought I was hiding money, she'd sulk all day long." Her blithe attitude toward money, and Pete's notions of grandeur, were a dangerous combination, not only for the household bank account but also for the children to observe. Meanwhile, MaryAnn continued to get pregnant.

In 1967, while Pete was with the Fleet Marines, the couple's second daughter, Regina, was born. A few months before "Gina's" birth in October, the Cunanan's purchased their first house, for $12,500, in scruffy National City, San Diego's outlying shipyard town. Squeezed between two freeways, the community was a far cry from the palatial setting Andrew would later brag about coming from. By the time Andrew made his arrival two years later, Pete had been transferred to the Naval Hospital in San Diego.

———

Andrew's birth was not easy. Delfin Labao says that MaryAnn lost a lot of blood, and a few months later she suffered a postpartum depression so severe that she could not even comb her hair. She required hospitalization for three months and was unable to care for her baby. It was the first of several breakdowns. Pete says he tried to fill the breach, coping as best he could while caring for the infant, who almost never cried. The experience created an ineffable bond. "I raised that boy from the cradle," Pete Cunanan says. "I changed his diapers and fed him his bottles." Once, when Andrew was a baby, he burned his foot by stepping on a floor heater, but Pete scooped him up and kissed him and marveled that the child didn't cry. From birth Andrew was his father's clear favorite. To make ends meet with four young children and a wife disabled by mental illness, Pete took a second, part-time job as a lab technician.

Christopher and Elena, the two older children, were raised differently than Gina and Andrew. Their mother calls them "street kids." They were not given the advantages that Gina and Andrew got. To all of his siblings, it must have appeared that Andrew was the favorite one. His brother called him "the white sheep." While Christopher was left to shift more or less on his own, Elena, blond and beautiful, began to take dance lessons from a neighborhood lady known as "Granny Dancing," and dancing became a big part of her life. Gina, also attractive but more cerebral and tomboyish, did not compete with her older sister. She grew up secretive and private. Andrew, from the beginning, was the adored little prince.

When Andrew was three, Pete retired from the navy with a full pension after twenty years as a chief petty officer. His dream was to become a stockbroker. While working as a lab technician, he continued to pursue his studies in business administration and eventually earned a bachelor's degree in 1976 and a master's degree in business administration in 1977. "It was upward mobility from that point on!" Pete boasts. "Wherever there were rich people, that's where you would find me!"

When Andrew was four, MaryAnn considered using the money she had recently inherited from her father to start a new life without Pete. Instead, with Pete cosigning, she bought a bigger house just a few miles east, in Bonita, for $96,000. The three-bedroom California ranch, in a middle-class neighborhood with good schools nearby, was a big step up.

Bonita, meaning pretty in Spanish, was once the lemon capital of the world, a paradise of lemon groves and dairy farms. Its rock quarry provided stone for the fashionable Victorian Hotel Del Coronado in San Diego, whose guests would take the train and spend the day picnicking at the site of Bonita's Sweetwater Dam, once reputed to be the tallest in the world. In 1916 a flood broke one side of the dam after a prodigious rainstorm. The rains had supposedly been brought down by a professional cloud seeder, who became the inspiration for the Broadway play, *The Rainmaker.* By the time the Cunanans bought there in the early seventies, the lemon groves had disappeared and the dairy farms were on their way out. Bonita was still, however, a horsey, countrified retreat with a mild climate in a lush valley surrounded by canyons overlooking the Pacific. Cookie-cutter tract developments were just beginning to cover the hillsides when the Cunanans moved to 5777 Watercrest Drive, the last house on the block at the bottom of a hill, across the street from a little league baseball field.

The Cunanans' house was standard-issue California ranch, but on the road above Watercrest were some very expensive homes with stables, where it still felt like the country. Many people who lived in Bonita were well off, and most residents sent their kids to public school. Because Bonita was surrounded by lower-income areas such as Chula Vista, however, and because the Mexican border was only ten miles away, there seemed to be a strong sense of pecking order in play there. Andrew's parents were always careful to see that he had what the rich kids had.

Andrew was a handsome child with a precocious sparkle. When he was ready to enroll at Sunnyside Elementary, he was a comely combination of his parents, with skin that looked permanently tanned, thick dark eyebrows, and large hazel eyes. It was not immediately apparent that he was half Filipino, and in school he never said he was. He was extroverted and happy in Miss Bobbie Hatfield's kindergarten. Although his parents believed he was a genius, Miss Hatfield, who has taught for over thirty years, did not find him exceptional. But it was enough that his parents did.

Part of the family lore that Andrew's parents and siblings have told on television—apart from the fact that they considered themselves a normal and typical American middle-class family—is that Andrew had read the Bible by age seven and could memorize long passages of the encyclopedia. Reading, it seems, became his retreat early on. According to his father, Andrew would opt out of the flare-ups at home with a book. "Andrew had a way of defending himself. He'd put on a nice smile and walk away. He had this expression—'Gosh, Mom. Gosh, Dad.' He'd grab his encyclopedia, lie down on the bed, and read."

Pete dealt with the misery of his marriage by staying out late and not being home very much. In 1979, when Andrew was ten, he began a training program to be a stockbroker with Merrill Lynch—a cause of great pride to him, which he communicated in no uncertain terms to his family. "Hey, I could talk—a man who is a stockbroker with his social standing, his intelligence, and I'm not bad looking either." Pete was a strict disciplinarian, however, and everyone knew he was the boss. If the children were watching television, for example, and Pete came in, they would automatically vacate the room so that he could sit down and eat his dinner by himself on a small table in front of the set.

MaryAnn kept the house spotless per his orders—there were plastic runners on the carpets—and stayed home most of the time. She devoted herself to her kids, and when she was alone with them, things were often pretty happy if precarious: Too much pressure could trigger a breakdown. But the Cunanans did not socialize a lot and had little interaction with other people on the block. The neighbors considered MaryAnn nice but somewhat eccentric—with her hair pulled back in a tight bun, wearing layers of clothes even when it was hot, and apt to say the first thing that popped into her head in a childlike voice. She had trouble with her weight and would attempt various diet programs to reduce. Rarest of all in California, she did not drive the freeways but stayed on surface roads.

Most of the driving she did was to church and back. MaryAnn was a very religious Catholic who sent all of her children to Mass on Sundays as well as to catechism class. She hoped that someday Andrew would become a priest, another point of contention with his father. He did become an altar boy, and the trappings of the church, at least, seemed to exert a strong influence on him.

Given the almost perfect climate in Bonita, most kids lived outdoors year-round, riding bikes, playing kick the can, catching lizards in the nearby canyons, playing baseball. Not Andrew. He preferred to be indoors with his mother, reading the encyclopedia and watching TV. "He loved Audrey Hepburn and Katharine Hepburn," MaryAnn says. Another favorite of his was Robin Williams's TV sitcom *Mork and Mindy*. Andrew would recite Williams's manic dialogue by heart. Andrew's neighbor Scott Ulrich remembers once yelling for Andrew to come outside—they needed more kids for one of their games. Andrew came to the door, but his mother pulled him back. "You can't do that," she told him. "He was more of a loner," says Ulrich. Charlie Thompson, another neighbor, calls Andrew "the epitome of a mama's boy."

Andrew's relationship with his mother was complicated. Her personality was fragmented, and after having been used as a doormat by her husband for years, MaryAnn was both needy and smothering. She brags that when Andrew was a little boy they "were inseparable." Since Andrew's parents vied for his attention, MaryAnn's closeness to Andrew infuriated Pete Cunanan. "You cannot cling like that to your son," he says. "She suffocated him by his necktie. She clung to his belt loop. It was that kind of relationship—mothering in a different way."

Perhaps MaryAnn thought the other neighborhood kids were too rough, but by keeping Andrew apart and to herself, to dress up and dote on, she was helping create a personality who began to see himself as superior, which his father encouraged. "The one impression I got from Andrew back then is he *knew* something good would happen to him. He knew he would turn out better than his peers, than everyone around him," says Gary Bong, Andrew's junior-high classmate. "This sense of superiority was his defining characteristic."

Pete also lavished attention on Andrew. They had pet names for each other and baby-talked with each other even after Andrew was well into high school. Pete says they would refer to certain funny things as "coocoo or poopoo. He was more than a son to me. He was a friend.

We'd kick tires together. We'd loaf around. I'd say, 'Hey, kid, let's go for an ice-cream ride.' He learned very quick . . . of course the first thing I did with him is throw Amy Vanderbilt at him. I said, 'I want you to memorize every fuckin period and comma in there.' If you grow up in this society, you've got to give yourself a walking cane, to be a cut above the rest."

"Of all the children Pete has, he put so much attention towards Andrew, maybe because he thought Andrew was so good-looking. It was not healthy," says Delfin Labao. "His father spoiled Andrew, made him feel he's got to be somebody, and maybe that rang a bell in his uncertain mind that that was what life was all about." Pete was beginning his bumpy career as a stockbroker. After being so proud of his training by Merrill Lynch, he didn't stay there. He left after two years to work for Prudential Bache. He lasted there only thirteen months before being "terminated for compliance," meaning he was fired for breaking the rules. But no one would ever know that he was having problems from the way he treated his son.

On their ice-cream rides Pete would tutor Andrew on labels and image. "He knew I made some money. We'd stop by a store and I'd say, 'You want those Ballys, those Johnston and Murphy shoes, a Cerutti jacket? Hey, you like the blazer?' He'd say, 'Gee, Dad, look at this one!' "

At an early age Andrew dressed in suits and preppy clothes, much more formally than most children his age. He liked to be noticed. "He was always a loud kid, very boisterous," says Charlie Thompson. On the school bus, Andrew would speak in loud tones from the back so that the other kids would be forced to turn around and look at him. He was mimicking his father's bravado, but that didn't necessarily mean that he felt secure.

At Bonita Vista Junior High, which began with seventh grade and ended after ninth, Andrew became part of the MGM—mentally gifted minor—program. In order to qualify for the accelerated academic course, one's IQ had to be at least 132. In the third grade at Sunnyside, Andrew's IQ tested at 147.

Bonita, a sprawling hilltop structure with ten full basketball courts and three soccer and football fields, was socially very competitive. The elite of the school were divided into the "soshes," or the social kids, and the "smacks," the smart ones in the gifted program. Andrew was a smack, and a rather showy one. Pink and black were the big colors during Andrew's years there, 1981–83, and students voted on who was best dressed. Andrew, perhaps taking his father's and Amy Vanderbilt's admonitions altogether too seriously, was beginning to define himself by cultivating an image of wealth and breeding. While most kids wore jeans, Andrew set himself apart by dressing in pressed khakis and Izod shirts. He wore an argyle vest and Sperry topsiders and put dimes in his penny loafers. His aim was to portray himself as a sophisticated, eastern, boarding-school student in an area where most kids considered Colorado "back east."

By seventh grade Andrew had developed a line of patter and a penchant for telling stories based on what he had read, and embellished for effect. The disturbing grandiosity that would mark his personality had already begun to take hold. No one knew he was half Filipino, and he never befriended the other Filipino students. "He always wanted to be part of a richer crowd," says classmate Gary Bong. "Andrew said he owned a lot of stock in junior high," remembers Andreas Saucedo, now a stockbroker himself. "He said he owned Wrigley Chewing Gum and Coke. He was always saying, 'My father did this and I've got stock in this.' I thought to myself, God, *I* want stock!" The fact that Andrew's parents never showed up at school and that almost no one was ever invited to his house shielded him. He would even often wait outside his house if he was being picked up. He clearly did not want his myth to be shattered.

A lot of Andrew's classmates got a kick out of his ability to con them and to tell funny, colorful stories—he had picked up enough information from his reading to be able make himself stand out in a crowd. Girls especially found it easy to talk to Andrew, because he was interested in celebrity and fashion. But Kristen Simer notes, "Even back then he was a pathological liar. We didn't take him seriously." And to some he seemed bizarre—flamboyant and stuffy at the same time. "In those days preppy meant sissy," says Charlie Thompson. "People would whisper on the playground, 'He's a fag,' " says Lou "Jamie" Morris, who had known Andrew since first grade.

Andrew began to hang out with Peter Wilson, a pudgy only child who became his adoring sidekick. Together they memorized *The Official Preppy Handbook,* taking it more as the Bible than as satire. At Christmastime the two were driven to a local mall to shop, but they blew all their money on lunch in the Neiman Marcus shoppers' dining room—in Andrew's mind, the height of chic. Perhaps because MaryAnn was a good cook, Andrew, who later became a connoisseur of restaurants and a gourmet of sorts, showed an early interest in food as a manifestation of his snobbery. When Mrs. Wilson asked what she should serve for Peter's Halloween birthday party in the eighth grade, Andrew floored her by suggesting cracked crab. "I was thinking pizza," she said.

It was a costume party, and Andrew came as the Prince of Wales, dressed in a blue blazer with a crest and a silk ascot. He suggested to tall, pretty, blond Jennifer January, a friend from the MGM program, that she come as Princess Diana. The fact that Jennifer looked a great deal more like Diana than Andrew looked like Charles was of no matter—in Andrew's mind he was a prince. "He put on an air—'I'm royal.' And he was. He carried it off," says January. "I think he was looking for something a little better than what he came from."

Andrew called Jennifer's father, a retired navy pilot, to ask if he could take his daughter out to a lobster lunch. Her father refused. Not to be deterred, Andrew invited her to have the same lunch with him at school—clam chowder and lobster with rice and drawn butter from a nearby seafood restaurant. Jennifer was mortified that he offered this expensive spread to her in front of all the other kids, who were eating out of their brown bags. Worse still, Andrew's mother delivered the meal. When Jennifer asked Andrew how he had gotten his mother to bring such an elaborate lunch to school, he said, "I told her to buy it and that it had to be here right on time." Today January says, "I felt she was controlled by Andrew. There was never a question he ran the show."

Sometimes Andrew's instructions on what it took to become a worldly sophisticate grated on people's nerves. At Lou Morris's twelfth birthday party, Andrew complained that there was no Perrier to drink, only tap water, and he told the Morrises that the salad should be eaten *after* the meal. "That's the European way," he said. But, unlike his classmates, Andrew never reciprocated with parties of his own, and Morris, who knew Andrew from the fourth grade on, finally got fed up. He was sick of inviting Andrew to his house and never being invited back in return. Who was Andrew to put on airs? Morris was the one with the big house who was asked to the invitation-only Junior Assembly dances—not Andrew. "I always knew the family didn't have as much money as he let on," Morris recalls. "He would say he spent the summers in Europe. It was all lies."

Morris says he could see that Andrew's values were becoming distorted. "I stopped being friends because he'd be loud and obnoxious, and he became so materialistic and preppy. He put other people down." Lou was shocked when he and Andrew were in the school yard one day and Andrew pointed across the hillsides to the dramatic canyons overlooking the Pacific. On clear days you could see north to downtown San Diego and south to Mexico. "If someone were smart, they'd put condominiums up on all those hills," Andrew said. "You could make a lot of money." Lou was appalled. Those were the cherished open spaces they had grown up with, and every day developers were threatening to encroach. Why would anyone want to spoil such pristine beauty? (Since then Andrew's vision has come true: there are identical tract houses all over those canyons.)

Because Andrew was clever and upbeat in class, most of his teachers genuinely liked him. He was always very polite to older people. As for his pretensions, parents like Mrs. Wilson thought he'd get over them. Mrs. Jerelyn Johnson, Andrew's English teacher, viewed him as "very verbal and one of my better writers. He was very bright, among the brightest, and I get the best and the brightest." For one class project with Mrs. Johnson, Andrew, Peter Wilson, Jennifer January, and Jennifer's pal Kristen Simer acted out a passage from *The Great Gatsby*. Andrew, ironically, did not portray Jay Gatsby, the great aspirer; he played Nick Carraway, the narrator.

Religion was becoming an increasing source of conflict for Andrew. He was growing up under the tutelage of his mother in a strict Catholic household. The Gospel was not about Cerutti blazers and Bally loafers;

what was wrong and what was right were clearly defined. But Andrew was getting mixed messages. If he really was special and superior, perhaps the Commandments didn't apply to him. On the other hand, he was beginning to feel attractions for other boys, and those feelings had to be suppressed if they were sinful.

To his family, Andrew gave no hint of any such internal struggle; in fact, he made quite a good impression on a nun from his parish, Sister Dolores, who led Andrew's catechism class on a field trip to a Mexican orphanage just south of the border in Tecate. Unlike the rest of the kids, who were content to drink McDonald's orangeade on the way, Andrew took his own cream soda on the drive down; "He said cream soda was posh," Jennifer January remembers. But once there, he seemed to be deeply affected, spending a happy day with the children, giving them piggyback rides and playing soccer. "He had an awakening experience," Sister Dolores says. "He told his mother he had a calling from God; 'I want to become a missionary.' He got such a thrill helping little kids. He thanked me for letting him go. He was so grateful. His mother wanted to send him to Catholic schools—his father said no." Sister Dolores adds, "You move hundreds through for one hour every week. He stood out." On the other hand, she had no illusions about the Cunanan family. "Right from the beginning it was a dysfunctional family. Between the mother and the father, the kids were tossed back and forth. They didn't have any money. MaryAnn was one hundred percent Italian, and he was Filipino. It didn't take. Andrew picked up that to get ahead in this world you have to own things."

With anger constantly boiling beneath the surface, the tense situation at home was a trial for Andrew. Despite all the attention he was getting from both parents and their unspoken affirmation that he was the crown prince, he was being asked to shoulder an enormous burden; they expected him to justify their staying together, perform according to their expectations, and become either a priest or a rich socialite, though he was without the resources to do so. From early childhood on, there were several Andrews: the happy kid, the worshiped baby idol, the growing boy being drawn into an adult world that was filled with problems. What child wants to marriage counsel a clinging mother or calm down an abusive father? On the other hand, if he had authority over his parents, it would be easy to break the rules and go beyond the established bounds.

Still, there were so many secrets he felt he had to keep. They began with the apprehension he felt coming from a racially mixed family, which in the seventies, in that community, was not as readily accepted as it is today. His mother's embarrassing illness, his father's explosive, unpredictable temper and brutal treatment of his mother—in one way or another, the whole family suffered from the parents' sick dynamic. Various children have had to battle eating disorders and substance-abuse problems. More than one family member had threatened suicide.

Elizabeth Oglesby, a psychologist who later lived next door to Andrew in Berkeley and befriended him, believes that Andrew was a narcissist. "Narcissists look at people as objects they can consume or use. His parents were just there to serve, adore, or cater to him." It is not unusual, according to psychotherapists who have studied narcissism, that in unhappy families the mother may choose a son to lavish her attention on and may use him almost as an emotional stand-in for the husband who has rejected her.

The perils run deep for such children, according to Oglesby. While their loyalties are torn between their parents, they are taught that they are superior, little Prince Charmings. Yet they are not able to process such feelings of intimacy—which include elements of seduction whether there are sexual overtones or not—so they end up pushing down their confused feelings of guilt, fear, or anger in an effort to avert them. When feelings are repeatedly suppressed they end up not counting for much. What is left in their place is a certain coldness along with the idea that one's image is more important than having feelings at all. The explosion comes later, when the child is unable to get his way; then the image crumbles, and all the pent-up rage erupts.

A few months after Andrew's own bloody explosion, Pete Cunanan decides to return to the United States for the first time since 1988, when he "flew the coop," leaving his family feeling stunned and abandoned and selling their house out from under them. Pete has flown in from the Philippines to tape a Larry King interview. In emulation of King, known for wearing colorful suspenders, Pete is sporting suspenders with a Golden Gate Bridge design. His gray sport shirt with a tab collar looks expensive, and it covers the paunch that hangs over his belt. His dark eyes are alert but puffy, the latter intensified perhaps by jet lag. MaryAnn has accused him of embezzling more than $100,000 of clients' funds and fleeing from the law; his former boss claims he filed a complaint with the Securities and Exchange Commission about him. Pete maintains that he was never officially charged with anything, and that the statute of limitations has run out anyway.

Pete wants to snag a book-and-movie deal about Andrew. He has run the numbers, he says, and his movie would cost eleven and a half million dollars to make. He also has a "most optimistic" analysis of the film's gross, "$115 mil" and a "least likely . . . $34 mil." He is asking $500,000 for the rights. The title is *A Name to Be Remembered By*. "I will not agree to anything else. That was his dying wish." Pete insists that he was in communication with Andrew to the end, and that the few intimations about Andrew's story are just "a teeny whiff of what the whole pie is about. If I smell money, this is it. It's prestige on the line. It's power." However, he can have no contracts within U.S. jurisdiction. "America's laws don't breathe without creating liabilities."

Today Pete feels his life has turned around. He is living with his "Filipina wife—all the partner I could ever want." He spends his days scheming to find buried treasure—$55 billion in gold bullion that the Japanese supposedly left behind in the Philippines during World War II. Pete is a follower of Clare Prophet, leader of the Church Universal and Triumphant, a cult based in Montana and San Diego, whose followers took to underground survivalist shelters in the hills of Paradise Valley, Montana, in 1990 to prepare for doomsday. He calls her Mother Chiara.

If he could just sell his book and screenplay ideas, Pete emphasizes, he could "bring in the bulldozers and backhoes." He could find the treasure that has had conspiracy buffs and fortune seekers drooling for decades. "Then you've got the problem of how do you dispose of eighty metric tons of gold—I'd have to talk to the IMF," he says. "If you let go with eighty tons of gold, there'd be worldwide crisis. If you float so much gold, you'd ruin the world economy. I could make a deal with the United States government. We could go fifty-fifty on my share—will you take care of it? But I have conditions. I want you to take in twenty-four engineer trainees from the Philippines every year. That would be my deal with Congress—just like what the Rothschilds did during the revolutionary years. If it wasn't for the Jews and their gold, General Washington would have failed."

Now Pete is setting out to make a little gold of his own through his son's tragedy. His proposal in part reads:

> *The movie story would certainly negate most, if not all, of the perverted lies and misinformation and malicious invectives weighed {sic} waged against Andrew Cunanan and which had been notoriously fed to the American people and peoples the world over in order to mask the sordid cover-up of the errors, misjudgment and miscalculation of the corrupt ones in state and society. "Somebody got paid. That's life is {sic}." So, Andrew Cunanan was murdered.*
>
> *I had never known my son, Andrew, to be a homosexual. For a very definite purpose he was being made to act as such. Who was calling the shots?*
>
> *I'm Andrew's father. I had known all along what had been happening: Names, places, events and motivations, not to mention the modus operandi.*
>
> *. . . Please indicate your interest and/or counter offer . . . time is of the essence.*

Like MaryAnn, Pete is in denial about Andrew. MaryAnn does not believe that Andrew killed Versace, but admits that he probably killed the others. Pete believes Andrew was forced to kill Versace, but he will not acknowledge that Andrew killed anyone else. "I was teaching him to be a diplomat. If I lucked out digging gold, we wouldn't need any money. My dream was that Andrew would be a philanthropist and an

American on duty as counsel in the Philippines. With this kind of personality who was outgoing, young, ambitious, and nice-looking, articulate and intelligent, with money, educated. And"—Pete pauses—"he has a big daddy in Washington."

A big daddy in Washington?

"You put two million in his campaign fund, and all you ask for is a lousy counselor post, wouldn't he give you the choice? Hey, you got to work your way up there, through the corridors of power. Hey, the only problem is I didn't get the money."

Pete still blames MaryAnn for dashing his dreams. He is bitter and outraged that the rest of the family cut him out from having any say in Andrew's "estate," whatever that might be. "Twenty-seven years I put up with that nut. I was a simple guy in the navy. Every time I'd leave the house, she had somebody," he fumes.

"I didn't even have time to scratch my head and she would lie and lie and lie. She's a neurotic psychotic with a psychiatric record. All she did was eat, shit, fuck off, and sleep for twenty-seven years!" He avoids answering whether or not he beat her, but he is just warming up. "I was a good provider. Would you believe that I could take her to parties with my rich clientele? I couldn't take her along with me. She belonged to the gutter crowd. I fell in love with her until she loused it up. She made a cesspool out of our married life so she could wallow in it, so I gave it up."

Pete vehemently declares that Andrew was trapped in a vast conspiracy of evil, that he was not a homosexual, and that he was tricked into dope dealing for a high-powered syndicate of very rich, older men, whom he probably met while working several years for an advertising firm in San Francisco. (There is no record that Andrew ever worked for an advertising firm in San Francisco.) "He stumbled into something so big they had to kill him." He claims he has names, dates, and places that he will reveal once he gets paid for the book and movie rights. He says Andrew communicated with him regularly before he died. In fact, these unnamed people are so dangerous that it would be better to call his manuscript "a literary forgery." He warns, "If you don't, your life would be in danger." At one point he asks, "What was Andrew doing in and out of Russia six times in 1996?" (There is no record of Andrew ever traveling to Russia.)

He blames law enforcement for targeting his son, and talks openly about killing people himself, his violent temper suddenly surfacing. "Many times I felt like walking to San Diego and blasting the devil out of the guys—the FBI, the police. I would be committing suicide, but I would take some guys with me."

People have wondered whether Pete and Andrew could possibly have had an intimate relationship when Andrew was growing up. Pete is not upset by the question. He coolly takes a drag on his cigarette, and says no. He would rather talk about getting the movie made. He has a leading man all picked out—he'd like help in contacting "John Junior." He wants John F. Kennedy, Jr. to play Andrew.

"Their mannerisms are very very close, almost the same," he explains. "I watch John Junior very carefully. The guy has a lot of moxie in him—that dignity." Pete says he is "willing to spend twenty-four hours a day" to teach John Kennedy, willing also to "get a seasoned director. There's enough money there. It's all a matter of cutting the pie!"

3

Bishop's

"I'M GOING TO BISHOP'S! I'm going to Bishop's!" Andrew was ecstatic. He had been accepted to the most highly regarded private school in the area, the Bishop's School in exclusive La Jolla. He couldn't contain his excitement when talking to his classmates at Bonita Vista Junior High, some of whom actually bought the idea that he was a rich kid going off to a fancy school. But others, and certain parents, were surprised. "Going to Bishop's from Bonita is like going to Vassar from Podunksville," exclaimed the mother of one of Andrew's friends. "Those kids have catered graduation parties. Where was the money coming from?" Andrew's best friend, Peter Wilson, was also going to Bishop's, because Peter's parents felt that "Bonita was changing."

Tellingly, Andrew wrote in Kristen Simer's eighth-grade yearbook, "Remember when I used to always sit next to you on the bus last year and everybody thought I liked you? (How preposterous!) [*sic*]. Maybe some day you'll date Tom Selleck!" Andrew was already beginning to hint that he wasn't ever going to have a girlfriend.

The idea of going to Bishop's was Andrew and MaryAnn's more than Pete's. MaryAnn sent applications to several private schools, believing that Andrew should be exposed to the best. Bishop's tuition in those days climbed from $4,000 to $6,200 a year, and the few students receiving financial aid rarely got more than $1,500. For the Cunanans,

Bishop's would mean a considerable financial sacrifice. But once again Andrew was being singled out by his family as the special one, not to be denied.

He clearly had looked forward to Bishop's, "invisioning (*sic*) ivy covered walls, spacious classrooms and teachers the like of Mr. Chips and Miss Jean Brodie." Andrew wrote a handwritten letter of application that is both compelling and revealing. "I imagined it as the West Coast version of Groton, Deerfield and so on . . ." Really. Very few of Andrew's eighth-grade classmates from Bonita Vista Junior High in Chula Vista, California, would have ever heard of Groton and Deerfield "and so on."

Andrew's answers to a series of questions labeled "Student Personal Information" are particularly telling: "What household duties do you have at home?" "None," he said, citing frequent disruption by his family as the cause for "things which make it difficult for you to complete your school work." When asked what he did with "time to do just as you please," Andrew responded, "I am a fanatical reader. I also enjoy chess, clothes, Mercedes' and running." He listed his "special talents and abilities" as "dramatics, ability to learn foreign language." Among titles of books "read this year," he quoted not only *The Catcher in the Rye* and *The Scarlet Letter,* but also *The World According to Garp* and *The Hotel New Hampshire,* both of which have strong gay characters, as well as *Henry V, Part One.* When asked "Who usually helps you with your problems?" Andrew wrote, "The Heavenly Father."

All of Andrew's pent-up aspirations and desires, and his inherent conflicts with his emerging identity, came tumbling out in his response to, "If you could make one wish, what would it be?" "Success, a house overlooking the ocean, two Mercedes, four beutiful (*sic*) children, three beutiful (*sic*) dogs and a good relationship with God." Mercedes were a constant desire throughout his life, but even then a wife was not mentioned. Nonetheless, Andrew wanted it all.

The decision to go to Bishop's School altered Andrew's life profoundly. He entered an environment of achievement and luxury that might have inspired others to buckle down and learn how to fulfill some of their aspirations. But Andrew was used to being handed everything without having to earn it, so instead of being grateful he was secretly resentful. "In high school Andrew had a quick intelligence, openness, ambition, easy camaraderie, and a sort of Mediterranean lust for life. But they were vitiated by negative and potentially explosive subterranean veins of darkness," says a Bishop's faculty member. "One such vein was envy. Andrew secretly regretted his classmates' wealth and lifestyles, which were continually all around him."

Although Bishop's strove to be nurturing, it only intensified Andrew's underlying anger and already well-developed penchant for pretending to be someone he was not. Outwardly Andrew was flamboyant, exuberant; inwardly he was deeply insecure and worried about what people thought of him. Few of his new friends knew that he was half Filipino, and very few knew he had a brother or sisters. His family was never seen at school. Rather, he masked his anxieties with bluff and bravado, acting almost maniacally happy-go-lucky—a "real lampshade-on-the-head sort of guy," according to former classmate Sarah Colman Jordan. "Simplicity, Sincerity, Serenity"—the school motto—hardly described Andrew Cunanan. Today Andrew's mother blames the "wrong crowd" at Bishop's for his downfall.

Originally founded in 1909 by the Episcopal Church as a girls' boarding school, Bishop's is a historical landmark of Spanish mission-style buildings grouped around a quad and anchored by a bell tower, which students sometimes sneak into and climb for a sweeping view of the Pacific. The school sits on a prime parcel of land donated by a member of the Scripps family—one half of the Scripps Howard newspaper fortune. The Scripps Institute of Oceanography and the Salk Institute for Biological Studies are nearby in an area celebrated for its overwhelming beauty.

La Jolla (pronounced la hoya, Spanish for "the jewel"), the northernmost township of San Diego, is perched on flower-strewn palisades and lushly landscaped hillsides overlooking miles of dramatic coastline. Billing itself as a "seaside village" in the manner of the French Riviera, La Jolla has always been synonymous with affluence and scenic wonder: sun-dappled coves, white sand, and sea lions sunbathing next to tourists. Bronzed surfers put on shows in the waves, while visiting scholars from the nearby think tanks stroll by with their pants legs rolled up.

But La Jolla is far more insular and conservative than its Côte d'Azur counterparts. Until the 1950s, blacks were confined to two streets reserved for maids and chauffeurs. Jews were kept out by covenant until the seventies, and most wealthy gays remain closeted to this day. Andrew's class at Bishop's had a Republicans Against Welfare Club.

Privileged La Jolla natives have a certain ease both indoors and out that Andrew could never comfortably absorb or imitate. He was already too deeply concerned about his image and too dishonest ever to let his guard down—though he covered his fears well with outrageousness and constant emoting at high volume. Try as he might, however, he never did perfect the slightly smug insouciance of those to the ocean views born. These were the Reagan years, the go-go eighties, and excess was the height of style. Bishop's students—the girls in preppy plaid pleated skirts, the boys in blue blazers—did of course come from all over the region, but the vast majority were very different from Andrew.

Bishop's bends over backward to prove that it has students on scholarships and that the other students do not act like snobby rich kids. But sometimes the students can't help themselves. An acquaintance of Andrew's from the class above him explains that Bishop's kids were so eager to play down their elite status that they "almost" thought it was cool to be poor. "The fact that your family had fifty million dollars as opposed to one million—that wasn't really a big deal among people." Unless, of course, you were among the 99.5 percent of the general population then who didn't have one million, as Andrew's family certainly didn't. Pete Cunanan probably never made more than $50,000 a year. "From Andrew's perspective," admits his former classmate now, "perhaps there was a huge gulf the rest of us didn't see."

Once you're there, Bishop's is tolerant and liberal, in the nonpolitical sense, within its own cocoon. Andrew joined a school body that assumed that anyone who gained entry became "one of us"—possessed not only of brains, but also of a fifteen-going-on-thirty level of sophistication, replete with ski trips, sports cars, and holidays in Europe. In fact, Andrew was soon going to debutante balls, dining out in fine restaurants, and attending parties in classmates' drop-dead houses. The good life of materialism his father had taught him to covet was spread out in front of him every day, close enough to touch. Andrew yearned to belong to that charmed circle, and since he hadn't been born to it, he would just have to pretend he had. "He very much carried himself as coming from a very highly cultured family," says his former classmate Kim Burgart Weir. "Because he wasn't from La Jolla, it was easier not to know the truth, because all the families from La Jolla know each other."

At first Andrew made the forty-five-minute commute from Bonita in a carpool with an older girl, who drove, and three others. Immediately he began to show off, to entertain, to charm. With Andrew along, Sarah Colman Jordan remembers, the ride to and from school "went from being silent hell to being fun." Andrew would tell hilarious stories. "He was very interesting. He knew how to talk and how to listen. He was very good at taking what interested you and tailoring his stories to that." Girls who did not otherwise receive a lot of compliments received them from Andrew. They've never forgotten.

"I was an ugly duckling, and most boys are cruel at that age," says Burgart Weir. "Andrew was one of the few boys who was nice to me, who always had a compliment on my clothes or hair." Andrew often hung out with the girls on the quad to trade gossip about celebrities. "It was very *Clueless*," says his classmate Heidie Hamer, referring to the Alicia Silverstone movie about the posh of Beverly Hills High School.

In his freshman year Andrew became close to twins in his class, Matthew and Rachel Rifat, who were bright and well traveled. Andrew was impressed that their mother, Anne, was on the debutante committee. He spent many weekends with the Rifats at their house in the Mission Hills district of San Diego. Anne Rifat, who is soft-spoken and warm, sensed that Andrew came from an unstable family. "That's why I let him come here so much." Andrew would put on one of Anne's capes and twirl around in it, but he could sense immediately if she thought he was going too far. "He was intuitive," she recalls. "One look from me and he'd stop." In his carpool, Andrew began to make obvious cracks about where his desire lay—remarking on various boys and their "cute butts." At school, however, he was relatively quiet as he sized everything up, and he even let the Rifats meet his parents.

Of course, it was all very staged. When his mother rang the Rifat's doorbell, Andrew would run and throw open the door, saying "Ma-ma!"

and blowing kisses. MaryAnn Cunanan is fond of telling people that Andrew always assured her that he preferred her to the other kids' mothers, "those phony women," the society ladies of La Jolla. "You are real," she quotes him as saying. "They are not."

But nobody who knew Andrew believed that. "Andrew was not interested in sharing the limelight with anyone, and they [his parents] were not part of his world, really," says Anne Rifat. "He'd come into the kitchen and talk to me. He treated MaryAnn like a child. 'Little Mother' he would call her. He would get frustrated and very upset with her. I got the idea that he didn't particularly want her around. She was too ethnic for him; I got the sense he was a little bit ashamed of her."

To his father, Andrew was affectionate and loyal. Pete drove Andrew and Rachel, who was his date, to their first Bishop's Christmas formal. To keep up appearances, Pete steeped himself in debt, but Andrew and Rachel went to the dance in his Lincoln Town Car. And Pete always dressed very formally in front of the Rifats, wearing suits and silk shirts. He even gave Andrew a credit card, which Andrew promptly overspent.

Andrew and the Rifats quickly became enthralled with a beloved member of the faculty who was the head of the upper school, Dr. Otto Mower, a former Catholic priest from Lugano, Italy, who had left the priesthood and married. Erudite and genteel, Mower preached the Renaissance ideal. He taught art history and philosophical ethics in a spellbinding manner, and art history and architecture soon became Andrew's passions. He became a Mower acolyte, and once again the ex–altar boy, "who had a profound respect for the church," says Matt Rifat, fantasized about becoming a cleric—a worldly priest who smoked and drank, certainly not one who took vows of poverty and chastity. Andrew posed in the Bishop's chapel in mock prayer for Matthew Rifat's camera, and also as a drunken altar boy. Andrew viewed the priesthood as a way to live surrounded by art, in Rome, without having to work very hard.

Certain faculty found Andrew bright but not truly intellectual; he could snow people with his uncanny recall of detail and trivia, but skimmed a lot of surface rather than developing his powers of synthesis.

He was an avid reader of magazines, particularly magazines that gave glimpses into the chic world he wished to inhabit. Reading GQ one day, he came upon an article about men's clubs in England that got him thinking. Soon he and Matthew Rifat with Dr. Mower formed the Gentlemen's Club, an excuse to spread out the school's linen and silver in Mower's classroom for lunch on occasional Mondays, when the three would discuss the arts and philosophical issues. Rejecting the usual cafeteria fare, Andrew or Matthew would go to a nearby French deli and bakery for brioches and Brie to bring to these elegant repasts. There, Andrew could fantasize about a life where he would never have to get his hands soiled with the hoi polloi. Now he, too, had a club to belong to. The lunches ended with the boys' sophomore year, but Andrew showed up to pose for the Gentlemen's Club picture for the next two Bishop's yearbooks.

The twenties and thirties in France and England were favorite points of reference, particularly because Andrew thought of them as "gay eras." He loved to throw French phrases around, but he never bothered to learn to speak French, or any other foreign language, though he often claimed to speak several. He thrilled to *Victor Victoria,* the Julie Andrews gender-bending movie set in the Paris of the Roaring Twenties: "Poochie, I'm horny," he would greet Rachel Rifat in the school corridors, copping a line of the movie's dialogue. He adored equally *Chariots of Fire,* the Oscar-winning ode to the 1924 British Olympians. And so enthralled was Andrew by the PBS series *Brideshead Revisited,* based on Evelyn Waugh's novel recalling his louche days at Oxford in the twenties, that he pictured himself as Sebastian Flyte, the rich, handsome, affected, Catholic aristocrat. In emulation of Flyte, Andrew took to carrying a teddy bear he named Bully around Bishop's. He also loved to imitate the book's lisping aesthete, Anthony Blanche, quoting "The Wasteland": "I, Tiresias, have foresuffered all . . . Enacted on this same d-divan or b-bed, I who have sat by Thebes below the wall, And walked among the l-lowest of the dead . . ."

"Andrew's personality developed as a pastiche," says Rifat. It was any life but his own. Once again Andrew was exhibiting the traits of classic narcissism. "Narcissists get hung up on their image. In effect, they cannot distinguish between an image of who they imagine themselves to be and an image of who they really are," writes psychiatrist Dr. Alexander Lowen. "Narcissists do not function in terms of the actual self image because it is unacceptable to them."

In the early spring of his freshman year, Andrew threw a tantrum when he had to miss a class outing to see the opera *Carmen* because he was sick. To make him feel better, his father went out and bought him a brand-new sports car, a Nissan 300ZX Turbo. Although Andrew was only fourteen and couldn't drive, the car was his. His father later bragged, "It was the first one that came out in San Diego."

When Andrew told Rachel that he had got the car, he also confessed to her that he was gay. Rachel wrote in her diary, "I can't believe it. I'm blown away." Although he wasn't her boyfriend, she told Andrew she hoped he was kidding. He said he wasn't. Rachel asked him, "What does it feel like to kiss a girl?" Andrew said, "It's the same as if *you* were kissing a girl. It feels awful."

Except for his family, whom he managed to keep away from the many activities for parents at the school, Andrew eventually wanted everyone to think he was gay, and his behavior grew increasingly outrageous and flamboyant. "We thought, it can't be real—it's so out there," says his classmate Anne Murray. The Bishop's faculty not only tolerated Andrew's conduct but stressed the virtues of kindness and civility. Some faculty members later confided that he was the first openly gay person they had ever known.

Andrew quickly realized that playing the "flaming fag" got him the renown he was so desperate for. When anyone called him a sissy, Andrew would rejoin with lightning speed, "You want some?" His classmate Jonathan Miner recalls, "If people jabbed him about being gay, he always had a comeback. Ultimately it got him attention, so it didn't bother him." His classmates were divided. While many liked him, describing him as suave, generous, and genuinely concerned for people, certain other classmates found his behavior sad and pathetic. "Whatever he was looking for, he was getting it, and he just got progressively worse—louder and more exaggerated," recalls one. "You could hear him halfway down the hallway, and he was fun to be around, just the same way a train wreck or a streaker is fun to be around," says Matthew Rifat. "It's outrageous, it's a mess, and it's fun to watch."

Despite their cash-flow problems, Pete and MaryAnn mortgaged the house in Bonita and rented it in order to buy a $189,000 town house on Via Embeleso in Rancho Bernardo, a retirement community twenty-seven miles northeast of La Jolla. The four-bedroom split-level, which MaryAnn referred to as a mansion, had a combined living and dining room with a small galley kitchen. Andrew told the Rifats he was mortified that the kitchen floor was linoleum, not tile.

Pete practiced pistol shooting in the backyard, which was covered with cement. Andrew told friends that Pete's target practice was to keep his bona fides with the Filipino Mafia. The Rifats remember the house as having an almost "tomblike silence," because Andrew was usually buried in a book when he was at home. The house, barely furnished, had ostentatious white carpeting throughout. Andrew would explain that it was one of many houses the family owned. He let the Rifats know that the Cunanans were really very rich back in the Philippines.

Nothing indicates Andrew's status within the Cunanan family more than Pete's decision to give his youngest son the master bedroom in the new house. Pete figured Andrew needed more space, and Andrew promptly moved in. "I told him I'd have to come in to use the closet," Pete says. MaryAnn says that she slept in the maid's room and Pete slept on a couch. By this time Pete and MaryAnn were no longer sharing a bedroom or much else in their lives, except an interest in Andrew and, to a lesser extent, his sister Gina. Andrew told friends that he thought his brother and sisters were jealous of him, "because I can get what I want and they don't."

Andrew had stopped mentioning his hope of getting an appointment to Annapolis. Despite his intelligence, he chose not to compete for the upper reaches in his class standings. Rather than apply himself in order to ensure acceptance at a prestigious college, which he felt was his due but for which he would need to earn a scholarship, Andrew preferred to give the impression that he was above it all and was breezing through.

He didn't run for office or work on the school paper, but in the one sport in which he competed when he was a junior—cross-country running—he made the All Academic Team for scholars and athletes sponsored by the *San Diego Union-Tribune* newspaper. He made the team mainly because he had a 3.65 grade point average.

Andrew was more remembered for his stunts—for always being the first one to take his shirt off during running practice and at school dances. In the class standings he remained in the top twenty. Andrew received an A from Dr. Mower in his History of Art Advanced Placement course, easily remembering the factual details of individual paintings, but experiencing difficulties in comparative essays and interpretation of periods. He also received an A from Dr. Mower in Philosophical Ethics, proving that at least once in his life he was able to grasp moral principles. But they seemed to have fought a losing battle against his predominant weaknesses.

"Andrew desperately wanted the type of intelligence, insight, and judgment that Dr. Mower had, but he wanted it instantly," says Matthew Rifat. "He wanted to experience the arts, culture, important people. But his longing bypassed intelligence, insight, and judgment to become histrionic: Look at me, I'm flamboyant, I'm entertaining to be around—take me out to dinner. Andrew was extremely interesting to talk to and to observe—basically that was the role he played. He had no value apart from that. He didn't have common sense or business sense, so he couldn't get what he wanted."

In his last two years at Bishop's, Andrew broadened his range of friends, seeking out a more worldly crowd, a few of whom were called "the druggies." Drug and alcohol use were common among a certain set at Bishop's, and as soon as Andrew could drive he began staying out late and telling stories about cruising Balboa Park, a well-known gay hangout. He spoke of an older boyfriend named Antoine, who gave him presents. Nobody at Bishop's ever saw Antoine, though. Eric Simon says Andrew smoked pot and took ecstasy and psychedelic mushrooms. Others say he also snorted cocaine. Andrew loved to think of himself as moving among the glamorous but screwed-up "spoiled youth" personified by the drugged-out rich kids in Bret Easton Ellis's novel and subsequent movie, *Less Than Zero*. He liked the concept of "live fast die young." (Ellis's bisexual protagonist eventually destroys himself.)

"He was a master of cover-up stories for his family," says his classmate and close friend Stacy Lopez, one of the few people to whom he spoke openly about his family. He told her his mother was "a mess" and neurotic and barely mentioned his siblings, except to note their jealousy. Perhaps because of his parents' vaunted expectations and his Catholicism, Andrew could never bring himself to tell them what he made a point of telling the rest of the world: that he was gay. Instead, Andrew at sixteen "loved money" and boasted of "the men who take care of me" to Stacy. "I never thought he prostituted himself. I thought it was more men gave him gifts and stuff, which I used to tease him about all the time—'Ah, you got yourself another sugar daddy.' " He also told Stacy that he enjoyed being "the feminine one in the relationship."

The high point was a tight red leather suit that Andrew proudly showed off to Stacy, crowing, "Antoine bought it for me." Although there were some boys in his class who would later adopt a gay lifestyle, no one at Bishop's then would dare wear a tight red leather suit. To add to his reputation for outrageousness, and to introduce the element of danger, Andrew also began bringing a gun to school. He kept it in his car and showed it to several of his classmates, sometimes telling them his father gave him the gun for protection.

Andrew lied so often and so compartmentalized his life that no one could see his life as a continuum. Even the classmates who thought they had him figured out saw only a part of him. But they wouldn't have had to be very astute to pick up the underlying anger and envy that drove him. Disturbing signs were there. Andrew always wanted more. On his senior-class ski trip, he was accused of stealing money from a condo where a group of his friends was staying. He denied taking the money and nothing was ever proved, but people wondered.

As high school came to an end, everyone in his class was consumed with going to college. Curiously, Andrew said nothing. His college boards were a respectable 1,190, but not high enough to win scholarships to top schools. His grades had suffered in his senior year; he had a C− in both Shakespeare and Algebra 2. Nevertheless, he got a glowing recommendation from Bishop's: "Andrew is a true intellectual with a ready sense of humor and a concern for others. He relates very well to adults, discourses brilliantly about culture and history and is capable of profound thought. He is independent, occasionally self-indulgent and at times only interested in pursuing areas that truly interest him. A fascinating individual in every way, Andrew can't help but enliven a college campus! . . . All of us applaud his originality, his fascination with ideas and his imagination."

Applause aside, Andrew's father was so overextended at this point that Andrew must have begun to realize there would be no money for him to go away, so he evaded the subject of what his next step would be. "He was a master of vagueness," says Stacy Lopez. By his senior year, Andrew had also gotten coarse. He would go around saying that his "two favorite things" were sex and defecation. "There's nothing like a good crap." His gestures and his laugh became edgy. Matthew Rifat remembers being slapped on the back by Andrew in an ostensibly hale-fellow-well-met way, but the whack was so hard as to be jarring, and Andrew would grab Matthew's arm the same way.

Throughout high school Andrew was never reticent about the life-styles of the rich and famous he wished to experience, but he had no plan for how to get there. Because he was surrounded by success and wealth and had a great longing for the finer things, he tried to convey that he was already in the upper reaches. But since he wasn't willing to work, and he was frantic to be noticed—to the point of secret fury at times if he was not taken into account—his outsized behavior escalated, as if fueled by simmering anger.

"Anger powered him through his insecurity," says Matthew Rifat. "Andrew would erupt, basically—whether he was going to laugh, or arrive at a party in a red jumpsuit, it was Andrew *erupting* onto the scene."

When they were still young boys, Andrew and Matthew had a conversation about their goals in life. Andrew was clear that he wanted to be someone people would remember. "There was no specific goal in terms of 'I want to become president of the United States and people will remember me because of that.' It was more 'People will remember me because of my behavior rather than any achievement, because of my personality.' It was important for him to have a spot in the minds of people who impressed him."

When senior year ended, Andrew knew he was being left behind. He never again communicated with Dr. Mower. From then on, he was listed among the Bishop's "lost alumni," never submitting a forwarding address to the school's alumni newsletter. Interestingly, for the boy who tried so hard to belong, Andrew chose not to write anything to go next to his graduation picture in the Bishop's Class of 1987 Miradero Yearbook as all of his classmates did. Nevertheless, his classmates voted him "Most Likely to Be Remembered." Under his picture, Andrew even declined to reveal where he was born—National City was not a place he would rush to claim. Instead, grand as ever, Andrew quoted the powerful spendthrift mistress of Louis XV, Madame de Pompadour: *Après moi le déluge.*

4

Pete

THE SAME MONTH THAT Andrew graduated from Bishop's, Pete was fired from his stockbroker's job at Crowell, Weedon & Co., and the family began to slide deeper into debt. Andrew's sister Gina was enrolled at the University of California at San Diego. In September, Andrew followed her there and chose history as his major. Pete was suddenly faced with putting two children through college, but to hear him today, one would never guess that he had suffered serious financial setbacks at the time. "In the U.S. money and power and Wall Street mean upward mobility—hey, hey, that's the name of the game. I was making money and living a very very comfortable life," Pete says. "I gave seminars in a country club. Can you imagine me giving seminars in a country club? I paid $2,800 for dinner on my expense account—hey, you got to prime the pump. Big deal: You spend $3,000 and get orders for $30,000 in commissions."

Pete apparently let Andrew think that he was doing a lot better in business than he really was, and he continued to indulge him at every turn. "As Andrew got older, I was able to give him a lot of good things—except one thing: This marriage I was into was very unhappy," Pete says. Pete told Andrew that he should enroll at Georgetown University and become a diplomat and a philanthropist. As a result, Andrew acquired a strong sense of entitlement without any foundation to support it.

Andrew, always the con man at school, was himself being conned at home. "Pete always wore expensive suits, would buy expensive cars and expensive homes, and I think Andrew believed this was all for real," says Ronald Johnston, who worked with Pete at four different firms. "Andrew was led to believe by his father that he could attain anything he wanted to attain. And I know his father spoiled him rotten and gave him everything that he could possibly want."

The truth was that Pete was becoming increasingly desperate. Johnson continues, "He had very definitely a pattern of spending over his head—spending over his income capabilities. I think he was constantly trying to get out of debt." Nevertheless, when Johnston bought an expensive Alfa Romeo coupe, he recalls, "Pete had to go out two weeks later and buy one as well."

During the nine years Pete Cunanan worked as a licensed stockbroker, from 1979 to 1988, he was employed by six brokerage houses; he never stayed more than two years at any job. Some of the companies where he worked no longer exist, and the National Association of Securities Dealers guards the confidentiality of brokers' records prior to 1989 very strictly. There is no disclosable disciplinary action with the NASD on record, but Pete was let go more than once.

Although he began at the top of the line with Merrill Lynch, and was then recruited for Prudential Bache, by the time Andrew graduated, Pete was in the outer tier of brokerage houses. From the mid-eighties, in fact, he had been struggling to keep up. After one of his terminations—in 1987, for "lack of productivity"—Pete next landed a job at Trademark Investment Services, Inc., a small San Diego outfit that Johnston had founded with James Rattan. Johnston then sold his share to Rattan, so it was Rattan who later had to contend with clients' complaints that allegedly stemmed from Pete's previous work for other firms.

"He had been accused of taking clients' money," says Rattan, a former naval officer. "I don't know the exact amounts, but he had been doing this apparently for quite a long period of time. He had done it at several major securities firms."

Johnston, who had supervised Pete previously, says he was not aware of anything untoward. But Rattan and his secretary, through intercepting Pete's calls and mail, discovered numerous apparent misdeeds. "We started getting funny little phone calls. Usually people who are taken don't want to admit it," Rattan says. "After talking to these people, we'd find he'd taken them to the cleaners for five thousand to ten thousand dollars. He was stealing." The securities industry requires you to put authorized products on your sell list. He was selling unauthorized securities. One client was in her nineties.

Pete would allegedly sell nonexistent stock and take the money. Rattan says he reported Pete's actions to both the Securities and Exchange Commission and the National Association of Securities Dealers, but not all of the records can be verified. Records do show that Trademark reported to the NASD that Pete had taken $26,750 from one customer—$1,220 as a personal loan, which he was supposed to pay back from the sale of his property, and the remainder as an investment in a convenience store. But Rattan was never able to confront Pete directly to tell him he was fired—he had already stopped showing up at the office.

While Pete was at Trademark, he indulged in some of the same kind of ego enhancement that his son did. For example, he went by the title Pete Cunanan, M.D. "I asked him what the M.D. stands for, and he said Maintenance Director," says Lee Swift, who sat next to Pete for two years. According to Swift, Pete's reach vastly exceeded his grasp. He remembers Pete's last big deal—a half million dollar pay-telephone underwriting scheme that never panned out. "You know, he took the money, cashed the checks, and 'See you later!'"

MaryAnn later accused Pete in a lawsuit of embezzling over $100,000, which Pete laughs off by saying, "The securities business is the most regulated industry there is." Pete claims there are no court records of any wrongdoing on his part, adding, "She made it up." When pressed, he asks, "How could I be a failed broker? I was nominated in the 1986 California Who's Who among stockbrokers." Although such books are often published to draw investors, no such book can be found.

After the crash of October 19, 1987, working in the market became more difficult, and during the first half of 1988, with Andrew and Gina at UCSD, Pete was trying to put his pay-phone deal together. "He was going to be the underwriter. He didn't have the expertise to do it," says Swift. In the two-month period beginning in July 1988, Pete, realizing that Rattan was becoming suspicious, allegedly took his spoils from the deal and sold his Alfa Romeo and his heavily mortgaged houses in Bonita and Rancho Bernardo. Then he disappeared.

James Rattan told Lee Swift to call Pete's house to find out where he was. MaryAnn professed not to know. "Nobody knew where the hell he was," says Swift. "I think he left in a hurry. I think once he had that money in his pocket, he got the hell out of here."

Pete Cunanan fled to his native Philippines on a tourist visa.

The family had literally had their home sold out from under them. MaryAnn was reportedly left with seven hundred dollars, even though she had financed the down payment of $41,000 for the house in Bonita. In California, a community-property state, after twenty-seven years of marriage she was entitled to half of everything. All Pete left was his navy pension check—$650 a month. Today he remains unapologetic for abandoning the family the way he did, and bitter that MaryAnn used the money to live, insisting that it was supposed to be for Andrew's education. "She took it all."

The family tried to hide the shameful secret of Pete's departure, which precipitated a major downward spiral in MaryAnn's emotional health. She needed psychiatric help and made multiple suicide threats. Andrew and Gina dropped out of college. The family was set adrift. The experience was clearly shattering for Andrew, whose image of his dad as a powerful and reliable protector was smashed. "If Pete did not get into trouble financially, I think he could have stuck it out with his family," Andrew's godfather, Delfin Labao, says. "But he played a big stake and lost. He abandoned his family, and they were heartbroken."

Soon, however, Andrew followed his father to the Philippines, but he stayed only five days. His father says he spent most of the time "sweating in a motel room," since he was unused to the intense humidity of the tropics.

Pete at the time was planning to look for buried treasure, but Andrew wanted no part in his father's diminished life. Pete says Andrew had an airline ticket and $900 when he left the Philippines to return home. From then on, Andrew's stories about how rich the Cunanan family was in the Philippines, and how many sugar plantations they owned, became ever more fanciful. In Andrew's imagination, his father—an enlisted man who had once taken flying lessons but had not earned his pilot's license—now became a Filipino general who flew then dictator Ferdinand Marcos around. Even Andrew could fly.

"When Andrew saw the crude poverty in which his father was living," says one of his teachers from Bishop's, "a driving madness took over his mind."

5

Berkeley

WITH HIS FATHER GONE, Andrew found his tenuous moorings cut out from under him. Unused to fending for himself, he was bereft and increasingly unstable. By forcing so much concentration on status, Pete had nearly obliterated whatever genuine sense of himself Andrew may have had. But Andrew had one more ticket to ride before having to yield to the grim truth that he was broke, that his father was a con artist, that his mother was sick, and that he would have to work his way through school if he wanted a college education.

How unfair it must have all seemed to a spoiled teenager brimming with secret anger and self-pity. But once again Andrew found a way to sustain the pretense. He decided to accept the hospitality proffered by his rich and spacey debutante friend Liz Coté, who was about to be married and live in Berkeley, just across the bay from the most liberated gay community in America, the Castro district of San Francisco. Andrew would be able to live comfortably for nothing, and he would be on the cutting edge of gay life.

Through Lizzie, Andrew could also cozy up to the carefree affluence he so desperately wanted but could never attain by himself. Lizzie was used to having her way. She rode horses and drove a brand-new BMW; she was only too happy to take Andrew out to dinner, because he entertained her. Lizzie was the niece of Emmy and Raymond "Bud"

Coté, a prominent, wealthy couple from Rancho Santa Fe, an enclave of million-dollar-plus houses north of La Jolla. Set among palms and euca-lyptus groves, with Mercedes parked on winding driveways, Rancho Santa Fe was the place Andrew would later call home even though he had never lived there. (In March 1997, shortly before Andrew began his murder spree, Rancho Santa Fe gained its own notoriety as the site of the mass suicide of the cult members of Heaven's Gate.)

Andrew and Lizzie had first met through the Rifats—Lizzie had made her debut one year after Rachel, and Matthew had escorted her to her debutante ball. Lizzie did not attend school; she was a born-again Christian who was being reared as their daughter by the Cotés. Bud Coté, a car dealer and developer, and Emmy, an active socialite and arts patron, presided over a household where one observer said the two most important questions were, what did you eat for dinner last night, and what are you wearing.

Lizzie loved the idea of having a retinue. She and Andrew mixed with a young crowd once described as "fresh enough, if used." Fasci-nated with the ideas of sexual license, self-destruction, and drug abuse in a group of screwed-up, spoiled rich kids, Andrew was once again reminded of Bret Easton Ellis's novel *Less Than Zero,* whose protagonist is forced to pay off his drug dealers by moonlighting as a gay prostitute. Straitlaced though Lizzie was, she and her faithful sidekick Andrew constantly referenced the self-preoccupation and hollow materialism of the novel and the film based on it. To Andrew, who rapturously identi-fied with Ellis's fictional world, it was all terribly chic.

Lizzie lived in a big house with a dining room painted in red car enamel. Emmy favored red leather Chanel suits. With the Cotés, there-fore, Andrew was definitely in the pink, though without any political connotations. The Cotés' Rancho Santa Fe garden was the site of former president Jerry Ford's son Jack's wedding reception, which Bud de-scribed as "a wingding" and a "hell of a deal." Longtime Grand Old Party supporters, the Cotés threw a big bash for out-of-state delegates in 1996, when the Republican National Convention was in San Diego.

Among the Cotés' close friends from Rancho Santa Fe were a very rich, quiet couple named James and Marne DeSilva, prominent San Diego art collectors. The DeSilvas, who had collected for years and now lent their Lichtenstein, Warhol, and Johns to museums, had endowed the Stuart Collection of outdoor sculpture at the University of California at San Diego. (Stuart is James DeSilva's middle name.) As a student at UCSD, Andrew constantly passed Niki de Saint Phalle's "Sun God," a giant open-winged bird commissioned by the DeSilvas, which became the university's unofficial mascot. Emmy Coté was the founder and president of the Colleagues, a Stuart Collection support group, and Andrew, who was considered Lizzie's "poor friend," met the DeSilvas through the Cotés. Jim and Marne DeSilva thus became enshrined in Andrew's imagination as his inspiration. He eventually usurped their name and, without their knowledge, turned them into his proxy parents.

At first he used the DeSilva name just to book dinner reservations, believing that Andrew DeSilva would get a better table than Andrew Cunanan—a not uncommon Filipino name in California. Later, when Andrew moved back to San Diego, where no one in the gay community knew him as Cunanan, he would use DeSilva as his own last name. He borrowed other parts of the DeSilvas' life as well. Mrs. DeSilva once roomed with eighties rocker Deborah Harry at the Golden Door spa in Escondido, California, an incident that made an indelible impression on Andrew. For years afterward, he would brag in the bars in Hillcrest that "my mother spaaed with Debbie Harry" and that he himself dined with Debbie at least once a year.

While he was still at Bishop's, Andrew had taken boyish delight in assuming other identities, and he never got over it. When he arrived in Berkeley at the end of 1988, he would go out at night and try to get people to swallow that he was "Count Ashkenazy." He didn't really care whether they actually believed him or not, as long as they went along with the conceit. And while many found this charade harmless fun, psychologist Elizabeth Oglesby, who came to know Andrew well, as her next-door neighbor and house-sitter, didn't think it was funny at all.

"This whole conflict of 'Who am I?' He had no opportunity to form a cohesive ego, so the whole thing is image: Am I being projected? Accepted?" Oglesby concluded that Andrew's family dynamic worked against his ever forming a coherent internal structure. There was too much chaos, given his mother's illness and his father's volatility. Shame and image replaced security and identity. Ultimately, Oglesby says, "Andrew had this thing about humiliation and wanted to be something his family wasn't."

When Andrew met this new neighbor, he was very impressed. Elizabeth Oglesby had grown up in Asia, and her house in the steep and leafy Montclair section of the Oakland hills, near the Berkeley line, was filled with Asian antiques, which were later destroyed in a fire that swept the area in 1991. Andrew was delighted when she told him that she thought Eurasian people were beautiful. He told her that his father was a rich plantation owner in the Philippines and big in the Knights of Columbus, the Catholic fraternal order. "You know my middle name is Phillip as in Prince Philip." Oglesby was not fooled.

"He thought if he acted it, he would be it," she says of Andrew's many guises as a trust-fund baby. "I don't think he had a clue that anything was deeply wrong. I would say he was a borderline personality who goes in and out of psychosis. He wasn't reality-based. He didn't understand some of the most basic things in life: You go to school if you want to achieve in this world. You have to work. People with severe narcissistic character disorder think, If I am already that in my mind, therefore I am entitled to be that." Such a frame of reference might have worked had Andrew adopted a totally ironic stance, especially since he was so entertaining. But he wanted to be taken at face value.

"Andrew confided in me to a large extent," Oglesby continues. Although he didn't tell the truth about his family, he told her that he didn't get along with them and that he had basically rejected his parents. "He said his mother was 'mentally not there.' " Oglesby tried to comfort him over pieces of cake from his favorite bakery, Il Fornaio. "He wasn't a physically striking individual. Even at that time he seemed to be such a tragic person. There was this desperate person starving to get the slightest bit of approval, dying to have that smile of reinforcement. He was so animated, so hyper. I remember one night he was going on and on, and I must have been tired. When he saw me tuning out, he looked devastated. Rejection was a big thing to Andrew."

Interestingly, Oglesby did not consider Andrew brilliant, merely "very good with trivia. He was preoccupied with the accoutrements, the looks."

The reason Andrew lived next door was that Lizzie had decided to get married. She was not yet nineteen when she wed Philip Merrill, a computer writer in Berkeley, who had grown up in New York and was ten years older than her. They were supported mostly by her family, and once Lizzie bought the house in Montclair, Andrew became the permanent houseguest because Phil thought it wasn't a bad idea for Lizzie to have a friend or two her own age to amuse her. Andrew was more than willing to fill the role of obliging courtier and to live in beautiful surroundings rent-free. Phil and Lizzie bought and then remodeled three houses in Montclair and the Berkeley hills, which they then sold for a profit. All Andrew's food was paid for, and he was able to borrow their car whenever they didn't need it. He began living with Lizzie and Phil several months before their marriage at San Francisco City Hall in March 1989. He was their best man.

Andrew and Lizzie would buy $150 worth of magazines and spend an entire day going through foreign-language editions of *Architectural Digest* and debating the merits of different kinds of moldings and bathroom fixtures. If Andrew had time, he would usually try to fit in a daily sunbath. At night he would go out on his own or stay home and read. "Frankly, it was great if she had this guy who was harmless to have around and who would talk to her for hours about color tones and whether this dumb-looking Napoleon-era table clashed with the room, because they were doing a dumb neoclassical thing instead of a good neoclassical thing," says Philip Merrill. "I was just feeling like the wife watching football, to a certain extent: I guess I could get interested in this, but I'm not interested yet."

Andrew and Lizzie made dollhouses and subscribed to a dollhouse magazine. Lizzie was a miniaturist, and Andrew was fascinated with furnishings. His grandest creation was a ruined French château of the post–French Revolutionary era, complete with blackened windows.

Oglesby didn't think the friendship was very healthy. "Andrew had a real issue with boundaries. Frequently, he didn't know where he ended and the other person began. When he became close to someone, he became that person. It used to make my skin crawl. I didn't like to see them together." Andrew, she felt, was sickeningly servile while Lizzie prattled on, "impressed with her own family's success. They talked about '*the* social set of San Diego' over and over, what powerful movers and shakers her father and brother were. Liz could get any sum she wanted from Dad. That didn't happen for Andrew. While superficially he's getting the feeling of being among the elite, he couldn't support it in concrete terms."

On several occasions, for a few months at a time, Andrew got jobs as a temp in San Francisco, commuting to the city on the Bay Area Rapid Transit. Once, he worked in a big downtown bank and bragged that he was able to see some of Jim DeSilva's financial records. Andrew was not above smuggling out of the bank the financial documents of rich people who interested him. His working days were numbered, however. A few weeks after Lizzie and Phil were married, Lizzie announced that she wanted to have children. Their daughter was born in early 1990, and Andrew became at once the godfather, the full-time companion, and the sometime nanny. He and Phil evidently took to parenting a lot more naturally than Lizzie did.

"He had a gift for taking care of children," says Merrill. Phil and Lizzie, who were supercautious about whom they would leave their baby with, had no qualms about Andrew, who cared for the little girl frequently and gave her, her father says, "a naughty sense of humor." Andrew photographed the baby and made an elaborate album with a running narrative. When Phil and Lizzie had a second child, a boy, in 1992, Andrew took care of Grimmy for the two days Lizzie was in the hospital. In 1995, Andrew was asked to be the little boy's godfather.

Yet, for all his candor about his sexuality at Bishop's, and as close as he felt to Lizzie and her family, Andrew would never admit to Lizzie and Philip that he was gay. Just as he skirted the question with his own family, he also danced around it with them, declaring a possible bisexual preference, a profound respect for the church, and an occasional outrage at open homosexuality. "We walked around the Castro last night looking at fags," he'd tell Phil. His remarks got to the point of sometimes being politically incorrect, but if Phil said anything, Andrew would get "cocky and grand" and treat the whole subject cavalierly. But Andrew knew when to back off if he became too obnoxious, and as a result he was allowed to stay on with the family.

"Hey, listen to this," Phil said one day when he and Lizzie and Andrew were riding in the car together. He read them a passage from a pulp thriller, of two detectives discussing why the bad guy they are pursuing may have used a .40 caliber weapon. The idea of using an unconventional .40 caliber, the detectives conclude, was arrived at either because the killer was very stupid or because he was making a statement—leaving a .40 caliber calling card. "If I ever killed anybody," Andrew said casually, and perhaps prophetically, "I'd use a .40 caliber gun."

Guns fascinated Andrew. Although he rarely brought up his father to Phil and Lizzie, who knew the truth, when he did, he would be cryptically admiring of Pete's ability to handle guns. Andrew would transform Pete's target practice in the cement backyard in San Bernardo into Pete's role as a kind of dashing James Bond figure. A couple of times he let the pain flash through, however, by referring to his father, with a thin smile and a grimace, as an embezzler.

Phil concluded that a propensity toward violence lurked just beneath the surface in Andrew. "There was always something at least Zorro-esque, Errol Flynn–esque, in the sense that, while his manner was deliberately foppish and fey, there was an express willingness, he'd talk about, to allow things to become violent if they needed to."

From Andrew's reading of the Marquis de Sade or *The Scarlet Pimpernel,* for example, he would exhibit "off with their heads," noblesse-oblige attitudes, suggesting that having superior knowledge or status keeps one above the law. Even more chilling was Andrew's frequent use of violent expressions in his speech. Instead of repeating the common phrase "going ballistic," Andrew would often substitute "going on a five-state killing spree." He'd say, "If I found out I had AIDS, I'd be so mad I'd go on a five-state killing spree," or "This is outrageous enough to make me go on a five-state killing spree." Andrew's frequent use of this phrase to be humorous was disquieting to Phil, who later told the

FBI about it, after Andrew had actually committed murders in four states.

Phil always thought that Andrew had a dark side, a reservoir of pent-up anger that was better left unexplored. Andrew once claimed to Phil that his generation was obsessed with just two things: money and death.

6

Capriccio

WHILE ANDREW WAS DENYING his sexuality to Lizzie and Phil, he was energetically networking with other young gays around the Berkeley campus and keeping a journal of his nocturnal encounters in the crowded Castro bars in San Francisco. The Castro was like a liberated small town, populated mostly by gays and lesbians. Andrew could converse about current affairs, but he didn't seem much interested in the politically charged atmosphere—his upbringing of spoon-fed San Diego conservatism wouldn't have been embraced in the Castro. He concentrated on his social life.

While Andrew appeared very devil-may-care, he really wasn't. By the late eighties the Castro was reeling from the AIDS epidemic, and Andrew, like so many others, was filled with anxiety that he might contract the disease. Even as far back as the 1970s, 40 percent of the 1500 gay white males in the San Francisco area interviewed by two researchers from the Institute for Sex Research (later renamed the Kinsey Institute) said that they had each had more than five hundred sexual partners. By the time Andrew arrived, a great political battle was raging over whether or not the number of sexual partners one had was relevant to one's susceptibility to the disease. In the earliest days of AIDS, some gay leaders in San Francisco were reluctant even to publish scientific data showing that the disease could be spread by sexual transmission.

Later they continued to be sensitive about any suggestion that promiscuity was responsible for the plague ravishing their neighborhood. Andrew, however, apparently thought that numbers counted. He was having frequent, furtive sex and was feeling both scared and guilty. Elizabeth Oglesby found Andrew's journal after he had moved away. (Unfortunately, the diary was also destroyed in the 1991 Oakland fire.) "It was amazing, like the journal was his friend," she says. "He talked about being too promiscuous—his fear of AIDS and his fear of too many contacts. It was all about the men he met in the bars." In his journal, at least, Andrew could be candid and "unsophisticated."

In fact, he was so secretive about his sex life that many people thought he was asexual. Just as he suppressed and numbed his feelings, so he hid rejection. Never one to score easily, he affected nonchalance when people he liked were unresponsive to him. That didn't keep him from eyeing or trying—he was smitten, for a while, for instance, with a graduate student in Spanish whom he'd invite to the opera—but much of what he really felt remained hidden, even in a place where being up front was a way of life.

In Berkeley, among the evergreens and eucalyptus, between the early morning fog and the mild, sunny late-afternoon breezes, one can find pairs of every class, race, ideology, and gender preference in the world. For Andrew, there was an ample sense of choice and competition in gay interaction as well, which mirrored the vast spectrum of Berkeley itself.

For instance, Andrew, who hated to work out, did not have to cope with the rigorous cult of the body that is practiced in gay society almost everywhere. In Berkeley, Andrew cultivated a mussy professor look older than his years. Not even his closest friends knew how young he was—they all thought he was close to thirty. Every day he wore the same lime-green Ralph Lauren sweater and khakis and brown Cole-Haan shoes. He also wore glasses and carried a cane, perhaps remembering his father's earlier symbolic admonition that "You've got to carry a cane to be a step above the rest." He soon acquired a brainy group of fun-loving friends, but was very select in what he let be known about himself. "He hung around very intelligent, talented people, because he wanted these people to be responsible to him," says former Berkeley student Doug Stubblefield, who was his close friend in those days.

His hip new friends heard all about his father, the Filipino general. "Yeah, the General's calling me back to fly the Buddy Holly death planes," he would say. He was a pilot, he went on, and he was referring to rattletrap aircraft he named after the fifties rock legend who had died in a small-plane crash. His family in his stories was super-rich, but had lost much of its fortune when Marcos was overthrown; he told hilarious tales of Imelda Marcos.

Yet other friends barely heard him mention that he was half Filipino. Jerome Gentes, who met Andrew at Berkeley in the fall of 1989, says that even though "Filipino was the hot race on campus that year, Andrew wanted to be blond and blue-eyed." Gentes, who was twenty-five at the time and had lived with an older man, found Andrew a kindred spirit. They both joined a gay group sponsored by the Berkeley Student Union and open to the campus community. Andrew talked about going back to school, but he hadn't done well at UCSD, so he was probably not in a position to transfer, and going to a junior college would have been way beneath the image he had of himself.

Gentes liked Andrew, but he found that for all of Andrew's big talk, he pulled away sexually. An ex-Catholic himself, Gentes felt that Andrew was like a lot of young gay Catholics and former Catholics—he had a prudish streak that wouldn't allow him to explore his sexuality.

"Andrew talked a lot about how nasty he was—I really didn't believe it. When I became intimate with him, he was really withdrawn." He also often talked about pornography and "leather"—a neutral word for sadomasochistic sex. "It was shocking to the other guys in the group—so many hadn't explored it. I got the feeling Andrew had explored it but hadn't gone through it."

The most amazing thing Andrew told the group was that his father was gay and had a young boyfriend, whom Andrew resented. Andrew said his father had bought the boyfriend a better car than Andrew had. One day he announced that his father was in town, driving around in a Rolls-Royce, and that he was going to go shopping with him and the boyfriend. No one, of course, ever met the General.

"I would try to press him for details," Gentes says. "He made it sound so perverse—an Oedipal thing." But Andrew never said there had been anything sexual between him and his father, which left Gentes to wonder. "What he did say was that his father had stolen a boyfriend away from him." At the same time, Gentes realized that much of what Andrew said was lies. "I felt Andrew was searching for connection, for some point of reference." Over time, Gentes concluded that Andrew's father was not gay, but others completely accepted what Andrew told them about his father's preferences. As Gentes says, "He really was a bundle of contradictions."

Finally, Gentes realized that Andrew wasn't ready to be honest and he told him that if he couldn't be honest he didn't want to be his friend. Gentes began to distance himself from Andrew. Over the years, the rupture of friendships over the issue of truth would become a recurring theme for Andrew. People would go through a process of confusion followed by frustration, and finally begin to realize that he was simply not able to be forthright. Many didn't mind, because they considered him cheap entertainment. But others did mind, and they would back off or drop him altogether. Over and over, Andrew's inability to deal honestly caused him to lose the people he most cared about. He never had trouble making new acquaintances, however.

In those days Andrew never really had any money, but that didn't seem to deter him. "Andrew would leave the house with three dollars and thirty-five cents and come back with change left over after dining, et cetera. I believe he took the art of getting other people to pay for him to a level of real excellence," says Phil Merrill.

Andrew would normally wait for his friend Doug Stubblefield to give him a ride across the Oakland–San Francisco Bay Bridge. "He would go out and have one drink. And if he didn't go out, he would read *Vanity Fair* and books," says Stubblefield, who also bought him *W*. The two would take *W* to a café and read about the jet set. Andrew loved feeling part of that world, and with his facility for memorizing he knew dozens of the international set by name and castle.

Andrew brought Doug home once and told him that he was half owner of the house he was living in with Phil and Lizzie. To Doug, Andrew was a graduate of Choate, the elite Connecticut prep school, and later he had gone to Bennington and Yale. As proof, he proudly wore a Choate sweatshirt. "His story was always that his family had money, not that he had money." Doug also heard about Andrew's rich Filipino father, the landowner with sugar plantations, and Andrew confided to him that he was writing a novel about his experiences in the Philippines. He let Doug hear some of the material he was dictating into a tape recorder, and Stubblefield was impressed. "It was filled with subtle allusions and metaphors."

Doug found the stories Andrew told him very entertaining and didn't care whether or not they were true. He liked the fact that he got "the good stuff" and not the same old bar stories Andrew told everyone else. He appreciated that Andrew, with that manic voice and laugh, tried to be good and sincere about listening to others, "but he still required being the center of attention." Doug realized that Andrew had built up a shield no one could ever penetrate. "He'd turn around with one phrase, and get the laugh, and yet would never let you in." Andrew confided to Doug Stubblefield—as he had confided to Matthew Rifat when he was barely thirteen—that he was convinced that he would one day be famous. "He didn't know where he fit in but he knew he was exceptionally talented and had something to give, but didn't know what that would be, and that was frustrating for him. He knew he could be famous if he just got the right match."

In San Francisco, as at Bishop's, Andrew was once again pasting together an identity so that he would be instantly noticed in the bars and cafés he frequented. The fact that so many young people in the Castro, as in Hillcrest in San Diego, were from out of town and were just coming out, reinventing themselves along the way, helped Andrew get by with his tall tales. The city was thoroughly welcoming; the Gay Pride Parade featured every group from Dykes on Bikes to the Sisters of Perpetual Indulgence. Within that wide arc, says one of Andrew's friends, "he carried off the bon vivant. He didn't need to do what ordinary mortals do, and he was a man with a million masks. Everybody knew a different Andrew."

His favorite hangout was the Midnight Sun, a yuppie gay bar in the heart of the Castro filled with "employed eligibles," "prissy queens," and older men looking for pick-ups. A long bar extends along one wall, with colorful banners hanging over it at an angle. Throughout the spacious room, video screens are suspended over small high round tables that patrons lean against while watching everything from comic routines—which Andrew was very good at mimicking—to gay pornography. It was a perfect setup for Andrew to dart around and mingle in, and to begin his eventual career as a greeter and matchmaker.

At the Midnight Sun, Andrew and Doug hung out with a bright young redheaded attorney named Eli Gould, who represented clients in Silicon Valley. Eli would buy Andrew an Irish whiskey, which he'd nurse all night, and then Joe, the bartender, might give him another. The Midnight Sun was right across Eighteenth Street from Gould's favorite restaurant, Lupann's, where a brass plaque commemorates his place at the bar. From that bar Andrew could see everyone who walked into the Midnight Sun, and if he felt so inclined, he'd follow.

Eli Gould, whom Andrew greatly respected and admired, was the third of the Tres Amigos, along with Andrew and Doug Stubblefield. Gould was Jewish and dignified, and before long Andrew began telling people at the Midnight Sun that he, too, was Jewish. This process of changing his religion from Catholic to Jewish had begun in San Diego. At first, Andrew's letting people believe he was part Jewish was a tool of convenience, but it could also carry an ugly ethnic slur. One naval officer who knew Andrew during his first year at UCSD, in 1987–88, was witness to the transformation. Some nights Andrew would be so "on" when he hung out at the West Coast, a now defunct dance club in Hillcrest, that he would bellow, "I'm so loud I sound like I'm a New York Jew!" Within a short time he was actually claiming Jewish blood, complete with parents who lived on Fifth Avenue.

But the reference could still be disparaging. "What do you expect from a Jew?" Andrew asked on another occasion. The surprised naval officer asked, "Since when are you Jewish?" Andrew didn't answer.

The half-Jewish, half-Filipino claim was baffling, but Andrew actually got people to believe him. Steven Gomer, who is Jewish and works for a San Francisco brokerage house, met Andrew in the Midnight Sun shortly after arriving in San Francisco from New Jersey in 1990. At first, Andrew introduced Steven to just about everyone he knew. "He just seemed so gentlemanly, and the way he introduced other people and the way he knew everyone and everything was so gracious. He was just much more mature and refined than I was—more than any of my other friends at that point were."

To Steven, Andrew "mentioned his mother being like a Filipina/ Jewish kind of princess. Not a princess, specifically, but a real maven of the arts and a real pampered woman, who knew the finer things in life." Steven recalls asking, "Was her father Jewish? Was he Filipino? Then it was, like, 'It's much more complex than that, Steven.' He was extensively Filipino, but he knew everything about Judaism, and I couldn't see the tie." Steven never got an explanation. "These were just 'little lies,' " he says. "Was he a wonderful friend? Did he remember everything I ever confided in him, provide me with valuable advice, teach me a lot about social graces and academic fields of study?" The answer was a resounding yes. Andrew would tutor Steven from whatever "seven-hundred- or eight-hundred-page book he was reading." Steven, who already knew Eli Gould, says, "Eli, like me, comes from an upstanding Jewish family. If he considers Andrew to be a quality individual and someone worthy of being his best friend, that's good enough for me."

Andrew told Gomer, who grew up in the northern part of New Jersey, that he was from the southern part of the state and a graduate of Lawrenceville, the prestigious prep school, but had studied at Choate as well. When Gomer teased Andrew by saying that Choate had once had a cocaine problem, "he pretended to take offense, as if I were insulting him personally." But Andrew also set out to teach Gomer how to become a gentleman. "He was so much politer, more dignified, reserved than I am." Over Diet Cokes he would buy for Steven, Andrew explained "The Rules" to him. "He felt very strongly that only fools work. But he did so in a way that was sensitive to my status in life. There was really no reason why someone should need to work," Steven recalls Andrew saying, "work with your own hands or work an hourly ledger when you can find others to do the work for you. He was not alluding to being kept by others—more to the fact that a smart businessman doles out responsibilities and has others take the work for him, and he collects on the backs of the employees' efforts."

Perhaps the greatest thrill Andrew provided Steven was an introduction one night at the Midnight Sun to the elegant blade about town, Harry de Wildt, a ubiquitous socialite who was a staple of the late Herb

Caen's gossip column. The flamboyant, Dutch-born de Wildt, a sixtyish dandy, is married to a younger, big-boned Mellon Bank heiress. A luncheon crony of Mayor Willie Brown's, he lives in a grand apartment on Nob Hill and prides himself, as he puts it, on having a "natural curiosity, whether I go to dinner at the Gettys' or visit the gutter," which may account for why he has been seen both at board meetings of the San Francisco Opera and at the Stud, a dance club in the south of the Market Street area, where Doug Stubblefield and Andrew would often go after the Midnight Sun. de Wildt says he thinks nothing of getting up at 4 A.M. to visit a new place. "I lead a full life, I'm curious, I'm invited everywhere."

"Harry was almost always there, and there were always our snide comments," says Stubblefield. "We would share jokes about Harry de Wildt." Andrew set out to meet Harry and "become his best friend," and he did succeed in becoming friendly with him. Several times they went out clubbing in a group. Andrew would also visit the health club at the Fairmont Hotel, which Harry de Wildt frequented, reportedly prompting de Wildt to quip that a workout for Andrew meant sitting in the club sauna. For Andrew, de Wildt was definitely someone to cultivate.

Andrew had a "pure admiration for Harry de Wildt," says Philip Merrill, and "came home all excited after the first time he met him." Thereafter, Phil would hear Andrew speaking to de Wildt on the phone to make plans.

But Harry de Wildt categorically denies ever having met Andrew Cunanan: "I haven't had the pleasure or displeasure of meeting Mr. Cunanan. I have never met him. I have never known him." Though his denial is contradicted by at least a half-dozen eyewitnesses, de Wildt insists: "Listen, I have the body of an eighteen-year-old boy. I keep him in a hotel in the Tenderloin! That joke was told me by a married man with five children! Anyone can say anything!"

"When I saw in the papers that Harry de Wildt is denying ever having met Andrew—I mean, not only can I laugh at that, but it was an exciting moment for me," Steven Gomer says. "I smacked Andrew on the shoulder and said, 'Oh, my God, look over there, it's Harry de Wildt!' And he said, 'You've never met Harry de Wildt?' And I said 'no,' and he said, 'Want to meet him?' And I said, 'No, no, no! Stop! Don't, don't, don't.' And he said, 'No, he's a good friend of mine.' "

Andrew took Steven over, and Steven says he will never forget the moment: "Harry was surrounded by gods—these smooth, bronzed, hairless blondes, six foot plus, tightly clothed, Matinique- and Versace-laden Adonises, and Andrew introduces him to me, and I'm just thinking, What must be going through Harry's mind? You know, Who's this schmo you're bringing here to pay homage to me?" Harry de Wildt and Andrew, it seems, went back a long way.

One night in the fall of 1990, Steven Gomer was in the Midnight Sun late when Andrew walked in dressed in a tuxedo. Steven greeted him by saying, "Andrew, how many people come into a bar to get a Miller Lite dressed in their finest Italian suit?"

"Oh, I just saw *Capriccio* at the opera," Andrew answered, adding, "I was with Gianni Versace."

"Oh, I was using my entertainment coupons at buy-one-get-one at the local movie theater," Steven countered.

Andrew laughed.

For all its cosmopolitan savvy, San Francisco can become positively gushing when it comes to visiting celebrities. Gianni Versace had been invited to design the costumes for the San Francisco Opera's production of Richard Strauss's opera *Capriccio,* which opened on October 21, 1990. He and his boyfriend, Antonio D'Amico, arrived from Milan for the premiere, and San Francisco's gay community was all atwitter that Versace was in their midst. There were parties surrounding the opening. The Opera Guild threw an official fund-raiser at the Inn of the Opera, a motel near the Opera House, and there was a party backstage after the opening.

Versace, who had been openly gay for some time and one of the biggest gay personalities out at the time, would also have a chance to meet members of the local gay community informally. He would come to the weekly Saturday night dance at the Colossus, a cavernous gay disco on Folsom Street. When Val Caniparoli, a choreographer with the San Francisco Ballet, who was helping escort Versace around, gave passes to Colossus's VIP room to Eli Gould, and Gould invited Andrew to come along, Andrew was ecstatic. He told Eli and Doug that he had been in Italy several times and knew the country well. He told Eli that he had met Versace before. When it became known that their friend Val would be working with Versace, Andrew claimed that he already knew the designer; "I know him. I've met him before." Andrew, it turns out, had never been to Italy.

That night, Eli and Andrew entered the Colossus dance area and went to the VIP room to await Versace. The designer walked in with an entourage, including Antonio D'Amico and Val Caniparoli, who quickly introduced him to a few people. After about fifteen minutes of chitchat and waves of young men eager to meet him, Versace began to survey the room. He noticed Andrew standing with Eli, cocked his head, and walked in their direction. "I know you," he said to Andrew. "Lago di Como, no?" Versace was referring to the house he owned on Lake Como near the Swiss border. Reportedly he would often use the Lago di Como line when he wanted to strike up a conversation with someone.

Andrew was thrilled and Eli couldn't believe it. "That's right," Andrew answered. "Thank you for remembering, Signor Versace." Then Andrew introduced Eli to Versace, who made polite talk about whether they had seen the opera. (They hadn't.) Eli and Andrew then drifted back down to the dance floor.

Versace visited Colossus three times during his stay. Whether it was that night or on another occasion, Los Angeles lawyer Eric Gruenwald, who was also in the Colossus when Versace was there, remembers meeting Andrew as well. Gruenwald had grown up in La Jolla, so he and Andrew discussed their hometown. Gruenwald didn't believe that Andrew had all the credentials he claimed, and he never saw Andrew again, but for years afterward he would tell the story of what Andrew had said about meeting Versace. Andrew told Gruenwald, "He came up to me and said, 'Hi, I'm Gianni Versace.' I told him, 'If you're Gianni Versace, then I'm Coco Chanel!' "

During Versace's stay, Doug Stubblefield was walking on Market Street to another gay club when a big white chauffeured car pulled up alongside him. Inside Doug recognized Harry de Wildt, Versace, and

Andrew. To show off, Andrew had the car come to the curb, and Andrew and Doug had a conversation. "It was very Andrew to do that, have the car pull over," Stubblefield says.

The next morning, Phil and Lizzie were still in bed when Andrew came bounding into their bedroom. Flushed with excitement he started jumping up and down on the bed. "You won't believe who I just went clubbing with!" he exclaimed. "Gianni Versace, his boyfriend, and Harry de Wildt! I'm so excited!" Phil Merrill also remembers Andrew repeating the "If you're Gianni Versace, then I'm Coco Chanel" line.

"Basically," says Merrill, "there was this sense of 'I've finally met one of the people who's like a god to me.'" Artist Julian Schnabel and designer Karl Lagerfeld were also in that category, says Merrill, "but Julian Schnabel didn't get talked about as much."

Although Harry de Wildt admits having known Versace at the Spoleto Festival in Italy and having had lunch with him during his stay for *Capriccio,* he says, "I categorically deny Mr. Versace, Mr. Cunanan, and I were in the same car." Nevertheless, it became kind of a running joke between Eli Gould and Doug Stubblefield that they both observed Andrew with Versace, and from then on, whenever anyone doubted Andrew's veracity, they would both say, "Ah, but remember he really did know Versace!"

7

Hillcrest

By the summer of 1991, Lizzie and Phil had decided to move to Sacramento. Lizzie wanted to be between Lake Tahoe and the San Francisco Bay. She was also going to try her hand at real estate there, hoping to avoid a downturn that had infected the usually buoyant Bay Area housing market. Sacramento was no place for Andrew. The California capital gets extremely hot during the summer, and Sacramento has none of the cosmopolitan glamour of San Francisco.

So Andrew returned to Rancho Bernardo to live with his mother in a small, $750-a-month, two-bedroom apartment. It was in a white stucco complex with faux Spanish windows across a busy boulevard from a strip mall. The living room opened onto a balcony overlooking a golf course. Their apartment was on the upper of two levels, and neighbors were at close quarters. Andrew decided to reenroll at UCSD, where his sister Gina had recently graduated. Once again he picked history as his major.

Although Andrew excelled at art history, knowing not only when many of the old masters painted but at what time of day and where they had hung, he never studied much. He got a job as a clerk at the Thrifty Drug Store in the mall across the street, a job he held for three and a half years. His mother babysat for two families and was a faithful member of her local parish church, San Rafael, up the hill, just a few blocks away.

At home, Andrew portrayed himself to neighbors and people who knew his mother as a poverty-stricken student, unable to afford the education he really wanted. Neighbor Hal Melowitz recalls, "Andrew talked poor in Rancho Bernardo. His mother was overjoyed when he was able to obtain financial aid to go back to school." Melowitz, a psychiatric social worker, understood how delicate MaryAnn was and befriended her. He remembers that she was under a psychiatrist's care and had suffered several nervous breakdowns, the first at age thirty-three, "when her husband broke a chair over her."

Andrew seemed indifferent to his mother, who chain-smoked, talked incessantly, and constantly threatened suicide. He forbade her to enter Thrifty Drug. "Andrew would become violent if I went into the drugstore," MaryAnn says. "He would fly into rages," says Melowitz. At one point in 1993 Andrew lost control of his anger completely and slammed his mother against the wall so hard that she fractured her shoulder and had to wear her arm in a sling. When she went to the emergency room, Andrew warned her that if she ever told anyone he'd kill her. Father L. V. Bourgeois, the parish priest, was upset and blamed it on drugs. "It's not normal behavior for a son." Despite the violence, MaryAnn clung to Andrew. According to Melowitz, "You'd need a crowbar to pry her away from her son."

Andrew, meanwhile, would party for days and then come home to crash. He demanded that MaryAnn remain absolutely quiet while he slept, often late into the afternoon. In order to comply with his wishes, she took the phone off the hook so that the ringing wouldn't bother him; she spoke in a whisper and cooked whatever he wanted, whether she could afford to or not. "Even if she had only fifteen dollars to her name, if he wanted steak, he got steak," says a friend of Gina Cunanan's. Andrew contributed toward rent and food, but MaryAnn, who referred to Andrew as the Prince, had to rely on Melowitz to drive her twelve miles to the military PX in Miramar to get her prescriptions.

"Andrew would wake up, take care of his personal needs, sit down, and eat," says Melowitz. "He had no interest in her. It was never 'Mom, how do you feel? What do you need? Thanks for preparing the food.' It was 'Don't bother me, I'm outta here.' " Nevertheless, MaryAnn would unfailingly ask Andrew when he was coming home, what did he want to eat, and when. "She was very smothering," says Melowitz. "It was an infantilization of him, no two ways about it."

No matter how squalid Andrew's days were, however, at night, the impoverished clerk from Rancho Bernardo would speed south down Interstate 5 in a big old LTD he usually kept out of sight, past La Jolla, past Sea World and the zoo, to hit the bars of Hillcrest, not as Andrew Cunanan on financial aid but as Yale-educated Andrew DeSilva, Mr. Congeniality, big-time spender, and heir to any number of fortunes— parking lots, car dealerships, sugar plantations, New York real estate, even a mattress distribution warehouse. Melowitz says, "He was a real Jekyll and Hyde."

To pull off the deception, Andrew was aided by the circumstances of his surroundings and a new friend. When he first got back to San Diego, Andrew began to hang around a gay fraternity comprised of young men from UCSD and San Diego State. One of the people he met on campus was a handsome, green-eyed surfer named Robbins Thompson, who was deeply in the closet. Robbins surfed on the professional circuit and did not want anyone to know his sexual preference; since surfing was judged subjectively, he felt anything that made others feel they had an edge would hurt his career.

Robbins loved the high life and came from the kind of exotic background Andrew wished was his own. Robbins was a Mormon and also a quarter Jewish, and he had grown up in the Moslem world. His mother was a onetime beauty queen, and his father had run a prosperous oil business in Lebanon until the violent political unrest that took hold in Beirut in the mid-seventies forced him to flee. He lost everything in the process. Robbins says his father spent his fortune in ransoms in order to get his family and his employees out of Lebanon alive. Then the family lived on a sailboat in the Caribbean for a few years before settling in Newport Beach, California. Robbins remembers Nicole Brown Simpson and her sister, Denise, from his high school days.

Robbins, who was six years older than Andrew, had largely given up pro surfing tours by the time they met, and was taking computer classes and trying to start up a contracting business. He was ready to come out, but only on the gay-party circuit. Like many gays who deal almost exclusively in the straight world and fear being unmasked, Robbins kept everyone, both straight and gay, at emotional bay; he needed someone who was a lot more outgoing to help him navigate the largely unknown territory of gay society.

Andrew and Robbins were perfect for each other. One was brazen and witty, the other, a vivacious, elusive hunk with the added cachet of the surfer mystique. At first they were lovers, but neither of them was much on sentiment. Robbins says, "We soon figured out that wasn't going anywhere, so we decided to become best friends."

Best of all, Robbins was not bothered by Andrew's lies. He focused more on what Andrew, who was extremely intelligent and very amusing, could do for him. Together they began a good-times roll with the rich older gays of La Jolla and San Diego, some uptight and closeted, some not. Andrew, who was conversant on many subjects he picked up from his reading, immediately hit it off with Lincoln Aston, a wealthy, sixty-year-old architect who had once been married. Lincoln was cultivated and possessed exquisite taste, but he had a fatal weakness for attractive young men. "Lincoln," says Robbins, "was a lech."

Lincoln and a couple of older Bishop's graduates took Andrew up. Soon Andrew and Robbins were going to parties with very prominent, closeted people. In San Diego, where gay wealth doesn't shout, these were often staid affairs. "We'd have cocktails and then either go out to dinner or have dinner there. They were very civilized and upper-class parties," Robbins says. Other men with money Lincoln knew were not so discreet, and they sprinkled their gatherings with "pool boys—clothing optional." Others hosted "video parties," where ten male escorts would be hired to liven up the party and eventually strip, and everything would be videotaped.

There was always a party, wild or not. Robbins remembers going with Andrew to a gathering at the home of David Copley, the adopted son of the owner of the conservative *San Diego Union-Tribune* newspaper and heir to the Copley newspaper fortune. Andrew would always hold forth on politics and the news of the day, and he managed to penetrate the highest circles. "But he was not a socialite," says Chris Fahey, who knew Andrew for five years in Hillcrest. "Andrew went to a party at

David Copley's and hung around with older rich guys. He was among them. He was among his betters."

Dr. William Crawford, a distinguished retired navy doctor who at one time had been one of six national test pilots for the navy, met Andrew at this time. Crawford and others quickly realized that Andrew would have to have been at least ten years older than he was in order to have done everything he claimed he'd done. Andrew, recalls Crawford, told him he was getting his Ph.D. in history. "He said he spent eight months to two years on a kibbutz. When you added that on, plus several years in San Francisco in the textile business, I said, 'Andrew, you haven't been alive all those years.' I knew it was invented, but it was not relevant to our relationship, which was delightfully correct, sophisticated, and enjoyable. He was wonderfully easy. We would match wits."

"You're the only one to keep up with me," Andrew once told Crawford, who says, "It was like keeping up with the celebrated jumping frog."

Andrew even told Crawford, an anesthesiologist, that he had worked from time to time as a pharmacy technician. "I didn't press how he knew drugs." Crawford was more concerned that Andrew was wasting his good mind on a frivolous life. "Andrew, all that brain power and it's sitting there idle."

"I enjoy my life. I like it this way," Andrew answered.

"Andrew, do you have a money machine somewhere?" Crawford asked on another occasion. "He allowed as that he had a trust. I said, 'When do you take possession?' He said, 'Oh, it sort of possesses me.' He was very deft at changing the subject. As a physician, I've never looked at my friends clinically. Andrew was consistent as Andrew, but not his stories."

Andrew and Robbins were new faces, zippy and fresh. Who cared if every little "i" was dotted or every "t" crossed? "Andrew told the truth. It was hidden in lies," Robbins insists. "You could see the truth of who or what he was describing if you took away all the dressing and embellishments around it. It was like a code you had to go through." Robbins most often was unique in that he understood the code. "Just sat back and watched the show."

Indeed, as the years progressed, the act was refined, and Andrew even used the circumstances of Robbins's life to pump up his own. Robbins spent a lot of time in Baja, California, where one local gringo was a convicted murderer, a former Hell's Angel who had spent twenty years in prison for killing a guard during a riot. He once asked a friend of Robbins's if he wanted his ex-girlfriend "offed" after she had betrayed him. That was just the sort of story Andrew lapped up. Andrew, who seemed to possess an inordinate fascination with violence, then bragged about his underworld connections, particularly a guy in prison he knew who could arrange to have people killed.

Aiding Andrew was the large transient military population of Hillcrest, a steady stream of newcomers whom he could entertain and eventually recruit for more sinister activities. Andrew was attracted to young military types, and gays with fetishes for uniforms found Hillcrest a bonanza. It was common knowledge that the military tests for HIV every few months; therefore, the gay military population is considered healthy and safe. "Going out to gay bars in San Diego is almost like being in an enlisted-men's club," says Steven Zeeland, author of *Sailors and Sexual Identity* and *The Masculine Marine.* "There is such an overwhelming military presence."

Once a year, for example, after the annual military dress ball, marines in full dress uniform can be seen drinking at one of the Hillcrest's most popular bars, Flicks, which is co-owned by Tim Barthel, a handsome ex-marine. Barthel says 30 percent of his clientele is military. Based on serving in the Marine Corps and running a gay bar for a number of years, Barthel estimates that at least 20 percent of the U.S. military is gay; official estimates are much lower.

San Diego also attracts teenage runaways and other homeless kids who bus in from all over the country and become easy pickings for unscrupulous predators in a still-uptight town where it's expedient to operate in secret. San Diego's longtime reputation for right-wing politics and its large military numbers meant that many of the men who had no qualms about being openly gay in Hillcrest were still firmly in the closet once they stepped outside that neighborhood.

"All of Andrew's supposed close friends had money—young professional types," says Brian Wade Smith, who once dated Jeff Trail and saw

Andrew in Hillcrest, San Francisco, and Minneapolis. "There was Andrew taking them to the places to go. They were lonely and didn't have
other people to go to these places with. Andrew would always say, 'Oh,
I have a friend I'll set you up with.' It was lonely people with money
and no place to go." In Hillcrest, where sex is often not only the coin of
the realm but also the great equalizer, Andrew was assured of having a
ready audience among those who were in need of a road map.

"You have the haves, the have-nots, the wanna-bes, the escapists, the
power junkies, the superior, the inferior—it runs the gamut—all played
out by one gender as opposed to traditionally what's been the rule all
down the line," says longtime Hillcrest resident Anthony Dabiere, a
former waiter and real-estate broker who knew Andrew and had observed him for years. Dabiere also points out that when a single gender
assumes both male and female roles, the rules become more intricate.
"Then the game is reinvented, and the natural proclivity of men to be
in competition is only heightened to sometimes absurd levels as men
compete with each other as both prizes and judges."

One of Hillcrest's attractions is that it is nonintimidating to, say,
transplanted gay Midwesterners, young men from small towns in Wisconsin, Minnesota, Illinois, or Kansas, who crave the freedom and the
climate of California but find that West Hollywood and the Castro have
too much attitude. "In the Midwest, to go to a gay bar you have to
drive two or three hours to get where there is a city feeling," says Tim
Barthel, who is from Michigan. "The attraction here is the pace. It's not
L.A. or San Francisco. When you walk into a bar here, you'll generally
know 50 percent of the people."

The small-town kids were far more apt to accept Andrew's stories
than kids from New York or Los Angeles. "He chose military boys and
boys from the Midwest and transplant people. In general, his group was
easily snowed," says Chris Fahey. "Very deliberately, that was his selec-
tion process. He replied to his skeptics with those willing to buy into
his act." Andrew eventually became a fixture of the neighborhood, a
combination cruise director and welcome wagon. In the bars, everyone
knew Andrew.

"In the gay world, you can be virtually anybody without needing to
advertise it. But if you choose to adopt a certain posture and broadcast

it, nobody will question you all that stringently," says Dabiere. "It's an open market, where the only real criterion is what you want to bring to your presentation. If you choose to go out in dungarees and sweatshirts, you will get to a certain level, and that may be your choice. If you want to supersede it, all you have to do is go to Nordstrom and buy yourself a nice new outfit and *voila*!"

Hillcrest, says Dabiere, is filled with people who live for the moment. "The relatively close proximity of a moneyed population from La Jolla alongside a youth-and-beach population gives elbow-rubbing opportunities for those who choose to pursue them. You can have a pauper alongside a prince without any trouble at all."

San Diego may be the seventh largest city in the United States, fast growing and spreading, with seventy miles of beaches and ninety museums, but in many ways it seems like a small town. Almost everybody is from someplace else, ingenuous enough not to laugh off somebody like Andrew's brand of audacious fabrication, and rootless enough not to be able to check it out. The outdoor life and climate are superb for tourism, and the burgeoning high-tech industry promises ever increasing prosperity. San Diego is less the sleepy naval headquarters and conservative country cousin to Los Angeles and San Francisco than in previous decades; it has the Old Globe Theater, a symphony orchestra, Sea World, and the famous zoo, but it also has some catching up to do.

In 1991, when Andrew returned to San Diego, the economy was firmly anchored to the aerospace industry. In the next few years that economy took a nosedive, as the Cold War wound down and defense jobs were phased out. The gay community, however, had by then begun to flex its economic and political muscle. One of its most visible leaders, Nicole Ramirez-Murray, who is billed as "the self-proclaimed mayor of the gay community," is a controversial Chicano Republican turned Democratic activist; a columnist; a public relations consultant; and a witty, performing drag queen.

"I have one side of my closet organized with gowns, dresses, and crowns," Nicole declares, sitting in her apartment filled with tchotchkes and faux Fabergé eggs, "and the other side with suits and ties. I wear both." In 1990, Nicole spearheaded the community effort to help raise early significant money for a city council race, and gays and lesbians have gotten the attention of local politicians ever since. "We have a swing vote in two assembly districts and one state senate district and in two city-council districts," says Nicole, "and more important, we have swing money, too."

Hillcrest, a gentrified neighborhood of rehabilitated storefronts, outdoor cafés, bars, restaurants, bookstores, and supermarkets, including many gay-owned businesses, began taking off in the late eighties. Announced in huge letters on a pink Art Deco neon sign that arches over University Avenue at the intersection of Fifth Street, Hillcrest has a friendly feel to it, and Andrew Cunanan soon began to call it his true home.

For those like Andrew who make the bar scene and want to be considered A-listers, the neighborhood is segregated into highly stratified cliques. These include the rigid "cult of masculinity" prevalent in urban gay ghettos, fueled by drugs and the promise of hot sex. The gay media is filled with images of pumped, hairless "muscle boys," all signifying what author Michelangelo Signorile calls "a fast-food lifestyle for people with a fast and furious appetite."

Andrew bought heavily into every part of that mystique, just as he had slavishly lusted for the material goods of his privileged classmates in high school. Gay author Armistead Maupin says, "He was seduced by the democratization of sex—the idea that, if you have the right goods, at a certain point you can meet anybody and do anything." Andrew's whole life was now determined by the dictates of gay status.

The living in Hillcrest, shaped by the mild coastal weather, is fairly laid back. Yet, Hillcrest is just as susceptible as big brother Los Angeles, or many other gay communities, to falling prey to many "debated-from-within-the-community" issues: whether the only thing gay liberation has wrought is a docile market for a certain lifestyle based on appearance, labels, possessions, and the aforementioned, much-discussed cult of the body; whether people are too often judged by the kind of car they drive or by how buff their physique is, etc. Similarly, drug use, consumption of pornography, and the injection of steroids to build up muscles are commonplace. San Diego even has the advantage of being near the Mexican border, where liposuction is cheap. The buff boys often ingest various nutritional supplements like creatine to convert fat to muscle more quickly. They then appear tan, shirtless, and rippling— on weekends in Balboa Park—riding bikes, grooming their dogs, and playing volleyball in an informal beauty pageant.

Andrew, who had no patience for the gym, and to his peers, never appeared very comfortable with his body, was forced to find another way to compete. He frequently went to Black's Beach, the nude beach in La Jolla, but he never took his clothes off. The cult of the body was an arena that Andrew could not enter with his own age group, and he did not try. Rather, with his cultivation of the finer things—particularly art and classical music—and his penchant for quips, Andrew sought to become a throwback to an older form of gay stereotype, what Daniel Harris in *The Rise and Fall of Gay Culture* calls "the high aesthete with the rapier wit." Such an existence requires not only considerable leisure time, which Andrew had, but also ample financial resources—much harder to come by.

The question always being asked was where did Andrew get his money? While he was still living in the Bay Area, Andrew had apparently explored the possibility of being paid for his sexual services. From Berkeley, Andrew made frequent, secret forays down to southern California on weekends when he could hitch rides, apparently trying to ply himself as a paid escort or kept boy.

In December 1989, a young computer software salesman visiting Los Angeles from Cincinnati met Andrew at a party in the Hollywood Hills for two country singers. Andrew was with a man about seventy-five years old, a doctor from San Bernardino. The two young men struck up a conversation, and Andrew was very interested to hear that the salesman was staying at the Beverly Hills Hotel. The next afternoon, Andrew, who introduced himself as Tony Cunanan, paid him a visit there, calmly throwing down his duffel bag as if he were planning to stay.

The two spent a couple of hours lounging at the hotel pool, went out that evening, and then spent the night together in the salesman's room.

Andrew came across as smart and smooth. The next day the salesman dropped him off at a health club on Santa Monica Boulevard, and the two promised to keep in touch. But the salesman thought it had been just another one-night stand. Andrew told his new friend that he was rooming with an escort in Los Angeles who billed himself "the best face in L.A.," and left him a phone number and a box number in Newport Beach. The salesman returned home.

A few months later he got a Disneyland postcard from Tony, saying he'd like to move away from California. Meanwhile, the salesman had lost his job and decided to move to Florida. He became an escort at the now defunct Exotic Escorts Service of Fort Lauderdale. Tony contacted him again. "He said there were too many other guys trying to do what he was doing in California and he'd like to try Florida—some place where it was warm." The salesman offered to help him get set up in the escort business. Tony said thanks, but nothing happened. Nevertheless, he called every few months.

In 1991, about the time Lizzie and Phil Merrill were getting ready to move out of Berkeley, the salesman showed up at a party and a photo shoot for a male calendar of Exotic escorts at the Glow Lounge. According to the salesman, the owner of the service told him that he had been contacted by Tony from California, and that the owner had sent a few jobs his way. The owner said he was impressed that Tony had remitted the proper share of the take back to him. The owner then explained that Tony had come to Florida for a little while and had said that he was willing to go anywhere to work. The former salesman was a little put out—after all, he was the one who had recommended the service to Tony in the first place. Why hadn't Tony called him?

(Interestingly, the salesman remembers that some of his clients were executives of the Home Shopping Network, headquartered in nearby St. Petersburg, Florida. Marilyn Miglin, the widow of Andrew's third murder victim, has been associated with Home Shopping Network since 1993, and her husband took time off from his real estate business in the early nineties to help her run Marilyn Miglin Cosmetics. Could Tony/Andrew have heard of Lee or Marilyn Miglin through the Home Shopping Network connection? Could he possibly have met Lee Miglin?)

The escort service owner, now in poor health, with a police record and retired, is extremely reluctant to answer questions about his previous activities, and will confirm little. He remembers clients from the Home Shopping Network. He says he does not remember Tony, and neither does the woman who answered the phones. He recognizes the salesman's voice on the phone but not his name. The salesman has excellent recall, can remember minute details and has even saved the letter from the escort-service owner, asking him to be there. He believes that he met Andrew Cunanan, and that Andrew was in Florida trying to be a male escort on a few occasions. Andrew did tell people he had spent time in Florida. But Andrew lied so much to so many different people that this story cannot be completely verified.

There is a similar story. A well-known San Diego gay, who fixes up dates as a favor for visiting VIPs, definitely remembers Andrew being brought to him when he first returned to Hillcrest. "One of my boys called me up to meet him. He said, 'He's part Asian.' I said, 'I've never had a call asking for an Asian.' The guy said, 'Well, he's real smart and cute.' I thought, Maybe a dinner date, but it's usually sex they want. Andrew came over to my apartment. Right away, I didn't think he was that cute. I said, 'What are your best attributes?' He said, 'My smile and my eyes. I think I have sexy eyes.' I said, 'Anything *else?*' Andrew said, 'I'm OK, I'm about average there.' He looked around my apartment and talked about the art, so I took a mental note that he was a good conversationalist. He only fit with about four people in all those years. If someone wants someone just for dinner—the politicians—it was a quickie three hundred dollars for him and no sex." But the problem, the arranger goes on to explain, was "They're very specific about what they ask for. I have a congressman who asks for 'this many inches cut from his hair and his feet cleaned.'"

On that level of specificity, Andrew was hard to "reference." "My boy told me, 'He's really looking for someone to keep him,' but he never fit the mold." For years afterward, whenever Andrew would run into the arranger, they would merely nod. In the end, Andrew wasn't ornamental enough—nor "boyish" or patient enough. To really make it as a kept boy, one has to have both the right equipment and an obliging temperament. Some boys do, and "they wind up with Jaguars and property in their names," the arranger tells me. "Andrew was stupid."

Nicole agrees. "I've met too many Andrews. Andrew blew it. Instead of thinking stocks, investments, he wanted too much. If you're going to be kept like that, they don't want you going to gay bars—you have to be at their beck and call. Many are married, and they put you in a condo. But Andrew wanted to have a way of showing off. He needed the approval of his peers—'Oh my god, you're fabulous, you have so much money.' " Andrew, Nicole concluded, was not cut out for the boy-toy big time. But he never stopped trying.

"Very early on, in a young adult gay life, you can take a path and become a prostitute, a porn star, but there are others who are not that at all," says Chris Fahey, who works in Hillcrest restaurants and observed Andrew for years. "There are certain specifics to the gay world. It's tight knit and hush-hush about men who may be prostitutes. Most people in the straight community think it's the type of thing that strippers do, but it goes on in the gay community much more than you might think. People come out and take one path or another. If you wanted to be absorbed in the gay community [as a prostitute], you could be absorbed pretty easily."

Robbins doesn't believe that Andrew ever turned tricks. "I saw him with tons of older people, but I knew most of them and I knew their relationship—all the ones in San Diego at least. They all were above-board." Robbins knew Andrew was searching for a sugar daddy. "He definitely wanted somebody to keep him, there was no question." But he wanted more. His four criteria, Robbins says, were that the person be "rich, intelligent, artistic, and famous." Such a person was worth waiting for. "I would equate him more to a very beautiful woman who's just not going to slut around. She's definitely going to go after somebody, but she's saving herself." Otherwise, "once they get a reputation like that, who wants them?"

Fahey is less charitable in his assessment. He was a nineteen-year-old waiter at a restaurant called Canes California Bistro when he met Andrew in 1992. Andrew would come in four or five times a week with Lincoln Aston or another "older gentlemen." Andrew told Fahey that he could get him "any kind of fake ID I wanted from the Department of Motor Vehicles. He never produced it." Fahey, who is from the East Coast, says, "You can tell who has money. On the West Coast, lots of people had airs. It was obvious he didn't have money." Based on his own observation and other people's remarks about Andrew, Fahey says, he put two and two together. "It was obvious to me he was a prostitute." Fahey developed a visceral dislike of Andrew. "That guy is so creepy," he told Trent Smith, the maître d', "I don't even want to be around him."

"Andrew?" Smith replied. "He's harmless."

At home, MaryAnn would often find expensive clothes and shoes in Andrew's room. "He doesn't have any money," she told Hal Melowitz. "He's stayed out for days. Hal, look," she said, showing Melowitz $700 suits from Nordstrom with the tags still on and $300 shoes. "Look what he came home with now—Ferragamo shoes." MaryAnn also discovered matchbooks from gay clubs and bars. "Where are these clubs?" she asked Melowitz. She even called some of the places, and people there would tell her straight out that they were gay bars.

When MaryAnn was alone, Melowitz would try to reason with her. "MaryAnn, these are gay nightclubs." But MaryAnn was in total denial. Instead, "She talked about Andrew going back to school and on to greatness." Though Andrew claimed for years that he was studying for a Ph.D. at UCSD, he left school forever in June 1992. When people checked, no one could find an Andrew DeSilva registered.

Like a bat, Andrew took flight for his prey at night. From the beginning, there was a certain rhythm to Andrew's nocturnal wanderings. Mondays, Nicole held forth as the witty and acerbic emcee at the Hole, a funky outdoor bar with a shower stage left, located near the old Marine Corps recruiting station. Wearing sequined chiffon, a red ponytail wig, and gold sling-back heels, Nicole would race over after doing the introductions to the Monday drag show at the Brass Rail in Hillcrest and conduct the weekly Wet 'n Wild underwear contest.

In gay America, men treat each other as objects in a manner that most women today would consider blatantly sexist. In a raucous crowd

of closeted military men, gym rats flexing their biceps, and a few proper
La Jolla gentlemen, Andrew could be found many Mondays in a blazer,
watching as contestants were hauled up onstage, stripped to their underwear, and told to get under the shower and then come out and
dance. While they shook their booty, they'd be questioned by Nicole.

"You have a nice body," she told one young black. "Did you get it at
the gym?" "No." "Where? Running from the police?" The crowd
hooted its disapproval. "Hey, I'm Mexican," Nicole countered. "If
you're Mexican or black, you run from the police." To another man who
identified himself as "Irish/Indian," she said, "You must be one big
fuckin' drunk!" She told a navy man, "Don't ask, don't tell, just open
your mouth. I hate little teeny ones—they poke."

Tuesday was Boys' Night at the Flame, a lesbian bar north of Hillcrest on the grand boulevard bisecting Balboa Park. One of the habitués
of that era was a charming con artist named "Larry," who eventually got
strung out on drugs, arrested for fraud, and sent to federal prison. Larry,
with whom Andrew often hung out, allegedly knew mobsters and was a
master at credit card fraud. He came from a family that masterminded
car thefts and oversaw a fleet of over one hundred shoplifters—who hit
major department stores and brought out hundreds of thousands of
dollars of "product" to be sold at 25 percent of retail. Larry says he
arranged for Andrew to buy product.

One night Andrew watched Larry casually "pick up" a previously
targeted, fully loaded red Porsche right outside the bar they were about
to enter. He never forgot the incident. When Andrew bragged that he
knew people with connections to goods that "just fell off a truck," he
meant Larry. Larry knew of a certain "big room," he would say, and
Andrew allegedly had access to the source where a "Cartier watch,
Persian rugs, a Peter Max painting, a case of Dom Perignon, Cristal or
Perrier-Jouet champagne, etc., etc.," cost anywhere from 10 to 40 percent of list price.

The trunk of Andrew's old clunker was suddenly full of Polaroid
cameras, calculators, fans, heaters, *Jurassic Park* videocassettes, and
men's cologne, all of which he would distribute as presents. He could
easily have shoplifted these things from Thrifty Drug. "He probably
just paid a guy a hundred dollars to set a box from the warehouse to the

side for him," Larry said, implying that such pickings were way too slim for real pros. "Who's gonna hit a truck like that?"

Wednesday nights and many other nights, Andrew hung out at the West Coast, a three-story dance club with an outdoor bar, where he was the main attraction. "He held court. We all worshiped," says Sheila Gard, who worked at the West Coast for a time. "Yes, Andrew, whatever you want. You're the god."

Sometimes he'd get "wasted on vodka," climb up on a platform, and dance to "Copacabana." Other times he would say he was a recovering alcoholic. Even so, he would often have Mike Whitmore, the bartender, spike his espresso glass with Bushmills or Bailey's.

Andrew had a secret crush on blond, blue-eyed Mike and tried to come between him and his boyfriend, Matthew. But then, he also had a crush on Matthew, as well as the doorman, Stan Hatley, an ex–air force officer who was dark and handsome. "He always told me that Richard Gere and I were his two dream men," says Stan. However, most people remember that Andrew had trouble scoring. "He'd cruise and cruise, but I'd never see Andrew leave with a person," says Ronnie Mascarena, another pal from that era. Andrew claimed that he preferred paying for sex to having a relationship. "He said he'd hire hookers," remembers John Beuerle, another regular. "Andrew liked them because there were no complications. 'When I'm done with you, see you later.' "

Now old friends realize that he was probably also talking about himself. "He often showed up in a tux at bars," says Shane O'Brien who was just coming out at the time and who became part of Andrew's clique. "He'd always be going to dinner parties requiring a suit and tie or tuxedo. I don't know who they were with. I guess they could have been tricks." Stan Hatley recalls, "Andrew was associated with limos and taxis and private screenings. He'd be all decked out in tan khakis and a navy blazer. We'd say, 'Where did you go?' He'd say, 'The opera, this or that show, that benefit.' We're finding out now he was a hired guest, so to speak. [But] I was proud I knew Andrew. He was the type of person, you could walk into a room of a thousand people, and the one guy everyone wanted to be around was Andrew."

As for Andrew, he wanted to be around anyone who looked like he had money. "He carried a wad of cash. He flashed around fifty and one hundred dollar bills. To those of us who came from the background he wanted to come from, he wouldn't buy *us* drinks," says Stan Hatley, who was supported by his well-to-do dad. "It actually became a sore spot with me."

In 1991, to impress Shane O'Brien, who was also supported by his family, Andrew said, "I go to dinner with Gianni Versace once a year." He then proceeded to tell Shane all about the dinner he had had with Versace at Stars Restaurant in San Francisco the year before, when Versace was doing the costumes for the opera there. He told similar stories to Robbins, but Robbins had no idea who Versace was or any interest in finding out. Andrew also told Shane that he dined annually with Debbie Harry. "Whenever she came up on a video in the bar, he'd say, 'I get to have dinner with her and you don't.' "

By 1992, Andrew DeSilva was telling everyone he was Jewish and had a commission in the Israeli military. To some he boasted that his father was a ranking member of the Mossad, or Israeli intelligence. He took a shine to a pretty young Jewish woman named Elisa Denner. "He could speak with a Jewish New York accent about going shopping and to lunch. He acted like a Jewish American princess in a guy," Elisa says. Andrew told Elisa, "We could be married. I'll take you to Hollywood." He begged her to go with him so that they could break into the movies as a couple. Elisa's close friend, Ronnie Mascarena, told him, "They'd never allow anyone with your voice on TV!" Ronnie explained that "Andrew had a very nasally gay voice. He felt he needed a beautiful woman on his arm to become famous and wealthy." Elisa adds, "He used to tell people I was his ex-wife. He told me he had a daughter."

For years Andrew flashed pictures of Lizzie and her daughter as proof of his marriage, but he said he never saw his family because "my wife has a restraining order against me." His excuse for never letting Denner or anyone else go to his house in Rancho Santa Fe was that, "he was in the closet because of his parents—they'd cut him off." Once, friends caught him driving his old beat-up LTD. "He said it was his maid's. We knew it was his," says Ronnie. It was easier to let Andrew indulge his fantasies about being rich and a member of the Israeli army.

"What would an active officer in the Israeli army be doing in San Diego?" asks Hatley. Spies, after all, wouldn't be announcing themselves. "With Andrew, you kind of pacified him. It was easier to pacify than hear him tell it all night," Sheila Gard says. "If you disbelieved him, he'd push it. Or he'd get real defensive and almost pouty. We were all there for Andrew, so it wasn't any fun if the life of the party was pouty."

8

Jeff

ALTHOUGH ANDREW WAS a practiced phony, he knew the genuine
article when he saw it. Jeff Trail, a handsome, authentic all-American
kid with dark hair and an engaging smile, was Andrew's ideal. Jeff was
a graduate of Annapolis who knew how to fly before he knew how to
drive; he was an excellent marksman and a skilled sailor. Many of
Andrew's now tarnished dreams were embedded in Jeff. Andrew was in
awe of Jeff, and he claimed they were like brothers, pointing out that
they were born only six months apart and that he too had once hoped to
go to the Naval Academy and pretended that he knew how to fly and
sail. Actually, Andrew had never had a flying lesson, and going out on
the water made him seasick.

In many ways, Jeff was everything Andrew was not. From the beginning, Andrew was highly possessive of Jeff, who had grown up in
DeKalb, Illinois, a small university town sixty miles northwest of Chicago, where the big crop is corn for corn flakes. Jeff personified the solid
ideals of the land he sprang from. He was loyal and law-abiding and
kept his word; he made friends easily and loved to be needed; he hated
being alone. He liked to cook, play cards, sit around a fire and talk.
During his entire childhood and adolescence, Jeff lived in the same
house, on the edge of Northern Illinois University, where his father
taught mathematics.

Like Andrew, Jeff was the baby of the family. His mother had had four other children, a son and three daughters, before being widowed at a young age. Ann Davis then enrolled at Oklahoma State University, hoping to become an elementary school teacher in order to support her family. There she met Stan Trail, a kind and thoughtful math professor, who is now emeritus at NIU. Ann eventually earned a master's at the University of Chicago and became a reading specialist. Jeff was the only child Ann and Stan had together.

The family was close-knit—even today they take their vacations together—and Jeff, the youngest by nine years, was doted on. In return, he adored his parents. After he grew up, Jeff was still so respectful of his father that in the middle of a discussion with someone he would say, "Just a minute, I'll call my dad. He'll know the answer." Jeff was the family conservative, at odds with the rest of the bunch politically. Says his sister Sally, "We could never figure out how we got a Young Republican in the family."

At an early age, Jeff decided he liked the military. His older brother, Mike (who would die suddenly, less than a year after Jeff), was a Navy corpsman in Vietnam. Sally, seventeen years Jeff's senior, enlisted in the Air Force and later became a career naval officer, one of the first women to attend the Army War College. Jeff wanted to be a Top Gun pilot. "His room went from toy soldiers to an eight-foot mural of the moon and the stars," says his youngest sister, Lisa.

Jeff took flying lessons when he was a sophomore in high school. Later, his family and friends held their breath as he flew them over DeKalb in an old Piper Cub from the local airport where he worked after school. He was so determined to get an appointment to Annapolis that he earned nineteen college-course credits in trigonometry, calculus, and linear algebra before graduating from high school.

DeKalb High had a lot of bright kids, many of them children of Northern Illinois State faculty members. (When Jeff was a freshman, the senior-class valedictorian was Cindy Crawford, who won a scholarship in chemical engineering to Northwestern University.) DeKalb High in those days was superstraight. "If you smoked cigarettes, you were considered a burn-out and completely ostracized," says high school friend Chris Walker, who eventually worked in the Clinton White

House. "There were no drugs and no smoking and very little drinking. Jeff led by example. He was one of the leaders in that."

Jeff's honors humanities teacher, Joe Lo Cascio, who led his students through Dante's *Inferno,* describes him as "an ideal kid—Jeff was going to be a significant person." Lo Cascio remembers him for his "strong values and his great code of ethics, a sense of academic vigor and a wonderful sense of self, and a very supportive family, obviously." Elegie Lo Cascio taught Jeff honors English. "Jeff had a great sense of tradition and obligation and a tremendous sense of honor." His favorite book was *The Iliad.*

At Annapolis, with its rigid discipline, elite tradition, and tough course load, Jeff was faced with the greatest challenge of his life. Set on a picturesque point where the Severn River meets Chesapeake Bay, Annapolis is both awe-inspiring and intimidating. Whether midshipmen are listening to organ music filling the Academy's domed chapel, the cacophony of orders and questions barked out in the cavernous dining hall, or the roaring cheers of "Beat Army!", they are never ever allowed to forget what is expected of them: excellence.

Jeff took responsibility very seriously. He soon realized that he wasn't going to be one of the few chosen for Top Gun, and became a political-science major. His grades were mediocre at best—he graduated 839th out of 950—and his only honors course was in leadership. However, he earned two stripes during his senior year for being chosen as a battalion adjutant, a semester-long leadership position.

Jeff's sexual preference must have been gnawing at him, but he still did not know for certain that he was gay. In the pre- "Don't Ask, Don't Tell" era, his father remembers, several midshipmen discovered to be homosexual were thrown out. Jeff, a stickler for rules, told his dad, "They better not try to come back!"

Up to then, Jeff had dated but had had no real girlfriends. His best female friend there, Liz McDonald, recalls how she and Jeff, "did weddings and dinners and drinks. You just liked him instantly. He was warm and made you feel at ease. If Jeff was your friend, he was your friend for life." Jeff's middle sister, Candy, remembers that he visited her during a wild spring break for college students on the Gulf coast of Texas. Jeff told her, "I just feel so different from all these kids." She thought he meant that because of all the rules he was subject to, he couldn't identify with Margaritaville.

Jeff graduated in May 1991 and was posted in the fall to San Diego, to Surface Warfare Officer School, where he'd learn to handle ships on the high seas. Out clubbing one night, he met Michael Murphy, a student at San Diego State, and had his first homosexual experience. It threw him badly. Jeff was very uncomfortable when Murphy took him to a gay beach up the coast in Laguna, and left immediately. Jeff soon broke off the relationship. "He was really upset, pacing around with his head down," Murphy recounts. Jeff was frightened, saying, "I can't understand myself, me being this way. This is the first time I've not been able to understand myself. I've always understood myself before."

His fellow officers on the USS *Gridley,* a steam-driven cruiser built in 1963, had no idea that Jeff was gay. He was one of only two unmarried officers on the ship, which was deployed to the Persian Gulf to help keep the peace after the Gulf War. Jeff flew out to be with the ship in late spring 1992 and returned to San Diego in October. His father proudly sailed with him from Hawaii. Thereafter, except for a few cruises to Mexico and one to San Francisco, the ship stayed in port in San Diego, being refurbished and getting readied for engineering trials. In the end, the *Gridley* was scheduled for decommissioning in January 1994.

During his time on the cruiser, Jeff worked in the boiler room in the engineering division. He commanded forty-two men and was very popular. It was almost as if he had made a conscious decision to identify with them instead of with his fellow officers in the ward room. "Jeff was proficient and a real good guy. He stuck up for his men—sometimes to the detriment of the mission," says Ted Cudal, his chief engineer.

One incident that sunk Jeff's chances for a brilliant naval career occurred while he was on the *Gridley*. The new commanding officer in the engineering division had just gotten out of Department Head School and appeared to the men to be very green. Even the other officers in engineering joked that he was clueless. He was soon transferred, and at his "Hail and Farewell Party," Jeff had to give a gag gift. Handing him the board game Clue, Jeff said, "We've all been talking and we pretty much decided you never had a clue, so here it is." Suddenly the party went silent; junior officers did not say such things to superiors even in jest. The captain of the *Gridley* was not pleased, and Jeff got a B in judgment on his final fitness report. "If you didn't get straight A's as a junior officer, you were never going to get anywhere," says Scott Silsdorf, also a junior officer on the *Gridley*. "If you got a B as a junior officer, it was a big black mark to get over."

Once Jeff accepted his homosexuality, his feelings of discomfort on board ship could only have greatly increased. In late 1992, Jeff spoke anonymously about what being closeted in the navy was like to a TV interviewer for a segment on the government's policy toward gays in the military on the CBS newsmagazine, *48 Hours.* "I am not able to share my life with those around me," he said in silhouette, in an interview that went on far longer than the bits actually aired. For himself, Jeff continued, "being gay is a half natural and half conscious choice." He sounded relieved to say that "I finally reached a point that, yeah, I'm gay and I can admit it to myself." But he certainly didn't sound as if he would have voluntarily put himself in such a difficult position. "When I sit down and think about it—I torture myself. I'm between a rock and a hard place." He couldn't reveal his true self to the navy or to his parents. "The way I do it—I'm very closed about how I feel. I'm very protective of my emotions, and I try not to be very emotional about anything. I tend to disassociate myself. I'm very good at putting the blame on other people and not myself."

He wasn't certain, he said, how much longer he could keep it up. Ever the conservative, Jeff decried the waste of taxpayers' money on training for qualified people who then had to leave the military simply because they were gay. When Jeff gave the interview to CBS, he had three years left of the mandatory five he had promised to complete.

That period roughly coincided with the time Jeff got to know Andrew—late 1992, early 1993. There was a mutual attraction. The closeted military man was in awe of the utter flamboyance and ease with which Andrew handled his sexual orientation. More important, Jeff couldn't believe all the cute boys Andrew could introduce him to. Andrew was always very solicitous of Jeff, though almost everyone who knew them insists that they never had a sexual relationship. "There was some strange bond there between Andrew and Jeff," says Jeff's closest friend, Jon Wainwright, then a real estate executive in La Jolla. "Andrew would hook up people for J.T. It was kind of strange, actually. My belief is that Andrew was very infatuated with Jeff."

J. Buchman, who was a marine when he met them, witnessed an interesting dynamic between the two—an elaborate mutual deference. "Jeff was kind of needy for attention, and Andrew would give attention," Buchman says. "And Andrew would require a certain amount of attention and respect given back to him. They massaged each other's egos—the alpha male thing. Andrew stooped down and acted like an ape (mimicking a chimp opening its legs and exposing its genitals, as homage to the leader of the pack) in deference to Jeff. That is one of the things Andrew would do for Jeff."

In gay karaoke bars, Jeff discovered he had a singing voice. "On karaoke nights, if Andrew asked Jeff to sing, Jeff would sing," Buchman relates. "Jeff would stand up and be Sinatra. He did a stellar impersonation. Andrew loved that. And in turn Andrew loved being listened to for his anecdotes. He and Jeff listened to each other."

As a handsome Naval Academy graduate, Jeff was a catch, and Andrew, according to Buchman, "always had a bevy of military men around him." In the parlance of the closeted military world, however, Andrew was not known as a sexual "chaser" of gays in uniform. Buchman's roommate, Steven Zeeland, author of *The Masculine Marine,* says, Andrew was a chaser in the sense that he often tried to impersonate a military officer, claiming to be in the Israeli army or U.S. intelligence. "Andrew was the only one I ever met," says Zeeland, "who posed as a military officer for any reason other than reasons of sexuality."

To Jeff and the other gay officers he knew, all of whom had to walk the perilous tightrope of the new policy of "Don't Ask, Don't Tell," Andrew was valuable as a networker and a connector—the Dolly Levy of Hillcrest. "Andrew was very considerate of people," says a career naval officer who was a close friend of Jeff's. "He was one of those people who could introduce himself and you to just about anybody. So we always met a lot of people when we were with Andrew." For the newly out gay man arriving in San Diego, explains the officer, Andrew was one-stop shopping. "He seemed to really enjoy meeting people, introducing people to each other—he seemed to like setting people up,

as far as introducing them to people he felt would be good for them."
Plus he was the one who was buying.

"Jeff was a military officer and wasn't making great money, and
Andrew always had money," says Judy Fleissner, Jeff's former neighbor
and close friend. "He used to buy all of Jeff's drinks and buy him a
really nice dinner, and this and that. I think if you had taken all of
those away, I don't think the friendship would have been the same."

Once Jeff came to terms with the fact that he was gay, he began to
make up for lost time in pursuing men—the younger the better. Andrew, who almost never went home with anybody, was blown away by
Jeff's insouciance. "That heartbreaker," he called him. But Jeff still
retained a sense of courtliness. "You know how people will go out
sometimes and sleep with somebody and then in the morning not even
remember what their name was?" asks Judy Fleissner. "Jeff was never
like that. And that's why there were so many guys who wanted to be
part of his life, because he always treated them nice as a person." "Guys
would flock to him," says Lou Feuchtbaum, an Annapolis graduate who
knew Jeff and Andrew in Hillcrest. "He was so charismatic people
sought him out." Jeff acted like a kid in a candy store. He got a Marvin
the Martian tattoo on his left ankle, wore a silver ring on one of his toes,
and even had his left nipple pierced.

"Between the stalls in a men's room on one of San Diego's Navy
bases is a waist-high hole barely large enough to accommodate a man's
finger. Lunchtime is the best time to visit it," Steven Zeeland writes in
the article "Killer Queen," published in Seattle's gay magazine, *The
Stranger*. Holes like this are known as glory holes. In 1995, Zeeland
says, he told J. Buchman about an especially beautiful man he'd seen
there three times. "The guy was shy, and only once, briefly, did he
kneel down and, in accordance with the prevailing etiquette, stick his
penis under the stall. Most of the time we just watched each other
through the hole, or took turns sticking our pinkies through it, touching, just barely, the tips of each other's penises." Zeeland learned to
identify the man by the cartoon mouse tattooed on his ankle. When he
finally met Jeff one night at the West Coast, he says, "We shook
hands—he looked at the floor."

Clearly, the military was receding as a career option. "I think that he decided that the navy was incompatible with the lifestyle he was beginning to enjoy, and he didn't want to pursue the navy anymore," says a naval officer who once was Jeff's roommate. "Andrew was the typical life of the party, and Jeff liked to party. But there were times when it wasn't all roses. There were a lot of times when Andrew could get on your nerves after a while. Then Jeff would have Andrew butt out, and then they'd go to dinner and make up. Things were back to normal again. I think they both had that personality that they never wanted anyone to drift out." In fact, Judy Fleissner, who is a lesbian, and her partner, Chris Gamache, warned Jeff that Andrew was over the moon about him. " 'Well, there's your man, right there,' " Judy says they'd joke as Andrew approached. " 'He would do anything for you.' And Jeff was, like, 'No way!' 'Come on, Jeff, go for it,' and Jeff said, 'No way. Never.' "

Judy and Chris would sit having coffee with Jeff until the moment Andrew showed up; that, Judy says, was "our cue to leave." The women didn't bother to conceal their contempt, and the feeling was mutual. "God, Andrew, you look like shit," they'd say. "Look how big you're getting." The two apparently saw right through Andrew. "Because we were such good friends with Jeff, we were, like, 'You need to get this guy out of here. He's a jerk and an idiot.' And Jeff was just very adamant about the fact that he wasn't. Jeff was like that with friends— that was part of the reason people loved him so much. He would do anything for you and back you a hundred percent."

Early in 1994, when the *Gridley* was put into mothballs, Jeff transferred to the Assault Craft Landing Unit One, based on Coronado Island, near the Hotel Del Coronado. His transfer to a unit that did not go to sea was a tacit admission that his ambitions as a career naval officer had expired. Instead Jeff was enthralled by law enforcement—his favorite TV show was *COPS*—and his new career aspirations turned in that direction.

In January 1994, Jeff purchased an unusual Taurus .40 caliber, Model PT-100 handgun at a San Diego discount store. At $400, it was several hundred dollars cheaper than the .40 caliber Smith and Wesson favored by police agencies, including the California Highway Patrol. Law-enforcement officers found that the S&W packed more power and had less kickback than other powerful revolvers. Still, it was a heavy gun, weighing about three pounds. "The forty S&W is an effective man-stopper based on data from shootings and will probably be around a long time," its consumer evaluators wrote. Jeff had learned to shoot at Annapolis. He was qualified both as a Navy Expert Pistol and as a Navy Expert Rifle. He and Andrew used to go target shooting together with his new gun. "Andrew knew calibers, sizes, weights of guns," says his friend Tom Eads. Jeff could always count on Andrew to accompany him. "If nobody else," says a former roommate of Jeff's, "there was Andrew." At one point Andrew showed friends a handgun of his own.

The one thing that Jeff would not tolerate in those days was smoking dope. He once came home early from a much anticipated date because the guy had pulled out a joint. "I can't hang out with somebody who does that," he told Chris and Judy. They, on the other hand, kept trying to tell him that Andrew was a dope dealer—where else would his money come from? "When we were sitting around drinking coffee, we'd be, like, 'He's a drug dealer!' And Jeff would say, 'No, he's not! He's got money from his parents.' Andrew always had these stories about where his money came from."

Though they kept the truth from Jeff, various friends and observers learned during 1994 and 1995 that Andrew did deal drugs. "I was witness to Andrew doling out drugs in bars—Percodan, Vicodin, Darvocet," says Anthony Dabiere, then Andrew's favorite waiter. He'd say, " 'This will give you an overall sense of well-being.' We were given to understand he was using. We were also reminded that he had access to coke and high-grade marijuana as well."

Eventually the news reached Jeff. J. Buchman who had been introduced to Andrew by Lou Feuchtbaum, and who also knew Jeff, told Lou of incidents that left no doubt about the source of Andrew's income. Buchman related that on the beach one day he had accidentally stepped on a stingray, and Andrew had given him a Vicodin for the pain. "When I knew him, he liked prescription drugs, not street drugs," says Buchman. "When I asked him about it, he said he worked at a UCSD medical facility. He said he was going for a Ph.D. there."

When Buchman confided to Andrew that he could use some extra money, Andrew proposed that they deal drugs together in the bars of Hillcrest. Buchman refused, without even bothering to ask what kind of drugs. Andrew showed Buchman the gun he carried and suggested that if Buchman ever felt betrayed by his roommate, Andrew could have him killed through his Mob connections.

Buchman, who defines his role with Andrew as "lackey," recalls sitting next to him once at the Landmark Theater Hillcrest Cinemas as Andrew hooted and shouted and clapped in glee at the over-the-top violence of *Pulp Fiction.* "He screamed the most when the guy in the backseat got his head blown off," reports Buchman. "He said it was probably one of the best movies ever made. He liked it for its graphic portrayal. He said the violence was dreamlike."

Buchman, who wanted to become a marine biologist, was also shocked by Andrew's cruel treatment of marine life. "We were just walking down Black's Beach [the nude, gay beach in La Jolla]. We came to a rock outcropping encrusted with marine animals. There was a particularly large anemone sitting in a tide pool," Buchman says. Andrew decided to feed it a live crab. "The crab was pinching at him—it didn't want to get caught." Andrew couldn't get his hand into the crevice where the crab was hiding, so he smashed it to death with his car keys. "Then he picked out the pieces and fed it to the anemone. And then he looked for another one to feed it."

Buchman told Jeff's friend Lou Feuchtbaum, the former naval officer, about Andrew's involvement with drugs, and Feuchtbaum felt it was his duty to warn Jeff off. He and Jeff used to have breakfast on Saturdays at a French bakery. "I told him, 'Hey, Andrew isn't one of my favorite people, hasn't been one of my favorite people, and I'm really scared that there's a lot more there than is on the surface.' And I told Jeff everything I knew about Andrew selling drugs and threatening people. Jeff was not just a moral person as I would define him. Jeff was even a little righteous, or self-righteous." Lou recalls that Jeff said he understood, but Andrew wanted to be his best friend, "so I can't just leave him out in the cold." Jeff even filled Lou in with additional details, including correcting the idea that Andrew got his money from his rich parents. "This is kind of sad," Jeff said. "I hear he's a clerk in a drugstore."

When a fellow naval officer went to Jeff's to watch the Army-Navy football game on TV, he tried to dissuade Jeff from seeing so much of Andrew. " 'I've known Andrew all these years, and none of his stories have ever matched. There's something wrong with the whole scenario. Why do you spend so much time with him? What's there?' " he wanted to know. "Jeff said, 'You really got to get to know him. He's a great guy. Warm heart. And he means well.' "

If Andrew was at times scary and callous, he could also be considerate and giving, especially with the items he had started pilfering from Thrifty. He would take to friends who were ill food and medicine from his vast supply. That was "the June Cleaver Andrew," as Buchman says. He was even capable of becoming the "Marcus Welby Andrew," says Ron Williams, a friend from the West Coast bar, who remembers a visit from Andrew when Williams was sick with strep throat. "He came over with a little black doctor's bag. He took out the thermometer and looked at my throat and gave me some Augmentin. He said friends at school were becoming doctors and they supplied him. It worked."

To Ron Williams, Andrew bared his insecurities about not being attractive and about having to buy his popularity. He also said his father had mistreated him. "He had pretty down times. He would be real quiet and reflective and talk about growing up with an abusive father. He said his father used to beat him up." (There is no evidence of this.)

Jeff did not socialize exclusively with Andrew by any means. He became especially friendly with a married couple, Kevin and Laura Gramling. Kevin, who was in Assault Landing Craft Unit One with Jeff, taught him to surf, and through a joke played on Jeff by another gay officer learned that Jeff was gay. It had no affect on their friendship, but Jeff still felt that his men must never know. "Hey, Kevin, if any of my men found out I was gay, it would be difficult to command the same respect from them." One night, to educate Kevin or to soften his attitude, Jeff took him and Laura to Flicks. Various patrons came up to Laura to advise her lasciviously on "how to keep her man." "I wanted to punch them out," Kevin says. He and Jeff got into a heated argument, but they made up the next day.

Lou Feuchtbaum, who was frequently invited to Jeff's house for dinner or cards with other guests, says, "I can't remember ever having seen Andrew at Jeff's home." Jeff's former roommate, a rising naval officer, agrees. "Andrew didn't just drop by." In addition, over time, Jeff had become more wary. "Until we were clear about what his background was and what he did with a lot of missing parts of the day, we just weren't too willing to get involved," says the former roommate. "I think everybody recognized that he made up a lot of fiction about his life—everybody just kind of accepted that." However, whenever Jeff was challenged about Andrew, Lou Feuchtbaum says, he would say, "Hey, this is really pretty sad, and it's pretty pathetic, and I can't turn this guy away. He looks up to me."

It soon became apparent that Jeff had more important things than Andrew to worry about. At the end of 1994, another incident occurred that irrevocably marred his military career. The navy had recently agreed to comply with federal and local environmental regulations. No longer would Assault Landing Craft in Coronado be allowed to carry hazardous waste on board; it had to be stored at a special "Hazwat" station. Jeff's men had removed ten cans of lead-based paint from the ship but the hazardous-waste site was so overwhelmed that Jeff's chief petty officer ordered the crew to put the paint back on the ship, where it could not be stored properly. Then, to avoid an impending inspection by the Environmental Protection Agency, the chief arranged for a "training exercise" to take the craft out to sea. Jeff was not aware of the infraction until the ship was about to get underway.

But someone had tipped off the EPA, and an inspector boarded Jeff's craft at sea from a coast guard ship. The improperly stored materials were found. Jeff, another officer, and three enlisted men were accused of conspiracy, with the implication being that they were trying to dump the hazardous waste in the bay. Jeff always insisted that that was never their intention, but as the officer in charge he took full responsibility. However, he was not supported by his command, and the EPA appeared to want to make the incident an example. In the spring of 1995, Jeff was called before a hearing presided over by a naval administrative judge. "It's nonjudicial punishment where they could pretty much destroy your career, at the very least, and certainly make your life unpleasant at most," says Lou Feuchtbaum. "Jeff didn't back down. He stood his ground." Jeff's sister Lisa Stravinskas, a lawyer, flew to San Diego to be co-counsel for Jeff, and went to dinner one night with him and Lou and Andrew. "The only reason the navy pursued it as much as they did was because the EPA was pushing them to make an example out of Jeff," says his former roommate, the naval officer. "I think he was a little upset that his superiors threw him to the wolves, basically. They didn't support him at all."

In the end, Lou says, "Jeff wound up getting a nonpunitive letter of reprimand, which means if he wanted to stay in the navy, it would have hurt him." But Jeff had no intention of staying. Hoping to become a police officer, he took the California civil service exam. Judy Fleissner, at his request, took the test with him so that he wouldn't feel alone. In May 1996, Jeff left the navy as a lieutenant. In July he was set to begin a training program in Sacramento for the California Highway Patrol. He was looking forward to a new life.

9

Crystal

Even the most dedicated barflies in Andrew's group went home when the clubs closed at 2 A.M. But not Andrew. The predawn hours were when the really wild parties began, and anyone who stayed up night after night, as Andrew did, immersing himself in the after-hours places, was almost certainly "tweaking." Tweakers are users and abusers of the drug methamphetamine—"crystal meth" to the gay world, "crank" to the straight. Yet despite Andrew's typical drug behavior— his habitual nocturnal lifestyle, his volubility, his brash self-confidence in public, all of which are hallmarks of the effect of crystal—no one ever thought of him as a tweaker. But evidence now points to another of Andrew's closely held secrets, one that many of his friends either did not suspect or chose to suppress or ignore: Andrew was a habitual closet user and dealer of crystal meth. It is a rough and extremely destructive drug, and it would strongly affect his future behavior.

At Wolfs, an after-hours leather bar near Hillcrest where Andrew would often drop by in the wee hours, alcohol is not served after 2 A.M. Most patrons don't care—they are already high on meth and don't want to spoil it with a drink. Instead, they are sipping bottled water, chewing gum, and frequently smacking or licking their lips. With pupils dilated and hearts racing, they play billiards at warp speed—grinding the ends of their cue sticks into the chalk, racing around the table to gauge a shot, then quickly lining up the cue and feverishly firing the white ball. Wolfs patrons, often tattooed and in leather, are mostly tweakers running on empty, hoping to score more drugs, have sex at dawn, or find a party with multiple sex partners.

Before Viagra there was crystal. Crystal meth doesn't necessarily make you hard, but it certainly makes you easy. San Diego is the crystal-meth capital of the world. "The biggest gay thing to do is the drugs," says Ronnie Mascarena. "Everybody in San Diego is doing it." Andrew Cunanan was right in the middle of the drug scene.

Methamphetamine, or speed, is a synthetic drug first used widely during World War II and later, in the fifties and sixties, by motorcycle gangs who took it to stay awake on long road trips. Speed has always been associated with aggressive and churlish behavior. Think of the Hell's Angels at the Rolling Stones concert at Altamont in 1969. Crystal has come back recently with a vengeance, particularly as the gay party drug.

In the last decade on the West Coast, and more recently in the Midwest, crystal meth—cheaper than cocaine but harder-edged—has been used as a sex enhancer and as an enabler for "club kids" and others to stay up dancing for hours on end. Crystal, also known as ice, quartz, tina, crank, and even crack, is an appetite suppressant, and it has become the drug of choice for a significant substratum of the gay community; its use is thought to be on an epidemic rise in Los Angeles, San Francisco, and San Diego, and it is spreading across the country. In the Midwest, for example, in certain communities, the use of methamphetamine has increased 300 percent in the second half of the nineties. "Crank," in the straight world, has replaced crack as drug enemy number one, especially among white and Native American youth.

Thus, what used to be called speeding is now called tweaking, or bumping up, in the gay world. Tweaking lowers inhibitions—often, reports say, among gay men who still feel ashamed of gay sex—enhances the intensity of the sex, and relaxes the rectum. Along with MDMA (ecstasy), Special K (anesthetic ketamine, a horse tranquilizer), and GHB (an aphrodisiac "date rape" drug), crystal is a fixture at "circuit parties"—frequent large gatherings of gays with enough money to fly to Palm Springs or Miami Beach, for example, for long weekends filled with drugs, alcohol, and sex. One of Andrew's crystal dealers also ran a circuit-party business. In *Life Outside,* Michelangelo Signorile describes a circuit party at a hotel in Palm Springs with a drug dealer on practically every floor. At times dealing drugs supersedes or underpins the particular business of running the giant party itself.

Such drug use is commonplace throughout various sectors of gay life—a dark secret not much publicized outside the community—and San Diego certainly is no exception. "In order to fit into the gay community in San Diego you have to do drugs," says Joe Sullivan, a former Hillcrest bartender who used crystal meth daily for eight years. "To be on the A list for people's parties, you have to do drugs. And when I say drugs, I mean crystal. If you abstain, you don't get invited."

On the West Coast, crystal meth is also widely integrated into the multimillion-dollar gay social-networking industry of sex-phone lines—which help link men seeking sex or sexual service—as well as bars, bathhouses, and clubs. "It gives you a gung-ho sex drive," says one crystal dealer. "That's why there are all these bathhouses and late-night places that are so busy. The majority of them go all night long." According to a report on methamphetamine use among gays in Los Angeles published in 1997 for the AIDS coordinator of the City of Los Angeles, Dr. Cathy J. Reback states, "The creation of social settings where crystal use is common—or in some social situations, expected—serves to normalize crystal in gay culture."

Crystal, which can be snorted, smoked, drunk, eaten, injected, or absorbed through the rectum, is made with everything from asthma medications to battery acid. The ingredients are easily obtained in Mexico, and recipes on the Internet lend themselves to home manufacture. (Each pound of meth produced leaves behind five or six pounds of toxic waste.) Meth labs in garages or warehouses are found throughout "East County," the eastern part of San Diego county, which is heavily Hispanic. But crystal, which is primarily used by whites, can be "cooked" anywhere—makeshift labs can fit in a suitcase.

Crystal retails for about $600 an ounce in San Diego, but it runs higher if purchased in smaller amounts. AIDS-prevention workers are alarmed that tweaking often means throwing caution to the wind during sex. Popular now, especially among young gays and those already infected with AIDS, is the practice of "barebacking" while on crystal—having unprotected anal sex, an extremely high-risk behavior for acquiring HIV. Reback goes on to say, "Crystal use has been described as a way to dissociate from the fear and responsibility associated with sex within the era of HIV/AIDS." As such it is highly prized.

Crystal makes braggarts like Andrew even louder, filling them with bravado and enabling them to focus speedily on tasks at hand. Yet despite its reputation for providing great sex, crystal is also known for giving users a nasty down. "Terrible Tuesdays" is an expression in San Francisco applied to those who have partied all weekend on crystal, gone to sleep fitfully Sunday night, gotten up and worked on Monday, and then faced sleeplessness, irritability, or depression on Tuesday as the drug makes its way out of the body.

In order to sleep at all, habitual crystal users like Andrew are often forced to use powerful downers—Vicodin, Xanax, Valium—to even out the high. Crystal, aggressive and edgy, artificially stimulates the pleasure centers of the brain to produce a positive feeling. But later it can leave a person feeling so depressed and down that the only solution is to bump up again. Or the high is too good to pass up one more time. In any case, more of the drug is eventually needed.

Each person reacts to crystal differently, but in time it makes people depressed, mean, irritable, and paranoid. In extreme cases, their behavior can resemble pronounced schizophrenia. In addition, crystal addiction is considered among the hardest to overcome because of the way it physically alters the brain. Even after the acute effects of withdrawal fade, addicts hit "the wall," a period of six to eight months "during which the brain recovers from the changes resulting from meth use," according to the 1998 Koch Crime Commission Report. "During this period recovering addicts feel depressed, fuzzy headed, and think life isn't pleasurable without the drug. Because prolonged use causes changes in the brain, will power alone will not cure meth addicts."

Friends often suggested that Andrew was tweaking. Nevertheless, he was a skilled liar, and he appears to have been careful with his use—there were periods when he even castigated others for being on crystal—and he always ate heartily, thus avoiding the emaciated, hollow-eyed look of many tweakers. "He probably got used to it," one of his ex-dealers says. "You can sleep on it and eat and drink on it. He had the money. I'm sure most people didn't even know he did it."

According to this dealer, Andrew began using crystal regularly in 1993, at parties during Gay Pride Week in San Diego, which takes place in the summer. That corresponds to a period when he in fact lost weight. Crystal can act like a permanent diet pill. The dealer says Andrew wanted his drug use to be a secret. "He tried to lay low with it; he was pretty closeted with it. I knew all the important people that nobody was supposed to know were using it—he was one of them who wanted it very quiet."

The dealer, who ironically had a close family member who was a high elected official in a Midwestern state, says Andrew began buying small amounts of drugs through the dealer's partner in the fall of 1991. Then his use escalated. Over several years, beginning in 1993, Andrew purchased a sizable amount of crystal meth at least twice a month. The dealer says Andrew's monthly outlay sometimes was $4,000.

Early on, Andrew apparently realized that he could sell crystal in the Midwest and make a handsome profit. "He can get it here for six hundred dollars an ounce. Then he could turn it around and sell it in the Midwest for three thousand dollars an ounce," the dealer says. "That's a quick turnaround." Andrew also worked as a mule for the dealer, flying first class. Many dealers used to send crystal through commercial shipping services that never checked—"anything could make it through," the dealer recounts. "But now you're taking a risk for something being mailed." In 1997, the dealer says, these services began to "buckle down. Now you have to fly."

That setup was perfect for Andrew. He would tell people in Hillcrest that he was traveling on the weekend, jetting off to one spot or another, but he hadn't decided where. He would insinuate that he knew famous gays such as entertainment mogul David Geffen, referring to Geffen by his first name once to Dr. William Crawford, for example, after having come back from a weekend in Los Angeles. David Geffen says he never met Andrew.

What seems more likely is that Andrew traveled either on tickets purchased through credit-card-fraud schemes—one convicted airline ticket fraudster now in jail serviced Hillcrest—or that he was recruited by a San Diego porn star who made his real money as a high-priced call boy. (Porn stars are the supermodels of the gay world.) The porn star would receive invitations from rich, often famous gays, as well as closeted married CEO's, and he would ship pretty boys or willing young men out for weekend trysts. They often traveled first class. "The escort once opened a FedEx package containing ten thousand dollars in hundred dollar bills in front of me," says Joe Sullivan, the former bartender. "That's what he was being paid for the weekend."

Joe Sullivan says that he, too, was recruited to be a jet-setting escort, but he refused. "Andrew ran with the crowd which spent time with these men. The clients were just very beaucoup-bucks wealthy. You'd literally get fifteen hundred dollars a day to fly to New York, plus tip, plus first-class expenses." Even so, a sexual relationship was not always assumed.

"Sex isn't involved a lot of the time," says Sullivan. "It's just companionship. You have a nice, young, attractive person who can make your friends jealous." At first Andrew, he says, just "started hanging around these people. And then, from everything I could tell, he became one of them. It's all done out of state."

Though Sullivan himself did not see Andrew using crystal, he knew that Andrew was hanging around with the circle of one of his former employers—among them his former boss's partner and fellow dealer. (This dealer later confirmed in detail Andrew's drug use.) According to Sullivan, "They were the white guys that you could go to and buy drugs. They would get it from the Mexican Mafia." These dealers were hardly a secret, but people rarely spoke about them. "The gay community in San Diego is very weird," says Brian Wade Smith, who knew Andrew there. "There are a lot of homeless kids, a lot of drugs, but it's all very hidden. I live in Minneapolis now. If I took Minneapolis people to San Diego, they would be really shocked. Everybody's on crystal in San Diego."

One night in 1995 at Rich's Bar, Andrew said to his friend Shane O'Brien, "I need you to follow behind me walking down the street. Walk twenty feet behind me and wear my jacket."

"I knew at that point he was dealing drugs," says Shane. Andrew explained that he was working in a pharmacy and getting the drugs there. Shane said no. "I could look like him. I said, 'I'm not going to get shot walking down the street because people think it's you.' He got put off and said, 'Fine. I'll find somebody else.' "

Twice Andrew had Shane drop him off at an adult video store on University Avenue. "I just made a 'purchase,' " Andrew told him, when he came out carrying a brown paper bag. "Want to see what's inside?" Shane said yes. "And he opened it. There were stacks of bills inside the brown paper bag. I said, 'Did you sell something?' He said yes. That happened twice, that he made a 'purchase.' "

The brown paper bag became an accessory of sorts for Andrew. One Monday night at the Brass Rail, a Hillcrest club with a drag show, Eric, a blond waiter with spiked hair, remembers, Andrew was perched at the bar when he suddenly pulled a huge wad of cash out of the bag and said, "I'm going to buy me some drugs and sell me some drugs."

Taurey Willis, a rave disc jockey originally from England, saw Andrew doing lines of crystal and dealing drugs at a 1995 party thrown by a wealthy gay couple from the Midwest at a mansion in nearby Del Mar, the site of the famous racetrack. "There was group sex and fetishing going on, and a couple of guys dressed in heavy leather gear," says Willis. "Way too wild for me." One room was the drug room. "I saw Andrew in that room doing business. He was selling."

Taurey believed that Andrew was also some kind of sexual middle man. On Fridays at Flicks, Taurey says, "really attractive younger guys" would go up to Andrew, who would make quick introductions, and the guys would then hastily leave together. "There was no standing around talking or having a drink or anything."

The wealthiest and most celebrated men in San Diego would not even go into a gay bar. "The social life is totally private invitation," says Nicole Ramirez-Murray. But for someone like Andrew, who was happy to trade in drugs and sex and make arrangements, there were constant opportunities. Joe Sullivan once answered an ad in La Jolla soliciting bartenders and waiters for a season of private dinner parties. "The pay was great," says Sullivan, who was told by the middle-aged business-man who interviewed him that the guests would be prominent local businessmen, some of them married. "Everything sounded great until he brought out this picture book of some of the waiters and bartenders at these parties." They were wearing G-strings "with strategic holes placed in the G-strings, and they were dressed up as bunny rabbits with genitalia as their noses." The interviewer explained to a suddenly disinterested Sullivan that "at the end of the season of dinner parties, a cash prize would be given for 'the best service.' "

Andrew enjoyed this rich, coastal, closeted crowd. And just as he had once been taken to the gay leader to be fixed up, Andrew could now be the silky hustler, the one who traded knowledge and favors and drugs for access and travel. A major Hillcrest drug dealer was familiar with Andrew's activities. "There'd be the wealthy locals, and then they'd have guys in from out of town. I think he was probably in charge of maybe organizing the tricks and the sex parties." The dealer adds, "They're wealthy and retired. Even these guys—a lot of them—do crystal sometimes. A lot of people into their fifties do it heavy out here. That's why they call San Diego the crystal capital."

In the world in which Andrew now sought to elevate himself, where looks and wealth ruled, and where sex was the commodity and drugs were the fuel, crystal meth was bringing to the fore practices long confined to the seamy underbelly of gay society. Bootleg "candid" videos in which subjects, some of them drugged, had no idea they were being filmed during sex acts, became widespread. The drugged subjects were said to be in the "K hole," able to perform physically but completely non compos mentis because they were on the drug Special K, notorious in the mainstream press as a date-rape drug. Secret videotaping went on constantly. Andrew wanted to be part of it all, and he plied himself against a backdrop peopled with murky characters and marked by surprising violence and brutality. It just wasn't talked about.

The most notorious party giver in Hillcrest—the ringmaster of the Evil Circus—was a diminutive ex-seminarian, half-Irish, half-Greek, who claimed to be both a chemical engineer and a Catholic priest, and Andrew desperately tried to keep up with him. Theodore "Vance" Coukoulis certainly knew his chemistry, and he applied that knowledge as a con artist, but he had no degree of any kind in science. Yet he and two real priests once got all the way to Kiev to deliver to the local branch of the Russian Academy of Sciences a paper on a chemical formula he had helped develop that might decrease low-level radiation in the aftermath of Chernobyl. Although he had passed through several Catholic seminaries across the country, Vance Coukoulis was never, nor will he ever be, ordained. He is not in a state of grace.

Vance Coukoulis was a premier party-giver in Hillcrest, and Andrew constantly sought invitations to Vance's parties. But in 1994 Vance had gotten busted for possession of drugs in Hillcrest after neighbors complained about his noisy parties. He then served a short time in jail, after which he was put for five years on summary probation, which carries no sanctions. He was arrested again in 1998, in Sedona, Arizona, for the "sexual exploitation of minors" by means of pornographic videos. A mother charged that her missing fifteen-year-old son had gotten drugs from Vance, who allegedly had sex with the boy and enticed him into posing for pornographic videos.

The state offered Vance a plea-bargain, which he refused. Preparing to go to trial, prosecutors launched a further investigation and uncovered enough additional evidence to expand the original four charges to eighteen counts of sexual exploitation of minors—the sum of which carry a penalty of over three hundred years in prison.

A court document alleges that Vance "introduces himself to young people as a priest who worked in the Vatican with the Pope, or as a former priest. Once the young males, many of them under eighteen years of age, trust the defendant, he then takes them to his home, or locations such as hotels, where he gives them alcohol laced with drugs." The document subsequently describes videos in which "young boys appear to be either unconscious or drugged to the extent that they cannot resist the sexual advances made upon them." Vance then "often uses sadomasochistic sex toys and paraphernalia on the boys, the defendant shaves the pubic and anal areas of the boys, the defendant diapers the boys, powders their buttocks with baby powder, the defendant places a baby bottle in the mouth for the boys and the boys are shown sucking brown fluid from the bottles, sexual acts including anal, oral, and masturbation are displayed and the defendant appears in the video wearing a baseball cap."

Interestingly, among the items found at the time of Vance's initial

arrest in March 1998 were a leather collar, a whip, a leash and restraints, a spiked leather bracelet, a vibrator, a pacifier, diapers, and a
magazine article and documentary about Andrew Cunanan.

Having sat in the Yavapai County jail for several months without
visitors, Vance, who claimed his arrest was false and ridiculous, talked
about his past with an eye toward his future. "If I become a priest and
get ordained in the next year and a half, I've got to be careful about
some stuff," he said. Still, he didn't hesitate to acknowledge the source
of his unique social standing in Hillcrest. "Out of fun I had a dungeon
built in my home."

Vance's dungeon was notorious in Hillcrest, a must-see venue for a
social animal like Andrew. The son of an Air Force officer who retired as
a general, Vance liked to teach young, fresh, newly out gays about S&M.
His walls prominently displayed pictures of himself with the pope
along with S&M paraphernalia, and he boasted that one day in St.
Peter's Square, "out of a million people in the crowd, the Holy Father
saw me, walked over to me, and asked me if I wanted to work with
crippled children in the Vatican." He claimed that he had lived in
Rome for two years. The truth, however, which Andrew and his friends
in Hillcrest never knew, was even stranger.

According to Father Charles Shelton, a Franciscan priest who accompanied Vance to meet the pope on more than one occasion, Vance had
once worked for a shadowy underworld intelligence figure in Phoenix
with ties to both the CIA and the Chinese; his aim in meeting the pope
was to try to pressure the Vatican into opening a consulate in Phoenix,
so that the Chinese could use it to negotiate South China Sea oil deals
without being spied on by the Russians. "Then Tiananmen Square happened, and it all fell apart," says Father Charles. "I have photographs of
Vance with the pope. But the meetings were always very short and sort
of puzzling for the Holy Father."

Father Charles, who says he knew nothing of Vance's behavior
toward minors, was also the instigator of a trip to Russia for Vance. The
idea was to offer the formula for Chernobyl as a bribe to get Russian
help to release missing-in-action (MIA) prisoners—a cause with personal significance to Father Charles, whose father was an MIA, and
whose late mother, Marian Shelton, founded the National League of

Families of the Missing in Action and Prisoners of War in Southeast
Asia. But once in Russia, Vance started flashing money at the hotel bar,
got beat up and robbed; while the attack brought Vance in touch with
Gorbachev's personal physician, who treated his injuries (he lost his
spleen), Vance thus missed his chance to address the Academy.

In a place like San Diego, it was inevitable that Vance and Andrew
would meet and conspire—they often favored the same quarry. Vance,
born in 1951 and openly gay from an early age, dropped even bigger
names than Andrew did. Like Andrew, he cultivated pretty boys as well
as the promiscuous, very wealthy architect Lincoln Aston. Vance says
that on several occasions Andrew proposed to him that they should
work together. Andrew enjoyed bringing people over to the dungeon,
where, Vance says, Andrew would just walk around and laugh his piercing laugh. "Whenever he got nervous or unsure of things, he laughed."

Vance recalls Andrew's proposal: "He would be more than willing to
travel with me, spend time with me, do whatever and just have fun.
And if that meant sexualness in between, then fine, but it wasn't the
initial motivation. The motivation was to have someone who had a lot
of contacts, who had a lot of fun, who invited people around. I never
needed that."

Vance regarded Andrew warily and he resented Andrew's influence
with Lincoln Aston, who came from big Texas oil money. Vance had
probably hoped that Lincoln would be susceptible to his schemes, so
Andrew was an impediment. "All of ninety-four, you could not see
Lincoln without Andrew at his side," says Vance. "It was disgusting.
Every time I tried to get Lincoln to talk to me, Andrew wouldn't let
me. He was like a bodyguard." Through Lincoln, meanwhile, Andrew
was solidifying his closeted La Jolla connections.

Vance claims that Lincoln had grown disillusioned with Andrew and
was trying delicately to extricate himself from his clutches by giving
him "twenty or thirty thousand dollars to go away." Suddenly, however, on May 19, 1995, Lincoln Aston was bludgeoned to death with a
stone obelisk from his art collection by a mentally disturbed drifter he
had picked up in a bar. Because Andrew bragged to people that he had
been with Lincoln the night of his death and had found the body, many

in Hillcrest still believe that he had something to do with his murder. The San Diego police, however, flatly deny any connection. The drifter pleaded guilty and is now in jail.

Vance and Andrew's relationship began to fall apart a few weeks after Lincoln's death. When Vance went up to Andrew in Rich's Bar one Saturday night, he was appalled that Andrew expressed no remorse for their friend's death. "He acted like he felt absolutely nothing." Vance decided then and there that he truly despised Andrew. Yet despite his animosity, Vance maintains a cool, analytical appraisal of Andrew's abilities.

"In the gay world you're either very good-looking or you're very wealthy in order to obtain any comment or be invited anywhere," says Vance. "It's unfortunate, it's a very shallow thing." Andrew stood out, he says, because Andrew wanted so much more than anyone else. "Being both with good-looking people and being surrounded by people with money was unique to Andrew. He was a pro. Most people didn't work both ends of the rope. Most guys either just hung with all the good-looking guys or they would work all the older men and stay away from the good-looking guys, because the good-looking guys were competition."

Not Andrew. "One of his ways of winning people over and making them think, 'This guy really has money,' was handing out large amounts of drugs. It was more of a favor, because that impressed people more than anything," Vance says. "What Andrew did was be a PR man. And that's a lot more important in the gay society." Not only did Andrew connect people, but he did so without charging. "How convenient. How nice. It's unusual to find a person who would do that, so I don't have to go through a legalized or escort service where I'm tracked. So he found a niche that provided favors, and people are willing to pay for favors." Vance says that sex didn't matter with Andrew. "He provided a much greater favor. He provided people whom these people wanted, or drugs or whatever, and a connect like that is very powerful."

Mood altering was Vance's specialty. People in the know in Hillcrest would never accept a drink from Vance. Guests claimed his champagne was sometimes spiked with rohypnol, a date-rape drug that seems to eliminate free will. "People walked away from there doing things they really did not want to do," says reformed crystal abuser Hank Randolph.

Joe Sullivan believes he had a mickey slipped into champagne Vance gave him on Christmas night in 1986. "I called him and said, 'What happened?' He said, 'I guess the champagne got to you.' Well, I guess it did. He had done this to a lot of different people." Franz vonRichter, Andrew's close friend at the end of his life, also thinks he was drugged some years later.

Buzz English, another young Hillcrest resident, recalls something far more sinister, however. Between 1992 and 1994, when Buzz was seventeen and eighteen, he was part of a young, pretty-boy group who were routinely admitted into the bars and clubs of Hillcrest even though they were under age. They would constantly see Andrew in these places. At 2 A.M. they would be asked to join bartenders and bouncers from the various clubs at early morning parties. "We used to go to these parties as tokens," says Buzz, who was raised on a Pennsylvania dairy farm. "We'd be partying in the back room, there'd be sex in another room, and people playing games and watching TV, socializing and mingling. We were there to make the old guys look good."

Buzz saw Andrew at several of these gatherings. "He would only talk to people with money. We were told he was a little off." Although Andrew tried to appear "prude and pristine," he was definitely on crystal, Buzz says. "He was basically a closet user. Crystal meth is dirty, and people don't have good lives on it. They lose everything. He didn't want to be a part of that or look like that."

Buzz remembers a party at Vance's when Andrew was not present. "One of us in our little clique was locked and tied up for hours. Vance is crazy, and I guess a couple of guys from the bars gang-banged our friend. It was a big hush-hush thing, and they advised him to leave town, and he did." Says Joe Sullivan, "He would get people who were seventeen, eighteen, who were just coming out and just beginning to explore their sexuality, and he would invite them to these parties where all of these very attractive young guys would be running around doing drugs, and it was sort of, 'You want into the gay world? This is it.'"

Vance denies all of these allegations. He says the dungeon was used only, "out of a sense of humor. I never took it seriously. I would laugh at people who said, 'This is so disgusting,' and I would say five hours later, 'Are you disgusted enough?' *Please!* I just love human nature." As far as drugs are concerned, he says, "I would only invite one person. And if they ended up having a good time, they better have a good explanation if their other half found out about what happened. 'Oh, I was drugged' or 'I passed out.' Anything to give an excuse for their own personal behavior." He denies seducing young boys. "I have a lot more morality and class than that. The truth of it is, I had some pretty wild parties, and I wouldn't invite everybody. And it was the people who weren't invited who spread the gossip."

One of those specifically not invited was Andrew Cunanan, whom Vance had come to dislike so intensely after Lincoln's death that he personally told him to stay away from his parties. But Andrew usually managed to show up with somebody who was invited. "After the third time it happened," Vance says, "I wasn't surprised anymore, and I even had bodyguards looking for him."

Andrew simply had to be in the center of the action, even if he was not wanted—even if the circle he was crashing was way beyond his imaginings. Because of his use of crystal meth, Andrew knew a number of users and dealers who came to sad and sordid ends. Lincoln Aston's death, for example, was preceded by the farcical tragedy of Scott Sloggett, the owner of Another Video Company Ltd., a gay pornographic studio in San Diego.

Andrew loved to associate with porn stars and tried repeatedly to act in porn movies himself. According to Vance, he would attempt to refer male models to Sloggett for pornographic videos; he also spent time with Sloggett in his house at Pt. Loma, an exclusive San Diego neighborhood. In addition to being a pornography purveyor, Sloggett was also a crystal dealer. He owed Vance a lot of money—supposedly for real estate deals—and Vance was looking to collect. Sloggett's onetime video art director and former partner, Glen Offield, had the largest collection of Barbie dolls in the world. The collection of five thousand dolls, along with thousands of Barbie dresses, purses, shoes, houses, and Corvettes, was appraised at more than one million dollars and had appeared on the cover of the *Smithsonian* magazine. After spending his workday on hard-core porn, Offield would come home to five thousand pristine unviolated Barbies, which he said, "had never been played with." Apparently, Sloggett saw this valuable collection as a way out of his money woes.

Vance claims that on October 10, 1992, while Offield was at a doll convention, Sloggett went to Offield's house and mixed a batch of crystal meth that blew up and started a fire. The police say Sloggett set another fire in Offield's house the following night in order to provide cover for the theft of thirty-seven cardboard moving boxes filled with dozens upon dozens of Barbies, Kens, and Skippers, which he dumped in a self-storage locker under a freeway overpass. The locker just happened to be rented in Vance's name.

Meanwhile Vance returned from a trip to Europe. The first thing he did was call Sloggett, who must have felt guilty about holding a million dollars' worth of Barbies hostage, because he cried and told Vance that things weren't going well.

Before Vance could get over to see Sloggett and demand his money, he was told that Sloggett had taken a sedative and was sleeping. In fact, Sloggett had committed suicide by swallowing forty morphine pills. Vance felt the suicide might be a trick, but he had no way to check, because the police would not let anyone see the body. Finally the police allowed the body to be blessed by a priest: Vance Coukoulis.

To make sure Sloggett hadn't faked a suicide with someone else's body, Vance says, "I put on my Roman collar. That was the only way the police would allow me in, to bless the body. And so they brought him out and I blessed him. And I made sure it was him! And also I truly, truly blessed him because I was very concerned about his soul and, because I didn't want him to be buried and not be blessed. And I must tell you," says Vance from his jail cell, "the expression on his face was the first expression that ever told me there was real evil."

The Barbies were later found in the storage locker room rented in Vance's name while Vance was in Holland where, he says, "I have an office." The story made headlines around the country, but Vance Coukoulis was never mentioned. Glen Offield, the owner of the Barbies, had a news conference to announce their retrieval. "I'm, like, I'm numb," the *Los Angeles Times* quoted Offield as saying. Brandishing a

1961 ponytailed Barbie for the TV cameras, he cried, "I've got them back!"

For Andrew, Scott Sloggett was a trifecta: he appeared to have money, he dealt drugs, and his business was pornography. "Crystal and pornography go hand in hand," says Vance. "It's a sex drug, and all it does is just heighten your whole sexual feeling about a million times." Andrew constantly got crushes on porn stars. His friend Erik Greenman, who would become his last roommate, had acted in a few pornographic films as "Josh Connors," and pornography held a prominent place in the world Andrew inhabited. "It's a big business," says Nathan Fry, who plays the piano for many events around town. "Every day I hear about another friend who did one. People think it's a high compliment to be wanted in one—it means you're sexy."

Andrew became an avid consumer of adult videos, particularly rough and violent S&M videos. As his crystal use continued, pornographic videos were probably his most consistent form of sexual release. Yet an obsession with pornography, says Vance, "wouldn't make Andrew look out of the usual at all."

Though gays are estimated to compromise only about 10 percent of the population, a 1996 Adult Video News Statistics study says gay video rentals and sales account for approximately one-third to one-half of total pornography-industry sales. These sales run to the hundreds of millions of dollars. About three thousand official gay titles are produced a year. It's anyone's guess how many more "candid videos" there are and what they bring in.

In *The Rise and Fall of Gay Culture*, Daniel Harris decries "the yuppification of gay pornography," where "the porn star is increasingly the embodiment, not only of the gay man's sexual desires but of his social and economic desires as well, his aspirations to lead the carefree life of a lounge lizard swimming in disposable income and basking in the sun around his crystalline pool where beautiful boys in bikinis silently skim the leaves from the waters and then succumb wholeheartedly to his sensual whimsies." For a lazy materialist like Andrew, these fantasies must have taken on a special vibrancy. "Contemporary pornography eroticizes all kinds of extraneous things," Harris continues, "chandeliers and Persian carpets, Porsches and convertible coupes, jade figurines and silver candelabra, all of the status symbols crop up on the inanimate fringes of the picture, where they are invested with erotic significance as searingly intense as the sexual images in the foreground."

Unfortunately, these pleasurable fantasies, coupled with crystal meth, can turn ugly and perverse, and the squalor of this reality is far away from crystalline pools and silver candelabra. Once again, in March 1996, the drug precipitated murder right in Andrew's backyard.

On March 16, 1996, Lou Ball, an "audio-video specialist" from an upstanding Philadelphia family, was murdered by ex-con neighbors who stole his safe—which contained cash from his methamphetamine drug deals—and some of his camera equipment. As it turned out, Nathan Fry had been with Ball just before he was murdered. Fry had gone back to Ball's apartment to get help with some audiocassettes, and he noticed that the position of a closet door had moved from when he first entered the room. "I got a sick feeling in my stomach and told Lou to get out of there," Fry says. "Then I left." Ball was found stabbed to death, and Fry became the principal prosecution witness at his murder trial. Two ex-cons living in the apartment next door to Ball were convicted and are now in jail.

The untold story, according to Fry, is one in which police seemed to display little curiosity: Ball's role as a child pornographer. "They weren't really interested in whatever kind of things that Lou was doing with videos—they were mostly just interested in getting these guys who killed him," says Fry.

Fry charges, however, that Ball and Vance "were in coproduction." Vance would recruit young boys, whom Ball would secretly videotape. "Vance and Lou had a thing going where Vance would get the talent and perform various acts while Lou had video or audiovisual." The equipment was rigged from an apartment below. According to Fry, Ball ran wires up and installed a false wall that concealed a camera and a peephole.

"They could pick up somebody who was really too young to even be walking outside at night, and get them on tape, and then sell that to his buddies, who would pay good money for those types of videos," says Fry. "The person who had rented this apartment [after the murder] showed me where it had been restored back to normal, with the wall being plastered up."

At the time of Lou Ball's death, his apartment was full of kiddie-porn videos, but the police found little evidence. According to Fry, "Those were all missing when the police came around, because Lou's friends had run through and gotten all the stash of videos."

Vance claims, "I was sitting outside his home when he got murdered. And I didn't know that until a whole month later." Vance says that Ball "was a pretty heavy drug dealer, that [his murder] was drug-related, and I know that all of his drugs disappeared except for a small quantity after his death." And what does he have to say about the videos?

"In the gay culture it's not uncommon for an individual to have a hundred tapes. It's just not uncommon," says Vance, sidestepping the question. (He denies any involvement with Lou Ball and kiddie porn.) "I would say out of fifty thousand people who used crystal, forty-five thousand would watch pornography, because pornography and that drug go together like milk and ice cream," he continues. "I'm sure it exists in the straight world as well." Vance blames crystal for "making you think about sex twenty-four hours a day. The whole system's become so promiscuous it's frightening. I believed in the devil after I got involved with the gay society and crystal meth, and then I realized evil existed in human nature and that human nature can be of good or of evil, and I really believe in evil now. Period. And I believe an evil spirit can overtake people, and I believe that's what happened to Andrew. He changed through the use of that drug."

10

Kept Boy

WHEN ANDREW MET Lincoln Aston and started to frequent Lincoln's gay salon, he also began to network in hopes of finding a way to be kept. He was perfectly at ease with these men at least thirty years older than he was, either in groups or one on one. He was particularly adept at discerning and then reading up on whatever his targets' interests might be—literature, art, flying. He did this whether those he targeted were younger or older.

Like a geisha, Andrew could converse knowledgeably, make entertainment arrangements, and provide comfort, sexual or otherwise. But few men found him sensual—his feelings had been long buried, and he was generally perceived as unemotional and largely cerebral.

With people his own age, he made comments about sex that were usually rough and easily dismissed. He was also known to make wicked asides, which could be very amusing if one was not the target. Lincoln Aston, who had spent many years living in San Francisco and who referred to San Diego as "Omaha by the bay," saw Andrew as a budding bon vivant, a young sophisticate. He would tell friends, "Andrew is the smartest young man I ever knew."

"It was like Andrew was the king of England. He threw out a platinum card to pay for dinner," says one fiftyish La Jolla man who was treated to expensive meals by Andrew on three occasions. A Bishop's graduate who had married but had eventually made his way to Hillcrest, the man listened to Andrew DeSilva tell what had become his "story" for the more established set: He was half Portuguese-Jewish and half Filipino, had once been married to a Jewish princess, and was the father of a little daughter. He loved to ride in his grandmother's Rolls-Royce. He had gone to Choate and to Bishop's and had spent two years in the Israeli army. His wealthy parents, who lived in Rancho Santa Fe and Manhattan, had thrown him out when they learned he was gay.

Andrew's careful re-creation of his life was designed to place him as the social equal of his betters, brilliant and exotic, certainly not some boy toy who could be easily dismissed. "Andrew DeSilva" could elicit sympathy from older men who had once been married themselves or who had had to give up a family and suffer in order to become who they were. Yet Andrew was so careful not to appear to be wanting anything that his Bishop's alumnus dinner guest says that it was only in retrospect that he realized what Andrew was up to: "I think these dinners were come-ons to see if I had money and would bite on the hook, which never occurred to me."

Andrew was definitely trolling, though, and in mid-1994, he caught a big fish. Through a long-established gay couple in La Jolla, whom Andrew had met with Lincoln, Andrew was invited that July to a dinner with Norman Blachford. Like his hosts and Lincoln, Blachford was a member of Gamma Mu, known as the "pink Mafia," a private, exclusive gay men's fraternity which Armistead Maupin makes fun of in *Tales of the City,* disguising it as "the Millionaires Club." It was the perfect group for Andrew to penetrate—secretive, slightly snobbish, and filled with potential sugar daddies.

Tall, with reddish-brown hair, a long face, and an aquiline nose, Norman Blachford, then fifty-eight, looked as if he preferred to be outdoors, working the land. He was reserved, soft-spoken, extremely conservative, and very, very rich. Norman's home was in Phoenix but he traveled frequently to La Jolla, as so many of the well-off of Phoenix do, flying over in less than an hour. La Jolla is Phoenix's East Hampton. Although rich Texans prefer nearby Del Mar for the races in July, the

"Zonies" gravitate to La Jolla. Norman owned a condo in a choice building on Coast Boulevard overlooking the ocean, two minutes away from Bishop's School.

Norman's partner of twenty-six years had recently died of AIDS, so Norman was alone and very eligible. His fortune came from selling the company he had owned, which developed special sound-insulation equipment for the film industry; the company had once received an Oscar for technical achievement. Norman was rumored to be worth scores of millions of dollars—a fact Andrew's friends say Andrew researched thoroughly. In Phoenix, Norman was a significant donor to the symphony. He was also very much interested in art, so Andrew was quickly able to impress him. Norman, however, was cautious by nature and did not part easily with his money, which was a source of frustration to Andrew from the start.

The relationship did not spark all at once. Andrew continued to spend evenings with Lincoln, deal drugs, and remain a fixture at Flicks and Rich's, as well as at the upscale restaurant next door to Flicks, California Cuisine, where he always requested a table next to the window. It was not unknown for Andrew to dash out into the street and haul in a cute boy he'd seen passing by, whom he'd invite to join his group for dinner. Then he might try to fix him up with somebody as a favor and leave a tip for the waiter—sometimes $200 for a $400 dinner for eight. Andrew had it down pat. He would leave a small tip on the credit card slip, a larger amount in cash, and then, when everybody could see, he would press more cash into the waiter's hand on the way out—godfather style.

Andrew was so fond of California Cuisine that on Mother's Day he arrived with flowers for Stella Kalamaras, the owner, telling her, "You're my family." His own mother nearby was ignored. Stella's husband had owned a restaurant in Chicago, and she and Andrew would discuss the Windy City—he seemed to know it well. He told Stella that he was part Italian. She was surprised, however, when Andrew described the part of Italy he said his family was from; she told a friend she recognized it as a penal colony!

On the weekends, Andrew would sometimes travel with Jeff. They would take advantage of Southwest Airlines' policy of giving two tickets for the price of one full fare. One of the places they liked to visit was Chicago, near Jeff's hometown of DeKalb. Andrew was nothing if not well traveled.

In the fall of 1994, for example, Doug Stubblefield was surprised to run into Andrew at the San Francisco Opera with "an old man" he passed off as "a friend of the family." Doug recalls, "It really shocked me to see him with a sugar daddy." But Andrew finessed it, and once he had made the introductions he joined Doug and his friends for drinks. Yet from then on, says Stubblefield, "his material circumstances were very odd. He was always driving different people's cars and staying at different people's houses, with never much explanation or friendly conversation about them."

Stubblefield was one of those who always saw Andrew's behavior as "very druglike. He was erratic, and he had his up and down times." Doug says, "He was always flighty and strung out, so that stood out." No one in San Francisco ever thought Andrew was a dealer, though. "A lot of people questioned whether he was doing drugs—no one questioned that he was *selling* them."

While Norman and Andrew were becoming acquainted, Norman continued to reside in Phoenix, and Andrew would visit him there. Andrew set out to show Norman how valuable he could be as the ultimate passkey to gay culture. They traveled together to Europe, and Norman was amazed by how much Andrew knew about architecture and paintings. Andrew took care of the details and organized the travel plans. He was a lively traveling companion, and for someone like Norman, who was naturally subdued, Andrew was also a great connector. In San Diego, particularly, Andrew knew virtually all of gay society. If Andrew's stories gave Norman any pause, he did not appear to be bothered. When they were with other people, Norman would listen to Andrew tell his tales without comment.

On his own turf, Andrew was a walking Baedeker. He knew the best places to see and be seen, the correct fund-raisers to attend. Andrew proved himself an adept acolyte of Lincoln, who continued to teach him a great deal. "Andrew was always at the right social functions and always tried to impress people," says Dr. Russell Okihara, who observed him on the social circuit. For Norman, as Robbins Thompson, Andrew's closeted surfer friend from UCSD noted, Andrew would be the perfect wife.

Nevertheless, whenever Andrew attempted to gain sympathy from one of the pretty young boys he tried to lure at the same time he was going after Norman—mostly by buying them drinks and dinner—he would complain that he was their victim. He said he thought they used him. With Ron Williams, the young man he had once helped nurse and had had quite a crush on at the time, Andrew would drop his happy-go-lucky pose and become very morose.

"We went out to dinner and dancing and we kissed, never anything more. He wasn't my type; he liked me, I didn't like him," Williams explains. "He was hurt. He thought people hung around him because he had money. He felt if he stopped paying, he'd lose all his friends. I put it to him once—he didn't answer me directly. I always thought he was insecure and wanted to be the life of the party. He was an A-lister, wanted only pretty boys around and only sparkling personalities. I told him, 'I've seen people like you paying everyone's way. You're good-looking.' He didn't think he was good-looking. I said, 'You think unless you [pay] you'll be out sitting in a corner eating mud. Why waste your money on these people?' He wouldn't answer me, and changed the subject. A couple of times he said, 'I could leave today and nobody'd know I was gone.' He had pretty down times." But such sentiments Andrew would never display in front of older men.

In April, Phil Merrill picked Andrew up and they drove to Los Angeles so that Andrew could be the godfather at the christening of Phil and Lizzie's son. By then it seemed that Andrew was wearing out his welcome with Lincoln, and in May 1995 Lincoln Aston was murdered by the male hustler. Before he died, "Lincoln had begun to tell people they should avoid Andrew," says a close friend of Lincoln's, who heard Lincoln say that Andrew would have to be "at least ten years older than he was to have done everything he said he had done."

For Andrew, losing Lincoln meant losing a lifestyle and a part-time piggybank. He quickly quit his job at Thrifty Drug and moved out of San Bernardo. In July 1995, two months after Lincoln's death, Andrew moved into Norman's condo in La Jolla. It had been exactly a year since they'd met. "They both knew what they were getting into," says Robbins. "This is not a situation of an older guy taking advantage of a younger guy. If anything, it was the other way around." It certainly was. "Andrew was kept before Norman," says Jeff Trail's friend Michael Williams, the restaurant owner. "Jeff told me there were others. I said, 'How did he become involved with these people?' Jeff said, 'He investigated them and put himself in those circles with them.'"

Andrew's departure left his mother high and dry. Contrary to the stories Andrew spun of a rich mother staying with her husband just so that her children could have their inheritance, MaryAnn was practically penniless. That November, Pete Cunanan suddenly stopped having his $650 navy pension checks sent to MaryAnn because he says, they were intended for Andrew's schooling. Unable to afford the rent without help, in December 1995 MaryAnn moved back to Illinois where her two eldest children lived. She later went on public assistance.

Meanwhile, Andrew enjoyed the swell life. After years of trying, he had finally landed someone to support his dreams. "In the gay community, Andrew opened every door he set out to open," says Robbins admiringly. Norman was generous with Andrew. He paid his credit cards and gave him a new, $33,000 Infiniti to drive around in, and an allowance of $2,500 a month. Andrew was also allowed a measure of freedom to travel on his own to see his old friends. Norman still had his house in Phoenix, which Andrew didn't much care for and eventually convinced him to sell. They continued to fly back to Phoenix for social events. From the beginning, however, Andrew's relationship with Norman was a cautionary tale of "be careful what you wish for."

"When he moved in with Norman, he basically knew he was going in there on a strictly financial basis," says Robbins. "There was obviously a great deal of affection. There was no question about that. But they were both clear-thinking guys, and they knew what was going on." Still, Andrew kept his new life largely a secret, and he did not like to admit that he was no longer in control or that his relationship with Norman included sex.

Shane O'Brien remembers being taken to the La Jolla condo by Andrew once while Norman was out of town. "I got to the bedroom and I said, 'Andrew, why are there two beds in here?' He told me they didn't sleep together. These were twin beds like you see in an eight-year-old's room—in the master bedroom. They used the other bedroom as a study. These two teeny beds on the opposite ends of a huge room— really weird. Andrew said, 'He doesn't expect that, he doesn't want that.'" Shane was incredulous when Andrew insisted, "No, I've never had sex with Norman." "I know that wasn't true," says Robbins. "I think that's what Andrew had hoped. They had a very close relationship, and basically it got to the point where, hey, we're in a relationship and that's part of a relationship. Either we're going to have a relationship or it's going to end."

Caught in a trap, Andrew never gave Norman a clue about his S&M leanings or his need for pornography. He busied himself being the decorator. At a cocktail party Norman and Andrew threw, one guest remembers Andrew saying, "I just hate living on the beach. I'd like to live up on Mount Soledad." The highest hill overlooking the bay in La Jolla, Mount Soledad is topped by a large white cross, and the views are spectacular, particularly at sunset. It was only about three weeks later, the friend recounts, that Andrew told him, "Norman's bought a house for me on Mount Soledad." The condo at the beach, Andrew said, would be kept for guests. What he failed to mention was the identity of the new house's previous owner—Andrew was moving into the house that had belonged to Lincoln Aston.

Almost immediately the backbiting queens started to gossip, says a friend of both Norman's and Andrew's, who defends the couple, saying, "I remember them in group situations exchanging fond glances across the room." He concedes that in Norman's circle of stable professional people, wealthy retirees, and "tight couples who travel together and have been aligned for forty-five years," Norman and Andrew were an anomaly. "There was no other couple like that—a man that rich with a guy that young."

Rumors began making the rounds in Hillcrest that Andrew had found himself a rich sugar daddy. Only close friends were supposed to know about Norman. There was still a stigma attached, on the surface at least, to being kept. But Andrew managed to convince his younger friends, such as Tom Eads, that he was actually doing Norman a favor. By dedicating himself to Norman, he said, he was foregoing his family inheritance.

Norman and Andrew shopped on Melrose Avenue, Los Angeles's expensive Decorators Row, for furnishings and rugs, real antiques and expensive reproductions. Jeffrey Marks was the official interior designer, and he remembers Norman introducing Andrew to him as "a friend of mine helping me pick out art." Andrew, he says, knew quite a lot about how a period of architecture related to a period of furniture, and was extremely intelligent about history and architecture for someone his age.

Still, Andrew would complain to his friends that Norman was cheap. He was always pushing Norman to do more, repaint everything, buy more expensive accessories. That wasn't Norman's nature. For his part, Norman kindly urged Andrew to continue his studies and acquire a profession. He would gladly have paid for Andrew to do either—he wanted Andrew to put his brain power and talent to work. But Andrew refused.

Too many years of hustling and dope had made Andrew both lazy and greedy—he had the classic narcissist's preoccupation with image and no interest in earning his way, it was easier to exploit others and to feel sorry for himself. Andrew professed to be bored with studies and said he didn't want to start a business. Anything less than total success would have ruined his image. Chafing more and more at being so much in the quiet company of older men and having to account for his time, Andrew started looking for ways to get out of the house at night. He found Project Lifeguard, a San Diego AIDS Foundation HIV prevention and safe sex instruction program. Andrew's job was to visit bars to pass out literature, give away condoms, and snag people for meetings.

Project Lifeguard may have had special significance for Andrew, who more than once feared that he might have AIDS, even though he wouldn't get tested for HIV at the time, according to Ronnie Mascarena to whom Andrew once confided, "I think I'm sick." It was also good cover for Andrew when he wanted to hit the bars. Andrew had apparently never stopped using or dealing drugs, and after he moved in with Norman word of his dealing began to reach old friends like Stan Hatley and others. And his extravagant spending had begun to be noticed by at least one of Norman's contemporaries, a longtime friend of Lincoln's who says that Andrew was now spending "far more than twenty-five hundred dollars a month," Norman's allowance.

So distinct were Andrew's two worlds that for Andrew's twenty-sixth birthday, at the end of August 1995, Norman gave him two parties: one for people his own age and one with their mutual friends. Perhaps because Norman's party for their older friends came first and included a curator for the Smithsonian, Andrew saw the party with *his* friends as an opportunity to shine in front of Norman. He left nothing to chance. Andrew told Jeff Trail not to say that he was in the training program for the California Highway Patrol but to say that he was an instructor there. He handed Jeff a brand-new pair of expensive Ferragamo shoes still in the box and told him, "Give me these shoes." Jeff was supposed to wrap the Ferragamos and present them as his birthday gift. Andrew still wasn't finished. He then gave Jeff yet another pair of Ferragamos and ordered him to *wear* that pair, saying, "You can't afford them—say you're a doctor."

Another invited guest, a flight attendant who was supposed to pretend he was a country western singer, balked. He said, "I'm proud of what I do," thereby annoying Andrew, who ignored him the whole night.

In the fall, Gamma Mu was having its semiannual fly-in to Seattle, and Norman, who would become a Gamma Mu board member in 1997, was taking Andrew. At last, Andrew would be in the inner sanctum. Gamma Mu fly-ins are always elaborate. The fee is $300—the cost of drinks—and members pick up their own hotel and travel. The schedule never varies: Wednesday night is the early bird cocktail party. Thursday night is the first official cocktail party. Friday is the traditional, dressed-up businessman's lunch where new members are introduced along with their sponsors. Saturday morning there is another brunch, and Saturday night is the gala. For the stragglers, there are more cocktail parties on Sunday. At registration, members can pick up packets listing daytime activities such as sails and shopping tours, and each host city tries to outdo the others in the lavishness of the spreads laid out and the beauty of the decor and locations where the parties are held.

Founded in 1967 by Cliff Pettit, a Fort Lauderdale travel agent who realized that closeted, affluent gays wanted to relax with one another on vacation, Gamma Mu has always been discreet and the subject of intense speculation. Is it the Gay Shriners or the Bohemian Grove? Hopelessly retro or fabulously fun?

Ian Gibson, a defense consultant, gallery owner, and former Gamma Mu, will never forget his introduction to the exclusive group of 650 men from all over the country, many of whom are still closeted. After being referred, Gibson joined Gamma Mu's gay ski week in Aspen in 1989. For $300, he said, he was expecting this "dirty little motel in the middle of nowhere." Instead he got a plush condo with Picassos on the wall, located next to Little Nell, the chic hotel at the foot of Aspen Mountain. "I walked in and there were three men in their early forties. Making chitchat, one told me when I inquired, 'I have a hotel.' I said something about, 'Isn't it nice you run a hotel,' and he said, 'No, I own a chain of 146 hotels.'" Ian Gibson promptly joined Gamma Mu, which stands for good men.

The following year he went to some events in Washington, D.C. "The D.C. ball had three hundred men in black tie, the average age the forties, and all were deeply in the closet. I remember one of the high officials of the Republican National Committee. Many were accompanied by a lot younger gentlemen, who became the flavor of the week. In the closeted Republican gay communities, it's far easier to find young protégés to train as you go up."

Not long after, Gibson was invited to a Halloween party hosted by a prominent Washington nuclear physicist, also a Gamma Mu member. "A lot of these people are high up and very discreet," Gibson recounts. "My partner and I showed up in these Renaissance costumes—we tried to gauge it carefully. We got there, and the host answers the door wearing this floor-length gown in a gorgeous red. I said, 'Oh, that gown looks very much like the one Marilyn Monroe wore in *Gentlemen Prefer Blondes*.' He said, 'It *is* the gown Marilyn Monroe wore in *Gentlemen Prefer Blondes*!'"

At the twenty-fifth-anniversary celebration of Gamma Mu in Houston in 1992, Neiman Marcus put on a fashion show for the men. Gibson recalls that a young man came down the runway wearing a $150 swimsuit. One member shouted from the audience, "I'll give you a thousand dollars." The model said, "What?" The man said, "I'll give you a thousand dollars for that right now!" Feeling no pain, the group then demanded that Neiman's open its ladies' hats area so that they could buy elaborate straw chapeaux to wear to the businessman's lunch the next day—which they did, to go with their colorful Willi Smith blazers.

"A lot of Gamma Mu members are closeted in their home environments," explains Washington, D.C., public-relations executive Wes Combs, thirty-three, who briefly was a member of Gamma Mu but found it too costly and the membership a bit senior. "Fly-ins cost two thousand dollars, and I'd rather go to South Beach." Of the membership he says, "They're prominent bankers and lawyers, and they like to go on fly-ins so they don't have to worry they'll run into clients." Founder Cliff Pettit has been known to tell groups of sixty or so traveling abroad to "tone it down" lest the closet door fly open. "Believe me," says Combs, "it's pretty obvious."

Many older gays and gay couples, says Combs, "assume because people see them together, most people understand they're gay, but they don't say anything about it—they're of that generation. The secrecy is based on physical safety but also [the fear of] ostracism. Older gays say, 'Why are you shouting it from the rooftops?' Homophobia becomes internalized from the time you're one to two years old. Boys playing with dolls are taught that that's bad."

Combs was referred to Gamma Mu by his cousin, Billy Ruben, who thought the group would be a boost to a young man like him looking for role models. "In Hawaii, we met a guy so high up in the navy his finger was practically on the red button," says Billy Ruben's partner, Howard Greenfield. "So I said to Bill, 'This would be a marvelous thing for somebody like Wes, who's uncertain about his life and what life holds. Look at all those different people and how they would make him feel great.' "

Billy Ruben and Howard Greenfield have been together as a gay couple for fifty years. They have been Gamma Mu members for more than twenty and have traveled to Gamma Mu fly-ins in Los Angeles, San Diego, San Francisco, Dallas, Houston, New York, Washington, Fort Lauderdale, Boston, and Seattle, as well as Hawaii. They have traveled with Gamma Mu to Tahiti and New Zealand, and have been part of 166 Gamma Mus sailing around the Caribbean on a sailboat from St. Bart's. They have barged down the Burgundy Canal in the south of France and have been taken on hot-air balloon rides with champagne. That trip began with Oktoberfest in Munich. Other Gamma Mu trips include sails around the Greek islands and a cruise on the *Queen Mary II.*

Naturally there are times when romance blooms. "We met a doctor who had just separated from his wife on a flight down to Puerto Vallarta," says Greenfield. "And on the flight he met his mate. It was his first fly-in and he was alone. Before we knew it, he had met that someone, and they've been together ever since."

Billy and Howard, both builders from Miami, were the hosts at the last Florida fly-in for a Banana Republic party. At their Fort Lauderdale home, a live jaguar met guests, and torches lit the paths into the tropical garden, where there were white cockatiels and an African band.

"Bill and I have always lived a diverse lifestyle," says Howard, who sports a tiny gold earring. "It was much different twenty years ago. There were some people who didn't belong who thought it was an excessive society group. We have met some of the most wonderful people we know through Gamma Mu. What could be more fun than meeting people once a year during holidays without hearing about any problems? Only wonderful things. One of the many advantages.

"There is not a city we go to where we don't have connections to Gamma Mu who can tell us where the restaurants are, where the bars are, where the action is. In New Orleans, a woman in the French Quarter lent us her home. She wasn't even there; she just said, 'Here are the keys.' It was marvelous." In Houston, a handsome young married doctor, "also gay who has children," gave the big gala. "He had a tented, sit-down dinner for three hundred, and he looked as if he had the entire state of Oaxaca, Mexico, as staff. He had wines and violins and an entertainment area with bleachers set up and a dance floor." Where were his wife and children? "Oh, they went shopping."

"When you go to their city, they really go all out," says Billy Ruben. "We form friendships all over the country. You meet people like you. If you go out to bars, it's not the same thing. There are some people from Gamma Mu who *never* stay in any hotel. They always stay at members' houses."

The advent of AIDS has changed Gamma Mu, just as it has changed so many other aspects of gay life. In the last decade Gamma Mu has set up a foundation that helps AIDS sufferers in rural parts of the country, where few support systems are in place. "I was unhappy with the foundation at first," says Howard. "I loved Gamma Mu because it never ever pretended to do anything but have fun. We're constantly besieged to go for charities. Once the foundation came in, I was afraid it'd be the same." Today Howard says his fears were unfounded.

In earlier times, Gamma Mu members were richer and overwhelmingly Republican. But the politics of AIDS and the current Republican leadership's coolness toward gay rights have made Gamma Mu more democratic and Democratic. In order to attract younger members, it also had to go a bit downscale, so it now counts among its members "a blackjack dealer on the Mississippi River and, of course, those who want to play cops and cowboys!" For the most part, however, "these are patrons of high opera and the symphony," Ian Gibson says. "They are big readers of the *New York Times* and *Vanity Fair*—the older and richer queens."

When Gamma Mu members flew into the nation's capital in 1996, for instance, they had brunch on the terrace of the Kennedy Center, sipped cocktails in the rotunda of the Capitol, and had a catered dinner in a Georgetown mansion. At the annual Gamma Mu Foundation fundraiser, the Stardust Ball, in Washington in April 1998, 250 male guests in black tie, representing "the highest echelon of closeted Washington," sat in gilded straight-back chairs at tables covered with peach tablecloths and centerpieces of fresh spring flowers. Their silver heads bobbed in conversation, their diamond studs flashed off the candlelight. It could have been any chichi charity ball, except that there were no tiaras, no rustling silk and taffeta gowns, and not even a drag queen in sight.

The ball, held in the sunken marble galleria of an opulent downtown Washington building, featured a bandleader in white tie and tails wailing on the sax. As the band swung into "Misty" and "Unforgettable," one hundred male couples got up and danced cheek to cheek, some with arms entwined, others doing the big dip. When the band started playing "La Bamba," the whole room immediately formed a long conga line that snaked up and down the stairway.

Andrew Cunanan fit right in. By all accounts, when he arrived in Seattle with Norman he made an excellent impression. He was well dressed, he kept his laugh down, and his manners were impeccable. Although Bud Riley, a Gamma Mu who flew up on the plane to Seattle with Norman and Andrew, found Andrew rather boastful—"no matter what you were talking about, Andrew would interject as if he was knowledgeable on every subject"—another Gamma Mu, Phil Flick, from San Diego, thought Andrew "well read and interesting. If you were going to Paris and Italy, Andrew knew all the places—where to go, where to stay." Art Huskey, head of San Diego's chapter of Gamma Mu, says merely, "We always assumed Andrew was hired to be Mr. Blachford's decorator."

A storm cloud passed over the businessmen's lunch on Friday, however, when Andrew was welcomed as a new member under Norman's tutelage. Tradition dictated that Andrew introduce himself and indicate his sponsor and his profession. According to a San Diego city official who was present, "When Andrew got up, he said, 'Hi, my name is Andrew DeSilva. My sponsor's Norman Blachford, who is also keeping me.' " Andrew got a big laugh, the official says. "But Norman got pissed off. It was a very memorable introduction."

The year 1995 proved to be memorable all around for Andrew. He not only found the man who could support his dreams, but also met the man who was his dream.

11

David

ONE WEEKEND IN November 1995, Andrew was in San Francisco staying at the posh Mandarin Oriental Hotel, the city's third tallest building, in a $520 room with a marble bathroom featuring a picture window over the bathtub looking out on the Golden Gate Bridge. He had returned to the city flashing big bucks. None of his closest friends from his Berkeley days even suspected that he was being kept, or even knew of Norman Blachford's existence.

Andrew was as hyper as ever and filled with tall tales. "I always thought he was a little too happy," says Jesse Cappachione, the longtime bartender at the Midnight Sun, "always laughing and smiling—a little too good to be true."

On Friday night, at the "no name" restaurant on Market Street at the entrance to the Castro, Andrew was having dinner and holding court—making friends laugh by telling people in the restaurant that he was Count Frescobaldi—when he noticed a handsome blonde alone at the bar. He immediately sent over a drink. The blonde, whose name was David Madson, was definitely Andrew's type—preppy-looking, not too tall, with deep blue eyes. An architect from Minneapolis, he was in San Francisco for a few days on business. "It was pretty sparky," says a friend who witnessed their first encounter. That night they had a "non-sexual sleepover" at the Mandarin Oriental.

For Andrew, to whom image meant everything, there was much about David that he could instantly fall for. David was vivacious, talented, and accomplished on many levels. What could be more perfect for Andrew than a dashing young architect? A waspy-looking golden boy? Architecture was one of Andrew's passions, and he had always been attracted to blondes. Plus, David was considered by his friends to be "so charismatic that he blew people away" personally and professionally. David also had the gift of gab; he had won medals in forensics all through high school, and he could talk his way out of anything.

David was driven and hardworking, the opposite of Andrew. But he too dealt in image, and Andrew, who started pouring on the rich-kid persona, seemed pretty interesting, especially if he was really as wealthy and cosmopolitan as he was letting on. Both of them loved clothes, knew food, and were very much aware of trends. Back home in his loft in Minneapolis, David had three closets stuffed with clothes, plus another closet in the basement. But unlike Andrew, David was willing to work ninety-hour weeks to support his tastes. He had always held a variety of jobs, from selling ladies' shoes and gifts at Saks Fifth Avenue, Donaldsons, and Target, to washing dishes and finally becoming the maître d' at a trendy Minneapolis restaurant. For several years he had worked part-time at a prominent law firm, helping with plans and graphics in the preparation of asbestos cases. Then—without a degree—he parlayed an internship into a job developing and publishing an urban development plan for the Downtown Duluth Waterfront Renovation Project.

It had taken David a while to find his professional niche, but when he graduated from architecture school at the University of Minnesota, he was awarded the President's Medal as the architecture student with the most outstanding thesis for the class of 1995.

Like Andrew, David was the youngest of four, the adored little brother, "but not spoiled," says his brother Ralph. "David got the best of all of us." He was also a performer. The little old ladies in his tiny hometown, Barron, Wisconsin, still talk about David as Harold Hill, the starring role in *The Music Man,* in the high school production fifteen years ago. "In high school they had talent shows. It was nothing for him to get up to the microphone and sing 'Bridge

Over Troubled Water' or anything that was popular," says his mother, Carol. "He could just do it." She describes David's high school years as "filled with absolute fun." One of his buddies then, Monty Shearer, says he learned from David, "A good one-liner is a good thing to always have on hand."

David was the quintessential Boy Scout, taking groceries to the needy at Christmas, helping others to learn. He was an aerobics, ski, and swimming instructor. "He taught half the kids in this town to swim," says his father, Howard Madson, who owns the local hardware store. Madson moved his family to Barron, a quiet community of cornfields and turkey farms an hour and a half north of Minneapolis, in 1979. Madson was a branch manager for J. C. Penney, and David, who was born in Waterloo, Iowa, spent his boyhood in three other small Wisconsin towns before arriving in Barron for high school. Growing up, he acquired a strong work ethic and solid Christian values. "All my sisters and David were certainly goal-oriented," says Ralph Madson, David's brother. "There's this belief if you set your goal and work hard enough, you work smart. It has served us well."

David, like Andrew, loved to be in the center of the action, but as a peacemaker. He was the mediator in neighborhood fights, and later the gung-ho resident adviser in a University of Minnesota, Duluth, dorm complex. As a hot young professional sailing through a presentation for his boss, David snowed clients, telling them, sure, they could have the impossible.

He seemed so animated and involved that he inevitably drew others to him. Wendy Peterson, one of his closest friends in college, remembers seeing him first from afar in the dorm dining room at Duluth. "Gee, I thought, I want to get to know that person, because he looks like a bunch of fun. I think people always wanted to be around him because of the electrifying magnetism of his personality."

When the Salem Lutheran Church bus had a flat tire on a trip to North Dakota, David, whose family is devout Lutheran, entertained the group while the tire was being fixed. When a college friend felt sad and gave herself a one-person "pity party," David showed up at her door in a tux to take her out for a night on the town.

"He wanted to save people. He liked the underdog. David was kind of drawn to people who needed him," says his former coworker Kathy Compton. "He had just seen the movie *Jerry McGuire* and he said, 'Jerry McGuire reminds me so much of me—always trying to make things OK!' "

But his easygoing charm and need to help attractive, screwed-up cases made David a target. Before meeting Andrew, David had been deeply burned by a handsome lover of two years, who began stalking and harassing him after he asked him to move out. The stalker, Greg Nelson, who spread false rumors that David had given him HIV, finally had to be jailed after repeatedly violating a court order to stay away from David. Sometimes Nelson would call him as many as 120 times a day. He gave David's number to sex-phone lines so that people "looking for action" would call. He sent pornographic literature along with a nude picture of David to senior partners in David's law firm, saying, "Do you know what your employees do?" Rich Bonnin, David's close friend and former roommate, explains: "David liked people to rely on him. Greg became very dependent on David. Then, when he no longer had David, he became obsessed."

This episode, which went on for more than two years, even after David had met Andrew, caused David untold misery and numerous court appearances. Nelson was arrested more than once. Meanwhile, David was afraid to open his door and he changed his phone number frequently. He never knew if he was going to find his car scratched and damaged.

David hated violence. Once when he was little, his father took him duck hunting. "David did not like to see anything killed," his father says. "We shot this duck, and he cried so bad I finally hid the thing over by a tree, and that didn't do it, so a fellow happened to be next door, and unknown to David, I gave the guy the duck to get it out of there, because David was just beside himself we killed this duck." When David was a dorm adviser, an angry student mistook him for someone else and pushed him through a pane of glass. He was uninjured but very shaken. "He was white as a ghost, very startled, and needed someone to calm him down," says Wendy Peterson. "He was very scared. David wasn't a big guy. He couldn't rely on size. David was not a physical person."

For years David searched restlessly for a career that would satisfy him. "This was a standard joke," says Doug Peterson, Wendy's dentist husband. "It seemed like anytime he would go anywhere, like a store or a restaurant, he'd say, 'Maybe I could get a job here.' It was always the trendiest restaurant." David's personal life was also in turmoil. Not wanting to disappoint his family, he struggled all through college with his homosexuality, dating numerous girls, even falling deeply in love with one, but constantly churning over whether he was straight, bisexual, or gay. "It was a very scary thing for him to confront." says Wendy. "When we went to college, everything was, like, status quo. Conformity was the way to be."

Wendy adds, "David was the biggest prep monster. He wore very preppie clothing. He was very studious and conformed very well, but this was one area where he couldn't conform. And it was a very disturbing area for him." David wanted to have a family. "But as time went on he couldn't ignore his underlying attraction to men." The day came when David went to his father to tell him he was gay. His father's strong religious conviction made it difficult for him to accept.

"I can't say that it didn't make any difference with me, because I disagree with that type of life. However, that had nothing to do with what I thought of him or how I treated him," says Howard Madson, who believes that Jesus came down from the cross to save sinners, not winners. "I'm not going to go there perfect, and neither are you. We're gonna go as sinners. What's the difference whether you lie, cheat, steal, you're homosexual, you murder. If you believe that forgiveness is there, if it's on the cross and by the grace of God, you've got just as good a chance as anybody else. So I don't look at David as any different. Yet I do look at him as different because he was homosexual. But that didn't create any problem between David and me. My feelings for David were no different." When David told his brother, Ralph, and his wife, Cindy, that he was gay, they were relieved. They thought he was going to say he had AIDS. Ralph told him to be careful: "There's a lot of kooky people out there."

On many levels, David's struggles were complicated by the fact that he was so talented and had so many options. When he was a little boy, he would take blueprints thrown into the Dumpster at a nearby design company and build Lego models from them. He majored in political science at college and thought he wanted to be a lawyer. Although he did not do well on his law-board exams, he moved to Minneapolis and went to work for a law firm, but he kept being drawn to architecture. In 1990 he gained one of forty entering slots at the University of Minnesota Architecture School in Minneapolis, where he was seen as a cockeyed optimist.

"David could take a project in architecture class and the professors would see it and say, 'That's terrible,'" says Rich Bonnin, his onetime roommate and fellow architect. "Then, after he'd talk it and market it, they'd say, 'I love it!' He had this ability to skim, to cajole, to charm and talk his way out of anything." Along with his talent, he could sell. "David was a salesman. He was good at sales pitches, he was creative, and he liked money," says Wendy, who thought he should go into advertising. "Architecture didn't pay enough. David was a very money-motivated person." Yet by the time David met Andrew, he was making architecture pay off.

He became a guest lecturer for an advanced urban-planning course at Harvard. He worked for the John Ryan Company in Minneapolis, designing "retail financial centers" for large banks, a $70,000-a-year position that took him all over the country. "David was an absolute joy to be around and an immensely talented person, on the precipice of becoming a leading designer in the world in his field," says John Ryan.

Tragically, however, he met Andrew Cunanan.

From the beginning theirs was a long-distance romance. At the end of their first weekend together, Andrew had to return to San Diego, to Norman, who thought San Francisco was where Andrew's ex-wife was. Norman believed that Andrew was making his numerous trips there to see his little daughter. Meanwhile, there was nowhere David could call Andrew. There was no address to which David could send letters—just a post office box that didn't get opened very often. Andrew's excuse was that his rich family needed to keep a low profile; they changed their phone numbers constantly because they were potential kidnap victims.

In one of his numerous postcards to David, Andrew cautioned him when writing to send only a sealed envelope with no return address. "Sorry to be secretive, but it's very important."

Andrew was in control. He would do the contacting.

Not long before Andrew met David, Stan Hatley broke his shoulder and showed up at Flicks one night with his arm in a sling. Andrew got a big kick out of parading Stan around the bar, saying, "I shot him. If you're not careful, I'll do this to you, too. This is what happens when people upset me." Everyone treated it as a big joke and indulged Andrew, who was buying drinks as usual. When Andrew returned from San Francisco after meeting David, he acted as if nothing had changed. "We never heard about Madson when he met him," says Stan, who a few months later moved to Minneapolis himself.

When David got back to Minneapolis, he confided to Rich Bonnin, "I met this really intriguing guy." He described Andrew as the person "he was least attracted to but the most persistent." Andrew had told David his real name, Cunanan, not DeSilva. David told Rich that Andrew looked Spanish, even though Andrew had said his family had plantations and a publishing empire in the Philippines. "He seemed to have a good education, seemed to be going places and committed to a career," David told Rich. "He was away from the family to make a mark on the world . . . out from under their shadow."

David thought it odd he couldn't call Andrew, but he traveled a great deal, worked out at the gym at night, and had plenty to keep him busy. Unlike Andrew, who by now avoided straight society and most women, David had many straight friends, and always had strong female confidantes who watched out for him.

When they would see each other in San Francisco, David would freely introduce Andrew to his friends there, including Karen Lapinski and Evan Wallit, who were engaged and lived in Pacific Heights. Karen and David had gone to school together. Andrew immediately began to cultivate the couple as a way to insinuate himself with David. Like David, they freely accepted Andrew's largesse.

One of the first gifts that Andrew gave David was an expensive Gold File wallet worth several hundred dollars. David protested that he couldn't accept it, but he ended up taking Andrew's presents—that was easier than having to watch Andrew pout. Andrew was elated at having met David. He told Doug Stubblefield that he was in love, and that David was brilliant. "He used lots of terms of endearment," says Doug. "David was the first person I ever knew him to date, romantically or seriously."

Even though Andrew and David were seeing each other every two or three weeks, and Andrew had set out to wine and dine David, Andrew had once again begun to frequent a gay San Diego bathhouse where drugs were prevalant—all while still living with Norman Blachford. He also planned to get David to participate in S&M sex with him in order to indulge the fantasies he cultivated from the rough pornography he had been watching for the last several years. He told his friends, however, that David was "introducing him." According to Doug Stubblefield, "We had a conversation about experiencing the S&M thing with David. He seemed not to know much about it." Andrew told Doug it "was awkward because he was the top and David was the bottom, but David was telling him what to do." Later, says Doug, "It became, 'David won't let me do everything that I want to do.'" Andrew boasted to Doug, however, that he had gotten wrist restraints: "David lets me tie him up. I really like tying him up. I'm really getting into this stuff. I want to explore more."

San Francisco was the perfect place to do so. The Castro has a long-established leather scene where what would be startling to the rest of America is treated as commonplace. On the same day Andrew killed Lee Miglin, for example, Jack Davis, one of the most powerful figures in San Francisco politics—a combative political consultant who is gay and frequents S&M clubs—had his fiftieth birthday party. The entertainment—staged in front of some of San Francisco's highest elected city officials, including the sheriff—featured a "blood-and-urine show," in which a dominatrix carved a star into the back of a trussed-up satanic priest. She then urinated on him and sodomized him with a bottle of Jack Daniel's whiskey. There were also strippers, both male and female, from a nearby porn theater. The ensuing brouhaha in the press centered largely on whether Davis had hurt the chances of having a new football stadium built, financed with a controversial $100-million-bond issue Davis had been hired by the San Francisco Forty-Niners football team to push through. (It won by 50.4 percent of the votes.)

There are gay sex clubs in San Francisco with large, dark areas of fetish stations. Patrons can copulate in an English taxi, a police car, a telephone booth, a jail cell, or a dentist's chair. And it's OK to watch— whoever wants privacy can go behind piles of old tires strewn around. A leather bar has theme parties—"latex fisting night," for example. Every third Wednesday of the month is "piss night." Private "associations" hold by-invitation-only parties in undisclosed locations designed to weed out "novices and voyeurs."

Mr. S Leather Co. and Fetters USA of San Francisco, where Andrew shopped, is four stories high and publishes a 289-page catalog of sex devices ranging from elaborate suspension cages and electrotorture equipment, to butt plugs, flogs, gags, masks, handcuffs, hoods, "the latest in hospital restraints," tit clamps, and nineteen handkerchiefs of different colors, each with a different sexual meaning when worn on either the right or the left side: red on the left means "fister," red on the right means "fistee"; gray on the left means "bondage top," gray on the right means "bondage bottom"; hunter green on the left means "Daddy," hunter green on the right means "wants Daddy." Mr. S is a gay father-and-son business. "We're just like Macy's," exclaims proprietor Richard Hunter, "with slightly different displays!"

Whether Andrew Cunanan had engaged in S&M before or not, he had been flirting with it for some time. In San Diego he consulted a dungeon master whom he got to know through Project Lifeguard. As with crystal meth, he definitely wanted his behavior kept secret. "The type of sex he had, the S&M-type sex, not everybody is into," says the dungeon master. "He didn't want others to know about it." According to Stan Hatley, "He knew too many people in San Diego and was too into his reputation to let somebody find him doing that there. He saved it for out of town."

On several occasions in 1995 Andrew pulled the dungeon master aside, wanting to talk about leather and bondage. "At first I took it as a joke." Andrew had been trying before to pump him for information without admitting anything about his interest. "He would ask me about bondage and flogging: Where do you go? What do you do? Where do you buy things?"

The dungeon master is on the committee for the San Diego Leatherfest, a yearly gathering of seven hundred or so. (In 1997 the leather fair was held at the Comfort Inn.) "Leather enthusiasts, bondage, S&M people sell their wares, hold demonstration seminars, workshops on safe, sane, consensual flogging," he explains. "For example, if a lover is into flogging, how do you safely tie someone up? How do you take someone to the breaking point and bring them back?"

Andrew, the dungeon master says, started "calling about mixing blood and semen together. Not a lot of people are into doing that. You cut into your skin, make a small incision into the chest or arm. The incisions are micro-thin so you heal without a scar. Lesbians self-mutilate on the chest. People ejaculate into the blood and mix it. It's very strange. It's one way HIV spreads."

The dungeon master says Andrew spoke to him about David Madson on several occasions around the time he was getting involved with David. Erik Greenman, Andrew's former roommate, says Andrew told him many times about his S&M sex with David. "He said David liked it just as much as he did." San Francisco friend John Semerau claims that more than once Andrew invited him to have three-ways with him and David. "I had dinner with him and David on two occasions. They wanted me to have sex with them. I never had sex with them," Semerau says. "Andrew then invited me to come to their hotel room to see the new leather underwear and cock rings they had bought."

There is also a leather scene in Minneapolis, and Minneapolis police say that David was acquainted with it. Just a few minutes' walk from the downtown Minneapolis loft where David lived is the Gay Nineties, a large and lively club that presents drag shows and male go-go dancers. The Nineties has a large dance floor and several bars. The back room is the "S&M-leather-boy-type place," says Stan Hatley, and patrons follow a dress code to get in. "Either you wear leather, you take your shirt off, or wear Levi's and black boots for S&M, or wear a leather harness." People are not there for "the vanilla-boy-type sex," says Stan. "I would see him [David] in the Nineties on those nights," though he admits, not specifically in the leather area.

A couple of blocks down the street is Y'All Come Back Saloon, a popular gay bar that on Sundays features "tank night." "You can put a wall between two pool tables in the back and section off part for the tank. People have sex on the pool table, people perform fellatio right then and there. Nobody pays attention, because that's what happens in a hard-core leather bar," Stan Hatley reports. His onetime roommate worked there. It, too, has a dress code, and Hatley says he saw David Madson at the Saloon on tank nights. "I guess you could say he was dressed appropriately." Stan explains that Monday night the Saloon's "S&M night," is more for straights, who congregate on a big dance floor. "You go there; they hang people in cages and whip people with whips." On Thursday, the S&M night is at yet another Minneapolis gay bar, Ground Zero, where the cage is in the main room.

"I had seen Dave Madson in these types of places," Hatley maintains. Nevertheless, the Madson family and many friends do not believe that David was ever involved in rough sex.

"I know on two occasions David talked to me about experiences with bondage and it really wasn't his thing," says Rob Davis, who added, "On a personal level, David was submissive in bed, and he'd rather be manhandled than stroked. I'm a teddy bear at home and David would ask me to be more aggressive." He conceded, "So I think there was a tie-in about his being dominated."

For David, the relationship with Andrew was an exercise in frustration. All signs pointed to disaster, but he was blinded by Andrew's erudition, experience, and wealth. After their second weekend together, David returned home and told Rich Bonnin that sex with Andrew was basically lousy. "The first time they spent the night together and then on several subsequent ones, David told me that, number one, it wasn't very good sex—Andrew made him uncomfortable—and that Andrew wanted to do things that David didn't want to do. It was actually a source of quite a bit of strife in the relationship." David claimed to Rich Bonnin that he never let Andrew be on top. "David always said that Andrew wanted very strongly to have intercourse with him that way and David always said no." David said Andrew got very upset. "He stormed out of the hotel room downstairs to the restaurant. He threw a little tantrum."

Andrew would toy with David. David could write only to the post office box and it would take Andrew a week or two to call and say, "I got your letter." David began to guess that Andrew was in another relationship. When he asked, Andrew would say, "I never said I'd be exclusive, when we've only gone out on a few dates." David said he thought, "Well, you know, I guess that's fair."

In truth, Andrew was in hot pursuit of David, but he was partly stymied by Norman. He would call David and try to make plans, but then he would not commit until the last minute and sometimes he would cancel. "It's that Pavlovian thing," says Rich, "where random reinforcement is the strongest form of behavior modification." If Andrew did things to encourage David to pursue him, Rich Bonnin claims, "David wouldn't perceive that *he* was being pursued." Andrew would send postcards saying how much he wanted to see David, then be totally noncommittal about whether David should extend a given stay to California or not—obvious passive-aggressive behavior, leading to David's complaining about Andrew's refusal to commit. David was not used to that attitude; *he* was the one who usually remained aloof; *he* was the one to make the plans. "At the same time, he thought, I'm being challenged, this is interesting," says Monique Salvetti, David's closest friend in Minneapolis.

While Andrew was showering David with expensive presents and staying in chic hotels with him, he was also going deeper into S&M. He asked Doug Stubblefield—who had done his thesis at Berkeley on Michel Foucault, the homosexual French philosopher who articulated "going beyond the boundaries of normality"—for advice on which S&M videos to rent. Stubblefield became concerned that Andrew was violating a fundamental tenet of the pain-and-pleasure principle—that it has to be equal and balanced. Doug thought Andrew had trouble drawing the line—he was trying to dominate David too much. His sexual behavior was being carried over to "public spaces where it wouldn't be so stylized but it would still abuse." According to Guenter Frivert, a San

Francisco store owner who knew Andrew through Karen Lapinski, "Andrew treated David like a slave. He'd give David the key and bark, 'Here, go get the car.' "

It wasn't until April 1996, that Andrew visited David in Minneapolis. He lied to Norman that his sister was an anesthesiologist working there. That weekend Andrew ran into Stan Hatley at the Saloon with David, but pretended he was just in town looking around. David took him to dinner at Manny's, the expensive steakhouse where he had once been the maître d'. Rich Bonnin was impressed by Andrew's immaculate appearance and by how articulate he was, but David's suspicions were growing.

Yet Andrew knew how to counter David's doubts even before they could come to the fore. At the table with Rich Bonnin, he played the poor-little-rich-boy victim, saying what a hard cross it was to bear, being from such a wealthy family: "People are jealous, and they make up *stories* about you," Andrew whined. "It was his way of trying to address suspicions about any information getting back," Bonnin says.

In May, Andrew and David met again in San Francisco, and David got an explicit warning. Karen Lapinski, Evan Wallit, David, and Andrew took an old crush of Andrew's from Berkeley to lunch to celebrate his getting his Ph.D. and becoming a professor. The professor says that Andrew's dodginess had always bothered him, but like so many others, he had let it go. He was aware that Andrew "hoped nobody referenced all the ways he was cut and pasted together. I read him like a very entertaining book."

The professor knew it had been rocky between Andrew and David. "David was just a person who demanded a lot of honesty. He wanted someone to be real with him, and that was not in the cards with Andrew." It was a beautiful spring afternoon, so the young professor took a walk around the block with David. "Andrew is a pathological liar," he warned him. "It's crazy. You don't know who he is. Don't put anything you're not prepared to lose in that basket." David listened, but the professor realized he wasn't willing to let Andrew go. "I think he wanted to make it work. He was a commitment-oriented person— very Minnesota, very trustworthy and reliable."

Then it was Andrew's turn to go around the block with his old friend. "I know you as well as anybody, and I don't know if that's saying much, you don't tell me a lot of who you are or what your life is like in San Diego. I think I have a pretty good idea." He looked at Andrew and said with heavy irony, "Your family's Filipino millionaires, right?" Andrew did not rise to the challenge. His only response was, "I'm not sure I'm in love with him." The professor considered that he had delivered two messages, but that Andrew, especially, was not going to be receptive.

"He didn't have anywhere to fit love in, no foundation to grow, because his whole life was a lie. In order to have David, he'd have to straighten it out." His friend wondered, "Would Andrew ever come to terms with the fact that he wasn't all these fantasy people he had become?"

12

Breakup

IN JUNE, ANDREW HIT the high-water mark of his life as a swell, sharing a house in Saint-Jean-Cap-Ferrat with Norman and Larry Chrysler, a Gamma Mu member from Los Angeles. Andrew told David that he was joining his family at "my summer home" in France and would not be reachable for the month. Before he left he mailed David a postcard from the Helmsley Park Lane Hotel in New York: "Have the best summer and someone very far away will be thinking of you." Once in France, Andrew continued to send David a steady stream of arch postcards with messages such as "France is very architectural and they have art there," or "Avignon is still full of scamps and vamps. C'est moi, ne pas? [sic]" In another card he told David, "You're much cuter than these hairy, dark-haired Frenchy boys . . . and I miss you and your jockeys more than anything." In his postcards Andrew often made oblique references to Norman, writing "food wonderful, company less so," and referring to a trip to Paris with his "business partner (the world's most romantic city with the world's least romantic guy)."

Andrew spent his days lying by the pool underlining passages in books, dining at the finest restaurants, and soaking up information "like a sponge," Chrysler reports. He acted as the tour guide and organized all the sightseeing. He told Chrysler he was descended from Sephardic Jews. Norman listened quietly as Andrew spun his tales and gave his opinions about everything. One night they were discussing the Mamounia, the old landmark hotel in Marrakech. Chrysler recalls, "Andrew said, 'Oh, nobody stays at the Mamounia anymore. It's been redone.' Two weeks later I pick up a magazine in the house and in there was the same direct quote about the Mamounia from [Yves St. Laurent's business partner] Pierre Bergé. Word for word. He was reading tomorrow's conversation."

Chrysler found Andrew "fascinating" if full of "b.s."; he knew so little French that he had to have menus translated. And he didn't always mind his manners. Going into one bar, he bellowed, "Here come the rich Americans!" He apparently did not know the area as he claimed to, but he would point out a distinctive house and say, according to Chrysler, "that belonged to so-and-so, and then it was sold to so-and-so." On the subject of cars he was obsessed with Mercedes: "I *always* had a Mercedes." One day he came back from the village of Beaulieu with a tiny jar of jam that had cost twenty dollars. "I never look at any price," he said. "My family never looked at any price."

On their way back from France, Norman and Andrew spent several days of July 1996 in East Hampton, on Long Island, as the guests of a wealthy gay couple. They attended parties and dined at the trendy restaurant Nick and Toni's. As usual, Andrew charmed his older companions, but according to one of his hosts he said "inappropriate things about money" and told them stories that made them raise their eyebrows. He said that he had been married to a Jewish woman and that his father-in-law was the head of Israeli intelligence, the Mossad. "He was young and attractive, entertaining, good company—what's not to like?" said the host, who also found him "sad" on two levels: "He's got a lot going for him, I thought. He doesn't need all this sham. . . . He was also ultimately a young man with no career ambitions in any direction. He pretty much said he was interested in older men for their financial situations. He made no bones about that, and he would say it in front of Norman."

Norman apparently *did* look at prices. While in Europe, Andrew had decided that he should have a new $125,895 Mercedes SL 600 convertible, and even confided to David about the car in a postcard. "I may finally get my Mercedes SL 600!" he enthused. "I feel I deserve it even if nobody else does." Soon after they returned home, however, when Andrew told Norman he would leave if he did not give him the car, Norman refused. In a grand gesture, Andrew packed his bags and left a note saying, "I've moved on." But he also left the voice-mail number of his cell phone and fully expected it to ring immediately. Negotiations broke down, however, and Andrew had to move into a weekly studio-apartment rental on Washington Street in Hillcrest—about as far away from 100 Coast Boulevard in La Jolla as you can get. Furthermore, Andrew had been promising David for months that they would watch the fireworks on the Fourth of July together from a sailboat in Boston Harbor. But in June he sent David a postcard from Cap-Ferrat, suggesting unnamed sinister activity might keep them apart: "The situation in Marseilles has become extremely delicate and I may not be home in July." Later he wrote, "I may not be home July 4th." When Andrew didn't come through for the fourth David finally had had it. He, too, cut Andrew off.

Both blows were stunning. Andrew had demanded a new Mercedes because that was the level of living to which he was accustomed, he told friends. Norman should honor that. After all, by living with Norman, he was forfeiting his inheritance. His family was disowning him, he said, because "by caring for Norman" into his dotage, he was effectively outed. Many of his younger friends actually believed this story. "He felt he came down several steps in his relationship with Norman," says his ex-roommate Tom Eads. "He felt he should be flying first class. He felt he was giving up a lot. He gave up his inheritance to devote himself to Norman. Andrew didn't like the nickel-and-diming. They argued over decorating. Norman would only repaint so many square feet of the new house in La Jolla. He wouldn't repaint it all."

Robbins had thought Andrew would stay in the arrangement at least three or four years—that was Andrew's thinking when he and Norman first moved in together. But Andrew wanted control at least as much as he wanted money. It rankled him that Norman who, he told people, was worth $110 million, wouldn't fly first class—he wouldn't even fly business class. Flying coach was a low blow to a narcissist like Andrew, even if he and Norman stayed at five-star hotels and ate in three-star restaurants. In a fit of pique, Andrew listed his demands: a Mercedes, first-class air travel, an increased allowance, a place in Norman's will. Norman was willing only to increase his allowance. "Andrew really thought Norman would collapse without him and beg him to come back," says Tom Eads, who termed the ending, "a deal not continued."

Andrew next wrote Norman a letter stating that he would leave it up to him to decide the amount of palimony he should receive to compensate for his year of service. Norman gave him $15,000 and took off for Europe on a previously planned vacation with friends Andrew had introduced him to. Andrew apparently tried to deposit the money without having the bank give the standard notification to the IRS—any check in excess of $10,000 must be reported by law—but the bank teller he knew refused his request.

Now that he was cut off from Norman, there was no way Andrew was going to let David go. But David had long suspected that Andrew was mixed up in something shady. Playing the big shot, Andrew had once told David, "There's someone in prison right now who got my friends in trouble, and I've arranged to have him killed." David had no idea what to think, but such remarks bothered him.

On several occasions, David had brought up the possibility of ending their relationship. "You know, if you don't want to see me anymore, we don't have to keep doing this." But Andrew would send him a dozen roses at work to placate him, while refusing even to consider that their relationship was over. "No, no, no. Our relationship is too special to me."

Now Andrew begged David to visit San Diego, but David refused. It was beginning to sink in—Andrew had lost both Norman and David. Moping and aimless, Andrew next turned to Jeff, the second most important person in his life. He showed up in San Francisco just as Jeff was quitting the California Highway Patrol—it just wasn't what he'd expected.

Andrew said he was planning to stay just a few days, but his visit stretched into two weeks. Jeff lived on and off with his eldest sister, Sally Davis, in nearby Concord, California. Mostly, however, he was apartment-sitting with his latest catch: Daniel O'Toole, a twenty-one-year-old, blue-eyed blonde. Jeff had told Daniel he was in love with him a couple of days after they met. Daniel fell head over heels for Jeff, too, but he worried that Jeff seemed to want to control him.

Daniel had his first prolonged exposure to Andrew when they bumped into one another one afternoon in the Castro. Andrew, who was wandering around the neighborhood, invited Daniel to lunch, flashed a lot of money, and suggested that they both get haircuts. Andrew had his hair closely cropped—"just like Jeff's," Daniel said. "It seemed to me that he was copying a lot of Jeff's looks."

Andrew then managed to get Daniel drunk and took him into a video store, where he pawed through "stuff that looked like underage exploitation." Andrew picked out some raunchy bondage porn that was kept in boxes in the back, deemed too raw for the shelves. After another drink, Andrew took Daniel to his Infiniti parked nearby to show him a picture of David and listen to music as Andrew rhapsodized to Daniel about David—"the love of my life, the man I want to marry." He also told him the story of having a daughter in San Francisco. "It seemed to me that David knew Andrew so well. Andrew implied that he had an extensive relationship with this person."

When Andrew dropped Daniel off at 11 P.M., Jeff was waiting. He was livid at Andrew for getting Daniel drunk. In fact, Jeff was rapidly getting fed up with Andrew altogether. He called Daniel's mother to apologize, telling her in no uncertain terms "to do anything you can to keep Daniel from getting mixed up with Andrew." She asked when Andrew would be leaving. "Hopefully soon," Jeff answered. Daniel recalled for Jeff some of the things Andrew had told him about his daughter. "Oh, Daniel, don't listen to all those things. He tells a lot of things that aren't true." Daniel says, "Jeff didn't figure there was any mystery to Andrew anymore. His ideal situation was to rent a movie, go pick someone up in a bar, and bring them back to his hotel room."

Jeff told Daniel that Andrew embarrassed him in public. Andrew would start telling one of his exaggerated stories, and all of a sudden he'd put Jeff into it, expecting Jeff to back him up. But Jeff did not want to listen to lies, and certainly did not "want someone else to determine what aspects of his personal life to be revealed." But then why did Jeff take so much from Andrew, Daniel wanted to know. Jeff's excuse was that "he felt sorry for Andrew because Andrew considered Jeff to be his best friend. But Jeff didn't consider Andrew to be *his* best friend."

Nevertheless, Jeff was loyal. He also admired Andrew's generosity, whether or not it created a sense of obligation. He counseled Daniel that it was best just to let Andrew pay for everything. Otherwise he'd make a scene, and that was just too exhausting. But by then "Jeff was definitely tired of the act," Daniel says. "I don't recall a time I knew Jeff when he was comfortable with Andrew, when Jeff and Andrew were really close."

Late that spring, Andrew, David, Jeff, and a date of Jeff's had dinner with Doug Stubblefield and his friend Glen Setty at a sushi restaurant. Andrew was especially loud that night. He said how Jeff was his oldest friend, and they had known each other since kindergarten or first grade, so if anyone had any doubts about what Andrew said, they could ask Jeff. Jeff politely went along. He said, "I grew up on the other side of the tracks, but I know everything about him." Andrew said, "If you want to get the real scoop, go to Jeff—he has the dirt." Stubblefield says he felt a real sense of camaraderie between the two that night, but in fact, Jeff would later tell others that by asking Jeff to lie for him, Andrew had in fact pushed Jeff away.

Jeff went down to San Diego for Gay Pride Weekend in July, and he and Andrew bumped into a naval officer who had known them both for a long time. They had dinner, and for the first time the officer noticed that Jeff's comments to Andrew were edgy. He guessed that maybe they were fighting over a boy, but that wasn't the case.

Andrew made one last stab at trying to woo David, in San Francisco around Labor Day, but he failed. David demanded honesty, and Andrew couldn't unmask himself. He had created this phony persona that destroyed his ability to have a real relationship. Without the facade, who was he? In a community where looks and cash came first, Andrew was suddenly on the losing end where both were concerned. His image, so carefully and pathologically created, was crumbling, and his sugar daddy was gone. Now he had to face the fact that David was gone too.

Defeated, Andrew flew south for the holiday weekend. When Michael Moore picked Andrew up at the San Diego airport, he recalls, "he didn't say anything for a long time." An old Bishop's School buddy, Stacy Lopez, heard more. When she ran into Andrew at a Labor Day party, the first time they had seen each other in several years, she ran over to hug him. At first he hesitated answering her questions about what he was doing, but she pressed on. "Do you work?" she asked.

"No," he answered. "I've got money."

"Oh, you've got yourself a sugar daddy, huh?"

"I've got my ways."

"Have you been dating?"

Andrew didn't lie this time. He told his old friend Stacy the truth. He was devastated, he said. "I was in a relationship that really hurt me." He was embarrassed that he had put on weight and told her he felt very unattractive. "Just look at me. I'm awful. I'm horrible."

Stacy remembers, "He was not happy with himself."

The unraveling had begun.

13

Bad Manners

At the end of October, unable to find a job in San Diego, Jeff culminated a three-month search by landing a job in Minneapolis as a district manager for commercial accounts at Ferrellgas, a propane company that actively recruited ex-military people. Some of Jeff's friends, such as Michael Williams, tried to discourage him from leaving: "Jeff quitting so fast and moving so far, I was bothered by it and trying to talk him out of it." But Jeff was anxious to repay money he had borrowed from his parents, and promised friends he would come back in six months.

Even though Jeff had supposedly cooled toward Andrew, in September he had allowed him to fly along with him to a job interview in Houston. Jeff did not want to be alone. Now Jeff was leaving a warm and sunny place he loved to live in a far harsher climate. The news that Jeff would be in Minneapolis was all the incentive Andrew needed to mount a new campaign to reinsert himself into David's life. He called David's loft, and David's sister Diane Benning answered. "Don't even call him back," she instructed. His sister had warned David not to have anything to do with Andrew. But Andrew persisted, with the excuse that David could help show Jeff around. The only problem was that a few weeks before Jeff got the job, David had fallen in love with someone else.

Robbie Davis was a tall, self-described "BAP"—Black American Prince—from Washington, D.C., whose family owned a thriving commercial cleaning business. Robbie was cool and street-wise, the first of several black boyfriends David would have. "They came from a different upbringing, and he found that very intriguing," says Wendy Peterson. "He felt he had had bad relationships at the time, especially with white guys. He felt he had been stabbed in the back, stepped on, or taken advantage of." David also sympathized "with many of the minorities' struggles," says Monique Salvetti. Wendy believed that having a long-distance boyfriend suited David, who could be aloof when he wanted to be. He felt that distance gave him more "control."

Jeff moved to Minneapolis with a young ex-sailor named Casey Murray, whom Andrew had introduced him to one day at the beach. Jon Wainwright and others tried to tell Jeff that he hadn't known Casey long enough to have Casey pull up stakes and join him, but Jeff was stubborn and wanted the security of a relationship. Casey arrived in Minneapolis about a month after Jeff. Within a month, the two broke up.

Casey had no love for Andrew, whom he considered "fake and pathetic." In fact, Casey would knee Jeff under the table every time Andrew told a whopper. "I kept saying to Jeff, 'Don't you see?' But nobody would ever tell Andrew to his face—they didn't want to hurt him." Whenever Andrew's name came up, Casey says, "Jeff would roll his eyes," but he never told him to "butt out." He told Casey that Andrew was someone to put up with, "more like a brother."

"The spotlight had to be on Andrew. You'd say something about your life—he'd have to have done it too, only ten times better," Casey recalls. "He would come in dressed really nice, wearing a gold watch and carrying his phone. The phone would never ring unless he dialed it. He never had to go anywhere—he just said he did. He wanted to be busier than he was."

Andrew decided to visit Jeff for a few days to acquaint him with Minneapolis. But the visit lengthened, driving Jeff to distraction. "You try having Andrew in your house for ten days," Jeff told Stan Hatley, whom he ran into at Y'All Come Back Saloon. "I told him he could either check into a hotel or go home: 'You're driving me crazy.' " Jeff also told a young Minneapolis woman named Dana Evans, "I need him to get out of here. I want him to leave." David wasn't prepared to have Andrew around either. "From my understanding," Wendy says, "Andrew would come to town unannounced. He would barge in and put himself in David's presence, and David would not be comfortable."

Andrew knew all about Robbie, but he kept assuring David that he was "changing," and he would constantly thank David for helping to straighten him out. He was only changing for the worse, but he was clever enough to appeal to David's penchant for helping the underdog. "David was the type of person who always picked up the wounded sparrow—sometimes with disregard for his own interests," says Rich Bonnin.

Back in San Diego, Andrew continued to mope. To raise cash he was forced to sell the Infiniti. "He said that after he sold his car that was all the money he had," Michael Moore reports. He was piling up charges on his credit cards, and his use of both crystal and cocaine was causing even his carefree friends to notice mood swings. "He'd go from loud to somber and quiet. He'd be reading, and then wanted to be away from people. It would happen instantly," says Franz vonRichter. "He seemed a little lost," says Michael Moore. "Jumpy." He would assemble people "for a several-hundred-dollar dinner, then walk away to buy magazines on cars and architecture and read them at the table." Moore adds, "He had some poor table manners. He brought up sex toys having to do with electrocution at dinner. A dildo that had electric current. I was hearing more and more about it."

In mid-November, Andrew returned to Minneapolis for a weekend to attend a Design Industries Foundation Fighting AIDS benefit—DIFFA. David was having a party at his loft before the event, and Rob Davis, his boyfriend, was flying in. Andrew arrived on Friday, the day before the benefit. That night he and Jeff went to the Saloon, where they met Dana Evans and a friend of hers, an architect named "Joe." Andrew and Joe started a conversation. "The only reason I talked to Andrew is because I thought Jeff was cute," says Joe, who is from a well-to-do Chicago family. He had gone to Brown and to Harvard for graduate school, and had a brand-new Saab convertible, none of which went unnoticed by Andrew, who was very inquisitive about Joe's father's financial business. "He was really interested in *where* and what the place was."

Joe had recently come out of a three-year relationship, and Andrew was enthralled. He begged Joe to let him stay with him, because he had nowhere to go that night. They went to bed together, but immediately had an argument about who would be on top and who would be on the bottom. "I said, 'Andrew, I'm never a bottom. I don't like it.' He said, 'I'm not one either.' " Then Andrew, who had spent the previous two hours affectionately "all over me, smothering me in the pillow," would not allow Joe to touch him. "Every time I'd go to touch his boxers, he'd flip out. We never had sex. He kept saying, 'No, no, don't touch me.' "

The next morning, Joe remembers, "I woke up thinking, What is this guy doing to me? I had blood hickeys all over my neck." Andrew had also bitten Joe on his chest, which left ugly bruises. "I just thought it was fun," Andrew told him. Despite this behavior, Joe drove Andrew to Jeff's apartment the next morning. "I couldn't wait to get him out of my house." Andrew said he was cold and borrowed a $1,200 Andrew Marc jacket from Joe. Andrew showed up wearing it later in the week when he and David had drinks with David's close friend Monique Salvetti.

At the pre–benefit party David threw on Saturday night, Rich Bonnin was surprised at the change in Andrew's appearance. "He wore a nice tux which had fit at a different time. He looked a little plump. He looked more tired and worn. I was very struck by it, because when I had met him in the spring, he looked like the role he described himself to be." Moreover, Andrew's behavior was downright bizarre.

Jeff came to the party, and so did a friend of his from work, Jerry Davis, an ex–Air Force officer, and another friend, Michael Reardon. Monique Salvetti, Rich Bonnin, Joe, and Dana Evans were already there. Rob Davis was playing host, and David was hanging back. "What is it you do?" Dana asked Andrew. "I'm a professional romantic," he blithely replied, and turned toward the canapes. Rob had specifically asked that no one feed hors d'oeuvres to Prints, David's beloved Dalmatian. Andrew filled a plate and gave it to the dog, who promptly threw up. What a jerk, Michael Reardon thought.

Then Andrew went over to a table that had a framed picture of Rob and David together on it. "This looks interesting," he said. He was trying to get someone to pay attention to him, and nobody would. He then walked over to the food table, which had two lighted candles on it, and nudged a paper plate toward one flame. A friend of Jeff and David's named Rick Allen pulled the plate away. Undeterred, Andrew put some napkins on the plate, and shoved it into the candle flame. He then dropped the flaming plate on the table and walked away as the smoke alarm went off.

Rob Davis grabbed the plate and held it under the kitchen faucet. When Andrew started whispering in David's ear and brushing up against him, Rob, who is over six feet, had had enough. He pulled Andrew into a corner of the loft and slammed him up against the wall. "Excuse me, I understand you're excessive. I'm not gonna have you pressing up against my man. While I am here, you respect my presence or you won't be here." Andrew backed off, saying, "All right, man. It was a whim." Rob reports, "David was, like, 'Thank you.' "

When the party broke up to go to the benefit, Andrew rode down in the elevator with Jeff and suggested that they all meet up later. Michael Reardon, who was walking with Jeff, turned to Andrew and said angrily, "You are such an asshole." But Andrew didn't react. "He just let it roll off as if, 'That's not the first time someone has said that to me,' " Reardon remembers. By this time Joe and Dana had arrived, and Joe wanted to know where his leather jacket was, but he decided not to make an issue about getting it back. "Andrew was so freaky." About a week later, Jeff asked Dana what she thought of Andrew. "I'm surprised you're friends with him," she said. Once again Jeff used the analogy of Andrew's being like family. "You may not agree with what they do, but you're there for them."

Both Jeff and David kept hoping Andrew would take the hint and ease off, but he never did. David took Robbie to Vail for a week of skiing before Thanksgiving, and Robbie bought David an *I Love Vail* bumper sticker for his 1995 leased red Jeep Cherokee. During this time, Andrew was staying in David's loft, taking care of the dog. "The only fear that David had about Andrew was his lies," Rob explains. Where did his money come from? Jeff, who had gotten to know David casually, and had gone to dinner and to the gym with him a couple of times, tried to warn him about Andrew: "You can't believe a word he says. He'll say anything just to get a reaction." Meanwhile, Andrew had told a friend that he was uncomfortable having the two people he cared most about living in the same faraway city without him.

In December Andrew, who had briefly left Minneapolis, found another excuse to come back, to loft-sit and take care of Prints. David confided to Robbie that Andrew had once told him that he had ordered someone killed. At a Christmas party, Andrew told Rob Davis that Jeff had come to Minneapolis because he had been involved moving cocaine across the Mexican border for Andrew; he had gotten scared because the California Highway Patrol was investigating him, and that's why he had resigned. Although Rob claims that Jeff had also once told him that he had had to leave California because things had gotten a little too hot, the police have no record of such an investigation and nobody who knew Jeff would believe that he would involve himself with drugs, Andrew did apparently try nonetheless. Jeff once talked to one of his Minneapolis friends, research engineer Rick Allen, about Andrew's attempts to recruit him for illegal business. "What Jeff told me," says Rick Allen, "was 'Andrew talked to me about doing security work for his "import-export" business.' "

"I don't even know what you're talking about," Rick Allen says he told Jeff.

" 'Drugs, Rick, drugs.' Jeff was very hesitant to talk about it at all. He told me, 'It's not something I tell anybody about.' I said, 'What did you tell him?' Jeff said, 'I said, "Fuck you." ' "

"Andrew also talked about having millions confiscated from foreign bank accounts through FBI subpoenas or warrants," says Rich Bonnin. "He told David that's what made him change his mind—he came so close to losing everything, he decided to go straight." Andrew's exact words, according to Rich Bonnin, were, "You just don't walk out on the Mob."

In retrospect, it is amazing that people tolerated Andrew as much as they did. Yet Monique Salvetti, who met Andrew at a DIFFA weekend, and joined David and Rich Bonnin for a drink with him the following week, pronounced him "a radiant personality." Andrew had gone right to her bookshelf, taken down a volume of Isak Dinesen, and promptly turned to his favorite passage and read it aloud. At drinks, Monique says, he turned on the full charm. "Andrew was very cultural. He knew a lot about arts and literature, and we were talking about things like that."

At one point he reached across to David and asked Rich and Monique, "Doesn't our David remind you of Tom Cruise?" Since the two looked nothing alike, says Monique, "I thought that was just so ridiculous." But later she told her friend, "He's really great, David."

14

Unravel

THE MUSTANG SPA, open twenty-four hours, caters to closeted bisexuals and an admiral or two. "On the weekends I get the gays," says owner Todd Kaufman. The Mustang is in North Park, a blue-collar area; not gentrified the way Hillcrest is, it is an easier place to hide. Early in 1996, Andrew started popping into the Mustang for quick sex. By the fall he was staying longer, sometimes for more than twenty-four hours. "I don't think he was having sex at all," says Kaufman. "I think he was annoying people." Andrew was wandering around without sleep and looking the worse for wear. Kaufman had seen the syndrome before. "People start acting like they live here. I got the feeling he had lost his job and was on the skids. His stories were out of this world." In his previous visits, Andrew had kept to himself and given the impression he was slumming. No longer.

"You pigeonhole people," Kaufman continues. "He went from being one type, dressed in nice clothes, to another—jeans, T-shirts, leather, bummy, sloppy. People start living at the baths because they don't want to focus on what's going on in their lives. They go into the bars till they close, then the baths till they close, so they're never alone and don't have to think about anything." Kaufman calls this "cocooning. They get very into themselves, very weird. You have to put them out." Andrew would come in at 2 A.M. on Saturday, after the bars closed, and would still be at the Mustang late the next day, eating out of the candy machine or getting an hour pass to go outside and buy something at the taco shop down the street. "*Roseanne* was on at five P.M. He'd sit and watch that."

About this time Robbins was in Mexico, attempting to get involved in the production of *Titanic,* hoping to help build sets for the epic film which was shooting there, but he wound up doing stunt work instead. Andrew, oblivious to the ridiculous impression he was making, would go around the Mustang bragging that *he* was building sets for *Titanic* and name-dropping about his Hollywood connections. "He got so desperate when he was trying to tell me these stories—he had to justify his worth," Todd says. What Andrew was really doing was dealing drugs. "He was hanging out with three leather druggie types. He came off like a Catholic schoolboy in over his head. He gave the impression he was trying to act as tough as they were, and he wasn't. They tolerated him because he was supplying. Two of them are in jail now."

Kaufman started keeping a sharp eye on Andrew, whom he thought was on ecstasy or cocaine. "I got the impression people were using him. He was trying to buy people's attention, and he was selling a lot, too," Kaufman explains. "He got on my and my workers' nerves, and I can put up with a lot or I wouldn't be in this business." Kaufman finally decided that he had had enough. "When he got too involved in dealing, I had to eighty-six him from the club. He made a bunch of threats when I kicked him out: 'I'm going to tell my friends not to come in here.' " Kaufman never considered Andrew violent; he was, as he says, "controllable. It was very easy to throw him out—that's not always the case."

Kaufman concluded that Andrew was suffering from depression and "very low self-esteem. He was leading several lives at once. He came across as someone drowning."

The previous September, Andrew had moved in with Tom Eads and Erik Greenman, a young gay couple he had introduced. Both were devoted to him, and he was crazy about their dog, a black Rottweiler named Barklee. They lived in a $750-a-month, two-bedroom apartment on Robinson Street, just a short walk from Rich's, Flicks, and the California Cuisine. Erik was a waiter at Mixx, an upscale restaurant

Andrew liked. Tom was in college and working part-time. In November he moved out, but he remained close to Andrew.

While living on Robinson Street, Andrew would sleep most of the day, rise late in the afternoon, and take Barklee for a long walk in Balboa Park. Once a week he'd stop by the cigar store and pick out a few eight-dollar cigars, which he'd smoke in the park. Andrew fussed over Barklee, and on their walks around the neighborhood he would buy him his own special *carne asada.* He'd return to the apartment in time to watch *Jeopardy!* and make plans for the evening. Often he'd call Franz vonRichter, another young, attractive, platonic friend, to have dinner with him. Andrew would sit in the backseat of the Infiniti he would soon be forced to sell and let Franz be the chauffeur. "Every time we went out, he'd say, 'Franz, stop by the Bank of America.'" Andrew kept his wallet conspicuously in his front pocket, and he would withdraw $400 or $500 at a time. "He went through a lot of money," Franz recalls.

During this period, Andrew also put on a lot of weight, the result of taking Franz out for elaborate dinners three or four times a week. "It was noticeable, bordering on gross. He looked something like a straight man would get," says Shane O'Brien. "Cottage cheesy all in one area—the gut . . . ugh." One day someone pointed out to Franz that he, too, had gained weight. "I went on a crash diet. I weighed 163. Then I got to 175, 180. In this community, that's ballooning," Franz emphasizes. "When I first met Andrew, he was 160, 165. Probably at the end he was 180 or 185." Andrew, he says, felt bad that his body was so different from those of the men he was attracted to. "He liked military guys—navy and marines—the thicker, the stockier, the better. Hard, worked-out, thick," says Franz. "If he said, 'Do you think that guy is cute?' it would mean short hair, lean, and hard."

When Andrew and Franz would go to Black's Beach, Andrew would be the odd man out. "God, Franz, you have a nice body," he would say. "There'd be all these people there with major bods, and Andrew would be eating a box of Oreos, smoking a cigar with a bag of Doritos, having a beer," says Franz. "There was this naked guy on a bike selling beer, and we'd buy beer from him. Andrew was never naked on Black's Beach. All his friends were good-looking." According to Erik Greenman, "Andrew was definitely not one to get dates. He had to flash money. A good-looking guy wouldn't look at him. That means an awful lot." On one occasion Andrew took Franz to meet an older friend of his. "This guy really liked me," Franz recalls. But Andrew became indignant, screaming, " 'I'm never going to take you out with him. Never! You stole the whole show. You embarrassed me in front of my friends.' " Franz says he told him, " 'Andrew, I only made you look good.' But Andrew's thing was *he* had to be the center of attention."

Although on the surface Andrew was pretending that everything was copacetic, as he gained weight and sank deeper into depression, his drug use was also increasing and his rage was barely controlled. Franz was often a target. Pretending to be playful, Andrew would grab him in a choke hold, throw him down on the ground, and twist his nipples hard. "He'd throw me down on the way back to the car or back to his house. There was an edge," Franz admits. "We'd always carry on, but he'd say, 'Franz, don't ever cross me.' " One day Andrew grabbed the pocket of Franz's shirt and tore the shirt right off him. He did it again later. "He had a streak about him, a sexual innuendo of being rough in sex. It kind of turned him on," Franz says. "Andrew had a thing of just grabbing everybody. He'd come up to people all the time and twist their titties. He'd grit his teeth and smile and say, 'You like that?' He'd come up to a guy, grab a crotch in a bar, and say, 'You fuck with David or Keith? He's got a penis as big as yours?' He'd grab their dick and say, 'Yeah, you've got a big dick.' Then he'd say, 'Here, let me introduce you. You have to meet my good friend Franz vonRichter. My Austrian, German, Bavarian bastard.' He'd do it with a fake German accent."

Andrew's anger and desperation did not seem to register on his self-absorbed friends, though; they continued to see him as the glad-handing money machine. "Andrew was losing his looks. What he lacked in looks he made up for with money," Franz declares. "Because of his personality and money, people just never questioned him. The money took care of everything."

Andrew's dark fantasies were fueled by crystal meth, cocaine, and pornography. "Everyone has his own sexual fetishes," says Erik. "His was watching that." Andrew especially liked the popular gay porn star Cort Stevens. "I told him once I was going up to San Francisco," Franz relates. "Andrew said, 'I want you to get me a video with Cort Stevens. Franz, I'm giving you fifty dollars. Rent the movie. You need a fifty-dollar deposit without a credit card. I want to keep the movie.' It was a weird movie," Franz says. "In every scene Cort Stevens is tied up, getting shocked. The other guy in leather has six or seven types of Tasers [stun guns], touching every part of Stevens with a Taser, and every time he'd get a shock."

Apparently Andrew would masturbate while watching porn tapes. "Erik was joking with me a couple of nights after I brought the videos," Franz reports. "Erik said, 'I came home, and that video was on the VCR, with a jar of Vaseline next to the TV, with a dirty rag.' "

Erik felt that Andrew's sexual proclivities were so extreme that they precluded the normal pickup, "tricking" situation. "Whether it'd be the whips or making the guy walk around in shackles—who knows? You need privacy for that. He's always had bondage videos. . . . Andrew always liked S&M—more the tying up, just the degradation, not the asphyxiation."

Within a few months, Erik says, Andrew was again delivering mysterious briefcases full of cash. He had a separate phone line under the name Andrew Cunanan for drug transactions. "Jeff flat-out told me that Andrew was dealing drugs," says Michael Williams. "Ecstasy, crystal meth, and cocaine. He said, 'He's up to his old profession.' "

Andrew had landed right in the middle of a drug ring that operated with impunity on one of Hillcrest's busier streets, fronted by several legitimate businesses. The San Diego police seem to know nothing about it to this day. Two retail stores share a common loading dock, where their large delivery truck allegedly comes up from Mexico or Arizona filled with crates of colorful ceramics and plaster garden ornaments, which in turn are filled with large quantities of crystal meth, pills, steroids, marijuana, and cocaine. The proprietor of a nearby pornography business is also allegedly involved and has a drop behind his store. The drugs are then shipped to the East inside the products of one of the businesses, and all payments are made with briefcases full of cash such as the ones Andrew carried.

This is by no means the only drug ring in Hillcrest, however. Several bartenders deal—one allegedly uses an old sewer pipe two floors below a decorating-business front as his drop. Anyone in Hillcrest can easily score drugs all over the neighborhood. "They're making an enormous profit," says former California Cuisine waiter Anthony Dabiere. "There's more than proof in the pudding. There's dipsy dooodly and you-you hoo." Andrew was working close to home.

That summer and fall of 1996 after Andrew and Norman broke up, Andrew started hanging around with Dominick Andreacchio, whom he deemed another Tom Cruise look-alike. He liked showing Dominick off, but he never stopped talking about David Madson. "He was so into him," says Dominick.

One day when Dominick was shopping with Andrew, he happened to see Andrew's credit card with the name Cunanan on it. Dominick recalls, " 'Oh yeah,' he said. 'I guess that's my other name.' And he showed me his other passport. He had a couple." But Andrew denied that he was mixed up in drugs, though he freely admitted to Dominick that he was into illegal activity of a different kind. He said that "things would just fall off trucks. And I was, like, 'What are you talking about?' " When Andrew gave Dominick a CD player, for example, he told him it came from an inside job. "Like big electronics truck ship-ments to someplace; he would be on the inside with other people and steal the electronic equipment."

Dominick had a boyfriend, so Andrew did not come on to him overtly. But he was very open with Dominick about what he liked sexually. "He used the electric-shock stuff. It was always very weird. He said stuff like, 'Oh, I'd like to electrocute *him*.' And I was, like, 'What-ever, you weirdo.' "

15

Spinning

IN SAN DIEGO over the holidays of 1996 Andrew had periods of uncharacteristic quiet, but then in a moment he would become the manic, witty Andrew of old. He and Erik gave a tree-trimming party, which he insisted also be called a Chanukah party. He boldly extracted a hundred dollar bill out of his friend David Gallo's wallet, declaring, "This is my Chanukah present," and told Erik that he didn't celebrate Christmas. Ken Higgins, one of Andrew's friends from his professional clique, invited him to a big seafood dinner at Christmas. In the middle of the meal, Andrew left the room to go and read a magazine. "Uh-oh, this is a mood swing," Ken would tease him at such times, but no one was really alarmed, not even when Andrew started using morphine and Demerol in order to go to sleep.

Late at night, Andrew's roommate, Erik Greenman, would see him injecting himself with his drug of choice, crystal meth. In the morning, "he'd be coming down and feeling awful," remembers Erik. Sardonically, he would tell him, "Never do crack, Erik. It's a ghetto drug." There was speculation that Andrew was also using heroin, but no needle tracks were found on his body. In Andrew's world, though, drugs and pornography were so prevalent that nobody bothered to wonder if the two might be feeding on each other, in his case, in a way to cause alarm. Experts on serial killer behavior say the combination can be explosive.

Andrew's narcissism and his pathological lying had already made him a borderline personality; mental illness also ran in his immediate family. But Andrew made sure that no single person had all the facts. Finally there was such a high level of tolerance for his behavior that in fact he was surrounded by enablers. When Robbins went to some of Andrew's friends out of concern for his rapidly depleting finances, for example, their response was, "Yeah, we sure are going through his money, aren't we?"

On New Year's Eve, Sheila Gard was shocked when she saw Andrew for the first time in months. She recalls saying, " 'Wow! What happened to you? You're disheveled!' He looked bad. His eyes were sunken, he was overweight, not talkative. He was completely different, all by himself. He seemed depressed—he was not running around, not being the life of the party. He was not in a good mood." He also had dark circles under his eyes because he was frequently staying up all night at Wolfs, the tweakers bar. Nevertheless, on New Year's David got a call from Andrew, who told him, "I've left my old ways. I realize how close I was to losing everything, and I just want to make an honest living." He thanked David for helping him see the light and told him that he was going to start a construction company in Mexico for building set designs—appropriating Robbins's life once again.

The truth was that Robbins had offered Andrew a job, and Andrew had refused his help. His phony grandiosity had kept him from being anything but slippery and scared. Andrew was boxed: If he admitted the truth, he would be mocked as a loser and a liar. But he had come to the point where his lies were costing him the only two people he really cared about. He had no job, and little money, and he was in the throes of a major depression. Where was the light? Andrew began spinning out of control.

Neither Jeff nor David wanted Andrew around, but they couldn't bring themselves to tell him that outright. At the end of January, Andrew returned to Minneapolis. He stayed with Jeff, who was suffering through the Minnesota winter and desperate to find a new job in a warmer climate. Jeff had also acquired some of Andrew's expensive taste and was piling up bills. Robbins Thompson began hearing reports that Andrew had lent Jeff several thousand dollars. If so, that may have made Andrew think he had license to pressure Jeff into helping him in his drug business. For even if cocaine was a no-no, one could still make a nice living in the Midwest selling steroids. Steroids did not carry the same stigma in the gay community as other illegal drugs; they were seen as workout boosters. Jeff may not have had much choice about having Andrew as his ever more frequent guest.

In the end, "Jeff and David were very supportive," says Robbie Davis. "If Andrew came into town for whatever reason, Jeff had Andrew stay at his house. Or if David was out of town, there was no problem for Andrew to stay and keep David's dog." Andrew seemed determined not to be forgotten by either of them.

After Andrew picked up a big dinner tab one night, Robbie asked David where all the money came from. "David said, 'He dabbles in cocaine, and he's got a sugar daddy who takes care of him.' I said, 'Hell of a sugar daddy to pay three hundred fifty dollars on a meal when you're only doing it to show off in Minnesota.'"

That particular weekend in late January 1997, Andrew went to a birthday party David gave for Robbie. Jeff was also there with a young date. Andrew told Robbie that he was kept by "an older, real-estate tycoon." He also mentioned that he had been in Chicago, but he did not link the two things. Andrew was so "giddy and jumpy" that Robbie thought he must be on cocaine.

"Are you messing around with whitey tonight?" Robbie asked him.

"Been there, done that" was Andrew's dismissive reply.

Robbie thought of Andrew as an intrusive wimp. "But David's explanation was, 'He's my friend. He's an ex. I don't see him that often, Rob. There's nothing to worry about.'"

By now, back in California, Andrew had shaved off most of his hair and forsaken his trademark glasses for contacts. He was heavier and wore loose, sloppy clothes. "What's up with the hair?" Franz asked him. "Low maintenance," Andrew replied. His moodiness continued, but he refused to let anyone penetrate his shell. One day he got up from the sofa in his apartment and said, "Erik, I'm unhappy." Erik says, "Then he's up and gone. He'd give you a glimpse, and then he wouldn't." Robbins attempted to reach him more than once. "He just said he was tired, and that was the closest it ever came." Robbins pressed him about what he was going to do, because he was "definitely at the end of his rope" and obviously running out of money. "I'm fine, I'm fine," Andrew replied, and announced that he was leaving San Diego and moving to San Francisco. He once confided secretly to Franz that he was mulling a job with a real-estate title company in North County, near Rancho Santa Fe.

Meanwhile, two bartenders at Flicks noted independently that beginning around February 1997, whenever anyone complained about somebody else's behavior, Andrew would say, "Well, we'll just have to kill him."

Andrew began drinking much more, often at Mixx restaurant. "He would order thirty-six dollar bottles of Stone Street merlot like there was no tomorrow," says maître d' Rick Rinaldi. Other nights he'd buy for the table one hundred twenty dollar magnums of Duckhorn merlot. Andrew would also eat rich foods—foie gras and desserts. (People who use a lot of crystal meth eat very little, but it is not unusual for long-time users to keep eating and for others to binge from time to time.) Andrew was so good for business and such a lavish tipper that Rick Rinaldi would rotate waiters to serve him. Andrew would jokingly tell Rinaldi that he couldn't decide whether to go to L.A. or Paris for dinner. In fact, around this time, he falsely told people that he hopped the Concorde with a friend who had a ticket for a companion, and spent four days in Paris. He "came back" raving about the hottest new restaurants.

One evening at Mixx, Andrew pointed to a man standing near the piano with a couple. "Do you know who that is?" he asked Rinaldi. "It's Joseph Wambaugh." Then Andrew went up to the man. Later, says Rinaldi, "I saw Wambaugh's name on the credit card." The famous crime author is a local celebrity, and Robbins claimed that Andrew once described Wambaugh's house in San Diego to him in great detail. Robbins, who was working on a construction job next door, realized he was accurate. "He definitely went into details. You definitely would have had to read about it or been there, because you cannot get in there—it's a guarded, gated community, very very exclusive," Robbins says. (Wambaugh has denied knowing Andrew.)

Rob Davis says he saw Andrew again in Minneapolis on the weekend of February 7, 1997. On Valentine's Day, David and Rob broke up, and David immediately starting dating another tall, good-looking African-American, a cable-TV producer. According to Rich Bonnin, Andrew briefly faded from the picture.

But not for long. Andrew confided to one friend in San Diego that he wanted to give David Madson a ring but David turned down his proposal. In mid-March, as Easter approached, David mentioned to Rich Bonnin that he had some frequent-flyer miles and was thinking of going to Los Angeles with Andrew to see his friends Karen Lapinski and Evan Wallit. By then David had a new African-American boyfriend, Cedric Rucker, the assistant dean for student activities at Mary Washington College in Virginia, whom he had met on a trip to Washington, D.C.

Andrew had proposed that Karen, Evan, David, and he take a European vacation together, but Karen had school, so they decided on Los Angeles instead. Andrew went to San Francisco and manipulated Karen and Evan into luring David west. Karen, whose father had died, asked David to walk her down the aisle at her wedding. Andrew grandly insisted that he would pay for the couple's wedding reception, and he also bought Karen a $900 leather coat. Karen and Evan were pleased to accept it all. He told them and David that he had fifteen thousand dollars that he had to spend for tax purposes by April 15. He thanked David again for showing him the straight and narrow and shrewdly appealed to his sense of compassion. At the same time, he dangled expensive gifts.

"David's weakness vis-à-vis Andrew was that he was dazzled by his materialism," says Robbie. David was susceptible to Andrew's supposed wealth, and even though he suspected Andrew of drug dealing and possibly worse, he continued to take expensive presents from him. Andrew FedExed David a $739 round-trip ticket from Minneapolis to Los Angeles and rented a $395 room at the Chateau Marmont in Hollywood for himself and David. He also took along a trunk full of sex toys—slings, harnesses, restraints, and dripping wax—he had picked up in San Francisco at Mr. S Leather.

The weekend was a moveable feast, all at Andrew's expense. The group lived at full-tilt boogie and dined in great style: a $1,400 dinner at Valentino Restaurant in Santa Monica on Friday night; a $1,300 sushi lunch for four at Ginza Sushiko, Beverly Hills's most expensive restaurant, where the rare fish is flown in fresh from Osaka; a $200 late supper at Coco Pazzo in West Hollywood on Saturday night.

In between meals, they shopped. Andrew bought a $1,200 Armani suit for David and $2,000 worth of clothes for himself and the others at Neiman Marcus and Zegna in Beverly Hills. Karen was an old chum of *Friends* TV star Lisa Kudrow, so one night they went to a studio party Lisa invited them to, and they had a meal at her mother's house, which Andrew would brag about for weeks. Naturally, Andrew tried to impress the celebrity—at one point he was taking credit for producing much of *Titanic*. She tried to blow him off. David called Cedric from the party and was on the phone for almost an hour. Back at the Chateau Marmont, Andrew wanted to have sex with David, but David balked. Andrew, who by then had charged about $8,000 on his American Express card, was furious and began to pout. "I think David used Andrew a lot," says Erik Greenman. "Andrew did shower him with gifts. David would readily accept them and then say, 'I just want to be friends.' "

Karen Lapinski later told police that Andrew clung to David, begging for sex. She also said it was obvious that Andrew was very much in love with David, but David did not reciprocate. David had told Karen that in the beginning his relationship with Andrew was "very wicked." She felt that Andrew wanted "a violent sexual relationship" while David needed "a loving relationship." In Minneapolis, for instance, the TV producer said that sex with David was "vanilla, vanilla, vanilla" and not at all violent. David told him that they had all had a "great weekend with a lot of shopping and they went to dinner at Lisa Kudrow's mother's house."

The producer, who sensed that David had a gift for listening and teaching, also came to realize that "David was pretty impressed with money and the power money can give people." One of the first things David had told him was "Successful people hang out with successful people." He says that David represented himself as having grown up in Chicago. "I had no idea he came from a middle-class family and that his father owned a hardware store." Now, David told him that *he* had bought an expensive suit on Rodeo Drive. "That whole weekend was about money and star-fucking," the producer says. Andrew, who so much wanted to control and who was so dangerously off balance, did not get his way with David that weekend. David was in control. And Andrew's rage was building.

Within three days Andrew was back in San Francisco, supposedly looking for a place to live. He stayed for two weeks, and rumors circulated about his drug use. Out of the blue, he called his sister Gina, who was living there, and they had a drink. She hadn't heard from Andrew in several years and was thrilled to have him back in her life. He took his young niece, who was visiting Gina for spring break, to the movies. That was the last time anyone in the family saw him.

Driving around in a rented red Mustang, Andrew told various friends that he had found an apartment in the Marina District, on Russian Hill, or in the Castro. He saw Karen and Evan frequently, and he stayed at the Sherman House in lower Pacific Heights and also at the Mandarin Oriental. To a bartender at the Badlands Bar whom he took out to dinner, he represented himself as an army intelligence officer. When the bartender called his room, Andrew answered the phone, "Commander Cunanan."

One night he met twenty-six-year-old Tim Schwager, an assistant manager in a San Francisco Denny's, at a gay dance club. Andrew offered to get him drugs—ecstasy or cocaine—but Schwager refused. "He said he was associated with people who dealt in San Diego," says Schwager. "He was kind of like a middle man." Andrew also bragged about knowing various celebrities—Lisa Kudrow, Elizabeth Hurley, Madonna. "He said he had lunch with Lisa Kudrow the previous weekend."

Andrew took Tim Schwager back to the Mandarin Oriental. Schwager's memory of what took place is hazy. "I think I was drugged that night, or I had too much to drink," he says. Like Joe in Minneapolis,

Tim also began to have "memory flashbacks of trying to fight him off during the night. I wasn't attracted to him sexually. I woke up with three hickeys on me." Tim Schwager remembers going to sleep in his underwear. "When I woke up, I had nothing on. After that night, I knew he had a rough side to him."

They ran into each other again the following weekend. "He kept his arm around my neck the whole time. He started to like me, but I rejected him." Andrew then went to another club, and when Tim got there, he saw him coming on to someone else. " 'You're a player, aren't you?' I asked him. He just laughed his sarcastic laugh."

Tim says Andrew told him he was moving to San Francisco, but before that "he said he had to go to Chicago to do something."

The weekend before he left for Minneapolis, Andrew stayed in San Francisco. The whole weekend seemed tinged with the dark foreshadowing of the tragedy about to unfold. Andrew was clearly on drugs. At the Midnight Sun he grabbed his old friend Steven Gomer from behind and spun him around. Steven remembers that his hair was so butch it made him look like "a terrorist commander ready to infiltrate." Steven reintroduced Andrew to his friend Philip Horne, an attorney. Andrew said he was looking for a roommate. So was Phil. Andrew told them all about an apartment he was renting in the Marina district—two bedrooms, two fireplaces, and Phil would have to pay only $630 a month, because Andrew would be traveling, overseeing his seventy-employee factory in Mexico, which constructed Hollywood movie sets. Andrew's lying was so ingrained that a few weeks earlier he had actually engaged Steven in a conversation about the Occupational Safety and Health Act regulations and how they affected his employees. Phil could not believe his good luck in finding an apartment. Andrew told him he would call him the first of the month.

That night, says Steven, Andrew was very "amped-up and aggressive," grabbing hard while pretending to be playful. "He was really over the top. When we were in the bar, he was jumping all over me, picking me up constantly, up and down." Steven says he felt like saying, "You're embarrassing me. It looks like you're humping me like an animal, and it's inappropriate and certainly not welcomed." But he didn't.

When Andrew ran into his old Berkeley friend, John Semerau, in the back of the bar, he was even more unruly. "He grabbed me around the neck so hard he was choking me by his grip," recalls Semerau. "He hurt me. He was very aggressive in trying to be affectionate, grabbing, choking, gripping his hands as hard as he could grip." Semerau told Andrew to cut it out. "Andrew, you're really hurting me. Stop it!" Andrew showed Semerau a flyer for an S&M party he was planning to attend the next night, and invited him to go. But Andrew never called. "He kind of spiraled," Semerau says. "Over the last six months, whenever I ran into him, he was particularly aggressive."

In the eight years since they had known each other, Andrew never allowed Steven to pick up the dinner tab, but that night he did. They walked around the Castro holding hands, and Andrew told Steven of his great love for David Madson. "He made no mention of the fact he was being rejected." Steven had never heard Andrew say such things as "David is the man for me."

"Why do you say that?" Steven asked. Suddenly Andrew's face contorted, and he let out a loud, manic laugh. " 'Well, he let's me do anything I want to him,' and he just started cracking up."

"What are you into?" Steven wanted to know.

Andrew started reciting a long list of S&M proclivities: cages, harnesses around the genitals, latex masks. "Latex masks? You mean, like with holes for the nose, eyes, and mouth?"

Andrew cut him off: "At least in the nose."

"At that time," says Steven, "we were no longer hand in hand."

They got on Steven's motorcycle and started riding back to Andrew's car. Then Andrew surprised Steven again. He came on to him, entreating him to go to the Mandarin Oriental with him. Implicit was the idea they could practice what they'd been talking about.

"Andrew, come on. We've been friends for eight years. Don't you think this is a bit silly?"

"Well, yeah, maybe so."

Steven says Andrew was much more open that night than he had ever been, but he was revealing a side of him Steven had never imagined: "Everything was always so upbeat and so happy, and he was showing me that he was unfulfilled, dissatisfied, and troubled."

Andrew begged Steven, "in a very puppy-doggish way," to show up the next day at Cafe Flor so that they could spend the afternoon together. "I promised him that I was going to keep to the plan, and I did not. I didn't show up, and I didn't spend the day with him, and I didn't call to explain. And that was the last we spoke."

Bud Moore, a good-looking blond friend of Jeff's who worked in advertising, ran into Andrew the next night at the Cafe, a Castro hangout that attracted a younger crowd than did either the Midnight Sun or Badlands. Bud had had a crush on Jeff, and they had dated casually, but since he was twenty-six, Bud says, "I was too old." Through Jeff and other friends of Bud's in San Diego, Andrew's reputation had preceded him. So Bud wasn't interested when Andrew started coming on, hooking him in a hammerlock and trying to keep his arm around him. "I knew he was a liar." Andrew grabbed Bud's baseball cap and he wouldn't give it back. He kept teasing Bud and hiding it behind him. Finally Bud went up to Andrew, leaned close, and let his full glass of water drop and break at Andrew's feet. "I'm asking you one more time, give me back my hat," he said. This time Andrew did not resist. Rejection was becoming his middle name.

On Sunday night, John Semerau went to the Midnight Sun to watch *The Simpsons* and again saw Andrew alone at the bar. He let him have it for not having called about the S&M party. "Andrew, I'm very pissed off. I'm tired of your superficial b.s. I've had it. And stay away from me." But later that evening Semerau relented. "I was feeling so damn guilty, I started talking to him. He didn't say much. He didn't say, 'I'm sorry.' " They walked out together, says Semereau. "He walked me to my car." There they said good-bye.

But Semerau continued to be haunted by the look Andrew had had on his face when he grabbed so hard and choked him. "Something had snapped in him." Only later did Semerau realize that "Andrew was hunting, getting the thrill of the hunt, the thrill of the kill. I saw it in his eyes. I saw it in his body. He had stepped over the edge."

16

Good-bye

ANDREW'S PLATINUM CREDIT CARD would no longer clear. He owed over $40,000 on two cards and was dead broke his last week in San Diego. In fact, Andrew DeSilva had even filed for bankruptcy. After an initial refusal from American Express, Andrew bluffed his way one last time into being allowed to purchase a ticket to Minneapolis, leaving on Friday. Then he would move to San Francisco for good. Yet in San Francisco Andrew had said he had business to take care of in Chicago, and while in San Diego he was telling friends, "I have unfinished business with Jeff Trail." In preparation for leaving, Andrew started giving his possessions away.

He summoned Tom Eads to claim a pair of black, buckled Ferragamo shoes. "He wasn't giving away his tux shoes," Eads says ruefully. But Andrew did give friends a cashmere topcoat and some fancy sweaters—things from his old life, before he had started gaining weight, shaving his head, and shooting crystal meth. Erik Greenman was well satisfied: "I'm the roommate. I got lots of stuff." Later, Erik says he realized, "Andrew was saying his good-byes."

On Wednesday night Andrew went to Mixx with mortgage broker Richard De Bethizy. Andrew told friends he might take a job with a title company and De Bethizy was in a position to help. On Thursday night, April 24, Andrew threw himself a farewell dinner at California

Cuisine, but he made it clear that he had no money to pay for it. Those who attended the last supper were his oldest friends, Robbins; Tom Eads, who had lived with him and Erik Greenman briefly; Ken Higgins, who owned the lighting company; and David Gallo, the lawyer from Texas whom Andrew had coaxed out of his shell. Franz vonRichter was working that night at a hotel, so he was unable to attend. "Dammit, where is he?" Andrew demanded. "I've staked him to dinners for a year!" Dominick Andreacchio, also the former recipient of three or four free dinners a week, managed to drop by. In retrospect, Dominick says, the hugs he kept getting from Andrew that night seemed "very final."

The dinner was a somewhat somber affair, as if Andrew were holding his own wake. David Gallo, who, along with Higgins, brought a couple of bottles of Veuve Clicquot champagne, was practically in tears, claiming that if it hadn't been for Andrew no one at the table would have gotten to know any of the others. "He was the glue that held us all together." Eads recalls, "Two people made that comment. Andrew helped them not to feel alone." Anthony Dabiere, Andrew's favorite waiter, wrote in raspberry puree around the edge of Andrew's plate of chocolate truffle tort, "Good-bye to You." When the time came for Andrew's toast, he was decidedly low-key. He said he was feeling bittersweet about leaving. What he was going to miss most, he said, was Barklee, Erik's dog.

On the way out, Andrew whispered to Higgins—who had helped pick up the check—that he would "have some money by Sunday." No one would have guessed, to hear him, that his ticket to Minneapolis was one-way.

In the Twin Cities, Andrew was like a character out of the old Bill Murray *Saturday Night Live* skit, "The Thing that Wouldn't Leave." Jeff didn't want to see him. Neither did David. As usual, nobody would tell him to his face, but Andrew was not stupid.

"I'm very uncomfortable about his coming," David confided on the phone to his boyfriend, Cedric Rucker, in Virginia. By this time David had met another man he liked in Atlanta, a graphic artist, and had begun a relationship with him, but he hadn't gotten around to telling Cedric. He was also apparently seeing a third man, in Minneapolis. "David was apprehensive about Andrew's visit," Cedric says. "He held suspicions that Andrew was involved in the international drug trade, bringing drugs into the country from across the Mexican border. He probably had ties to organized crime. I said, 'Why would you want to be affiliated with this?' He said, 'Because he's trying to make a change in his life. Andrew just needs help.' "

At this time, David was agitated for another reason. His old stalker, Greg Nelson, had reappeared. In a coffee shop in the uptown district, named Cafe Wyrd, David had looked up to see the stalker staring at him through the window. David immediately left and drove to Monique's in order to see if he was being followed. A few days later, when he went with his coworker, Linda Elwell, to the lot near work where he parked his Jeep, he found it scratched across one side and dented, a sure telltale sign.

On Monday Andrew left a phone message for Jeff: "I'm coming to Minneapolis next weekend, and I wanna see ya." He ended by saying, "So yeah, I'm excited. I hope I get to see ya." But Jeff was also uneasy. On April 7, Jeff's mother had undergone cancer surgery, and he and his sisters had gone home to be with her. There, Jeff confided to the sister he felt closest to, Candy Parrott, that he had a problem and needed her advice. "This has happened before," Jeff explained. "Andrew is coming to stay in a couple weeks, and I'm involved with this guy, Jon, and I don't know what to do about it." Until then Candy, who lives in Austin, Texas, had had no idea that Andrew wanted to be anything more to Jeff than a platonic friend. She had met Andrew the previous September, when he had flown to Houston with Jeff for Jeff's job interview. "I never read anything sinister into this," Candy says. "The way Jeff expressed it to me was that this had happened before. Andrew had come to Minneapolis in November, and at that time Jeff was involved with Casey."

Andrew, it appears, was carrying two torches simultaneously. First, in Minneapolis, he would see if there was any way he could get back with David, "the man I want to marry." If not, Jeff would apparently become the object of his desire. "He's always wanting more than I want to do, and I just don't know what to do about it," Jeff complained to Candy. But he did not mention any push from Andrew about going into the drug business—only that Andrew wanted a "relationship" with him.

Andrew, who had always been solicitous of Jeff, desperately needed to think that someone, somewhere, also cared about *him.* At the same time, the drugs and pornography he fed on kept his cruel and domineering sexual fantasies at fever pitch. Candy gave Jeff some rational, sisterly advice: "You owe it to Andrew to let him know you're involved with Jon and let him make the decision."

Jeff, it seems, did talk to Andrew, who was not happy with what he had to say. Not long after, Jeff phoned his friend Mike Williams in San Diego to say that he and Andrew "had had a huge falling out." He said he never intended to speak to Andrew again. Even a month before that, when Jeff ran into Stan Hatley at the Saloon one night and Stan asked about Andrew, Jeff had said, "I don't want to talk about him. He's pissed me off." By the end of April, however, Jeff had relented. It was clear that Andrew was going to stay with both David and Jeff the weekend of April 25, whether they wanted him to or not.

Thursday, David started casting around for something to do with Andrew. That night his ex-boyfriend, the TV producer, happened to call David, who explained the reason for Andrew's visit: "Andrew has some business to discuss with Jeff Trail." "What type of business?" the producer wanted to know. "It's a long story. I don't want to get into it right now," David answered. The producer recalled rumors about Andrew and Jeff and their "shady business dealings. I'd heard it was drug related." When David's former roommate Rich Bonnin learned that Andrew was showing up again, he was not pleased, but David waved him off. "I ain't going out of my way for him."

Meanwhile, Jeff was so broke he asked to borrow a hundred dollars from a friend at work to tide him over the weekend. Jeff had made plans to be out of town when Andrew arrived and maybe avoid him altogether. On Saturday he was taking his boyfriend, Jon Hackett, a student at the University of Minnesota, for an overnight in the country to celebrate his twenty-second birthday. They were staying at the Dancing Winds Goat Dairy and Cheese Plant, and Bed and Breakfast. Andrew could stay at Jeff's apartment in Bloomington Saturday night—he'd leave the key under the mat—but Jeff was making it clear by inference that he would have no time for Andrew.

Andrew packed one black Tumi duffel bag for his weekend in Minneapolis. He put in handcuffs, pornographic videos, and five 200-milligram glass vials of the illegal steroid ML testosterone. The fact that the steroids were packaged in vials and not Baggies, says a Hillcrest drug dealer, meant they were "upper-class," to be used by yuppies. Andrew may have taken the steroids to raise some ready cash. They could also have been a love offering to David, who was fanatic about working out and had bulked up in the last year, though his friends insist he did not use illegal drugs. It's unlikely that Andrew, who had weight problems and never worked out, would use himself.

Friday morning, Ken Higgins drove Andrew to the airport without much conversation. Later he would remember that Andrew had told him more than once how he hated Gianni Versace. Andrew was deeply jealous and resentful of the rich and famous Italian designer who "came from nothing" and who through "hard work" had become an international celebrity and gay icon. Andrew called Versace "the worst designer ever" and told Higgins he was "pretentious, pompous, and ostentatious." Outwardly, Andrew sought to keep his rage in check but inside he seemed to be keeping a little list. Yet nobody picked up on how seriously depressed and deranged he really was as he boarded Northwest Airlines Flight 576, scheduled to arrive in Minneapolis at 5:20 P.M.

David dutifully picked him up at the Minneapolis airport. Once again he was stuck with Andrew. Once again Andrew came bearing gifts that David accepted. Five of his friends from work had casually suggested David join them for dinner at the Caffè Solo, across the street from the loft. They were mildly surprised to find David and Andrew already at the bar waiting for them when they arrived. Linda Elwell, Laura Booher, and Kathy Compton all agree that David seemed rather quiet. "David was not at ease," says Kathy Compton. "He seemed bugged." Andrew urged him, "Show them what I got you." He had brought David a gold Cartier watch. It was "not new," David assured them, just a thank-you from Andrew for helping him turn his life around.

In fact, Cartier watches, never used but not exactly brand-new, were on Andrew's list of "what fell off the truck."

During dinner Andrew mentioned that he was planning to return to California Monday morning, but he wasn't very friendly. He told Kathy Compton about his grandmother's Rolls-Royce convertible, which he had ridden around in as a kid. He informed one of the women that he had a company that made sound-abatement equipment for movie sets— just like the one Norman Blachford used to run. Later David and Andrew met Monique and a colleague for a drink at Nye's Polonaise, a camp polka palace with Naugahyde booths and a crowded dance floor fueled by "the World's Greatest Polka Band." They stayed and talked for about forty-five minutes. Andrew told Monique he might be having brunch with Jeff on Sunday; maybe they could all get together after that. He said he was setting up a factory in Mexico to make prefab movie sets.

Then Andrew and David headed to the Gay Nineties to dance. David stayed longer than Andrew did. The next morning David was up by nine o'clock to work out at the gym. A little later he talked to Monique. "Is everything OK?" she asked. "Yeah," he said. They made plans to meet later that day, but Monique couldn't reach him. She had plans for Saturday evening, so David invited her to have dinner on Sunday. David also talked to Cedric, who overheard Andrew ask, "Who are you talking to?" David told him, and then carried on as if he weren't there.

The Harmony Lofts building, where David lived, was like a scene out of *Seinfeld*. Young urbanites, including "Kilo Bale," the drummer with the rock band, "Flip," lived there and were on friendly terms, visiting one another's prime loft spaces. David could frequently count on his neighbor across the hall, graphic artist Perry Del Ghingaro, to look after his dog, Prints. Jennifer Wiberg, the building's caretaker, was also friendly with David, whom Perry said at one time had glowingly described Andrew as "very wealthy and very intriguing." Yet Perry also characterized David as "very select." Both he and Wiberg felt "very honored" to make David's guest lists. "We were the only people in the building invited to his soirees." On Saturday Perry Del Ghingaro and Jennifer Wiberg both met "Andrew from California" in the elevator. Again, Andrew was not particularly pleasant and did not engage in conversation.

The weekend wore on, and Andrew was not getting his way. Around midnight Friday, Stan Hatley and a friend ran into Andrew and David walking toward the Saloon from the Gay Nineties. Andrew was anything but cordial to his once bar buddy Stan. "The meets and greets and talks were very forced," Stan remembers. "Hey, what are you doing?" he asked. "Nothing," Andrew answered curtly. "I just came out to visit Jeff." Stan thought Andrew looked "despondent and subdued."

Saturday night David and Andrew went to dinner at the popular Monte Carlo restaurant, but then separated. Once again, after hitting the bars, Andrew was alone. He apparently spent Saturday night at Jeff's apartment in Bloomington, not far from the Mall of America, but nobody knows for sure. David's next-door neighbor, Scott Carlson, was awakened about 3 A.M. by loud yelping sounds he heard coming from David's loft, number 404. They lasted several hours, until 7 A.M. He later told police he thought David "might be having sexual intercourse with his homosexual partner," a "white male with black curly hair, about five feet, eleven inches," whom he had been dating "for about a month." Later that morning David called a lawyer friend to cancel a brunch they had set up.

About 10 A.M. on Sunday, Andrew was at Jeff's when Jerry Davis, Jeff's pal from work, called to leave information for Jeff about Jerry's gay-softball-league game that afternoon. Jeff rarely missed these games. Andrew politely took the message and wrote it down for Jeff on a yellow legal pad, signing the note, "Love, Andrew." About 12:30 that afternoon, Joe, who had lent his expensive Andrew Marc leather jacket to Andrew the night before DIFFA, saw Andrew and David going into a book-and-record store on Calhoun Square in the Uptown area of Minneapolis.

While alone at Jeff's, Andrew apparently took the opportunity to call friends in San Diego. He left a message for Dominick Andreacchio saying he hoped to see him soon in San Francisco. And for the first time in months, he called Norman Blachford to say good-bye. He told Norman that he realized their relationship was really over and that he was moving to San Francisco and would stay in touch. Blachford was somewhat puzzled by the call. He already knew that Andrew was leaving.

Jeff drove Jon Hackett directly from the bed and breakfast to his job at the Old Navy Store in the Mall of America. On the way Jeff said that he had to talk to Andrew about something "pretty important," but that it would only take about half an hour. "Jeff didn't say he knew what it was about," says Jon. Jeff also said he would not be around on Monday or Tuesday; he had "personal business" to transact. Hackett says he did not question him further. He did not feel it was right to pry into Jeff's personal business. Jeff next showed up at Jerry Davis's softball game, making fun of the "prissy queen" ballplayers. Jerry thought he was in a mean mood, but another coworker, Ben Guzzi, who was there with his wife, later described Jeff as pretty upbeat. Jeff went home early to bake a cake for Jon Hackett's birthday. A few friends were coming over, he said.

The only other sighting of Andrew that afternoon was at about 5:30, when a tenant saw him get into the elevator by himself and get off on David's floor. He didn't want to make small talk. When Jon Hackett returned to Jeff's apartment at about 6 P.M., he took a nap, and Jeff turned the phone ring off. Jon Hackett slept through Andrew's call, but at 8:00 Andrew left Jeff a voice message without identifying himself, just giving Madson's number and saying, "Give me a call, because I'd like to see you." Jeff immediately called him back.

Still, Jeff was willing to blow off Andrew entirely, and he suggested to Jon that they go to a movie. "No way," Jon said. He wanted to dance on his birthday. At about 9 P.M., Jeff left in his 1996 Honda Civic to meet Andrew in a coffee shop. He said he'd rendezvous with Jon between 10 and 10:30 at the Gay Nineties. That never happened.

PART

TWO

17

Murder

The first blow to Jeff Trail's skull landed with knockout force. It was delivered with an expensive claw hammer that had been out on the dining room table in David's loft. David had been doing some renovation work to the kitchen, so he had his tool box handy. Jeff apparently raised his arms to shield himself, because he was hit several times on his left wrist and hand. He then crumpled to the ground as he was furiously struck by a total of twenty-seven repeated blows to the face, head, and upper torso with both the blunt and claw sides of the hammer. Either a hammer blow or the force of his own weight falling on his Wenger Swiss Army watch caused it to stop at 9:55 P.M.

David's caller I.D. noted that someone—presumably Jeff—had called David's loft at 9:08 P.M. from the nearby coffee shop where Jeff had planned to meet Andrew. The caller I.D., connected to the loft's intercom, also shows that David received a call from the intercom at the Harmony Lofts entrance at 9:45 P.M. David did not have a buzzer system, so Jeff would have had to have called and waited for someone to come down and let him in—either Andrew or David, who habitually walked his dog before the ten o'clock news came on, and may have been on his way out to do so at 9:45.

It takes at least three minutes to get from David's loft down to the front door, and an equal amount of time to take the elevator back up.

Whatever conversation took place once Jeff was inside the apartment was brief. There is a dent in the wall to the left of the door, suggesting that one of the hammer blows missed Jeff. But another, which connected while the door was open—before a neighbor heard it slam shut—sent a splattering of blood across the hallway. Pieces of brain matter lodged in the door frame itself.

Jesse Shadoan, David's neighbor across the hall, later reported to police that about the time Jeff arrived he heard someone shouting: "Get the fuck out!" Then he heard the door slam shut and thumping noises that went on for from thirty to forty-five seconds, after which he heard footsteps racing down the hall and water running. He stuck his head outside his door but saw no one. No other residents reported hearing anything.

When Andrew had requested meeting with Jeff on Sunday night, both of them were in precarious financial shape, Andrew far more seriously than Jeff. But Jeff was also overextended, addicted as he was to expensive toys—several TV's, a karaoke machine, a $300 blender from Williams Sonoma, two top-of-the-line tennis racquets, several $600 suits. Jeff was in debt mainly to his parents, but people in San Diego, Robbins Thompson for one, believe that he also owed Andrew several thousand dollars.

Andrew might therefore have been pressuring Jeff to sell steroids for him in the Midwest where great profits could be made; Andrew may have come to Minneapolis to collect what Jeff owed him; or perhaps he offered the steroids as a way of paying Jeff money that Andrew owed *him.* In any case, Jeff was unwilling to let him stay around, either as a pal or a business associate or the boyfriend Jeff told his sister that Andrew wanted him to be. Andrew had tried several times in the recent past to extend his stays in Minneapolis, but Jeff had always told him no.

If Jeff didn't want to have anything to do with him, and if David was rejecting him once again, Andrew was cornered. He had lavished time, attention, and money on both of them; he could not bear to think that he had been used. Now the two men he most cared for in the world were turning their backs on him, banishing him to struggle alone, insecure, depressed, and overweight. It was all their fault. They were forcing him to expose the sham of his grandiosity like a mangy peacock.

The years of pathological lying, combined with the habitual use of crystal meth and an addiction to violent pornography, had left Andrew dangerously unbalanced under all the layers of lacquered pretension. The moment in which Andrew lost hope and picked up the hammer encapsulated not only all of his envy and self-pity but also his cold-blooded willfulness to keep the con going. He would not allow these ingrates to cast him out. He would keep the mask on. He had never allowed even Norman Blachford a measure of emotional control, even though Norman was granting him his every material wish. How dare Jeff and David dump him? He suddenly unleashed his fury.

As a seasoned manipulator who had dominated David in rough sex, Andrew now had to convince him that Andrew could always say that David had been present during Jeff's murder—or perhaps even pin the murder totally on him—whether he had been there or not. How could David disprove it? After all, it took place in his loft. But even if David had been there, too horrified to intervene—and that possibility seems unlikely—wouldn't Prints have barked? It would seem so, but Andrew was a skillful dog handler, and Prints liked him.

But why wouldn't Madson try to escape? Certainly Andrew could count on David's abhorrence of violence to keep him in check. If he got out of line, Andrew could put the handcuffs and leg restraints and duct tape that they had once used for pleasure to a more practical use. By the same token, if David naively thought he could call on his famed powers of persuasion, he may have reasoned that he could cajole Andrew into telling the authorities a story and turning himself in. But if David wasn't 100 percent sure that Andrew didn't have Mob connections, or if David felt under threat, then he would have had to tread lightly and try to reason with the unreasonable. David did not have many options.

The first thing that had to be done was to get the body away from the front door. It had fallen on an Oriental area rug David had kept in the entryway. Jeff's body was then rolled up in the carpet, dragged ten feet past the dining room table, and rested against the back of the living room sofa.

Most of the nine-hundred-square-foot loft was open space—only the bathroom, at a right angle to the front door, was completely walled off. The kitchen area was next to the bathroom against one wall, and the dining room table mostly occupied a middle area between the kitchen and the living room. A partition defined the sleeping area behind the living room in the front of the loft. The sofa, which faced several feet away from, and parallel to, the dining room table, was the other border for the living room area. Jeff's body resting against the sofa could be seen from the front door and the whole kitchen dining area. His legs were sticking out and covered with a neatly folded, off-white afghan.

There was a lot of blood to clean up. Cloth and paper towels were used to wipe up the floor. Nevertheless, two sets of bloody footprints— one barefoot, one shod—were left on the hardwood floor. Jeff's watch and navy ring were removed and thrown into a plastic drawstring bag, along with a bloody Banana Republic T-shirt and the bloody hammer and towels, and the bag was placed under the table. Jeff's pager, which would be activated repeatedly and fruitlessly over the next few days, was left on his corpse.

Jon Hackett waited for Jeff at the Gay Nineties, wondering why he never showed up. At 3:00 A.M. he went to Jeff's apartment. Having no idea that Andrew was staying with David Madson, he did not immediately call there. When he woke up at 8 A.M. and realized that Jeff was still not home, he started calling hospitals and the jail. He also called Jeff at work, but there was no answer. All day Monday Jon tried to reach Jerry Davis, Jeff's closest friend at Ferrellgas, but he was out seeing customers and did not respond.

Jon asked his father, a jail administrator, whether he could call the police if he got the vehicle identification number, or VIN, of Jeff's car. His father said yes. But the Bloomington police weren't interested— they said that if he couldn't reach Jeff's parents, he'd have to wait seventy-two hours before filing a missing-persons report. "They advised me that Jeff was a big boy—twenty-eight—he could do whatever he wanted to." Jon Hackett knew Jeff had not told his parents he was gay—Jon hadn't told his parents either—so he was loath to call the Trails. He hoped that Jerry Davis would call them.

Jon attended classes on Monday and went back over to Jeff's at 8 P.M. "Everything was just as I left it. A light was still on over the stove. Nothing had changed." He searched records and tracked down Jeff's bank number. After listening to Andrew's message on Jeff's answering machine, he called David's number twice late Monday night but got no answer. He hoped to hear from Jerry, but Jerry did not return his calls all day.

On Tuesday, Jeff's employers began to be concerned and Jon was finally able to talk to Jerry Davis, who hadn't heard from Jeff either, which he said was unusual. Jon kept trying the hospitals and the police, who finally said, "Who are you? Are you his lover?" Jon said, "Well, yes. He's still missing. I want to file a missing-persons complaint." Both Jon Hackett and Jerry Davis begged the police to intervene, but the police told them, "We can't do anything until we hear from a family member."

On Monday David did not show up for work, even though he had an important meeting at 9 A.M. That afternoon David's next-door neighbor, Kathleen Sullivan, came down the Harmony Lofts elevator. When it opened on the ground floor, she was face to face with David and Andrew. "Hi," she said to David, smiling. "Hi," he answered desultorily. She thought he seemed "crabby or unhappy." Andrew said nothing.

On Tuesday morning, while having breakfast, Kathleen Sullivan looked out her window and saw two men, one of whom she thought was David, walking a dog along the river, where David usually walked Prints. The dog was on a leash—not David's usual custom. The man walking the dog was in shirtsleeves; the man he was with was wearing a jacket. Both were too far away to identify.

Meanwhile, at John Ryan Company, David's co-worker and friend Linda Elwell got a call from the woman who was David's contact for a big bank job he was doing. "I tried calling David all day yesterday. He has assignments due, and we have no idea where he is," the woman told her. "I really have a bad feeling." Linda said that she and Laura Booher would go check on him at his loft.

At 12:15, Linda and Laura went to David's loft, and as Laura knocked on the door she thought she heard whispering inside. The dog began pawing and scratching, but no one answered. Linda, who had been with David recently when he found his car scratched, was afraid that Greg Nelson might have come after David. Nelson was the obvious object of her anxiety.

The two women returned to the office and called the police to file a missing-persons report—Linda was afraid that David might have fallen in the bathtub—but police suggested meeting them at the building instead. About 2:30 P.M., two patrol officers arrived but they did not go past the foyer. "They put up so many barriers," says Linda Elwell, telling them that the locks and door could be damaged and that they and David would have to negotiate payment. They also said they might hurt the dog if it became aggressive.

The police were going by the book. From their point of view, the rules of forced entry depend on "probable cause." In order for anything found in a forced entry to be admissible as court evidence, there must be probable cause for police to have entered and searched the premises. In this case the police did not feel justified. David had been seen the day before. As for Prints, if he gave them any trouble, they explained, "Don't worry, lady, we'll just shoot him."

Linda and Laura didn't want the responsibility for anything happening to Prints, so they left a message for the building superintendent, Jennifer Wiberg, asking her to go into the apartment with her passkey. The women then asked neighbors if they had seen David. One tenant told them she had seen him walking his dog the day before, and that calmed them somewhat. But Linda left an additional message for Wiberg: "Based on my gut you may wish to bring police protection." Meanwhile, another co-worker of David's had telephoned Monique Salvetti to express concern. Monique promised to drop by the loft on her way home from work.

About 3 P.M., Ginger Beck, a first-floor resident whose large corner loft looks out on both Second Avenue North and Third Street, says she happened to see David and Andrew walking toward the building on the Third Street side. She can't remember if Prints was with them. "David's face looked blotchy, as if he had been crying. He was disheveled." But Andrew was gesturing and "talking a mile a minute."

Jennifer Wiberg, the building's caretaker, got the message from Linda and Laura about 4:00 P.M. Accompanied by her neighbor Perry Del Ghingaro, who also knew David, Wiberg knocked loudly on 404 and called for David. Prints started barking as he always did when someone was at the door, but there was no other response. Using her passkey, Wiberg opened the door.

"Oh, my," she exclaimed. "Oh, God." She immediately saw what appeared to be a body rolled up in the Oriental rug. The thought raced through her mind that the body looked larger than David, but the corpse had already started to swell. "Son of a bitch," Del Ghingaro said. "Someone killed David."

Wiberg called Prints and waited out on the stairwell—in shock—while Perry Del Ghingaro gingerly took a closer look. He saw blue-jeaned legs and feet in white tennis shoes sticking out and noted the large amount of blood. They returned to Jennifer's apartment and called 911. It took between fifteen and twenty minutes for the police to respond. The uniformed officers were the first police to go into the apartment, just long enough to smell the odor of the decomposing body and verify that no one was there. Then they called homicide. Police headquarters was in the old City Hall building just a few blocks away.

"We knew right away it may be a gay thing," says Sergeant Bob Tichich (pronounced titch-itch), a twenty-four-year veteran of the Minneapolis police force, who responded to the call at 4:55 P.M. "The caretaker knew he was gay. We made the assumption it was Madson's body—it was a reasonable thing to assume. He hadn't shown up for work—it was him!"

Tichich called police technicians to photograph the body and process the apartment. "We just did a cursory walk-through. They were processing. We were interviewing." On the dining room table was David's wallet, and inside the refrigerator were two partially eaten plates of food. A light had been left on. On the bedroom dresser they found two pairs of handcuffs with keys, leg cuffs, two empty drinking glasses, two partial rolls of duct tape, a bottle of For Play lubricant, and two packs of

Wet formula, another lubricant. There was a bag containing balled-up duct tape on the dresser, and more balled-up duct tape on the night-stand and on the floor in front of the dresser.

Next to the dresser was the black duffel bag Andrew had packed with clothes, pornographic videos, and steroids. Now it also contained an empty gun holster, an empty magazine, and a box with fifteen live .40 caliber Remington Golden Saber bullets in it. The other ten were missing. At first glance, the police assumed that a sex scene had gone on and that the bag belonged to David.

At 5 P.M., Linda Elwell called Jennifer Wiberg, who was talking to police. Elwell reiterated that Greg Nelson had to be a suspect. Tichich talked to Linda Elwell at about 7 P.M. He told her that they believed David had been beaten to death. His only question to Linda was "Did you touch the doorknob? This is important." She assured him that she had not. A few minutes later Lieutenant Dale Barsness, Tichich's boss came by. "It was a very brutal crime scene," he says, "somewhat bizarre—the body rolled up in the rug. We believed that the killer or killers planned on moving it."

There was no urine or feces in the apartment, which indicated that the dog had been taken out and walked for at least two days following the murder. Crime technicians sawed out planks of the hardwood floor with bloody footprints on them. Nobody went near the body. Police waited for the medical examiner, Dr. Eric Burton, to arrive at 7:20 P.M. before unrolling the rug to reveal the body. But the body was not removed from the rug for fear of losing valuable hair and fiber samples. As the hours ticked by, the police went on believing that the dead man was David. Moving the body off the rug for positive identification would not be done until it was at the morgue for an autopsy.

David's friend Monique Salvetti, a public defender, had arrived to check on David only to find the building surrounded by police. She would have been able to rule out David as the body in the rug and identify Jeff, but the body was still rolled up and she was kept out. Sergeant Steve Wagner took her to headquarters to interview her. Monique named Greg Nelson as a prime suspect. She also told Wagner that a man named Andrew, a dark-haired former lover of David's from California who might be into something "shady," had been staying at the apartment that weekend. She related details of his relationship with David and told what she knew of their activities the previous weekend, but she couldn't remember Andrew's last name.

Meanwhile David and Andrew were heading north on Highway 35 in David's red Jeep.

Ever since the O. J. Simpson trial, the rules of evidence have changed. Fearing that they'll be humiliated in court the way the prosecutors in the Simpson case were, in spite of a plethora of circumstantial evidence, state and county district attorneys have reined in police departments. They now demand a much higher threshold of proof before they will charge suspects with crimes, and they insist that police adhere to strict procedures in order to avoid potential defense motions and objections during trial. The situation has caused considerable tension in some police quarters. In this instance, in the first, crucial hours when they could have at least broadcast a bulletin for David Madson's Jeep, the officers involved were doggedly guarding the evidence.

"While it's important to identify the body," Tichich explains, "you cannot lose evidence that will lead you to the killer. So it has to be done in a methodical, painstaking way, so no evidence is ruined or spoiled."

Initially, even David's friend Linda Elwell and his boss, John Ryan, accepted the idea that the body in the rug was likely to be his. But soon, says Linda, they told Tichich that they didn't believe it: "David was a bodybuilder. He wouldn't let someone beat him." Meanwhile, Monique suggested that Sergeant Wagner call David's friend, Minneapolis attorney Jim Payne, to see if he knew Andrew's last name. Payne told Wagner he thought it might be Kunanen, but when Wagner tried to find such a listing in San Diego on the computer, there was nothing. He then called Monique, who said Andrew's name was definitely Kunanen or Cunanen (sic). Monique said Wagner could probably get it off of the Rolodex in David's office.

Monique also told Wagner that David's hair was blond—almost white in the back. In David's apartment, the police couldn't help but notice that the hair sticking out from the top of the rug was dark, almost black. After interviewing Monique, Wagner alerted the officers at the loft that David's hair was blond, which was easily verified by photos of him in the apartment. Moreover, it seemed that his unknown, dark-haired weekend houseguest, name of Andrew, might even be the victim.

"Oh God, we hope we're not in shit now," Tichich recalls thinking. "When Steve Wagner got the description, we realized that it very possibly was not Madson—the hair color, we could see, was black. So now this becomes a serious issue. We can't by law go in without a search warrant if David's not the victim." Tichich was convinced he might have made a major error in entering the apartment without a search warrant, although many law-enforcement officials would not have been so scrupulous. Wagner kept calling Monique back, asking for more physical details about David. Linda Elwell also called Tichich and described him: "Blond hair, baby-blue eyes, muscular." Tichich told her, "Well, then, based on your description, this body is not David's." At 8 P.M. the police removed the body; at 10 P.M. they decided to leave the loft and start fresh in the morning with a search warrant. David Madson's family still had not been notified.

Since David was fanatic about working out, the police assumed the steroids they found were his. Tichich had also learned that neighbors had seen David freely walking around with his dog. To Tichich, therefore, it was a no-brainer: David Madson was the chief suspect.

Around noon on Tuesday, Stan and Ann Trail went to their daughter Lisa Stravinskas's house in Elgin, Illinois, to pick up their two young grandsons. The family was going from one medical crisis to another. Lisa was eight months pregnant and experiencing an extremely difficult pregnancy that had culminated in premature labor. She had to be in the hospital in order for doctors to determine whether the baby's lungs were sufficiently developed for a C-section to be performed. Ann Trail was still recovering from cancer surgery she'd undergone a few weeks before. Nevertheless, the Trails would care for the boys while Lisa and her husband went to the hospital for an amniocentesis and a sonogram. Jerry Davis was unable to reach the Trails until late Tuesday afternoon.

At first Jeff's parents thought that their son might have taken off for

Texas to see his sister Candy because he couldn't take Minneapolis anymore. Jerry Davis called back the Bloomington police to verify that the Trails had not heard from Jeff, and made an appointment for himself and Jon Hackett to talk to a detective Wednesday morning. Finally the Bloomington police agreed to issue a missing-persons report.

"Be sure to let Jeff know that I might be having the baby," Lisa told her stepfather. "He wanted to be here when it came." Stan Trail answered, "I can't. Jeff is missing." Jeff's body was still rolled up in the rug in the Minneapolis morgue, when, at 9:47 P.M. on Tuesday, May 29, the Bloomington, Minnesota, police issued a notice for "Missing Adult Jeffrey Allen Trail." The report incorrectly stated the license-plate number of his 1996 green Honda Civic (it no longer said, "Navy 91"). The report also stated that Jeff had been going to meet an old friend named Andrew at a coffee shop, and that Andrew "lives with a man named Dave." It gave Madson's home phone number. The report called for a metrowide search. The police assured Jerry Davis that if nothing happened overnight they would do a national missing-persons alert on Wednesday morning.

At 6 A.M., on Wednesday, April 30, David Madson's Jeep pulled into a parking garage at 300 N.E. Water Street in Chicago. No one saw the driver. At 8:15 A.M., in Elk Grove Village, Illinois, Jeff's sister Lisa Stravinskas gave birth to a baby girl, Emmy. At almost the same time, a Bloomington detective calling Stan Trail to verify that Jeff had not contacted the family told him brusquely, "You know he's a homosexual, don't you?" Lisa Stravinskas says today, "As if that explained everything." In fact Stan Trail did not know Jeff was gay, but at that moment, he recalls, the discovery seemed "minuscule compared to the fact that Jeff was missing."

Meanwhile, at 9 A.M. in Minneapolis, the autopsy on Jeff's still unidentified body was beginning with Sergeant Wagner present as police witness. Sergeant Tichich, after getting the phone number of David Madson's parents in Wisconsin, was over at the courthouse, where, at 9:20 A.M., he obtained a search warrant to enter David's apartment.

When Jeff's fully clothed body was finally lifted from the blood-soaked rug, the medical examiner found a black nylon wallet in the right rear pocket of the victim's jeans. It contained all of Jeff's identification and forty-two dollars. Jeff was ultimately identified by a tattoo of Marvin the Martian on his left ankle. He also had a pierced nipple and toe ring. The wallet's contents easily led the coroner to the Trail family in DeKalb, Illinois, where a local Catholic chaplain accompanied by a police officer arrived at the Trails' home later that morning to tell them that their son had been murdered.

Sergeant Steve Wagner returned from the autopsy with the news that the body had been identified as Jeff Trail's. He had had a gut feeling, he confided to fellow officers, since hearing about Andrew and his relationship with David in his interviews with Monique, "that David didn't fit this whole thing. I think we're going to find David Madson dead." He also remembered that Monique had mentioned Andrew having a friend named T.J. or J.T. He called her, and she told him yes, Andrew's friend was indeed Jeff Trail.

Ferrellgas, Jeff's employer, was then notified, and Jerry Davis drove over to Jeff's apartment to break the news to Jon Hackett. Now they would no longer have to keep their Wednesday morning appointment with the Bloomington police.

While he was waiting for Jerry Davis, Jon Hackett restlessly dialed David Madson's apartment one more time. When the phone rang, Tichich, who was there with his warrant, had just been apprised of Jeff Trail's identity. He did not pick up the phone but was jolted to have the caller I.D. read "Jeff Trail residence." Oh, my god, Tichich thought, I'm talking to a dead man. He called back immediately and Jon Hackett answered. Who is he? Tichich wondered, thinking, Am I talking to the murder suspect? Hackett also was curious. "We got in this cat-and-mouse game," Tichich says. When Hackett explained that he had reported Jeff missing to the Bloomington police, it was the first Tichich had heard about it. But that was not unusual. Missing adults are routine. "Every day we get calls about people not showing up for work, and 99.9 percent of them want to disappear."

Tichich asked questions about Jeff's relationship with Andrew and about Jeff's tattoos, which Hackett was able to answer. Then Tichich confided, "I shouldn't tell you this, but we've found a body. We think it's Jeff." Jon Hackett was so stunned he had Tichich repeat this, twice. Just then Jerry Davis arrived, and he confirmed the horrible news.

Jon Hackett's parents were planning a birthday celebration for him that night at his brother's house, forty-five minutes to the north. Jon's mother picked up the phone to hear her shaken son say that he was gay and that his lover had been murdered. She told him that being gay was something they could discuss later; just come home. It wasn't until he was on the freeway and heard Jeff's name on the WCCO six o'clock news, Jon recalls, that it really sunk in: Jeff was dead.

Wednesday morning, on page B7 of the metro section of the Minneapolis *Star Tribune,* readers found the first two-paragraph press mention of the soon-to-be-giant story: "A man's body was found Tuesday afternoon in an apartment in Minneapolis' Warehouse District, and police were investigating his death as a homicide . . ."

A few hours after giving birth by cesarean section Lisa Stravinskas was told about her brother's death. Jeff's secret, kept until then by her and her sisters, was out. Under the most tragic circumstances possible, even as they had to begin making arrangements to get back the body of their brutally murdered son and brother, the Trail family for the first time as a whole was suddenly having to come to grips with the fact that Jeff was gay. Stan Trail thought back and remembered Jeff telling him that one of his reasons for quitting the California Highway Patrol was that "it was not tolerant of people with alternative lifestyles." Today Jeff's father says, "But he never said he was one of those people. Jeff never told his mother or me he was homosexual, but he gave us every hint. He never hid anything. He introduced us to people who were obvious homosexuals—I never made that connection. That's a remark on my perception. He did everything but grab me by the shoulders; he wanted me to ask him, but I never could. Maybe subconsciously there's something that didn't let me."

"It occurred to me," says Ann Trail, "but the one reason that I wasn't able to close on that was that Jeff was intolerant of people who deviated from his expectations on behavior—people who smoked pot and, for a long time, people who drank alcohol. I wanted to ask him, but I thought, if I ask Jeff a question like that, he's never going to speak to me again. I really thought he would be totally insulted and hurt if I asked him."

18

Suspect

THIS IS A WEIRD ONE, Sergeant Bob Tichich remembers thinking to himself when he first viewed the crime scene at David Madson's loft. I wonder how this is all going to turn out.

In the Trail murder investigation, which he headed, Tichich was destined to play the role of the "bad cop." To David Madson's family, he was the unsympathetic blue meanie who initially suspected David of being involved in Jeff Trail's murder and who then would not reverse his original thesis. Why? Simply because he didn't think the evidence allowed him to. He still says, "My gut tells me he didn't do it, but my gut doesn't count."

Stubborn and scrupulous, Tichich, fifty-two, is tall and balding, with a "just the facts, ma'am" demeanor. He speaks in a monotone and with a seemingly breathtaking lack of comprehension of how his blunt speech might affect others—he is tone deaf to feelings. A mountain climber who digs deep for his facts, he sees no need to conform. In the Madson case, he stood on principle. Actually, Tichich and his younger partner, Pete Jackson—a hip, black, fast-talking ex-narc—bickered like an old married couple and looked as if they had just stepped out of a TV sitcom about cops. The frustrated friends of David Madson who refused to believe he would have aided Andrew in any way, didn't see the TV connection. They used a closer-to-home film metaphor: For them, Tichich was *"Fargo* without Margie."

Tichich was trying to enlist Jerry Davis's help in locating Andrew. Would Jerry search Jeff's apartment for Andrew's phone number? Jerry wanted to know if he should keep everybody out of the town house. "Absolutely not," Tichich told him. "That's not the murder scene." When Davis asked if he could scrub the apartment down, he was told yes. "But Andrew just stayed there. Should I leave his bathroom alone, at least?" He said Tichich told him, "No, no, you can scrub it down." Davis decided not to take Tichich's advice. "I left the bathroom alone, and the room Andrew stayed in alone, but we went through everything." (Davis, worried that Jeff's family might find pinup-boy magazines, was intent on "de-gaying" the apartment.)

After Jerry Davis came up with Andrew DeSilva's name and San Diego phone number from Jeff's Rolodex, it was Jackson, at Tichich's direction, who later discovered Andrew's number on David's caller ID by going through all its long-distance calls. When Jerry had called the number, he got a message saying, "You've reached Andrew and Erik." The message also gave Andrew's cell-phone number. On Wednesday, Jackson asked San Diego police to try to locate Andrew and warned San Diego that two murder suspects might be heading their way. The San Diego police then confirmed Andrew's address, 1234 Robinson, and supplied the name of his roommate, Erik Greenman.

Wagner went to David's office to get his Rolodex and ask John Ryan to check and see if David was using his corporate credit cards or his phone-calling cards. The more he learned about David Madson, the less he saw him as someone who would be involved in a murder. "I was getting the impression of David as a nonviolent, peaceful guy, willing to do anything for anybody, including Andrew Cunanan."

It was only Wednesday evening at 9 P.M. that Tichich put out the first national all-points bulletin on David Madson and his vehicle, but there was no mention of Andrew as a suspect and nothing in it asking police to hold on to the driver. It would not be until Friday that a felony warrant was issued for Jeff's missing car. Sometimes police deliberately omit the names of suspects they are seeking because they don't want them tipped off. Other times they don't know who it is they're looking for. In this instance, says Steve Wagner, "It was a little bit of both." Jeff's car, which had been parked a couple of blocks from David's loft since Sunday night, had a new license-plate number, so it had not yet been discovered. And it was not until Wednesday night that police contacted the Minneapolis airport to see if David's Jeep was parked there. They had not yet tried to learn whether Andrew had flown home or not. But Tichich had contacted the Barron County sheriff in Wisconsin to find out where David's parents lived.

Although their son had been missing for three days and a body had been found in his apartment, Carol and Howard Madson were told nothing. On Wednesday evening, while Carol was fixing dinner, she saw a TV news report about a murder in a downtown Minneapolis apartment building. Gee, that kind of looks like David's building, she thought to herself. Just that day she had received an anniversary card from David, which he had mailed the previous Saturday.

If David's family remained unaware, the news that Jeff had been murdered and that Andrew was missing traveled fast on the gay tom-tom between Minneapolis and San Diego. On Thursday the police began to stake out Erik Greenman, who was nonplussed at being surrounded by police cars when he stopped at a traffic light in his San Diego neighborhood. He told the police that he had heard about Jeff's murder from Andrew's lawyer friend David Gallo, who had heard it from Stan Hatley, and that Andrew went by two names, Cunanan and DeSilva.

Erik said that Andrew was nonviolent and that he would never kill Jeff—they were best of friends. He also told police that David was the dominant person in the Andrew-David relationship, and he speculated that David may have become violent toward Jeff if Jeff had said or done anything to come between David and Andrew. (Thus it was a gay friend who offered police the homosexual-love-triangle theory that some in the media would subsequently seize on, angering the Trail and Madson families and causing considerable indignation in the gay press.) Erik volunteered to turn over phone numbers and addresses of Andrew's acquaintances, but no one asked to search the apartment, and no one ever warned him not to touch anything in Andrew's room to avoid contaminating the evidence.

At first, the very idea that Andrew was capable of committing murder was widely discounted. Jeff's closest friend, Jon Wainwright, contacted police in Minneapolis early on to say that he didn't think Andrew would do such a thing. However, Rich Bonnin and David's lawyer friend Jim Payne also contacted the police after reading the item in the *Star Tribune* about the body in David's building. Neither had been able to reach David, and the police would not give them any information. "All of David's friends told the police that David and Jeff Trail had lived in the same city for six months and nothing ever happened," says Rich Bonnin. "The weekend Andrew's here, Jeff is murdered. 'You need to look for Andrew,' I told Wagner. But all they said was, 'Where do you think David might be?' "

Tichich felt certain that David would try to return home. On Thursday, the police began staking out the Madsons' house. He warned Linda Elwell on the phone, "We think David is suicidal, and if he tries to call you, you better call me." Monique Salvetti, an officer of the court herself, was taken aback when Tichich warned her that she too had better call in. " 'Now, are you going to level with us or what? Can we count on your cooperation? If you hear from David, if you know something, you better come forward,' " Monique remembers Tichich saying. "I got the distinct impression that he was really saying, 'Don't fuck with us.' "

She and Elwell took umbrage, as did many of David's other friends, that they would be suspected of harboring a fugitive. They were also upset that the police seemed to be concentrating their effort on finding David and not Andrew, although Wagner assured them that was not the case. "I know co-workers of David's called and yelled at police, 'You better be treating this as a missing person because he's not capable of this,' " says Monique, "but the police said, 'Look, we see a lot of things you don't,' very dismissively. It was the tone of voice they used. They just concluded it was David, and didn't need to go into much more evidence." Elwell and Laura Booher, who had gone looking for David on Tuesday, could not understand why they weren't being formally questioned. If Tichich suspected David, they wanted to know, why wasn't it put out to the media and broadcast that they were looking for him? Tichich basically told her to mind her own business. "You don't know the facts."

On Thursday morning, May 1, Wagner telephoned Carol Madson, David's mother, for the first time to report that David was missing. "He was very soft-spoken," Carol Madson recalls. "He didn't alarm me. He said there had been a body found in our son David's apartment, and they were looking for David for questioning. I was kind of in a state of shock."

"We were trying to catch him," Wagner explains, by surprising him if he went home. Carol Madson told Wagner that they had not heard from David in about ten days but of course they would cooperate. "I hung up the phone and called Ralph at the store." She told her son, "Find Dad, and the two of you should come home together." She worried about her husband.

Howard Madson, David's father, was out of town making a delivery for the store, but not far away. He had had a massive heart attack three years earlier, had been operated on twice, and had undergone six bypasses. His wife was afraid that the news would trigger another attack. Just then Howard Madson walked through the door of the hardware store. "We have to get home right now," Ralph says he told his father. "Then I had to calm Dad down, because he thought something had happened to Mother. When we walked in, Mother was just in shambles. She relayed the story to us. It didn't make sense. It couldn't be right. We didn't get the story straight." They called Wagner who essentially repeated what he had told Carol.

Meanwhile, Greg Nelson called the police to find out if David was a homicide victim. He said he understood from his lawyer that if this were true he could be a murder suspect. To eliminate himself, he said he could fax copies of plane tickets that showed that he had flown back to Washington, D.C., where he lived, on April 23. He also accused David of "psychological and physical abuse." That and other evidence the police were gathering "to corroborate S&M activity," according to Tichich, continued to make them believe that David could have taken part in Jeff's murder. "It was well known that Madson was involved in S&M, and so was Cunanan, and it had gone on a long period of time."

When Sergeant Tichich called the Madsons at around 2 P.M. and reached Carol Madson, it was her turn to be jolted. " 'Your son is a homosexual who uses steroids,' " she says Tichich told her. " 'He flew into a rage and killed Jeff Trail. People who are on steroids can do that. He's wanted for murder. If he contacts you, be sure to call us.' I said, 'Well, that's ridiculous,' " Carol Madson recalls. " 'David's not on drugs. He's opposed to drugs of any sort,' which he was." She adds, "He [Tichich] had no proof, of course. He was just very blunt . . . his whole attitude was, 'Well, you knew this.' " She reported the conversation to her son and her husband, who says he heard essentially the same thing from Tichich two days later.

Tichich, who denies that he ever spoke to Mrs. Madson, claims that he believed at that point that David should have been formally charged with murder. The steroids in the gym bag, Erik Greenman's description of David's dominance in his relationship with Andrew, and the fact that Andrew and Jeff had been close, all added up to the first police theory: a homosexual love triangle murder triggered by " 'roid rage." "I first thought Madson because he hadn't showed up for work. There was a body rolled up in a rug," Tichich explains. "There's all this physical evidence. They tramped around in blood and had taken measures to conceal this body. You have to believe Andrew was able to control Madson for extended periods of time without the possibility of escape."

Tichich went to the Hennepin County attorney's office to ask for a warrant charging David Madson with murder. (His request was denied.) "The murder happened at his place and he was seen walking around after. I thought we should charge him," he says. Tichich was also quoted on local TV implicating David, saying "They rolled Jeff's body in a rug and intended to dispose of it." In another TV sound bite he said, "They took advantage of the opportunity to run out the back door and into David's Jeep."

By Thursday evening, the Madson family had begun to realize that "David's life was in serious jeopardy," says Ralph, who was already furious at the way Tichich had talked to his mother. When he called Tichich that night, he claims, the detective told him that someone had accused David of infecting him with AIDS, to which Ralph countered "Bullshit!" Ralph then called Steve Wagner to protest Tichich's offensive call to his mother and got a sympathetic ear. Wagner became "the good cop."

From then on, more often Steve Wagner dealt with the Madsons. (Ironically, Tichich says he does not recall any conversations that would have soured his relationship with the Madsons—"I had no hint or clue there was ever any problem between us and I have been mystified by this since this has happened," he says today—became the good cop for the Trails, calling them back promptly and treating them politely.) Thursday night Ralph told Wagner, "Something's happened to my brother, I know it." Wagner in turn had begun to take his cue about Andrew from his interviews with Monique Salvetti. "This Andrew guy is one bad hombre," Wagner told Ralph. "We fear for your brother's life."

Friday, May 2, was one of those frustrating days for the investigators. Armed with a search warrant and two technicians, Wagner went to Jeff Trail's apartment to retrieve the written message Andrew had taken for Jeff and to record the voice message Andrew left Sunday night on Jeff's answering machine. At first, however, neither Jerry Davis nor Jon Hackett could positively identify Andrew's voice. The technicians took photographs and dusted for fingerprints but got nothing; allowing Jerry Davis to clean up had been a mistake. The inability to find samples of Andrew's fingerprints anywhere would eventually become a major foil to building a case against him.

In Barron, the Madsons were beside themselves. They made numerous phone calls trying to locate David. Diane Benning, David's sister, was the only member of the family who had met Andrew and was aware of David's trepidations about him. "Right away I knew it was Andrew," she says. None of the Madsons is passive, but Ralph recalls that Diane was particularly frustrated and keyed up. "My sister was on the phone probably ten times, just hollering out, 'For God's sakes! You've got to find David!' "

That morning the Madsons were astounded to discover an entry in the "Bulletin Board" of the St. Paul *Pioneer Press*—a grab-bag page of mostly humorous contributions from readers (Howard Madson read it religiously every morning)—headed, "A joke for today: From David who is an engineer and I'm OK." The joke began, "An engineer, an architect and an artist are having an argument . . ." Jeff was a trained engineer, and Andrew billed himself an expert on art. Could this be a veiled message from David? They thought it might be, because David always kidded his parents about reading that page. They urged Wagner to call the paper and find out who contributed the item. "My jaw dropped when I read it," Wagner says. "I thought, It has to be from David. I showed it to Tichich. Everyone said, 'It's gotta be David.' "

But the *Pioneer Press* refused to reveal its sources, even lighthearted ones. Wagner was outraged. "I threatened to close down the paper," he says. That didn't go over too well with the county attorney. The paper said the item had come in via e-mail, and it would conduct its own investigation. When police did not hear back, Tichich got in a shoving match with a *Pioneer Press* reporter.

Friday after work, Howard and Ralph Madson delivered a riding lawn mower to a customer just outside of town. "It was pretty hard to hold it together," Ralph says. Father and son had a heartrending conversation. "Oh, God, don't you wonder what David's thinking right now?" Howard Madson asked. "Think how scared and terrified he is," Ralph replied. The talk was so emotional that Ralph later called Wagner. He made Wagner promise that if anything happened to David, he would be called first, not his parents. He worried that his father couldn't take the shock. "That's against policy," Wagner answered, but Ralph got him to agree.

In La Jolla, San Diego police left a message for Norman Blachford after they had found an address of his beach-side condo listed for Andrew Phillip Cunanan on a recent California driver's license. The police also found an address for MaryAnn Cunanan in Rancho Bernardo, but neighbors said she had moved to Chicago in December 1995. The single thumbprint Andrew had given to the California Department of Motor Vehicles for his license was the only one that existed anywhere to provide a basis of comparison. Otherwise, there were no records—none at all for Andrew DeSilva—and that fact alone made law enforcement's job much harder.

Tichich wasn't making much headway. He still thought David Madson was the primary suspect and possibly had AIDS. Other theories and questions kept popping up: Did Jeff tell David something that put a wedge between Andrew and David, causing Andrew to flip out? Or did *David* flip out? Tichich asked Jerry Davis, a former Air Force intelligence officer, to help the police find out if Andrew had had a one-way or a round-trip ticket to Minneapolis. Davis says Tichich thought Davis might have some pull with the military. "He gave me this big spiel about the police department can't just go into places and make people do stuff. They have to go through the court system."

Jerry thought he was being asked to do someone else's work, and blew up at Tichich. "What started to irritate me was that he was just asking me thousands of questions and wasn't sharing anything." Tichich, on the other hand, felt that he was just doing his job—he had no need to share. "At first I thought it was because it was a gay victim that they were just dragging their feet," Jerry Davis says. "But there are eleven openly gay officers on the Minneapolis police force." Some of them assured Jerry that he was wrong, that Tichich was merely idiosyncratic.

Finally, at about 8 P.M. on Friday, Jeff Trail's 1996 Honda Civic was found, two blocks from David's loft, where it had been parked since Sunday. It had now been five days since Jeff's murder and the police were hardly any further along than they had been Tuesday night, when Jeff's body was discovered. Worse still, no one had a clue as to where to look for Andrew and David.

19

Chisago

THE MOST FAMOUS THING IN Chisago County, population forty thousand, is the upscale drug-rehab center, the Hazelden Foundation, where an array of celebrities—Calvin Klein, Eric Clapton, Bob Packwood, Liza Minnelli, Kitty Dukakis—have all gone to detoxify. There is also a buffalo farm, but otherwise Chisago, just north of the Twin Cities, is a picturesque, peaceful rural county that grows corn, soybeans, and oats. Lake Woebegone could well be there.

Fishing season begins in early May, so on Saturday morning, May 3, 1997, Kyle Hilken and Scott Schmidt were out scouting potential camping sites for their next weekend's fishing trip on East Rush Lake, about an hour from Minneapolis. The lake is not visible from the highway, but comes into view a few miles down a county road and around a curve not far off the Rush City turnoff from Highway 35. The logical place to stop after you see the lake is an abandoned farmhouse with a red roof and turret on top. It's made of old-style pressboard siding, and the windows are broken and boarded. Tall pines form a border along the backside of the house; butternut and walnut trees grow in front. Nearby is the small, sagging barn, and between the two buildings, a gravel driveway leads to a steep slope of lawn about 140 feet down to the high grass and brush bordering the lake.

About 10:45 that morning, Hilken and Scott drove to the end of the driveway and Hilken got out. He had walked only a few feet before he motioned for Scott to come over. They looked down toward the water's edge, then ran back to their Jeep and called 911. A body, clothed in jeans and a plaid flannel shirt, was lying on its back facing the lake about twelve feet from the water. The right eye had been blown out and his left eye was open.

Madson had been shot three times. "I think he probably got taken by surprise," says Sergeant Todd Rivard, of the Chisago County sheriff's department, who supervised the scene. "He had these defensive wounds in his left little finger and his right knuckle. He was shot in the right eye and right cheek and in the back between the shoulder blades—the bullet lodged in his chest." A loop of tire tracks was visible in the grass, and the body had apparently been dragged about twenty feet from where the killing took place. The body carried no identification, just a bookmark in the pants pocket from a store in San Francisco. A set of keys and keyless entry device to David's Jeep Cherokee was found nearby. The car was gone.

To Rivard, a big bear of a man of forty-six with a mustache, who for seventeen years had been the sergeant "in charge of all homicides in Chisago," the body "looked fresh." The left eye, for example, appeared "moist." Although earlier in the week it had rained, and cold, hard winds had swept across the lake, the last two days had been clear. The sun, Rivard says, could beat down on a body at that time of year. Had David been there very long, his body would have decomposed to a greater degree. And the corpse was clean. "The condition of his clothes and everything . . . he looked great. I mean, he was clean, unsoiled, except for his back, where he had been drug a ways. Otherwise, the guy just looked great." Nevertheless, the corpse had bugs in its mouth. The county coroner, Dr. John Plunkett, a forensic pathologist for more than twenty years, who had seen "hundreds and hundreds" of bodies, came to the crime scene and said David had been dead thirty-six hours at most.

"We've had a lot of bodies dumped in our county, and it seems always by the water," says Rivard, "like there's some kind of mystique about water." Rivard theorizes that since the killer would have difficulty seeing the water at night, "he must have been killed during the daylight hours." In small counties like Chisago, they rely on a state agency, the Minnesota Bureau of Criminal Apprehension, to process the crime scene. The BCA also serves as a liaison between jurisdictions. BCA agent Jon Hermann was one of the first to show up at the old farmhouse. He thought David looked like a bodybuilder.

Rivard wanted to get the body identified as soon as possible, so he sent deputies out to tiny Rush City with Polaroids of the corpse to see if anyone recognized it. No one did. At about 7 P.M. the body was removed from the site. Processing continued into the night. In the grass, near the tire marks, the casing for a .40 caliber Golden Saber bullet was found. Another would be found with a metal detector a few days later, buried a few inches in the ground. A search for the murder weapon in the shallow waters of the lake, both by boat and by a scuba diver, turned up nothing.

Saturday night, Bob Tichich turned on the Channel 9 nine o'clock news. Unlike the Minneapolis police, who played their murder case close to the vest in hopes of catching David unawares, the Chisago police immediately publicized their discovery. When Tichich saw the story of an unidentified white male found on the shore of East Rush Lake, he quickly got in touch with Todd Rivard and they compared notes. The physical description Rivard gave him matched David Madson, and the fact that he was shot with .40 caliber bullets seemed to cinch the matter.

Rivard called Jon Hermann of the BCA, who volunteered to get photos of David from the Minneapolis police and compare them with pictures the BCA crime lab had taken in Chisago that afternoon. Wagner was on "dog watch"—the late-night shift—and Hermann told him that the probable time of death was late Friday. That would mean that David and Andrew had been together for five days after Jeff Trail's murder, but no one had seen them. A few hours later Hermann called back. He was certain the body was David Madson but positive identification would have to wait until Monday morning at the autopsy. Wagner requested permission to tell the Madson family.

––––––––

On Saturday, Howard Madson had another go-round with Tichich, who sarcastically told him David and Andrew were together on the French Riviera. Ralph Madson went to work at the hardware store that day, but he couldn't function. He recalls a customer asking for a gallon of orange paint to be mixed. "The first gallon was green. The second one was blue. The third one was brown. Finally, I turned around and said, 'I'll have to get someone else to help you.' We couldn't tell anybody—what do you say?" That night he went to bed at 11 P.M. His wife, Cindy, was crying. "Ralph, I have a very bad feeling now," she told him. "Let's just try to get through another night," he answered. About 2:15 A.M. the phone rang.

"Ralph, this is Sergeant Wagner." Ralph sat up on the edge of the bed. "This is the kind of phone call I don't like to make. We found David, and David's been murdered."

"That son of a bitch. He got him. That son of a bitch." Ralph turned toward his wife. "David's dead." She began to cry softly. "I want to make sure I heard you right. David has been murdered?"

"Yes. Is it OK if I call your sister?"

"Yes. But tell her don't call Mom or Dad. You've got to give me time to get over there."

Ralph called his pastor, who lived nearby, to come and help break the news to his parents. The two houses are separated by a field, and before walking over, the two men knelt and said a prayer for strength. When they arrived, the back door was locked, so Ralph pounded on the front door. His father came downstairs in his pajamas. "Dad knew—he knew what I was there for. He didn't know exactly what had happened, but he knew the reason I was at his house with the minister at two thirty in the morning was to tell him David had been murdered."

About 6:00 A.M., Ralph walked out to the field again and wrote a prayer. He gave it to a neighbor who was going to his church and asked him to read it and to give it to the other churches in town as well. "And that's how our community found out about David."

Shortly after he got off the phone with Ralph, Wagner asked that a criminal advisory be put out nationwide for Andrew Phillip Cunanan aka DeSilva—that he should be considered armed and dangerous; that he was wanted in connection with two murders in Minnesota; that he might be driving David Madson's red Grand Jeep Cherokee, license 543 LUG. Wagner also wanted to change the "pick up" advisory on David Madson's Jeep. It was now to be listed as "stolen" in the national supercomputer for missing vehicles that all police departments can tap into. It wasn't until the following night, Sunday, at 11 P.M., when he went back on dog watch, that Sergeant Steve Wagner called the Minneapolis airport police for the first time to see if an Andrew Cunanan or an Andrew DeSilva had left on any flight from Minneapolis in the last week. Within twenty-four hours the answer came back: negative.

For almost a week the emphasis of the search had been on the principal suspect, David Madson. With his murder, gears were abruptly shifted. But valuable time had been lost.

On Monday morning, while the Madson autopsy was going on, Tichich and Wagner called Monique Salvetti and asked her to come from St. Paul, where she worked, to the Old City Hall building in downtown Minneapolis. They wanted her help in identifying the black duffel bag found in David's apartment, the one filled with the empty handcuff and leg-restraint boxes, the steroids, pornography, a holster, and .40 caliber bullets. They had always thought the bag was David's— indeed, many of Tichich's basic assumptions about the case had been shaped by the bag's contents.

"Have you looked at the identification tag?" Monique asked, indicating a label enclosed in a grip around the handle. When she opened the tag in front of Tichich, there was the name of its owner: Andrew DeSilva. "Oh, wow, I'm very embarrassed," she recalls Tichich saying. "I guess you didn't have to come down here after all."

Todd Rivard, meanwhile, was assisting at the autopsy performed by a tri-county medical examiner, Dr. Lindsey Thomas, in Hastings, Minnesota. Apart from the shock of their son's murder, the Madson family was still reeling from the idea that David could have been considered capable of killing Jeff Trail. Now they had to contend with the fact that, for whatever reason, David had stayed with his murderer for almost a week. They couldn't believe it. But the evidence coming through convinced the Chisago authorities that he definitely had. On

Sunday, Rivard had received a call from a woman who owned the nearby Rush Lake Resort. She said that while she was out working in her yard the previous Thursday, she had heard two gunshots coming from the direction of the area where David was found. She knew the difference between rifle and pistol fire, she said, because she was a hunter. She had not seen a red Jeep, however.

In Illinois, the Trail family was both curious and confused. Who did kill Jeff? Was it Andrew, or David, or Andrew *and* David? When they heard the news about David, they were shocked and saddened. Nobody bothered to ask them, but as soon as the Trail family learned that David had been shot with a .40 caliber gun, they assumed that the police must know that Andrew was using Jeff's gun. Yet in the first week after Jeff's murder, the Minneapolis police hadn't checked whether Jeff had even owned a gun.

During the autopsy, Dr. Thomas took samples of blood from David and retrieved lead fragments from his brain. From the medical examiner's point of view, the use of the .40 caliber gun was unusual. Because of its heavy size, a .40 caliber is especially deadly. Moreover, the Golden Saber bullets left behind in the duffel bag and used in the murder weapon are designed to turn into a mushroom shape once they strike their target; that way they inflict more damage as they rip through the body.

She also took a sample of vitreous humor from David's eye. As the cells of the eye decompose, they release potassium, which can be used to measure normal potassium levels in the blood. The higher the level of potassium, the longer the body has been dead. After a week, the vitreous dries out altogether. But Dr. Thomas did not test the fluid, which was simply preserved. Some medical examiners test it routinely; others use it only when they need multiple gauges to determine time of death, particularly if the time of death is in doubt. "I don't know why," Dr. Thomas says when asked why she didn't test the vitreous humor. "I guess because it's so unreliable—I would never use it in court."

Larvae from the maggots found in David's mouth were also preserved, since they too have an exact life cycle and are considered a reliable measure if other factors, such as accurate climate data regarding where the body was found, can also be determined. The bugs were not tested, either, because the procedure is costly, few entomologists do it, and there didn't seem to be any real need for it. Dr. Plunkett and Todd Rivard saw David's body themselves, and it looked fresh. Moreover, the lady who owned the Rush Lake Resort had reported hearing gunshots on Thursday.

As for the exact time of death, "there really is no good way to do it," says Dr. Thomas. "Quincy could do it on TV, novelists can do it. In all honesty, the most accurate is when was the person found? When was the person last seen reliably?" She adds, "It's so dependent on what the weather's like; that's the trouble. If it's warm, the body decomposes quickly; if it's cold, somebody can stay fresh-looking for days. It depends on the ground cover and the position of the body."

On the autopsy report Dr. Thomas placed the time of death as Friday, May 2. The Madsons refused to believe it.

That same Monday, the Chisago investigators talked to Monique at length about Andrew and David, and she considered them "very professional." The Chisago police began interviewing many of the same people that the Minneapolis police had. Karen Lapinski told Rivard that she had seen S&M paraphernalia in Andrew and David's hotel room in Los Angeles, and that Andrew had told her he had had a relationship with Jeff. The Chisago police were going down the list of potential witnesses just as Minneapolis had done the week before. Now there were three police departments involved in the case, not counting the BCA.

In San Diego, Norman Blachford told the San Diego police that he couldn't supply much information about Andrew's personal life. He believed that Andrew's parents lived in Rancho Santa Fe and also had a home in New Jersey, and that his sister was an anesthesiologist in Minneapolis. He did give police the name of a San Francisco travel agent, however, who told police he had sold Andrew a one-way ticket to Minneapolis. The agent also recalled the two tickets Andrew had bought for David Madson to fly to Los Angeles at the end of March. The Amex numbers used to purchase the tickets led Tichich to discover that Andrew had run up $20,000 on two credit cards, and that his credit had been shut down.

Then David Gallo called the San Diego police. He said Andrew had mentioned having a seven-year-old daughter, an ex-wife in San Francisco, a sister who was a doctor in Minneapolis, and a brother who made canoes in Hawaii. Erik Greenman told San Diego police that he had gone through Andrew's personal effects over the weekend and had collected a box of things that might be useful in locating him, including some serial numbers for guns, cocaine, and pharmaceutical drugs. "The most useful information out of that box was it gave us an idea of all the money he had gone through," says Sergeant Wagner. Police found all the vehicle papers for the Infiniti and learned he had sold it for cash, plus receiving the $15,000 from Norman Blachford.

"We compiled a huge list of phone numbers from scraps of paper and gave that to the fugitive task force," says Lieutenant Dale Barsness of the Minneapolis police. "I believe every one got followed up on by the FBI. A lot of these people were being driven underground and didn't even want to live in their apartments because of fear." Erik had told Minneapolis police that news of Madson's murder made him fear for his life. Stan Hatley also called the Minneapolis police and said the same thing, adding that he had seen Andrew and David together on Friday night before Jeff's murder. Stan contacted Outfront Minnesota, a Minneapolis gay and lesbian project against violence, seeking guidance on how to protect himself. He went underground for a while and moved to a small town in Louisiana. Norman Blachford, preparing to sail on the *QE2,* had been warned by police that Andrew was on the East Coast—and that he shouldn't go where he could be found.

Panic became a common reaction. Andrew had known so many people in the gay community, and now many of them were beginning to wonder, Am I next?

20

Miglin

ANDREW CUNANAN HAD GOTTEN way ahead of the police and he stayed ahead of the law until he chose to end his life. Even before Jeff Trail's body was positively identified, Andrew had driven all night to Chicago, over four hundred miles away. From 6 A.M. to 7 P.M. on Wednesday, April 30, he parked Madson's Jeep in a garage near the tony, expensive Gold Coast area. With its graceful town houses, luxurious apartment buildings overlooking the lake, its proximity to chic shopping and lively nightlife areas, the Gold Coast was of course familiar turf to Andrew. He claimed to have visited Chicago on any number of occasions.

One of those people who had heard about Chicago from Andrew was Ron Williams, back in San Diego in 1994. Andrew had a crush on Ron Williams and used to confide in him. In a nice way, Ron had urged Andrew to get a life and to stop catering to the pretty boys, to stop buying all the drinks. Why didn't he get a job?

Andrew told him that apart from his family, he did have options, "an older friend, an investor," says Williams. "Andrew said he had an investor by the name of Duke in Chicago. He said he didn't know what he wanted to do but this good friend was willing to help him—to back him in business when he decided to go into business. He never said there was a relationship, but a good friend, very successful in Chicago."

Andrew's father, Pete Cunanan, also claimed that Andrew told him about a rich family he spent the weekend with in Chicago several years before. "First he met the son in New York and then the son took him home for a weekend—it was for some holiday. He mentioned what an impressive family they were." Rob Davis, David Madson's former boyfriend, was never told the name of the sugar daddies Andrew claimed were supporting him in November 1996, but he did tell Davis that one was a big real estate tycoon and he did talk about recently being in Chicago. Rob Davis also heard from David Madson that Andrew said he was being kept by "a real estate tycoon, an older man."

The same day that Andrew arrived in the Windy City, Marilyn Miglin, a fixture on the Home Shopping Network, was leaving for Canada to sell her self-named line of cosmetics and fragrances on TV. Marilyn Miglin had told her husband of thirty-seven years, real estate mogul, Lee Miglin, age seventy-five, that she wouldn't be home until Sunday. By all accounts they were a devoted couple with two grown children, Marlena and Duke. They lived on tree-lined East Scott Street, in two town houses that had been joined by a large kitchen in the rear with a picture window overlooking a garden. Their house was just two blocks west of the lake, and walking distance to her beauty institute on Oak Street. The institute was almost directly across the street from the Gianni Versace boutique.

The Miglins, though not well known to the average Chicago citizen, were certainly known at City Hall. Paul Beitler, Lee Miglin's partner in developing the vast real estate holdings that made up Miglin-Beitler, says he was Mayor Richard Daley's single largest contributor when Daley first ran for the office and lost in 1983. In 1989, Beitler gave $100,000 to the mayor's first successful campaign. "I told Richie that Chicago should get rid of the Beirut-on-the-lake image." Beitler was younger and brasher, the front man; Lee, although tough and thorough in negotiation, was more of a quiet workaholic. Says Beitler, "Wall Street ice veins he is not."

Miglin-Beitler developed or managed prime pieces of real estate downtown. Indeed, the Richard J. Daley Civic Center Plaza, named for the current mayor's father, was managed by Miglin-Beitler. They built the Chicago Bar Association Building and the forty-five-story Madison

Plaza, the world headquarters for the Hyatt Corporation. Miglin himself built the world headquarters for National Can and developed much of the industrial park area near O'Hare Airport. At their height, Miglin-Beitler managed over thirty-two million square feet of other buildings throughout the Midwest—sixteen million square feet in the city of Chicago and neighboring suburbs. No one leaving O'Hare could help but notice the crowing billboard on the Kennedy Expressway complete with twinkling ruby slippers: "If Miglin-Beitler managed the Emerald City, she would have never left."

Miglin-Beitler's own offices were in the elegant fifty-story white granite Cesar Pelli–designed skyscraper they built at 181 West Madison, at the corner of Wells Street; their Ayn Randian suite of offices boasted a luxurious conference room complete with a padded leather wall. Panels in the wall dramatically swung open to reveal under glass, stark white spotlighted models of the World's Tallest Building—The "Skyneedle," a nearly 2,000-foot-tall, 125-story skyscraper that had been Miglin-Beitler's dream to build for almost a decade, but had never gotten off the drawing board.

Marilyn Miglin, as driven and ambitious as her husband, but far less retiring, was an officer of the Chicago Convention and Tourism Bureau and served on the state of Illinois's Economic Development Board. She had made her civic mark as president of the Oak Street Association. The Miglins owned six pieces of commercial property on Oak Street where Prada, Armani, and Barneys, as well as Versace, are located, and she was instrumental in raising a million dollars toward its renaissance as the chicest shopping street in Chicago. The street had even recently been renamed Marilyn Miglin Way. In early April 1997, Marilyn Miglin had also been honored for her humanitarian work—providing cosmetic makeovers to burn victims—by a Jewish group hoping to raise money for a hospital in Jerusalem.

Although most people assumed they were Jewish, the Miglins were Catholics—she was Czech, he was Lithuanian—and were well known to the church hierarchy. Lee, born Albert Lee Miglin, one of eight children of a central Illinois coal miner, began his career selling stainless steel flatware door to door and premixed pancake batter out of the trunk of his car. His wife, Marilyn Klecka, was a leggy, onetime chorus girl who began by developing makeup that would not run while working up a sweat dancing. Despite her profession, she was extremely prim and not immediately attracted to Al, as he was known then. The couple would tell the story that on their first date she was so horrified by his kissing her that she ran inside and rinsed her mouth out with Listerine. Six weeks later they were engaged.

After ten years of marriage, they had Marlena, named partly for Marlene Dietrich, and then Duke, named for John Wayne. Marlena, twenty-eight, was married and living in Denver in 1996; Duke, twenty-five, was a fledgling actor in Hollywood. Duke had begun college at the Air Force Academy, partly because Lee had trained to be a flyer in World War II. But after two years, Duke transferred and graduated from the University of Southern California. He settled in funky Venice Beach, where he had lived unobtrusively with a roommate, aspiring composer Chris Lennertz, whom he knew from USC, for six years. Both children helped their mother with her business on a part-time basis—Duke sometimes traveled to San Diego for her. So far he had only acted in B-level movies that went straight to video without theatrical distribution. Duke's big break, he hoped, was coming in the summer—a bit part in *Air Force One.*

Lee was quiet and meticulous, always carefully and elegantly dressed, never without a fresh manicure. He had begun in real estate with a legendary and colorful broker/developer named Arthur Rubloff, Chicago's Mr. Real Estate, who ran a large company and died in 1986. Abel Berland, the vice chairman at Rubloff, remembers arriving at his office one morning at 8 A.M. to find the thirty-one-year-old Albert Miglin seated in the chair opposite his desk. "Who are you?" Berland demanded. Miglin explained that he could not get an appointment through Berland's secretary and wanted to come to work there. Berland turned him down but Miglin, born to sell, pleaded so eloquently about being a poor boy who knew how to work "before I knew how to walk" that Berland relented. His pay was $250 a month. Miglin began putting in six-day weeks working until 8 or 9 P.M. every night. "I'd say good night and Miglin was still working," recalls Berland. "It was more his persistence and tenacity that pulled him over the top."

"By the time I'm forty, I want to stand for something in this community," Miglin told Berland. "I want to be somebody." When Miglin was thirty-seven-years-old, he told Berland he wanted to introduce him to the twenty-year-old girl he was going to marry—Marilyn Klecka. "He brought her in; she was a part-time model for Patricia Stevens," Berland remembers. "I was tremendously impressed with the girl. She had her eyes on the ball and was going to the top. She was going to be the largest dispenser of cosmetics in the world." She also convinced Al Miglin to change his first name to Lee.

Starting "with nothing except their own energy," Berland says, they bought a house for $30,000 on the Near North Side (one of Chicago's most prestigious neighborhoods) and "literally with their own hands and hearts made it a home." They also cozied up to the boss, preparing elaborate dinners with fine wines for him and his wife. "In the early days they invited me and Mrs. Berland regularly."

Lee was both an optimist and a pragmatist "who believed in the future of real estate," says Berland. Although they began to acquire more and more valuable properties and amass a fortune, the Miglins were not flashy and did not throw their money around. Apart from the considerable holdings of Miglin-Beitler, Lee's personal portfolio of real estate included two dozen buildings on the North Side of the city. "Lee epitomized the American Dream," says his partner Paul Beitler, who lived far more luxuriously in a meticulously restored neo-Corbusian house by Richard Meier and loved to fly in the company's private jet. Although Lee had recently sailed first class on the QE2 by himself, "they didn't understand how successful they were," says Chicago social-ite-writer, Sugar Rautbord, a family friend.

Rather, the Miglins were fastidious early risers who ate dinner in the kitchen often by 6 P.M. They employed two housekeepers who lived out, and because Lee was so particular, everything was kept spotless. For example, a week before Andrew came to town, Lee had demanded a thorough scrubbing of the walls of their garage, across the back alley from the house where he kept his cars—his two-year-old black jade Lexus, a Jeep, and a Bitter, an exclusive, limited edition $80,000 German car designed by the race car driver, Eric Bitter.

Lee paid all the family bills and took care of business, and Marilyn relied on him to manage the financial end of Marilyn Miglin Cosmetics.

She too was a tireless worker, the creator of the $500-an-ounce fra-grance, Pheromone, with thousands of devoted fans on the Home Shop-ping Network; in 1994, the last year for which records are published, her cosmetics company grossed $25 million. But to certain tenants and employees, the warm friend of the mayor and bubbly TV pitchwoman was also known as an abrupt taskmaster who seemed to be looking for opportunities to do battle.

The potential for lawsuits and fights in the real estate business is naturally vast, and the Miglins, particularly Miglin-Beitler, had their share. One wealthy neighbor, Lou Richardson, fought with Lee all the way to the State Supreme Court and won, ending a six-and-a-half-year dispute over damage done to her property during the renovation of a Miglin-owned town house. A cosmetics employee went to court to charge that she was denied her $800 commission. The small stuff seemed to grate on Marilyn the most. If anyone happened to park in the alley across from her garden, she would take prompt issue, claiming it obstructed her sight line of the graveled yard beyond. She once mistook a city sanitation worker for a homeless person and chastised him for picking through her garbage.

"She's not a cream puff," says Miglin-Beitler's former longtime spokesperson, Mark Jarasek, who defended her as being only a latent Type A. "Marilyn hides it till she needs to bring it out." Many noted that Lee always walked a few steps behind her.

On Saturday afternoon, May 3, 1997, a few hours after David Mad-son's body had been discovered at East Rush Lake in Minnesota, Ste-phen and Barbara Byer were pulling out of their designated parking spot in the alley behind the Miglins' Gold Coast house at precisely 2:15 P.M. The Byers were art dealers who rented an elegant duplex town house from the Miglins just one street over on East Division. The rear of their house—the focus of Lou Richardson's lawsuit—faced the rear of the Miglins' across the alley, so they were used to seeing the Miglins in their kitchen, where the blinds were never drawn. The day was cloudy and rainy. After first noticing that the Miglins' garage across the alley was open, they checked to see if anyone was inside, and saw Lee Miglin.

"He was at the very rear of the garage, wearing a tan suede jacket with his back to us, and it appeared he was puttering with some plants," says Stephen Byer. Since Lee was hard of hearing and wore hearing aids, Stephen Byer didn't bother to call out, and they went on. When Stephen Byer returned to his parking spot at precisely 5:30—he checked his watch because he was running late—he noticed the kitchen blinds were drawn. He thought it odd but he really didn't pay attention. By then the Miglins' garage was closed. There was no sound from their aging retriever, Honey.

The Byers liked Lee Miglin. He had come over to their house two nights earlier to renegotiate their lease and wound up telling stories about his early days as a door-to-door salesman. Even for such an informal meeting, he hadn't changed, but wore a gray pinstripe suit, white shirt, and silk tie. He was a dandy with white hair and there was never a hair out of place—everything had its order. But that usual tranquillity was shattered on Sunday morning, May 4, at around 8:15. The Byers, on their way out to breakfast, came face to face with Marilyn Miglin at their backyard gate.

"Steve, Steve, come over quickly. Something's wrong!"

"Marilyn, what do you mean?"

"I just got back from Canada and something's wrong," she repeated. "Lee isn't home. Lee is missing. He was supposed to meet me at the airport and he didn't, and I took a cab and somebody else has been at the house."

Byer sought to reassure her. "Marilyn, try to calm down. I'm sure Lee is fine." But as soon as the Byers rushed across the alley, through the garden and into the kitchen with her, "I sensed she was right—something very bad had occurred. First, there in the kitchen was a pint of Häagen-Dazs ice cream with a spoon stuck in it. Half eaten and half coagulated. And secondly, there was an empty Coke can on its side in the sink. Lee was a serious, fastidious, compulsive kind of man," Byer explained. Lee Miglin would never leave anything out like that. He began to query Marilyn. "Was Lee going to pick you up?"

"Yes," she responded. "He always shows up."

"Did you try calling him?"

"Of course. There was no answer."

"Why don't I look around the house?" he suggested.

"I don't know if you should. I saw a gun in the upstairs."

"A gun?" Byer was taken aback. "Look, why don't you call the police?"

"I have been. I've been trying to get ahold of them and no one has come over so far."

"Well, how long ago did you call?" Byer asked.

"Like fifteen minutes ago."

At that, Stephen Byer told his wife, Barbara, to stay outside with Marilyn. He went upstairs to look around—and promptly got lost. The two town houses the Miglins put together had been joined at the kitchen level but not above. "You go up one stairway and you can't get across or down the other side. The two stairways don't meet." To add to his confusion, "The first thing I saw disturbed me greatly: I saw a ham, like a Smithfield ham on a bone. I saw that literally on the desk in the library with a slice cut out of it. The knife was stuck right in the ham and it wasn't even on a plate. 'Oh my God,' I said to myself. I guessed Lee Miglin would never have left a Coke can in his sink or a pint of ice cream on his countertop, let alone a ham on his desk. So it was pretty obvious pretty quickly that something very bad had happened."

From watching police dramas on TV, Byer decided that he better not touch anything. He continued on to a bathroom where he saw "other signs that really were troubling. There was a gun lying on the white marble sink and in the sink itself there were black whiskers. Lee Miglin had white hair, and these clippings were for a two- to three-day growth of beard. And then I looked over at the tub and there was a layer of scum in the tub—soap or body debris—and there were also a couple of towels on the floor between the sink and the tub."

Upstairs on the third floor, in what appeared to Byer to be a guest bedroom, a closet with Lee Miglin's out-of-season clothes had been opened, and casual clothes and shoes were strewn around. "I could see that somebody had gone through it and kind of pilfered it." By now Byer surmised that whoever had shaved and used the bathroom was somewhere in the house. "I assumed that it was a drug addict or some-one who had broken in and was now sleeping it off."

But everywhere he looked there was an eerie silence. Still, as Byer continued his search, he expected "to find some bad guy sleeping some-where—or Lee's body." Again mindful of the cop shows he had seen, Byer opened closets with the sleeve of his jacket, so as not to disturb any evidence. "I kept opening closets and kept expecting Lee might fall out of a closet."

After searching the top floors, Byer, who is Jewish, crept down the stairs into the dark basement to face the most jarring moment of all. He stumbled onto an altar with more than a hundred unlit candles. "They have a chapel in their basement and I really didn't understand what it was." He came back upstairs and repeated his search on the other side of the house, up and down, yet found nothing disturbed. "The house was totally quiet."

The police still hadn't arrived, so Byer took the keys to the garage to check whether any cars were missing. Sure enough, Lee's dark green Lexus, usually parked there, was gone. Byer looked into the two cars that were there—the Jeep Duke used and the silver Bitter parked be-hind it. But he didn't see anything awry.

He went back to tell Marilyn: "The Lexus is gone."

"Oh my God. I bet Lee is in the trunk of the Lexus."

"Marilyn, it may be that Lee's OK and we're misinterpreting what's going on here," Byer tried to soothe. "What's the car phone number?"

When Byer called the Lexus, he claims first he got a recording that the party he wanted to reach was unavailable. "Then the second record-ing came on saying, 'The number you are trying to reach is now out of state.' Which I have never heard on any cell phone before."

Marilyn Miglin, meanwhile, walked nervously into the living room. She kept repeating, "I know he's dead. I know he's dead."

"Marilyn, you don't know that," Byer contradicted.

"Yes, I know he's dead and they'll never catch him. They'll never find who did this." She began opening the living room drapes—they were not usually drawn either. Byer cautioned her about touching any-thing. "That doesn't make any difference," Marilyn replied. "They'll never find whoever did this."

Just then the police finally arrived, two uniformed officers, a man and a woman. Marilyn had reached a police captain she knew and told him he had better send someone right over. Stephen Byer took the male officer on the same search of the house that he had just made, pointing out what was out of place. Once again they got disoriented trying to figure out how to go from one part of the house to the other. When the two reached the bathroom, both thought the gun lying on the sink looked real. "I agree," the officer said. "Something appears to have gone very wrong. I'm going to call for backup now."

Just then, four more police officers showed up and one of them asked if anyone had been to the garage. Byer told him, yes, the Lexus was missing. Then Barbara Byer took the key and led two of the officers across the alley where she unlocked the garage by the side door and let them in. At first, things once again appeared normal. The three briefly looked around and came out. But Barbara Byer hesitated and went back in. She let out a scream.

From the Miglins' kitchen, Stephen Byer could see that his wife was crying and had to sit down on a bench in their garden. He ran over. "Oh my God, Lee's dead," she said. Byer went to enter the garage but was barred by one of the policemen: "I don't want you to come in here." Then Byer glanced down and saw brown wrapping paper and some blood coming from under the Jeep. It was parked at the rear of the garage with a garbage can placed to the side of its right front fender to obscure the body. He hadn't noticed the blood before.

"I just went back in because I knew there was something wrong with this wrapping paper on the floor," Barbara Byer told her husband. "Lee would never leave wrapping paper on the floor. And what happened was, I picked up the edge and his feet were sitting there!" Stephen Byer turned white and started feeling dizzy. He was on the verge of passing out when a policewoman rushed over. "Hey, don't collapse, don't crack up, the family needs you."

"You're right. I just have to catch my breath." Byer joined his wife on the bench. Barbara asked the policewoman, "Have you told Marilyn?"

"No," she answered. "I really don't know what to say."

"Oh my God, you have to tell her."

"I really don't want to."

"Someone has to tell her. All right, I will." Barbara Byer went across the alley to find Marilyn Miglin in the kitchen.

"Marilyn, I'm so sorry to tell you this. They've found Lee." Marilyn was obviously stunned, but she put up a brave front and marched right over to the garage to identify the body. "I knew it!" she said. "I knew it."

By then, sirens were blaring, racing police cars were skidding to a stop in the alley, and cops were suddenly everywhere.

21

Minefield

Fₑₐᵣ ₙₒw ᴳᴿᴵᴾᴾᴱᴰ Lee Miglin's upscale and eclectic Chicago neighborhood, where socialites from the quiet side streets and bar hoppers on the busy thoroughfares frequently mingled. But the Gold Coast had long been a notorious haunt of master killers. Two days after murdering eight Chicago nurses in 1966, Richard Speck hid out less than a mile away from the Miglins' at the old Raleigh Hotel on Dearborn Street, now an expensive office space. Six blocks away James Earl Ray, who assassinated Martin Luther King, was arrested for holding up a cab driver at gunpoint at State and Delaware. The Walgreens Drugs, around the corner from the Miglins' at North and Wells, sold one of the four tampered with, poisoned Tylenol bottles that ended up killing seven in 1982. Jeffrey Dahmer picked up one of his seventeen male victims at the gay movie theater, the Bijou, five blocks up Wells from Walgreens. And John Wayne Gacy, responsible for the deaths of thirty-three, helped remodel what was then the Winstons Doughnut House at State and Division, just one block from where the Miglins lived; because the basement where Gacy had labored smelled bad, police dug it up searching for more buried bodies, but found only rats. Ironically, both Dahmer and Gacy were also gay, and Speck was bisexual—they just weren't out of the closet the way Andrew was. Apart from the serial-killing notoriety, which was not publicized, and the affluence, which

was self-evident, the neighborhood also had a reputation for being closeted.

In Miglin's case, the police at first had no idea who or what they
were looking for. Was it a Mafia hit? Did Lee Miglin have enemies? Did
a real estate deal go wrong? Police quickly learned that $2,000 that Lee
Miglin's secretary had delivered to him on Friday afternoon was gone, as
well as several thousand dollars more that he kept in the house. Two
leather coats were missing, one of them Duke's, a couple of suits, along
with some insignificant ladies jewelry and a dozen pairs of new Sulka
black socks from the bedroom.

In the first few days, no one around the neighborhood reported
having seen anything unusual. Marilyn Miglin had last talked to her
husband at 2 P.M. on Saturday, when he told her that he was working
both inside and outside and was going to get a salad for dinner. The
time of death was estimated between 2 P.M. Saturday and 6 A.M. Sunday.

The crime scene itself was immaculate, with little blood, except
where the body lay, and a few spatterings on the wall near the service
door. Nevertheless, Lee Miglin's murder was horrendously brutal—the
most vicious of all Andrew Cunanan's crimes. Lee Miglin was found
lying on his back fully clothed, in the tan suede jacket, white shirt, and
jeans with one shoe on and one shoe missing. Once again, the shoe was a
Ferragamo, this time black suede. Inexplicably, a small tube of
Dermarest hydrocortisone cream was found underneath the body. Gay
pornographic magazines had been left not far away. The zipper of Miglin's jeans was open with teeth missing on the left side, yet there was no
overt sign of sexual molestation. Lee Miglin was wearing black Calvin
Klein bikini underwear trimmed in white.

Neither his white-on-white, patterned, tab-collared shirt nor his
sleeveless white T-shirt showed signs of being cut through, but in fact,
Miglin had been slashed numerous times in the neck and stabbed several times in the chest—two stab wounds, two inches deep, had pene-
trated his heart. Either he had not been wearing a shirt when he was
stabbed, and subsequently Andrew "redressed" him, or his shirts were
lifted up or pulled back for the attack.

The weapon appears to have been either a tree-pruning pole thrown into the garbage container or the bloody screwdriver later recovered in Miglin's stolen Lexus. Lee Miglin's ankles were bound with an orange extension cord wrapped tightly around eight times and tied with a double knot. His mouth was gagged with a white garden glove with numerous black rubber dots. There were over two dozen blows causing bruises or lacerations to his head, face, and chin; the blood from these wounds soaked through layer upon layer of three-quarter-inch masking tape that had been wound around his head mummy-style, except for an opening at the nostrils and at the top of his head.

Bruises do not usually form unless the victim is still alive. "He attacked him, I'm thinking, with an object—maybe with the handle of the bow saw found in the garbage container," says Illinois State Attorney Nancy Donahoe, the prosecutor in charge of the "felony review" on the Miglin case. "The blood could be from hitting him—he attacked him somehow first."

Using the blade of the garden bow saw that he also subsequently dumped into the garbage, Andrew nearly severed Lee Miglin's head with a seven-and-a-half-inch jagged gash, two inches deep, that wound around from the back of his neck to his throat. For good measure, Andrew also threw two bags of cement on top of Miglin's chest and fractured every one of his ribs. Then he covered the body with plastic garbage bags and put brown paper on top of those. Although not mentioned in the police report, a small Oriental throw rug was reportedly on the very top. The cement bags were found lying against the corpse.

There was massive internal hemorrhaging, yet despite all the brutality, no defensive wounds were present. Those close to Lee Miglin do not believe that he would have put up a fight. "Lee always said if anybody tries to rob you, give the person what they ask for and never trigger him, never give him an opportunity to shoot you," Paul Beitler recalls.

Because the missing black suede Ferragamo was later found in the trunk of the Lexus, one theory was that Andrew had originally tried to get the body into the trunk after knocking Lee Miglin out, or after killing him. But there was very little blood in the Lexus trunk, briefly prompting speculation that Andrew had surprised Miglin when he didn't have his hearing aids on—and kept him in the trunk while he entered the house. The blood was never tested to see whose it was.

There was also a one percent carbon-monoxide level found in Miglin's blood—far above the normal level, especially for a nonsmoker like Miglin, though he could have been breathing contaminated air from one of the leaky heaters that commonly caused trouble in the neighborhood.

One theory is that Andrew may have tried to put Miglin in the trunk to try to asphyxiate him. Or maybe he wrapped him first, leaving holes for the nostrils, and then beat him. But why were openings left for breathing if the purpose was murder? Was he tortured? If so, why? There is also speculation that perhaps Andrew was in the house before 2:15 in the afternoon, possibly as an invited guest.

Finally, Miglin's murder could have involved an element of sexual sadism, perhaps some form of fantasy fulfillment. Certainly the wrapping of Miglin's face resembled the latex masks Andrew seemed so intrigued with from watching S&M pornography, the masks he told Steven Gomer he was so fond of for rough sex. But Miglin's clothes were not mussed except for the zipper of his jeans. Though the jeans appeared to have been ripped open, the zipper could also have been damaged in transport from the crime scene.

Whatever happened, there's ample evidence that Lee Miglin's killer never had to struggle with his victim or hurry through his crime. By holding Miglin at gunpoint, Andrew could have learned that no one was expected home until the next day. But would Miglin have also told him—could he even have predicted—that no one else was coming over? Could it be that Andrew was invited to spend the night there? The family believes Andrew played the Miglins' telephone answering machine with a message from Marilyn Miglin telling which flight she was arriving on, although that too is omitted in the police report, which has never been made public.

For three days, until early Wednesday morning, the police had no suspects. Both the family and close associates knew of no one who would want to kill Lee. "We're all grieving the loss of my father," a dry-eyed Duke Miglin said, shortly after he rushed into the house at 6:30 P.M. Sunday, having just arrived from California. "We don't know any details of what happened and we're still trying to get in touch with some members of the family." His sister, Marlena, was vacationing in Italy with her husband and could not be immediately found, but high profile friends of the couple, like Sugar Rautbord, started coming over right away to comfort Marilyn.

First they huddled in Marilyn's opulent office on Oak Street while police technicians were dusting the house for fingerprints, putting black powder everywhere. Sugar found Marilyn Miglin alone in her office, guarded by the police. "Marilyn's office has a glass dome over it, so the sunlight streams directly down upon her," Sugar recalls. "And Honey the dog was seated by the side of her desk." (Honey was later the target of much anger from Marilyn Miglin for not having barked any of her usual warnings, and was banished for months to the country.) At that moment, though, Sugar was immediately struck by "this place so full of order—the desk is so neat, the office is immaculate, everything is per-fect. It's almost as if there is no room for any kind of chaos."

Marilyn was behaving very calmly and had not yet cried. "These are not people who cry in their sleep, who show their grief and sadness. These are people whose lives are in order," Sugar explained. "Marilyn stood up from the desk and we embraced and she started to weep. The policeman said, 'She needed to cry.' I didn't know what I was crying for, but I was crying because something so terrible had happened. Something like murder doesn't belong in a place where light is being refracted off the crystal chandelier and the fragrances have been mixed and you're almost in a staged setting of perfection."

Meanwhile, police who were questioning neighbors were gossiping about bits and pieces of the evidence. Betsy Brazis, another Miglin tenant, who had just moved into the other half of the luxe duplex town house where the Byers lived, got a description of the Miglins' bedroom and bath. "The police couldn't believe it. They said whoever murdered Lee had spent the night, had slept in the bed, and was relaxed enough to take a bath, to shave, and to leave the sink full of whiskers and a dirty bathtub. They said, 'We think it's a black man because of the texture of the hair in the sink.' Don't you think that's a little racist?" Betsy Brazis said.

At the same time, Marilyn and Sugar had come back to greet Duke who looked "totally numb." As soon as they entered the house, "There was a different, greasy smell in the house, like an oil the killer used," Sugar said. "You could smell evil had entered that house." Then Marilyn took Sugar on a "terrible House of Horrors tour," decrying the violations everywhere. "We went into the bathroom and she said, 'What do you do? Do you hurt somebody? Kill somebody? And then you cut your hair?' "

"All this dark, coarse, curly hair was on the bathroom floor. The policemen were there and she said, 'Sweep this up! Get this away!' Very kindly, they said, 'No. You can't touch anything.' And both of us bent down and stared at this dark curly hair on the bathroom floor. Lee had gray hair and Marilyn had blond hair. Everything in that house was white and sunny, and all of a sudden it's like something dark and awful and swarthy and greasy had moved into the house. There were greasy fingerprints on the wall walking up to the stairs." Sugar Rautbard noticed a picture was askew that masked a wall safe.

Because no one could touch the refrigerator or the kitchen counter, Sugar picked up the phone and called nearby Gibsons Steak House and told them what happened. "They started to cry—the guys who own the restaurant. Within twenty minutes they came over with all kinds of food." Marilyn was worrying, " 'Well, has that policeman had something to eat? This one?' Part of her was being in control, elegant and precise. She wasn't ready to fall into the abyss. But slowly you could see it etching its way into her face—this terrible look of shock and sorrow. I don't think I have ever felt such a sense of a house being invaded by evil before."

Within twelve minutes of the first radio call by police signaling that a body had been found, the first TV truck pulled up to the murder site. A millionaire getting murdered is a big local story anywhere, and the Chicago media are very competitive. The Miglins weren't just rich—they were social, they knew the mayor, Marilyn had hosted a fund-raiser for the governor. Within a few hours reporters and police were swarming.

Although it had taken the Chicago police awhile to respond, they were now blanketing the site. Reporters from Fox News and the local TV stations were leaning on neighbors' doorbells, begging for any shred of information. Stephen Byer got fed up and released his pet shar-pei/pit bull and his Doberman into the gated front garden. "These newspaper reporters and press people just scattered. I don't know if they thought the dogs would jump over the fence or what, but they literally ran away."

The first day, stories in the *Chicago Tribune* and the *Chicago Sun-Times* were filled with details about the crime scene that astounded the Minneapolis police when they read them—they claim they would not have told so much. Readers learned things only the killer knew—the position of the body under the Bitter, pruning shears as a possible weapon, the wrapping in masking tape. Marilyn Miglin herself was also far more forthcoming than the family would be just a few days later, telling the *Sun-Times* that the killer had possibly stayed overnight: " 'My first thought is, why does someone think they have the right to take someone else's life and so horribly at that,' said Miglin, adding that she was 'horrified that whoever did this evil, evil thing also apparently spent the night in our home.' "

Tuesday's *Sun-Times* incorrectly led with the story, attributed to police sources, that Lee Miglin was "run over by a car at least five times . . . and garbage was dumped on his body." It also reported correctly that his throat was cut with a saw blade and that the gun found in the bathroom was a nonworking replica. (The copy of the black semiautomatic Beretta had actually come out of Duke's room where it had been mounted on the wall.)

In Chicago, the police chief is known as the police superintendent, and the then superintendent, Matt Rodriguez, was almost voluble: "There are aspects of the homicide that indicate there was some torture," he told the *Sun-Times,* declining to get into specifics. He also confirmed for the paper what Marilyn Miglin had already told their reporter: that her husband's face was "bound up like a mummy," and that her husband never would have left the dirty dishes found in the kitchen, which she took as a sign that the killer may have spent the night.

Rodriguez went on to tell the *Sun-Times* that the killing "looks quite unprofessional. However, it looks so unprofessional that maybe it is professional." One sign of obvious unprofessionalism was the theft of the car. "When one takes a vehicle that is registered to a victim, you immediately are putting yourself in jeopardy if you happen to be an offender," he told the paper.

But the *Sun-Times* could only get so much information out of the police department. Significantly, Commander Joe Griffin of Area 3, the politically appointed officer in charge of the investigation, would not comment beyond acknowledging the homicide of "an elderly gentleman." Griffin was so tight lipped he later became the scapegoat for the lack of cooperation displayed by Chicago police toward other jurisdictions. And in the same story the reporters Fran Spielman and Phillip J. O'Connor described reaching Superintendent Rodriguez's boundaries of disclosure:

> *Rodriguez repeatedly talked about how the killer had made himself comfortable in the home. When asked how the killer did this, Rodriguez said:*
>
> *"Very frankly the specificity of your question and any response on my part would jeopardize the future investigation. Things that occurred there are best left unsaid right now by police officials because, in fact, they may contribute to a successful investigation and the arrest of an offender."*
>
> *Asked if blood were found in the home, Rodriguez said, "I don't want to respond to that question."*
>
> *Asked if the killer stayed with Miglin before the murder or remained in the home after it, Rodriguez said, "I can't say for certain if there was any occupancy by the killer before the killing. There is an indication the person or persons occupied and used the victim's apartment. And that is all I can really say."*

But that was a lot.

To an alert reader, the superintendent's repeated references to how comfortable the killer felt in the Miglins' house could easily be interpreted as the police believing that Miglin may have known his assailant. Most murders are committed by someone known to the victim—not a stranger. There was no forced entry. And of course the dog, which neighbors said barked frequently at strangers, did not bark and was not harmed.

Certainly the crime scenes of both the garage and house suggested someone who was not just randomly killing for money and a car to escape as fast as he could. "A robber gets in and out quickly," says Nancy Donahoe. "Can you say the same about Cunanan? No." Miglin's murder, states Medical Examiner Dr. Edmund Donoghue, was "very controlled and purposeful. He wanted control." The medical examiner's office was not comfortable with the idea suggested by Superintendent Rodriguez that Miglin had been tortured. Asked how long it would have taken to kill Lee Miglin, with the tying, the wrapping with tape, the almost four dozen wounds, the clean up—bloody rags were also thrown in the garbage container—Dr. Donoghue says, "Just a few minutes if he flew like the wind." But Andrew didn't fly anywhere—he hung around.

And what about the racy bikini underwear seventy-five-year-old Lee Miglin was found wearing? Dr. Donoghue saw no suggestion of a double life for Miglin. "She was high fashion—she probably bought it for him," he explained. Asked how he would respond if his own wife brought home underwear like that for him, Dr. Donoghue did not hesitate: "That would never happen."

Nevertheless, there were signs that would lead many investigators to consider the possibility of a sexual element to the crime. The sadistic aspects were consistent with a pattern prevalant among serial killers, whom experts say often need to act out their sadistic fantasies and repeat them till they get it right. According to Gregg McCrary, senior consultant of the Threat Assessment Group and former supervisory special agent of the FBI's Behavioral Science Unit, such killers typically have "compliant victims—they begin with sex partners who were complying with their fantasies. They get someone to go along with bondage and torture until the victim won't go along anymore, so the sadistic offender is not satisfied. By the time they reach their late twenties and early thirties, they've developed their sadistic fantasies. They're really vibrant at this point, and they need to act out these things, and they can't find people to go along with them. So now they find an unwilling victim to abduct, rape, or murder. There's a much higher rate of homicide if torture is acted out against the will of the other individual."

McCrary says motives here can be mixed—both sexual gratification and the extortion of money. What was done to Lee Miglin, for example, "is a window into [the killer's] fantasy." Even the psychological motives can be mixed. A killer's savaging of a victim's face indicates a "very personal" impetus, he says. "The destruction of the face is many times the personality of the victim—they want to destroy the person outright." Putting the victim in a mask, on the other hand, represents depersonalization. But while Miglin was masked, his face was also brutalized. The autopsy report notes fifteen facial bruises.

On Tuesday, Paul Beitler, responding to persistent questions searching for a motive to the killing, told reporters, "This was not a gangland hit." But he probably raised more questions than he answered when he added, "Everyone has their personal opinion about what happened . . . But it had nothing to do with business." The family had called a press conference to ask the public for help with leads to the killer. Although observers felt that the family's body language was oddly stiff and awkward with each other, going before the cameras was nothing they shied away from. Marilyn told reporters: "What can you say about a man you loved passionately for thirty-eight years, [one] who exemplified courage and honor and dignity and a code of ethics beyond what anybody I know has had?"

Until Tuesday midnight, police were stymied. Some officials were appalled that Superintendent Matt Rodriguez had used the word "torture," and that it had been falsely reported that Lee Miglin had been run over. Police questioned Stephen Byer—had he seen any strangers? Betsy Brazis told the police she had seen a red Jeep parked in front of her house on East Division, one street over from the Miglins' house, on Friday night. On Saturday she noticed it had been moved around the corner to East Astor.

The more rumors ran rampant—whether or not the murder was a Mafia hit, whether or not Lee Miglin knew his killer—the more the police lid on the investigation was tightened. The police were both bowing to the wishes of a powerful family and attempting to avoid potential legal perils. "You have to understand the outpouring of love and how the police protected her," Sugar Rautbord said of Marilyn

Miglin. Another high-profile murder was also, apparently, never far from the minds of the law enforcers. "Police in Chicago are very closed-mouth," says Paul Beitler. "Can you blame them given the Simpson debacle?"

Nothing moved. Then, nearly three full days after Lee Miglin's body was first discovered, Policewoman Olive Dickey noticed three tickets on a red Grand Jeep Cherokee parked on Astor Street, just "eighty-five steps" around the corner from the Miglins' row house. When she decided to run a license check for Minnesota 543 LUG, she hit the lottery: The Jeep belonged to homicide victim David Madson, and the suspect, Andrew Phillip Cunanan, was armed, dangerous, and wanted for murder.

Now the story would become far more sensational, catapulting the two previous murders that had first been thought of as "a domestic crime," albeit a gay one, into the alleged secret lifestyles of the rich and famous. That night, however, was quiet. The Jeep was dusted for fingerprints and towed away. The Jeep contained numerous items identifiable as belonging to David Madson, as well as a Chicago city guide with lines marking a map of the Gold Coast, and a copy of *Out* magazine. Perhaps the most interesting piece of evidence recovered from the Jeep, however, was the parking stub indicating that Andrew had first parked at the General Parking Garage on North Water Street, a couple of miles away, on the previous Wednesday, April 30, at 6:08 A.M.—about twelve hours after Jeff Trail's body was discovered in Minneapolis. That parking stub would eventually throw the whole time of death of David Madson into serious question.

The media immediately leaped on the story, but Chicago police would say little. In Minnesota, which Chicago media poached in the absence of information from Chicago, the motive still alleged in the first two murders was either a "homosexual love triangle"—much to the chagrin of the Madson and Trail families—or a scenario that had an HIV-positive Andrew killing for revenge, an assumption widely scoffed at in the gay press. (In FBI records later released, the HIV-positive revenge motive was attributed to a gay friend of Andrew's in an early report out of San Francisco.) There is no doubt, however, that with the addition of the older, richer, prominent Miglin to the list of victims, the visibility of the case was given a huge boost, not only with the press but with law enforcement nationally. Tiny Chisago County led the way.

At 6 A.M. Wednesday morning, Chisago County Sergeant Todd Rivard learned that a reporter at the Chicago NBC affiliate had informed the Sheriff's Communications Center that the Jeep had been found. Rivard had not yet been notified by Chicago police. The call began a pattern: Chisago would hear about major developments in the case from the media first. When Rivard called the NBC reporter back, he learned not only about Andrew's possible connection to Miglin's murder, but also that Miglin's Lexus was missing. Later in the morning, Rivard called the Chicago police, who confirmed both facts to him. Not long after, Karen Lapinski telephoned Rivard from San Francisco to tell him that a phone bill with numerous long distance charges Andrew had made had arrived in the mail. She also gave Rivard a full accounting of what she understood Andrew and David's relationship to be.

In the spirit of quick, decisive action, Sheriff Randall Schwegman and Sergeant Todd Rivard went to Chisago County District Attorney James Reuter to ask for a warrant for Andrew Cunanan's arrest for murder. He acceded. The decision raised prosecutorial eyebrows. Minnesota does not even have the death penalty, and by current big city prosecutorial standards, which downplay circumstantial evidence, they didn't have nearly enough to go on. But Schwegman and Rivard convinced the DA that finding the bullets in Andrew's duffel bag in Madson's apartment, coupled with the recovery of the Jeep near Miglin's house, was enough. "We had probable cause. We were concerned (Cunanan) was going to flee to the Philippines," says District Attorney Reuter. "We were early in our investigation but we found we would be developing additional confirmatory evidence as it progressed."

The taciturn Chicago Area 3 Commander, Joe Griffin, was livid. Griffin was known to be so cautious that he once reportedly refused to tell detectives investigating the mayor's brother's burglary what was taken from the house. A fur coat was among the items stolen from Secretary of Commerce Billy Daley and Griffin reportedly thought owning such a luxury item might reflect negatively on the image of the First Family of Chicago.

But Griffin was not alone in his concern. "Chisago issuing the warrant shocked everyone," said Chicago prosecutor Nancy Donahoe. "I got a call from Griffin screaming, 'How could they do this?' " The problem was that Chisago's complaint contained many specifics including the identity of the unusual .40 caliber murder weapon, names of numerous witnesses and, in some cases, where they resided, making them easy targets for the media to contact. "Our biggest concern was that [the warrant] would chase potential witnesses off," says Nancy Donahoe. "I could talk till I'm blue in the face promising we won't put this in the media, your family won't find out you're gay," but what good would it do if they saw or heard about Chisago?

There was a far more important reason, however, for Chisago to issue a warrant for Cunanan's arrest: The complaint paved the way for the FBI to enter the case. Ordinarily, each murder is the province of the local jurisdiction where it happens—unless the suspect crosses state lines in an attempt to escape and there is a warrant for his arrest. Such a complaint is used to trigger a federal UFAP warrant—unlawful flight to avoid prosecution. Then the FBI is able to jump in.

In the case of Chisago, Roy Tubergen, head of the FBI Violent Crimes section, concedes, "They were going out on a limb to charge." Even so, the FBI had already been eyeing the murders at the highest levels. Said former FBI Deputy Director William Esposito, "I got a call from our command center saying something was going on—there were a couple of deaths in Minnesota—they look like they could be connected. Then the third one happened and I think people started piecing things together."

"Murder in Minnesota is not as common as it is in Chicago or the East Coast," says FBI Deputy Assistant Director Roger Wheeler, "so the fact that a murder occurred in the city, followed by another murder a few miles outside the city, apparently by the same person, tweaked everybody's interest." After Miglin, "We have a murderer who has traveled into three states and three different jurisdictions. We thought because of the speed, and Cunanan's ability to get around the country as quickly as he did, that he deserved as much attention as we could put on it from the very beginning."

Still, before getting in, the FBI demanded certain assurances in writing from Chisago. According to Todd Rivard, "Jim Reuter had to prosecute for first degree murder"—although the complaint said second degree murder. "We just told him, 'Listen, Jim, trust us—we never let you down before.' " Rivard was confident they could develop evidence for first degree. But the FBI, knowing there was no death penalty in Minnesota, was not about to pledge its resources lightly. Rivard characterized the Bureau's attitude as, "We're not going to all this trouble without a commitment." Translation: We're not going to haul ass for a measly manslaughter conviction. The FBI not only needed a warrant with sufficient probable cause, it also "wanted a letter promising prosecution for first degree murder and a promise to extradite" if they caught Andrew. In other words, Chisago, the first to charge, had to promise it would not insist on trying Andrew first, thereby holding up a more promising Cunanan murder case that could be tried in a capital punishment state.

In Minneapolis, the news that David's Jeep was found around the corner from Lee Miglin's house was a bombshell. It threw all their theories into disarray. "We're thinking it's some sort of gay lovers' quarrel between Jeff and David and now we got a millionaire in Chicago involved and another missing vehicle," says Minneapolis police sergeant Steve Wagner. "From that point on, the FBI is very much involved and big-time it escalates."

Now the whole complexion of the case did change. With the FBI in, the investigation would expand—there would be a national manhunt. The Bureau immediately began dispatching its tools, including a Rapid Start computer team to establish a unified, computerized system for handling all leads pertaining to Andrew Cunanan. The case itself would be given over to a fugitive task force, part of a joint Safe Streets Task Force, which unites federal, state, and local authorities together under one roof, sharing command with the FBI to find the country's most violent fugitives. The task forces are supposed to reduce interagency rivalry and foster police cooperation—always a ticklish issue.

"Literally within hours of putting the word out in the task force arena, we had every major metropolitan police department or sheriff's office involved because most of them have representation in one form or another on task forces," says FBI Deputy Assistant Director Wheeler. "It's a tremendous advantage over five years ago. [The task forces] are a nineties vehicle. And it's an extremely valuable form of communication and networking"—if in fact, everyone is paying attention, which is by no means automatic.

Because Cunanan's crimes originated in Minnesota, the Minnesota Joint Task Force was in charge: Lee Urness of the Minnesota Bureau of Criminal Apprehension shared duties with Kevin Rickett of the FBI. "Their responsibility is to set leads to other divisions to follow," says Stephen Wiley, head of the FBI Fugitive Division. "Minnesota set a lead to San Diego giving them a list of things to do, to check the background of friends and associates." A common assumption is that fugitives will try to contact their families, or try to come home—although that was certainly not the case with Andrew.

The FBI's primary objective in fugitive investigations is neither to gather evidence nor establish motive. Rather, the Bureau is trying to figure out where the suspect is headed and how they can catch him. Along the way, the agents assigned often learn a great deal, but if the information does not directly pertain to finding their man, they might not pay much attention. Character doesn't count. "Our sole purpose here is not to find out who Andrew Cunanan is, or to find out what he's about," says Kevin Rickett. "Our sole purpose is to arrest him." In Cunanan's case, putting on the "fugitive-investigation-only" blinders did just that—the Bureau conducted hundreds of interviews but missed or ignored some important clues.

Nevertheless, the Chicago police and the other jurisdictions now had the FBI and its myriad technical resources to count on. "UFAP is very good at tracking down in various ways—by phone records, credit card records, cellular phones—where he is, where he's going, where we believe he'll go," says Illinois prosecutor Nancy Donahoe. Still, there had to be some ambivalence for Chicago police about where this case would eventually take them.

In their Thursday, May 8, story, in the aftermath of finding the Jeep, the *Chicago Tribune* opined, "If the admittedly tenuous threads police are following lead where some think they might, investigators will have to figure out how the killing of the 72-year-old (*sic*) Miglin fits in with the murders of the two young men." But Chicago authorities were not overly thrilled with the political minefield: dealing with an openly gay killer who was suspected of being a prostitute and had killed two other gays he was close to, when their victim was a wealthy, prominent family man with a politically connected business partner and a wife with a fancy street named after her.

Says Tichich's partner, Pete Jackson, "Chicago knew the guy packed some heat when the cardinal's office called up to ask how the investigation was going."

22

Fatal Error

ONCE AGAIN, Andrew had gotten away with a substantial headstart. By late Saturday night he was in Lee Miglin's Lexus headed out of Chicago. The FBI was able to trace his route with a piece of new, highly sensitive software called a "triggerfish," a triangulation device that can track cars with a high degree of accuracy once their cell phones are activated. Miglin's Lexus had a phone, but Andrew did not know the code number required to use it. The phone was apparently activated, however, as soon as the car's ignition was turned on. Andrew either turned on the ignition or attempted to use the phone twice—once at 11:25 P.M. Saturday night and again at 12:37 A.M. Sunday morning.

Those calls were monitored by a signal transmitted via a tower located in Grand Rapids, Michigan. Twice again, on Sunday afternoon, he tried to use the phone. Those calls were picked up at a tower in Union County, Pennsylvania, on a route that goes directly to New York City. "The FBI was spearheading the tracking of the cell-phone transmissions," says Chisago Sergeant Todd Rivard. "I was contacted by Lee Urness [the member of the Minnesota Bureau of Criminal Apprehension who was heading the Minnesota Fugitive Task Force with the FBI's Kevin Rickett], and he told me what was going on—that this was very top secret, that they had had one reading from the cell phone." By some fluke, the phone service was then turned off, and it was not reconnected until the middle of the following week.

It appears that Andrew drove straight to New York, because at 12:45 A.M. on Monday, May 5, he registered at the West Side Club, a gay men's bathhouse located in Chelsea, an artsy, largely gay neighborhood bordering on Greenwich Village. He was in a familiar environment, hiding in plain sight. Meanwhile, in Minneapolis and Chicago, the lives of the families and friends of his victims were being turned upside down. On Monday morning, David Madson's and Lee Miglin's autopsies were being performed, while in DeKalb, Illinois, Jeffrey Trail's funeral was being held, with no media in attendance. Minneapolis authorities had failed to send Jeff's ashes in time for the service. David Madson's Jeep was still parked near Lee Miglin's house, and the clamorous fallout from Andrew's three "spree killings" had not yet begun. Thus, while the bodies of two of the men he had killed were being probed for any remnants of his cruel violence, and his third victim was being eulogized, Andrew went shopping for a pair of jeans. He bought them at the Original Levi's Store, on Fifty-seventh Street near Fifth Avenue.

From the beginning Andrew frustrated law enforcement, because they had almost nothing concrete to go on. Since he had never been arrested, and his only existing fingerprint was the right thumbprint on his California driver's license, police had tremendous difficulty matching any fingerprints at the crime scenes. And because the authorities had not, for example, taken proper caution while investigating Andrew's apartment in San Diego or Jeff Trail's apartment, much of the evidence had been contaminated, so police had to compare hundreds of prints. Andrew also looked very different from one photo to another: Sometimes he appeared nerdy in glasses; sometimes his hair was long; other times he looked butch, with his head shaved close. Few of the pictures showed that Andrew had recently put on weight.

"What irritated me first when their big manhunt was on," says Jerry Davis, "was the pictures they were showing. Because the Andrew I knew was a fat, ugly guy. . . . I thought he was gross. And that picture they showed on TV—I thought he was nice-looking. That's what I kept trying to tell those guys." The other problem was that with his medium height and dark looks, Andrew looked commonplace. "He's a guy who could blend into a number of different communities— Italian, Greek, Hispanic," says Todd Rivard.

Then there was the question of whether or not Andrew was deliberately taunting the police, since many serial killers pride themselves on being able to outsmart the law. Or was the case just full of exquisite irony? For example, movie stubs found later in Miami show that on Wednesday, the day the FBI entered his case, Andrew presumably was at the movies in Chelsea, watching Jim Carrey in *Liar, Liar.* The next night he saw Brad Pitt in *The Devil's Own.* "He had an evil purpose for everything he did," says Minneapolis police sergeant Steve Wagner. "I don't see him as a genius. Al Capone, Lucky Luciano, John Gotti— they're a lot smarter than Andrew."

By the end of the week, half a dozen law-enforcement agencies were pursuing various aspects of Andrew's murders without knowing what his motives were or where he would land next. "He just kept moving," says Wagner, "going from one spot to another." But he was doing so under the beginning of the media's spotlight.

Finding the Jeep near Miglin's house was the catalyst the tabloids needed for turning up the heat on the "gay San Diego party boy," and the possibility that Andrew might have known or been involved with Lee Miglin spurred national attention. *Time* and *Newsweek* began preparing stories. Local TV was insatiable. On Thursday, recalls Ann Trail, Jeff's mother, "we came home and the entire street was filled with cars and people." TV satellite trucks were parked in front of the Trails' house ready to fuel *Live at Five.* "They descended on us like a horde of locusts. It was like a mob coming after me. I had had serious surgery April seventh. I still was not well. Stan said, 'You go inside—I'll handle it.' "

Perhaps there is no truer gauge of the potential interest in a crime story than a nod from *America's Most Wanted,* the Fox TV show beloved by the FBI and law enforcement everywhere for its audience of millions and the numbers of criminals it helps bring down—535 to date. At first, *AMW* thought the Minnesota murders were run-of-the-mill domestic crimes. "Half the crime in this country is domestic," says executive producer Lance Heflin, "so it goes on a slower track." But host John Walsh had his own take—that Andrew Cunanan "always was a wanna-be. He wanted to be in those circles. He wanted to hang with the rich and famous. He wanted to be in the Hamptons with David Geffen's crew." He wanted to be famous period.

When the third murder occurred, the producers paid attention. "It's big news in Chicago because Lee Miglin is so respected in Chicago as a real-estate developer, a philanthropist," explains Walsh. "I know Mayor Daley was a very original supporter of the show and a friend of Miglin's, et cetera, et cetera, so we get the murder on." *AMW*'s first broadcast about Andrew Cunanan was May 10, the day after Lee Miglin's funeral. It was only two minutes and forty-seven seconds in length, but it was a signal, especially to the large law-enforcement audience, that Cunanan had become big. "Here's the guy, he's inside Miglin's mansion. Now the elite, wealthy part of society says, 'You know, most crime happens in the ghetto. How could somebody get in Lee Miglin's house and kill Lee Miglin?' We start to look at it and say, 'We may have a serial killer on our hands here. What's the connection with Lee Miglin?' "

America's Most Wanted had company. A tabloid TV crew, finding the gate to the Miglins' garden open, marched right in and started filming the family seated around the kitchen table. The *Chicago Tribune* tracked Norman Blachford down via satellite phone as he and a friend, Peter Cooper, the former director of Project Lifeguard, were trying to escape by sailing for London on the QE2. Blachford refused to comment, so the *Tribune* had its London correspondent waiting on the dock like a chauffeur, holding up a sign saying, "Norman Blachford," because the bureau there had no idea what he looked like. Although Blachford did not approach the reporter, the intrepid journalist tracked him down in his London hotel room, where Blachford told him in no uncertain terms to back off.

Everybody wanted a piece of the story—with one notable exception. In Andrew's hometown paper, the conservative *San Diego Union-Tribune,* he was the invisible man. Six weeks after reporting the mass suicides at the Heaven's Gate cult in Rancho Santa Fe, the *Union-Tribune* actually ran an obituary on Lee Miglin the day after David Madson's Jeep was discovered, but it made no mention of Andrew Cunanan.

"That story was very sensitive around here," says longtime *Union-Tribune* financial writer Don Bauder. David Copley, the forty-one-year-old heavy-set son of the paper's owner, Helen Copley, was widely rumored to have been an acquaintance of Andrew's. Robbins Thompson and others say that they had attended a party at David Copley's house with Andrew, but Copley denies that he ever met him. When the *Union-Tribune* finally printed its first story on Andrew, on Thursday, May 8, it mentioned "authorities in several states looking for a San Diego man," but it was buried on page A9, included no interviews with any of Andrew's many nearby friends and acquaintances, and was sourced mostly by Chisago District Attorney Jim Reuter.

Unlike Jeff's funeral, which the media had ignored on Monday, David's funeral in Barron on Thursday attracted a swarm of TV cameramen. But they were mostly kept out. By this point the Trail and Madson families had been overwhelmed. For ordinary Americans, unused to the limelight, being caught up in the blinding media glare at the moment of their greatest sorrow is bewildering and often alienating. At David's funeral, the Madsons' neighbor from two doors down, an off-duty policeman, showed up in full uniform at the church and barred the door. "In a little town like this, when a tragedy happens, the whole community just kind of wraps its arms around the community," says Cynthia Madson, David's sister-in-law. Even so, both families felt obliged to seek the advice of media consultants.

Lisa Stravinskas's law firm and David's employer were helpful. "When I saw [the homosexual-love-triangle story] on the Chicago news, I called my boss," says Lisa. "He recommended a media adviser for the firm, who graciously gave us her time and gave us pointers. She recommended that unless you talk to everyone, don't do it. Have a family statement and give them something a little personal so they'll leave you alone." The Trails followed her advice.

In Barron the townspeople sternly made the media feel unwelcome—so different from the case in Miami and San Diego later, where palms on all sides waited to be greased. "They went to businesses downtown and got kicked out," Howard Madson says. "They tried to set up in the church parking lot. The highway patrol, the Barron County Sheriff's Department, and the city police absolutely cordoned that thing up there like you couldn't believe. At the cemetery, when we drove in, I looked and there were, way back in the woods, two highway patrol cars and policemen all over the place. They protected us without even telling us."

The police were also making sure Andrew did not return. But the Madsons saw their efforts in a more personal way. David's brother, Ralph, says, "The town knew David Madson and grieved, not just for David but for the family, because of the commitment the family has made to this community over the years—I like to think for the respect for my mom and dad. They just knew we needed to grieve."

In addition to their grief, the Madsons were filled with anger— stung and outraged that David was being tied to Andrew in any way. They objected to the idea that Andrew and David had been lovers, to any suggestion that David had been involved in S&M, and mostly to the very notion that David might have been implicated in Jeff Trail's murder. For these transgressions they blamed Tichich and the media. Ralph particularly objected to David's being referred to as Andrew's lover. He eventually came to accept that that might be true, but he wanted "a timeline" attached to the term. He categorized the media as having two approaches. "Number one, we want to tell the victim's side. The second thing is, 'Well, I'm going to write it anyway. So if you want to tell your side of the story, fine. But no big deal, I'm going to write it anyway.' We went through this with the press so many times. It's a type of blackmail."

At the same time, the family cherished letters that poured into them from David's co-workers and friends, telling of acts of David's kindness and recalling his humor. His employer had its own memorial, and Minneapolis friends who gathered at the Monte Carlo Room restaurant the night after the funeral in Barron to eulogize David, presented the Madsons with an album of remembrances. Little old ladies who still knew David as Harold Hill, "the Music Man," who had delivered groceries to them even on holidays, pressed cards into the Madsons' hands at the wake on Wednesday night. "All came with a card and two dollars," for a memorial fund, says Howard Madson, "which is really a lot to all of them, because they're on Social Security."

The family took great solace in these generous gestures and brandished them as proof that David was not who "they"—the police and the press—were suggesting he was. "Most of David's friends were straight," his mother insists, as if some other, sinister world had been visited upon her child. The Madsons, who had always respected authority, were now having their illusions shattered. "Until you walk in our shoes, you can't understand it," Howard Madson says. "It's difficult for us to separate fact from fiction too, because we're no different from you, and we're being treated as though we are possibly hiding a criminal."

Howard and Ralph Madson drove to East Rush Lake to see the place where David's body had been found. There they erected a handmade wooden cross with the epitaph BLESSED TO BE A BLESSING TO OTHERS. "It's a strange thing that always presses on you—that thread [of David's giving] that goes through everything he did," says Howard Madson. "This Cunanan thing is so far away in our imagination. How the hell could this have happened?" Yet for whatever reasons—shame, fear, anger, or legal considerations—the Madsons did not reach out to the Trails, who were also suffering. Instead, they vowed to clear David's name.

On Friday, May 9, members of both the Trail and Madson families were in Minneapolis. The Madsons had asked permission to go into David's loft to look for personal papers—bank statements and the like. Tichich was to be there, because he wanted to see if he could eliminate David as the owner of a bloody white Banana Republic T-shirt found in the loft, in the plastic bag with the murder weapon. Evan Wallit, Karen Lapinski's fiancé, had told Tichich that Andrew had recently purchased some T-shirts and had given one to him.

But David was a clotheshorse, so of course he owned some Banana Republic items. The possibility of clearing David was foreclosed in much the same way that the Ferragamo shoes found in the loft with blood on them could not be positively identified as either Andrew's or David's. They were almost the same size, and both wore Ferragamos. There were still a few piles of clothes strewn around in the sleeping area of David's loft that had not been checked, and they were left unexamined as were two dop kits in the bathroom. More police mistakes.

The visit was hard on the Madsons. They found that David had already purchased and wrapped Christmas presents for his nieces and nephews. Whether Sergeant Tichich realized it or not—and he seems not to have—they were becoming more infuriated with him by the minute. At one point Ralph Madson opened a drawer and saw a letter postmarked December 1996, which had been returned to the sender. It was addressed to Andrew Cunanan in La Jolla, California. According to Ralph, he turned to Tichich and said, "You may want this."

"Why?" Tichich asked.

"It's a letter from David to his killer."

"We don't know that he killed him," Tichich replied.

Ralph insisted: "Maybe there's some writing from David to Andrew or something."

Tichich took the letter, but Ralph felt he was getting a distinct message from the policeman. "I was really being made to feel, like, 'this is none of your damned business. I'm the cop. Don't tell me how to do my job,' " he says.

Ralph Madson is nothing if not confrontational. Next, he says, he demanded of Tichich, "Who's using the word 'lover' to the press? Man to man, tell me. Come on. I'd like to know."

Tichich first said "a friend" and then admitted "Miss Salvetti."

Ralph jumped to the conclusion that he was being lied to. "Monique had not talked to the press at all," he insists. But Ralph misunderstood. She certainly had told the police that Andrew and David had had an intimate relationship. The police had passed that information on to the press via the police PR office.

Now Ralph, who had not met Tichich in person before, clearly felt he needed to get a few things off his chest. "You were wrong about David, weren't you?" he demanded, referring to Tichich's claims that David had been involved in Jeff's murder. "You were dead wrong," Ralph reiterated. "It's David who's dead now!" Then he turned on his heel and walked out.

Relations between the police and victims' families are often complicated, and it is not unnatural for the surviving family to vent their frustrations on law enforcement. In this case the Madsons felt more than aggrieved, yet Sergeant Tichich says he really doesn't understand why they have it in for him. "I had two or three conversations that I thought were just fine with Howard prior to David's body being discovered, and all of a sudden he stopped talking to me and I had no hint or clue in any way that there was ever a problem between him and me. I have been mystified since this happened."

"We don't spend enough time with victims' families," says Sergeant Wagner. "The problem is just time. When we are focusing on suspects, normally the families are not kept abreast, and they have this tremendous desire for knowledge, to know everything. Some things we can say, others we can't."

Wagner later sent the Madsons a sympathetic letter assuring them that David was a wonderful person, which they took as vindication for the perceived stings from Tichich. But Wagner defends his fellow investigator. "His mind is always working. You have to have different personalities. Tich is rough on the edges, but he digs real deep."

While Tichich was at David's loft on Friday with the Madsons, he got beeped by Jerry Davis. Davis and Jon Hackett were at Jeff's apartment with Dr. and Mrs. Trail and Jeff's sister, Sally. They had found something. The Trails had come in for a memorial service for Jeff in Minneapolis. Like the Madsons, they wanted to hear as much as they could about what had really gone on with regard to Jeff's murder. At the memorial service the following day, Stan Trail, who had had a good relationship with his son, would say that he realized after Jeff left the house at age eighteen that there was a lot he didn't know about him. They lost touch. Jerry Davis, meanwhile, trying to make things as comfortable as he could for the Trails, filled them in on anything he could to ease their pain. But they never asked him a single question about Jeff being gay.

While at the apartment and going through Jeff's things with the Trails, Jon Hackett made an important discovery. On the top shelf in Jeff's closet—police had never searched there—he found a gun case and a metal military ammunition box with three holsters and an empty magazine. There was also a bill of sale for ammunition purchased in California in 1994. The gun itself was missing, but earlier in the week the .40 caliber shell casings had been found in the ground near where David had been shot. The police believed they had made a match. "As soon as we got that—that Chisago had received shell casings at the scene which marked the caliber of their gun—that discovery was a big deal," says Wagner. "We didn't have the gun, but we knew it was .40 caliber, and it's an unusual gun." He added, "We wanted to keep that information secret. It ended up in one of the Chicago papers."

Except for dusting for fingerprints, the police had never completely searched Jeff's apartment beyond the room where Andrew had stayed, nor had they picked up Andrew's eyeglasses, which he had left behind there. The day of the dusting, a neighbor who lived above Jeff saw the police and told them she thought she had seen Andrew out in front of Jeff's apartment, alone, the Monday night after Jeff's murder. But since she had come forward only after there had been so much publicity about the case, Tichich wasn't satisfied that her sighting was genuine.

When Tichich, whom they were meeting for the first time, arrived at Jeff's, the Trails wanted to discuss Jeff's murder with him. Jerry Davis, who had earlier had words with Tichich over the detective's request for help in finding out about Andrew's airline ticket, says he got upset again. Tichich began describing the murder in such graphic terms that at one point Ann Trail "got up and could barely walk. She had to catch herself on the table and leave the room." In Davis's opinion, "He was just way too blunt for somebody whose parents are sitting there, when their son was just murdered. Instead of just saying there was blood on this shirt, he said, 'When Jeff was getting bludgeoned with the hammer, blood just spattered.' "

Davis was frustrated that Tichich couldn't even figure out how to operate Jeff's answering machine—which caused Davis to spend several unwanted hours driving to and from Jeff's house twice to help him. The Trails, however, did not share Davis's opinion of Tichich. "He was graphic," Ann Trail says, "and it did upset me. But it didn't offend me. He was showing us what happened." The Trails had no quarrel with Tichich, who believed he was just doing his job.

For Andrew, it was time to move again. On Friday he barely missed getting caught. At 1:30 P.M. and again at 3 P.M. on Thursday, May 8, the tracking tower for Ameritech Cellular phone had informed the FBI and the Chicago police that the telephone in Lee Miglin's Lexus had been activated in the Philadelphia area. Chicago authorities informed the Philadelphia police, desperately hoping to be able to pinpoint Andrew's whereabouts. The next morning, Friday, the *Chicago Tribune* ran a story—which reporter Andrew Martin says was based on a law-enforcement leak in Chicago—saying that Andrew had used the cell phone and was being tracked.

Yet the Chicago police denied in the same day's Minneapolis *Star Tribune* that Andrew had used Miglin's cell phone. The Minneapolis paper did, however, quote Philadelphia police saying that a description of Miglin's car and license number was being broadcast every hour to all the squads in the City of Brotherly Love. "I think the description was made by the Philadelphia police and broadcast on their radios, which are not encoded," says Philadelphia FBI spokeswoman Linda Vizi. " 'Be on the lookout,' that's how the media picked it up." That's how some media picked it up, but nothing happened right away.

Complicating this version of events is the movie ticket stub later found for *The Devil's Own* on Thursday night in New York City. If Andrew was correctly tracked in the Philadelphia area and also saw *The Devil's Own* in New York, that would mean that he left New York, drove south to Philadelphia, then turned around and went back to New York—at least an hour and a half away in the opposite direction. Wherever he was on Friday, however, he bought the *New York Times,* the *Philadelphia Inquirer,* and *USA Today,* of which only the *Times* had a short item about him.

Thursday night, a Chicago network affiliate had also carried the information that there was an all-points bulletin out for Andrew in Philadelphia. Other media soon asked the Philadelphia police for confirmation on the APB and the cell-phone tracking story. Deputy Police Commissioner Richard Zappile announced that Miglin's cell phone had been activated on Thursday. As a result, all-news radio in Philadelphia broadcast to the world that Andrew was being tracked, as did radio and TV stations. Meanwhile, also on Friday, Sergeant Todd Rivard got another top-secret call from Lee Urness, who was heading the Cunanan investigation. "Don't tell your wife, don't tell anyone," Urness cautioned Rivard. "We got him on the hook." Apparently Urness, in Minneapolis, was completely in the dark about the leak.

"I was just pulling into a food store and talking on the phone to Lee

Urness," says Rivard. "I walk into the store and there it is. It was on the news." In fact, the Lexus phone had been activated Friday afternoon at 2:28 P.M., 2:30 P.M., and 2:33 P.M. in southern New Jersey, in the vicinity of the small township of Pennsville, not far from where five major thoroughfares—including two interstate highways—converge.

Clearly, Andrew was also listening. This unfortunate leak, followed by the police confirmation of it, was probably the most serious blunder of the entire manhunt. Its consequences, swift and direct, were later revealed in the inspection of the Lexus. "The phone antenna was completely torn out, so he obviously heard it right away and tried to dismantle the cell phone," says Rivard. The antenna was later found broken in two on the floor of the back seat. The actual power box for the phone, which allowed the signals to continue to be emitted, was in the Lexus trunk; Andrew never found it. The FBI later found holes in the lining of the Lexus roof, indicating that Andrew had frantically searched for a way to disconnect the phone. "Apparently he couldn't," says former FBI Deputy Director William Esposito. "That's when he decided to ditch the car."

The authorities would never knowingly get so close to Andrew again. "Everyone who was working on [the case] was outraged," Chisago County Sheriff Randall Schwegman told the Minneapolis *Star Tribune.* "I still believe that precipitated Reese's death," says Sergeant Steve Wagner. "He had to get rid of the car then." Andrew pulled into an information booth located at the Delaware Memorial Bridge, a major crossing between Delaware and New Jersey, thirty miles south of Philadelphia. He asked for material on historical sites and was provided with a packet that included information on Fort Mott State Park. The park is adjacent to Finn's Point National Cemetery, in Pennsville, New Jersey, a remote Civil War burial ground that would soon have its tranquillity shattered.

23

Whispers

LEE MIGLIN'S ELABORATE FUNERAL earlier that Friday was covered locally as a major news event. Had the funeral not been steeped in sensationalism and senseless tragedy, it would not have attracted such attention; the ordinary citizen in Chicago had probably never heard of Lee Miglin before his death. But the media turnout was so heavy that even reporters from *People* magazine and *Time* were among the crowd behind a barrier across the street from Holy Name Cathedral.

The family had requested that the new archbishop of the Chicago diocese, Francis George, Cardinal Bernadin's successor, say the funeral mass, but he had been installed only that week and was not available. Even so, more than a thousand mourners filled the historic church, which was filled with orchids, dozens of them sent over from the annual spring floral display at Marshall Field, the department store where Marilyn Miglin had once modeled. At the service Marilyn Miglin said of the deceased, "Let's never forget the spirit and the light of the great guy I call my friend."

In those first days after the killing, it took a tremendous effort for close friends to steel themselves against the rising tide of rumors. Nevertheless, many were startled by the family's composure. "Duke Miglin never shed a tear," claims Paul Beitler, "the whole time, not one tear for his father." Sugar Rautbord counters, "They're so private, people could mistake it—that elegant privacy for coldness. It's not. They're very dignified." Within two weeks of her husband's death, Marilyn Miglin went back on the Home Shopping Network to sell cosmetics. She said she felt safe in the studio. The ladies who watched her sent in thousands of cards, but privately she was shattered.

"She turned this into an event, to watch her like a soap opera," says Paul Beitler. "She told me, 'I have to go back on. I have a responsibility to these people; I have to do it. They all want to know, to see me.' I was incredulous."

The family had had a private memorial mass the previous Tuesday, shortly after giving a press conference. Paul Beitler, who had acted as the family spokesperson, considered Lee the father he had never had. Intense and emotional, Beitler had fought in Vietnam, and he compared the crime scene and the aftermath of Lee's murder to being in combat. "I saw people's lives destroyed in front of me."

Beitler's "hot" demeanor on television and in person could be disarming, even off-putting. He was criticized for gravitating toward the camera too often, even though, according to one observer, he looked like a "deer caught in the headlights." But his loyalty to Lee Miglin was never questioned. Beitler couldn't believe it when Marilyn did not invite him to the family visitation before the cremation. "I was not able to pay my last respects." It was the beginning of a painful rift, which he says he does not understand to this day. But a close business associate of Marilyn's explains that when a person is so devastated, logic does not always prevail. "She was angry that he's alive and Lee's dead."

At first, Beitler was the avenger, out to quash any doubts about Lee Miglin's heterosexual identity and to cut off press and police speculation about any sort of relationship between Andrew and Lee. "Our plan was to shut it down, go into seclusion, not answer questions," says Beitler. "Geraldo's producer called. Tom Brokaw called through his producer the night they found Lee's car." In fact, Beitler learned from the media that Miglin's car had been found. But as events unfolded, Beitler was by turns hurt, then confused, then tortured. He struggled to understand what had really happened to Lee. In the process, his relationship with Marilyn Miglin broke down completely. "Marilyn treated me very badly. She is not my friend."

Problems began right after the announcement of Andrew's connection to the Jeep. The Miglin family dug in—denying that Andrew had ever met Lee or Duke Miglin. At the same time, some of the Chicago police apparently felt that they were not getting a whole lot of cooperation from the family, even though the Miglins, thanks to Beitler's longtime links to the mayor, were being treated with kid gloves. "My recollection," says Paul Scrimshaw, the Miami Beach lead detective on the Versace case, "is the Chicago cops saying that the Miglins were not cooperating at all." But Paul Beitler says that Miglin-Beitler was cooperative. The company conducted an exhaustive search of their phone records and correspondence and uncovered nothing tying Lee Miglin to Andrew Cunanan.

The new buzzword was "random," as in "This was a random crime." Beitler insisted day after day, "We can say with absolute certainty neither Duke nor anyone in the family knew Cunanan." Over and over, Mark Jarasek, the spokesman for Miglin-Beitler, denied on behalf of the family any connection between Lee or Duke and Andrew. "Duke Miglin never heard of Cunanan, has never met him, doesn't know him." Or, "Beitler and Miglin's family have vehemently stressed that neither Miglin nor his son, Duke, who lives in the Los Angeles area, ever knew Cunanan, Trail, or Madson."

Privately, Mark Jarasek asked Duke to tell him the truth. At the house, he recalls, after Madson's Jeep had been discovered, "I took him into a private room. I sat him down and I asked him point-blank, because a TV reporter had come to me with the question and I blew the reporter off. We had both of Cunanan's names. I said, 'Do you know this person? Have you ever heard the name? Duke, it doesn't matter to me, and I'm not going to say anything, but I've got to know. This is serious.' I told him it was serious for him, for the company, for the family. It was odd—the way he said no reminded me so much of his dad. It was uncanny. The way he said no was exactly the way Lee would say no."

Jarasek reiterated how important his answers were. "I made it very clear to him, because I'm the person defending the whole thing. If something turned up later, it would be a hell of a lot worse than being truthful at this point." Once again, the answer from Duke was "No, I am not gay or bi. I have not had a sexual experience with a man." Jarasek says he "absolutely believed" him. Paul Beitler, however, never felt he could pin Duke down or get him to confide in him. "Duke would never answer my questions. He was always very evasive with me. He would never sit down and talk with me. I never got five minutes of Duke's time. Marilyn became withdrawn and snippy."

Nevertheless, to the press Beitler painted a picture of Andrew swinging in off the expressway, going up busy Rush Street, parking the Jeep around the block from where Lee Miglin lived on Scott Street, then happening onto the alley where Miglin's garage was, and by chance encountering Lee. Then in a split second, Andrew presumably decided to murder him brutally with the available tools at hand.

Police knew that that was not necessarily the case. Betsy Brazis, the Miglins' tenant, had told them that she had seen the red Jeep with Minnesota plates parked in front of her house on East Division Friday afternoon. She saw it again shortly before midnight on Friday night, after it had been moved a few spaces up the street. Then she saw it on Saturday, parked on Astor Street where it was found on Tuesday about midnight. Two other neighbors also said they had seen the Jeep parked on Astor Street on Saturday—and perhaps had even seen the killer himself.

At 7:30 that Saturday morning, David Arnold was out walking his dog when he came upon a man sleeping on the passenger side of the Jeep, with his baseball cap pulled down. Arnold and the dog stopped about a foot away. "We just walked up, took a look at him, and entertained waking him up," Arnold says. "He looked like somebody who had had a rough night in the bar area. He looked unshaven. When I saw a photo of [Cunanan] on the front page of the *Chicago Tribune,* I said, 'Definitely, that's the guy.' " Arnold adds that, since the neighborhood is "immediately adjacent to the lake and a significant bar area, it's not unknown to see nonresident cars."

Jill Dryer was house-sitting that weekend for her neighbors, who live at the southwest corner of Scott and Astor—right where the Jeep was parked. On Saturday afternoon between one and three she was carrying several loads of clothes from her apartment on Astor, a half block away, to wash in her neighbors' laundry. She too spotted the red Jeep with Minnesota plates. The windows were down. "There were two guys in the car—I only saw the one with his arm down on the ledge, eating a sandwich. The only reason he caught my eye is that he reminded me of this creepy person I know, and it gave me the chills." She passed the Jeep several times, but she doesn't remember what the other passenger looked like, other than that he was a white male. "We get a lot of people who camp out there—they park and go to the beach and use it as a stop. I thought, Oh, God, losers. They're using the Jeep for a hotel, and they've parked for the day in front of my house."

Dryer is a waitress, and as she was walking home at 2 A.M., shortly after the murder, she was stopped by two policemen who asked her if she had seen anyone in a red Jeep. She told them yes, related her observation, and got an odd reaction. "They didn't want to hear anything about it—two people in a Jeep," she declares. "I was so furious. I said, 'Do me a favor, check it out. There might be someone else dead in an alley.' I described the guy before they showed me any photos. Then later they showed me photos and I picked [Cunanan] out. He was on the passenger side." Dryer says she does not understand why the cops kept cutting her off, saying, "'OK, ma'am, we've got enough.' I certainly don't want to accuse people of not doing their jobs. Maybe they thought because I couldn't describe what the other one looked like, they dismissed me."

In the unreleased Chicago police report, Detectives Lawrence Aikin and Charles Gorski omit any mention of Dryer seeing two people in the Jeep. They mention only that she believed the photo they showed her of Andrew "was the same person she observed sitting in the passenger side of the Jeep Cherokee which was parked on the southwest corner of Scott and Astor at about 2:00 P.M. on 3 May 1997."

For potential trial purposes, according to prosecutor Nancy Donahoe, the police and the state's attorney appear to favor another eyewitness's account, which is at odds with those of Arnold and Dryer. Rather, it bolsters the random-killing theory the Miglin family is pushing. Lisa Douglas says that she and her mother were leaving Bloomingdale's, at Michigan and Walton, on Saturday afternoon about 5:00 or 5:15, when they were approached by a clean-shaven, dark-haired man. He looked like a "well-to-do foreign student," and he asked in an indeterminate accent, "Where's the Gold Coast?" He was carrying a laminated map and booklet. According to the police report, Douglas told him this *was* the Gold Coast. He just looked at her, so she pointed north, told him to go up Michigan a few blocks and turn left. She had to wait there for about ten minutes, and he continued to lean against the building. Douglas identified the man as Andrew Cunanan.

But if he was clean-shaven, where did the whiskers in the Miglins' bathroom sink come from? Moreover, Andrew knew the Gold Coast and Chicago. He used to chat about the city to Stella Kalamaras, the owner of California Cuisine in Hillcrest, whose husband had once owned a restaurant in Chicago. Furthermore, there was one person who was not telling the police what she knew.

Betsy Brazis, a tanned and fit brunette, did tell detectives that she had seen the Jeep parked in front of her house Friday night and on Astor Street on Saturday. However, Brazis says, "I saw other things that I never divulged to the police, because they did not ask me direct questions. I didn't respond out of respect for the Miglins."

Brazis had recently been divorced from a surgeon, her daughter was about to graduate from college, and she had moved into the $6,000-a-month duplex attached to the Byers' only two weeks before. Just before moving in, she had cut her hand and had to have more than forty stitches. It was not a tranquil period. "I was trying to deal with my own life. I wasn't getting involved in the Miglin case. I don't need to be on TV. I don't need that kind of notoriety." And she certainly did not want to cause any trouble for the Miglins, who, after all, were her landlords. Later, however, she did cross swords with Marilyn Miglin over her lease and she wrote her a letter telling her that out of respect she had not mentioned everything she knew about the murder. She never got a reply.

On Friday night, May 2, Betsy Brazis was home alone with her dog, Mimi, a long-haired Chihuahua. A girlfriend from North Dakota would be flying in for a visit the next day, so Brazis was getting Mimi accustomed to her new home and taking her out frequently. Like the Byers, Brazis had a view of the Miglins' kitchen and garden, and she too was accustomed to seeing her landlords, Lee and Marilyn, having dinner in front of their big picture window in semidarkness.

Sometimes when Brazis was out in her graveled yard with the dog, she would run into Lee. They usually nodded and spoke a few words. Just after dusk Friday, Lee passed her in the alley but didn't say anything. "I know Lee saw me in the backyard. I thought it was a little strange he didn't say anything—not that he would," she recalls. "He was with a young man with dark features wearing a baseball hat. I couldn't see the faces. It had to be dark."

Several hours later, Brazis saw Lee Miglin and the younger man talking together in the kitchen, where many more lights were on than usual. She did not get a close enough look to be able to identify Andrew Cunanan. Only after seeing Andrew's picture "a zillion times on TV" did she think that he was the one with Miglin that Friday night, but she couldn't be positive. Throughout the tumultuous days following Lee Miglin's murder she kept her secret. "I wasn't going to go there. I didn't speak of these things. I told my daughter." Betsy Brazis is positive, however, that on Friday night Lee Miglin was not alone. On several occasions, other neighbors claim, they had also seen Lee in the alley with a young man, though apparently not the man Betsy saw that night.

Betsy Brazis had another eerie experience that weekend. At 3:30 Saturday afternoon she was out again with Mimi, and the dog kept sniffing and growling at the service door to the Miglins' garage, not far from where Lee Miglin's body was found. "She wouldn't leave the side door alone," Brazis recalls. "I said, 'Mimi, get away. There must be something dead.' "

But Brazis heard nothing, and she believes the main garage door was closed. "Lee didn't usually leave the garage door open. I never recall the garage door being open." She too remembers seeing the kitchen blinds drawn, as Stephen Byer did, which prompted her to think that the Miglins must be away. Early Sunday morning, however, she says, "the gate was wide open."

Like the Byers, Betsy Brazis's life was disrupted long after the murder. "It was the buzz, wherever I went, for weeks." Male reporters would stop her on the street, asking her where she got her hair done. "It was ridiculous—just to strike up a conversation." She says that the reporters asked a lot more questions than the police did. She kept remembering oddities—how a few weeks before the murder she had run into the Miglins in the alley, walking toward their garage. Marilyn rarely said hello, but on this occasion she stopped to explain that they were on their way to a photo shoot. "That's why Lee's wearing makeup," Marilyn said. "I don't want you to think he always wears makeup."

Betsy Brazis was not entirely surprised to find that Lee's murderer was gay. She had long heard the rumors about Lee that by now were sweeping the Gold Coast, although they had never been substantiated. "Don't take this to mean Cunanan or Miglin never met," says Bob Long, media spokesman of the Chicago FBI, "but we never were able to come up with any information that Cunanan and Miglin knew each other, and we were really looking for it." Brazis, a nurse, had lost her brother to AIDS, and for years she had led an AIDS-education support group. Before she ever moved in across the alley, she says, she had heard Lee Miglin's name discussed in the group she was leading. "He was a well-known bisexual man. Because of his money and power, nobody would speak of it in social circles. I've done AIDS work for fifteen years—it was just known," Brazis says. "Lee's name would come up occasionally as a gay 'straight' man."

In Las Vegas, where he was now working, Ron Williams, whom Andrew used to take to dinner in Hillcrest, heard about Andrew's suspected connection to Lee Miglin's murder and was amazed to learn that Lee had a son named Duke. He remembered Andrew saying in 1994 that he could be backed in business whenever he wanted by a rich older Chicago investor that he named Duke. "I was shocked," Williams says. But Ron Williams was never contacted by law enforcement, so he too kept his recollection to himself.

In New York, Jack Shaffer, a Park Avenue real-estate financier who had worked with Miglin-Beitler on previous deals, and his partner, John Bralower, were also stunned to hear that Lee Miglin had been murdered and that Andrew Cunanan was the prime suspect. A few years back, they had run into the Miglins in the Los Angeles airport. Their flight to New York had been delayed for a couple of hours, and they were in United Airlines' Red Carpet Lounge. The Miglins were on their way to Hawaii for a family Christmas, and were waiting for Duke to join them. He finally arrived with a friend, who made a great impression. "If you saw him, you were meeting a very unusual individual," says Shaffer. He didn't remember the friend's name, but as soon as he and Bralower saw Andrew Cunanan's picture, they concurred immediately: That was the friend of Duke's whom they had met at the L.A. airport. "I know that that's the guy whose picture's been all over." But memories can be hazy and Duke, of course, has always maintained he never met Andrew and it has never been proven he has. "I just know that's what I know," says Jack Shaffer. Still, he admits that he and his partner could not swear to it in court.

24

Reese

If the corpse of a dead man is found lying in the open on the land which the Lord, your God, is giving you to occupy, and it is not known who killed him, your elders and judges shall go out and measure the distances to the cities that are in the neighborhood of the corpse.

—Deuteronomy 21:1–2
the passage by an index card found in the Bible on William Reese's desk

ANDREW WAS IN FULL PANIC. He knew from all the news reports that he was being stalked electronically. The all-points bulletin on the Lexus was being broadcast on KYW, the area's powerful, 50,000-watt, number-one radio station four times an hour. A witness had already seen him ripping the antenna from the Lexus's rear-window mount. He cut the wire to the phone receiver. He slashed the head liner at the rear window and removed the antenna wire. But because of the power box in the trunk that he could not find, the phone was still activated whenever he turned on the ignition. It would only be a matter of time before the police caught up with the Lexus, its trunk filled with the bloody residue of Lee Miglin's murder.

He crossed the Delaware Memorial Bridge. If he continued south on I-95, he would be heading toward Washington, D.C., in broad daylight on one of the most traveled routes of the eastern seaboard. Instead, he doubled back to an information center, where he nonchalantly inquired about points of interest in the immediate area.

Fort Mott State Park, he was told, was off Route 49, the first exit after the bridge in New Jersey. Employees at the fort, erected in anticipation of the Spanish-American War, are convinced that Andrew had already been there the previous Monday, the day he was also buying Levi's in New York. Carrie McIntosh, who worked in the welcome center, later said that a man she recognized as Andrew had told her that he was "touring from California." He had declined to sign the guest register. Even though it was a cool day, he was wearing khaki shorts, and maintenance worker Larry Creamer claims to have spotted him lying down on a small hillside. When other tourists passed near, he would cover his face with a calendar of events he had been given by McIntosh. The other tourists, according to McIntosh, had noticed his Lexus with the Illinois plates in the sparsely filled parking lot. "See, they come from all over," one woman remarked to her husband. "Even from the Land of Lincoln."

Adjacent to the state park is Finn's Point National Cemetery, a Civil War burial ground where casualties of both the Confederate and Union sides, but mostly Confederates, were buried in trenches. Later, graves for German POWs of World War II were also dug there. The site could not be more remote. In order to reach the cemetery, you have to go down a long, narrow dirt road through deep woods. Tall trees eventually give way to reedy marshland as you near the Delaware River. The road ends at the cemetery parking lot. An iron gate separates the parking area from the cemetery entrance and a curving driveway going up to the caretaker's stone house on the left and the barn and garage on the right. Most visitors are southern families looking for ancestors. Another road, which runs along the river behind the caretaker's house, is a favorite teenage spot for drinking and making out, but that's about as rowdy as it ever gets at Finn's Point. According to Park Ranger David Kirschbaum, "It's a very lonely place."

Bill Reese, who was forty-five, loved the peace and isolation. He had been the caretaker for twenty-two years and he took pride in his work; this land of the dead was totally alive and beautiful to him—he considered himself a caretaker of history, and he had been commended by the National Cemetery System for "superior service and dedication." He knew all about the two thousand Confederate and Union soldiers buried beneath the lawns he kept so carefully, as well as the battles they had fought. For twenty years he had taken part in reenactments of the Civil

War, even appearing in Turner Broadcasting's TV movie *Gettysburg.*
Bill Reese, in full black beard, cut a dashing figure. He had gone to
Albany, New York, to research the uniform of the 14th Brooklyn
company: bright red trousers with leather leggings, which he made
himself, and a navy blue jacket, modeled on the uniform of a French
chasseur. He also made his backpack, haversack, and gunpowder car-
tridges. "Bill was a handy man, very meticulous," says his best friend,
Bob Shaw. "Everything he did, even if it took a little longer, he'd do it
right."

Reese had grown up in South Jersey, in Vineland, a town of sixty
thousand. He was the oldest of four children. David Reese, his father,
was an electrician, and he and his wife, Nancy, were religious people
who belonged to an independent Christian church; their firstborn son
was equally devout. "He was never in trouble his whole life," says his
father. "He was a clean-living kid who didn't drink or smoke." Bill, his
parents, and his sister Fay rode dirt bikes and motorcycles together. Bill
loved the outdoors and animals and worked during high school in the
local SPCA. Schoolwork was never much of a challenge—he especially
loved history—and after graduating from Vineland High, Bill became
an electrician like his father. "Sometimes you just follow in your father's
footsteps instead of what you lean toward," says his sister Fay.

When Bill Reese was twenty-two, he and Bob Shaw and a few others
began researching the 14th Brooklyn, New York, State Militia, which
had fought at Bull Run, Antietam, and Gettysburg. Bill's great-grand-
father had fought at Gettysburg, on the Union side. They became so
involved that in 1978 they incorporated themselves as a historical society: the Society for the Historical Preservation of the 14th Brooklyn,
New York, State Militia Infantry. Bill was a "founding father" and first
sergeant. Today the 14th Brooklyn has 250 members and has been
reactivated as a branch of the U.S. Army National Guard, which troops
the colors in full regalia at Guard reunions.

In the course of pursuing his historical passion, Bill Reese became
friends with the supervisor of the cemetery and found that the supervisor needed an assistant. So Bill went to Finn's Point. When his mentor
retired, Bill stayed on alone. "Bill liked the idea of going to the same

place every day," says Shaw, "and then going home." He had found his
calling. "He loved his job, if you can love a job," says Craig Platania,
Bill's brother-in-law. "He enjoyed being by himself out in the fresh
air." Bill would even get in his truck and chase litterbugs. Once he
caught up with them, he'd wave the litter at them and yell, "How
would you like it if someone threw garbage on your front lawn?"

In 1978, Bill Reese married Rebecca Gunderman, the librarian in a
local elementary school. Their son, Troy, is thirteen. Not long after they
were married, they bought two acres of land and built a small house in
Upper Deerfield, about thirty miles from the cemetery. Bill and Rebecca liked to make things together: puppets, birdhouses, and wooden
ornaments to sell at craft fairs. Bill would hitch a trailer to his 1995 red
Chevy pickup and the family would go camping.

On Friday afternoon, around 2:30 P.M., just when Andrew was being
driven mad by the Lexus phone signal, Rebecca Reese telephoned her
husband to make sure that they were still going out that night. He said
yes. Being a man of habit, he always drove to the main road to pick up
the mail around 3:30. By 4:00 he was usually ready to go home. He
would lower the flag, lock the caretaker's house and the gate, and leave.

Bill's former boss had had two German shepherd watchdogs at
Finn's Point, but he took them with him when he retired. Even though
people said the stone house was haunted, Bill never had any fear. He
loved every inch of the property. If a visitor stopped by, Bill would not
hesitate to ask him in to show him the map of the grounds on a wall
inside the house. Generally, though, says Ranger Kirschbaum, the site
was so removed that "nobody knew he worked down there."

The phone in the Lexus was last activated at 3:33 P.M. that Friday.
Andrew may have seen Bill Reese picking up the mail in his truck and
followed him back to the cemetery. Or he may have arrived there on his
own, a complete fluke for such an out-of-the-way site. Certainly it
would not have taken Andrew long to deduce that the two of them were
alone. The red pickup he wanted was parked close to the house. Andrew
parked the Lexus next to the barn. A Christian radio station was playing
in Bill's office and his Bible was on his desk when Andrew entered
through the side door.

Rebecca Reese could not understand why her husband was not home by 5:30. He was always so punctual. She worried that the pickup had broken down, or that he had lost his balance and taken a fall. He had recently been diagnosed with the beginning stages of muscular dystrophy, so she was especially concerned. She took Troy with her and drove to the cemetery, on the lookout all the way. Meanwhile, someone in the park had seen Bill's red pickup racing out at approximately 6:10 P.M. It looked odd—Bill Reese would never drive that way.

Rebecca was alarmed to find the iron gate to the cemetery wide open. She and Troy went through the house calling for Bill and got no answer. "Bill, Bill, are you in here?" In his office, she picked up the phone and called her parents, who lived about an hour and forty-five minutes away. "Something's not right," Rebecca said. "Bill's not here, his truck is gone, and there is a dark green Lexus parked next to the garage." Her father told her, "Hang up the phone and get out of there now. Call the police from the road and wait for them there."

What Rebecca's father didn't tell her was that he had heard a news report saying that an armed and dangerous murderer driving a green Lexus was at large in the vicinity.

The nearest township was tiny Pennsville, about five miles away. Rebecca called the police and waited for them on the main road. When the Pennsville police arrived, they had her and Troy wait on the road outside the cemetery parking lot. They went inside the house but found nothing. Bill Reese was nowhere to be seen outside either. Then they noticed that the basement door was locked from both the inside and the outside. They broke the inside lock, went down the stairs from the kitchen, and found Bill Reese at the bottom, slumped against the wall. At first glance, the police thought it could be either murder or suicide, but since there was no weapon in sight, they quickly concluded it was murder. "This was just a cold-blooded, heartless killing," says New Jersey State Police Detective Sergeant First Class Tom Cannavo, who was in charge of the crime-scene investigation. "He had him kneel down and shot him in the back of the head."

Within minutes of running a license check on the Lexus, the Pennsville police had their answer: Andrew Phillip Cunanan had killed for the fourth time in twelve days. They called for backup. "To think the guy way back in there could be a victim is really hard to believe," says Chief Salem County Investigator Ted Vengenock. "It's very unusual." Lieutenant Patrick McCaffery of the Pennsville police adds. "No one even heard the shot. That tells you how remote it was." When the police phoned the county prosecutor to notify him of a major crime, McCaffery says, he was told that the prosecutors had been notified that Cunanan was in the area. Vengenock says they only heard it on the news. Tragically, nobody had notified the Pennsville police. Why? "That's a good question," McCaffery says. Later, law enforcement blamed the media for Bill Reese's death, but from the first leak onward there was enough blame to go around.

"Can I come stay at your house tonight?" Rebecca Reese's voice was very calm as she spoke to Linda Shaw, Bob's wife, about 11 P.M.

"Sure, you can, Rebecca." Linda thought maybe Bill and Rebecca had had an argument.

"Can I stay for three or four months?"

"OK. What's the matter, Rebecca?"

"Bill's dead."

"Was he in an accident?"

"He's been shot. He was shot because a guy wanted his truck."

Rebecca Reese had been taken to the New Jersey state police barracks in Belmar. She was frightened, and the police did not want her to stay in her house alone. When Linda Shaw arrived, the Reeses' minister was already there. He told Linda to keep an eye on Rebecca—she might be suicidal. Linda took Rebecca and Troy home with her; Rebecca's parents, who lived in Whiting, New Jersey, also came to spend the night. People took turns staying up, to make sure nothing happened.

At 3 A.M. the Lexus was hauled away on a flatbed truck to be processed. Inside Bill Reese's office, investigators found his Bible open to the passage in Deuteronomy talking about unknown murderers. "It was very strange and very eerie," says investigator Tom Cannavo. "It was similar to what had just happened."

At 4:30 A.M. the Shaws' phone rang. Rebecca answered. It was the state police calling to say that the victim definitely was Bill and that the investigators had completed their work at the crime scene. They wanted to know if Bill had any credit cards. Only then did Rebecca break down and cry. "Until then she wanted to believe that it was someone else—it couldn't be Bill," says Linda Shaw.

Meanwhile, panic was sweeping the surrounding area, mostly brought on, chief investigator Ted Vengenock says, by the sight of fifteen or twenty satellite TV vans racing through the sparsely popu-lated townships to the crime scene. "A number of residents were very concerned that evening," he says. Police heard a rumor that a woman was so scared when she heard a noise in her bedroom that she dove through the screen on her bedroom window and ran up the street in her nightgown and slippers. A cop reportedly smashed up his car chasing the wrong red pickup.

No one knew whether Andrew was still in the area or not, although police sought to calm fears by stating they did not think he would linger. "We were pretty sure that after that night he was gone," says McCaffery. "If that truck wasn't found within a certain number of hours, he was out of here." Privately law-enforcement officials felt that a bright red pickup truck with a license tag that was being broadcast throughout several states within minutes of the finding of Reese's body ought to be snagged in a flash. "It's a very visible pickup truck that should have been easily seen," says Vengenock. But apparently Andrew took off straight down I-95 with impunity.

The satellite trucks came equipped with searchlights that shone so brightly over the little stone house and cemetery that at times the scene resembled a night game of the World Series. Local reporters were doing stand-ups. Fox TV was shooting last-minute footage for *America's Most Wanted,* which would air the following night. The usually empty park-ing lot was full. The next morning, when Bob Shaw went to get Re-becca's car, the area looked like a space station with all the satellite dishes pointing straight up and "people walking up and down the road with clipboards." Shaw said he and Rebecca's father "tried to look like police, because if they had any idea who we were, we would have been besieged."

Pennsville police set up a command center for the various law-enforcement agencies involved behind the station house and tried to figure out where Andrew might be going next. "I thought he would have headed for New York," McCaffery says. But no one really had a clue. "Once he left the cemetery," says FBI Deputy Assistant Director Roger Wheeler, "he could be anywhere in the country or literally anywhere in the world, because he did have a passport. We really didn't have specific, exact sightings to put him anywhere at a certain time."

The FBI began an exhaustive search for Reese's pickup at every major airport between South Jersey and Boston, plus "hotel parking lots, shopping center parking lots, airport parking lots, bus terminals—any place where someone might park a car and leave it for a period of time," Wheeler says. "Literally, a logical fugitive lead in this type of case would be, Go check the parking lots." That weekend was also the climax of Gay Pride Week in Philadelphia. The FBI was on the scene and contacted various gay organizations in the area to be on the lookout for Andrew and to distribute fliers with his photo—all to no avail.

The autopsy took place on Saturday. The medical examiner concluded that William Reese had died from a single "gunshot wound of head with perforations of skull, brain, and face, aspiration of blood and massive bleeding." Reese's brother-in-law, Craig Platania, had been called in the night before to identify the body officially. On Saturday, the state police arranged things so that while they were briefing reporters at the crime scene Rebecca was being questioned by the police in another location. That way she was spared exposure to the media. The FBI quickly concluded that William Reese was not connected to Andrew Cunanan in any way but rather was the victim of a crime of opportunity.

In the ensuing days, the TV reporters wouldn't leave Rebecca Reese alone. She had to call police to get their vans off her neighbor's property. For several weeks they would intermittently pull up to her house at night without warning and shine their lights in her windows, "giving the effect of being in a Nazi concentration camp," said one observer. When that happened, Rebecca would have to get Troy and find cover in her own house, when all she wanted was the privacy to grieve alone.

Apparently Andrew had worn gloves to murder Lee Miglin, whose wallet and credit cards he left in the Lexus glove compartment along with a blank bank check on the account of Lee and Marilyn Miglin. A "creative thinking" cassette belonging to Lee Miglin was still on the tape deck. Inside a clear plastic garbage bag found in the trunk was the black suede Ferragamo shoe that matched the one on Lee Miglin's corpse, as well as the bloody screwdriver Andrew had punctured him with and an assortment of gloves: white cotton gloves with black rubber dots on them that matched the gag in Lee Miglin's mouth, with a piece of masking tape stuck to one; heavily blood-stained brown suede gloves; and blue cloth gloves with leather-tipped fingers, also stained with blood. There were also bloody paper towels, a Banana Republic shopping bag, and a Pratesi shopping bag with Marilyn Miglin's name on it.

In the pocket on the door on the driver's side, Andrew had left two photos, one of a group of his friends from Hillcrest at a party, the other of Robbins Thompson in bathing trunks standing next to his truck. Robbins had given the photo to Andrew, and it was the only print. Although the police had no way of knowing immediately who these people were, it was almost as if Andrew were dropping bread crumbs, Hansel and Gretel–style, to lead investigators on. Why else would he not get rid of all this incriminating evidence during the long drive between Chicago and the East Coast? He appeared to want credit for his crimes.

Employees of a truck stop about a mile down on the Delaware side of the bridge are convinced that Andrew stopped there for a pack of cigarettes after he killed Reese, although he normally smoked only occasional cigars. His image was captured on video but never positively identified. People were terrified, figuring that if Cunanan could find Reese in that isolated cemetery, he could find anyone anywhere. "That was a closed area none of us had ever even been to, and this man was floating around out here and the cops couldn't find him," says Andrea Pickman, who manages the Popeye's Chicken at the truck stop. "It seems like he was escaping through the loopholes and killing innocent people. He was like a madman. I was scared to death."

While Andrew was barreling down I-95, law enforcement was paralyzed at the Reese crime scene, seeking to resolve a jurisdictional question. Who had the authority? Did Reese's murder belong to the FBI or to the locals? "Originally it was thought to be a Pennsville police job," says Tom Cannavo of the New Jersey state police. "Then Salem County called us after I got there, and they advised me it was federal property, and I said, 'Whoa. Call the FBI.'" Everything stopped until the FBI arrived, about 11 P.M. Had Andrew left any special clues behind to reveal his whereabouts, they likely would have sat there.

When FBI Special Agent Paul Murray of Philadelphia arrived, he told Cannavo and the state police to go ahead and process. "He said, 'Look, it's a homicide; we don't do it much—you do it all the time. You handle it for us.'"

Finn's Point National Cemetery is on federal ground, so ordinarily the FBI would be in charge of any major crime committed on such a "government reservation." But someone remembered an old treaty that seemed to give local law enforcement jurisdiction over Finn's Point. It took several days to research before the FBI prevailed, taking the case out of the hands of the Salem County prosecutor and delivering it to the U.S. attorney in Newark. The park was closed for five days while the cemetery was combed for evidence. A .40 caliber shell casing found near Reese's body matched the shell casing found at the scene of David Madson's murder, and the bullet jackets revealed that both had been fired from the same weapon. The FBI later awarded the Pennsville police department special letters of commendation for their cooperation.

A second ticklish issue arose: Who was going to get the Lexus? Chicago wanted the Lexus back undisturbed, just as New Jersey had found it. New Jersey wanted to keep it. "We stepped in to say we wanted the Lexus and the contents for our own case. They said, 'We are still determining circumstances,'" explains Illinois State's Attorney Nancy Donahoe. "The overlap in the evidence was something you had to think carefully about." She adds, "There were so many crossovers in the crime scene that lots of discussion was going on over who was going to get what."

"We were not going to jeopardize our case," Cannavo declares. "We turned over the screwdriver and anything we had free to go. Anything tied to our case, we asked that they wait until our case was over." According to a federal official, "Chicago needed Miglin's car, but we had it and were processing it for our case. We are not about to release it without processing all this evidence." In fact, the Lexus contained such a cornucopia of evidence tying Andrew to both Miglin's and Reese's murders that it took five days to process it. "The FBI and us were working hand in hand," Cannavo says. "He left so much behind."

The quality of evidence was a matter of concern for Chicago, because Reese's murder occurred when the national FBI lab, which normally handled all DNA testing, was under fire for mishandling hundreds of cases. "Although they had always done superior work for us," says Donahoe, "the FBI lab was taking heat. We had to decide, Is it worth it or not to go with the FBI lab?" Again mindful of the O. J. Simpson case, Chicago wanted to make sure there were no screw-ups. They successfully fought having any testing done immediately to the small amount of blood found on the carpet of the Lexus trunk.

New Jersey argued that transporting the car a thousand miles to Chicago could easily cause damage and might disturb evidence. Fingerprints could be lost, for example. Chicago conceded that the argument made sense. Nobody had gotten any fingerprints so far. "Everybody wants something big," Donahoe explains. "They want a fingerprint or blood from the scene of the crime." Chicago had to settle for the screwdriver.

The U.S. attorney's office in Newark, which usually has to play second fiddle to Manhattan, was determined to go to trial first if Andrew was apprehended. "Whoever goes first ultimately wins," says Donahoe, and New Jersey was sticking to the old adage that possession is nine tenths of the law. Andrew was no longer an ordinary domestic slayer. With Lee Miglin's murder, he had become "a very dangerous, violent, psychotic killer," says John Walsh of *America's Most Wanted,* and Reese's murder proved that he was so bloodthirsty he would kill for nothing more than a vehicle.

For the ambitious state and U.S. attorneys involved in the case, Andrew Cunanan was rapidly shaping up as a career maker or breaker, and they were all eager to prove their mettle. "What a case to lose!" Donahoe remarks. Chicago was invited to send a crew to help process the car, but New Jersey was holding on to the Lexus.

25

The Lid

In Chicago, the media spread out all over town, trying to learn whether or not Lee Miglin was gay and whether Duke knew Andrew, but they came up short. "Everybody wants this guy to have been gay. I could never dig up a single thing," says Achy Obejas, a lesbian reporter on the *Chicago Tribune*. "Everybody was happy to confirm it," she adds, but in fact nobody had proof about Lee Miglin. At one point Miglin-Beitler was called by the owner of a gay bar. "Mark Jarasek and I were here late," says Paul Beitler. "Mark got the call that there was a TV crew from a local channel in the gay district in Chicago, going to bars there saying, 'We'll pay a reward for anyone who can come forward and verify if Lee was gay or having a gay relationship.' The bar owner said, 'What the hell is going on? They're cooking evidence like crazy.' " But the majority of reporters were far more careful. "There was terror around the story," says Obejas, with regard to creating negative gay images and inciting the family. Since Duke was not the victim, any reporting about him was ultimately dropped.

"How hard did I look to find out if Lee Miglin was gay? I looked incredibly hard," says Andrew Martin of the *Chicago Tribune*. "The problem was, the standards for saying it in the paper were so high it was almost a wasted enterprise. I'm not sure if I had [identified] four former lovers they would have run it." On the other hand, Martin says, "If

Miglin had been an active gay man in Chicago gay circles, I'm convinced that we would have known. If he was a regular at these places, I think we would have found out." Still, "to smear the reputation of a dead prominent Chicagoan, I don't know what I would have had to have. I would have had to have a hell of a lot. Things came out later, when my paper had lost interest. I thought they lost interest too soon." Obejas adds, "There were stones that were unturned."

For the Miglin camp, as well as for the Chicago police, the flow of information became the enemy, out of their control. Reportedly at Beitler's urging, the mayor told the police superintendent to clam up. Beitler himself called Superintendent Rodriguez, who stopped returning his phone calls. Beitler was incensed that an unnamed detective had speculated in the press that the Miglin murder might not be random. "That's when I picked up the phone and I called Rodriguez and said, 'Listen, unless you have hard evidence, get your detectives under control. We don't need them speculating in the newspapers about this murder. We could turn around and do the same thing in reverse to the Chicago police department—start speculating we have another O.J. problem going on here.' "

"It had all the earmarks of becoming the story it became," says Rodriguez, explaining police reticence. "Miglin was well known in the business and corporate world—he was not well known to people on the street, but in these kinds of cases the lid is put on because we have various jurisdictions involved. We don't know if what an individual says here adversely affects another case. The media is like a dry sponge. It would take anything."

In fact, the Chicago police were deeply embarrassed that a leak of theirs had inadvertently set off the chain of events that led to the murder of Bill Reese. And they were further upset by the information revealed in the Chisago warrant. The Miglin family was particularly rattled by a story that ran in the Minneapolis *Star Tribune* on the Sunday after Reese's death. Bruce Kerschner, the owner of Obelisk, a Hillcrest bookstore frequented by Andrew and located next door to California Cuisine, was quoted as saying that Andrew knew Duke Miglin very well. "He talked about him all the time. They spent a lot of time together."

Beitler wanted to sue immediately, but in the end Marilyn and Duke did not follow through on their threat to sue the paper for libel. Mark Jarasek says simply that "Marilyn wanted to get on with her life." At any rate, it didn't take long for Kerschner to back down. He called a press conference the next day to say that he had been misquoted, and disavowed having any knowledge that Andrew and Duke knew each other. "The reporter asked me if I had heard all the rumors, and when I said I did, he used me," Kerschner says. The newspaper printed Kerschner's denial, but it claims that the reporter quoted him accurately. "The FBI did hear that Andrew had mentioned Duke Miglin," says Minneapolis Police Sergeant Wagner. He thinks that Kerschner's recantation to the press seemed strained. "I'm sure Miglin's attorneys read him the riot act."

Another disturbing oddity was the flash of a picture of Andrew's modest bedroom in his San Diego apartment as part of the *America's Most Wanted* story on television. Among the books and magazines piled up was a 1988 issue of *Architectural Digest,* which Andrew had obviously saved. In it was a story about Paul Beitler's restoration of his Richard Meier house. Again Beitler chalked it up to coincidence, but he was becoming less sure.

Then, to add insult to injury, the Washington, D.C., *Blade,* a gay newspaper, published a story with anonymous sources saying that Lee Miglin had been recognized in the Unicorn, a gay bathhouse in Chicago. Lou Chibbaro, the reporter, was promptly contacted by the Miglin family's attorney, who protested the story. "We run into this all the time when we deal with the murders of gay men," Chibbaro says. "People like to hush things up. The man who saw him in the bathhouse—he knew him only because Miglin was a fairly well-known person, and my source knew him enough to recognize him." One of these sources was later tracked down without Chibbaro's aid, a male hustler kept by an older man. He had a friend who claimed to have seen Miglin at the Unicorn, but the Unicorn's owner, Rick Stokes, says he does not comment on his membership.

In the course of its investigation, the FBI picked up several second- and third-hand reports from gays in various parts of the country who knew Andrew and who said they had heard that Lee Miglin was gay or involved in S&M. These sightings were duly noted in their records, but they were only hearsay. And although the police went looking for anyone who might know Andrew on North Halsted, the main gay thoroughfare in Chicago, it is not at all clear that they were also asking whether Lee Miglin was known there. "The police never looked for Miglin up there," says Cook County prosecutor Nancy Donahoe. "If it was done, I wasn't told about it." Donahoe concedes that the cops don't tell her everything they do, but adds that "I have no reason to believe they did" go out of their way to place Lee Miglin on North Halsted. Andrew yes, Donahoe says. "We look at phone records. We know he knew people there."

What was the value of finding out if Lee Miglin was gay anyway? For the Chicago police, who were hearing from the archbishop's office about this case, making Lee Miglin out to be gay could quite possibly spell career suicide. "Why irritate everybody who's important in the city?" asks Donahoe. "The detectives are real good guys. They were under a tremendous amount of pressure. The mayor's wife is friends with Marilyn Miglin. If we knew [Lee Miglin] was gay, where are we going to go with it at that point? If *Cunanan* had said, 'I had a relationship with him,' then we would have had to make a decision about how to handle it." As it stood, they kept the lid on.

On Monday it was the *Sun-Times*'s turn to ruffle feathers. The paper had found Andrew's mother living in public housing downstate in Eureka, Illinois. She had moved there to be close to her elder daughter, who lived in Peoria. In the paper MaryAnn Cunanan described her son as a "high-class male prostitute." She later disavowed ever saying those words, but they were widely disseminated, and they were precisely the same words she would use to describe Andrew to the FBI. Apparently the FBI had not attempted to interview MaryAnn—or perhaps didn't even know where she was—until the *Sun-Times* appeared. Later that day, however, a Chicago detective and FBI agent knocked on her door. She said that she had not seen Andrew in two and a half years but that by chance she had talked to him on the phone in April, when he was visiting his sister Gina in San Francisco. Interestingly, he had told his mother he was about to take a job with an architect.

MaryAnn said she had suspected Andrew was gay from the time he was seventeen, adding that he would "befriend wealthy gay men and begin relationships with them, which enabled him to be supported by them. Andrew lived a rich lifestyle from gifts from male companions."

In this highly charged atmosphere, stories began to appear asking, Who's in charge here? On the same day MaryAnn was being interviewed by the FBI, the Minneapolis *Star Tribune* ran a piece headlined Hunt for Suspect Lacks Strategy:

> *As Andrew Cunanan continues to evade authorities, it appears that there's no coordinated strategy among local law enforcement agencies to help catch the man suspected in a nationwide killing spree that began in Minneapolis.*
>
> *No single agency is assuming overall responsibility for processing information, directing the investigation or developing an approach for finding the 27-year-old San Diego man who has been wanted since the first of four victims was found April 29.*
>
> *And there is no national model for local investigators to draw upon for coordinating their individual efforts.*

Andrew was moving too fast, killing and then each time vacating the premises. The Cunanan command post run out of the Minnesota Fugitive Task Force had links to the FBI in ten cities, but the Bureau had no authority to investigate homicides unless they occurred, as Reese's had, on federal ground. The FBI did, however, plaster Andrew all over its "Crime Alerts" and "Fugitives" pages on the World Wide Web—he became the first criminal suspect to get such extensive Internet attention from the Bureau. The FBI also contacted the National Gay and Lesbian Anti-Violence Project for help in alerting their members to the menace Andrew threatened. The effort was extremely uneven, however. In New York and San Francisco, where gays are well organized politically, thousands of fliers with Andrew's picture went up in gay neighborhoods. The New York chapter posted a $10,000 reward for information leading to his capture. In his own hometown of San Diego, however, where there hadn't been much contact between gays and the FBI, the effort was much weaker. In Miami it was almost nil.

The Minneapolis *Star Tribune* article quoted a criminologist who said, "We have a centralized law enforcement reporting system for stolen cars, and nothing for human beings. When you have this kind of thing, nothing is set up for it."

That was painfully obvious in the backstage drama going on with the Minneapolis police, the county attorney's office, and the Chicago police. In the beginning according to Sergeant Tichich, "I couldn't even get the county attorney to return my phone calls" regarding the murder of Jeff Trail. And the county attorney was not only keeping the case but also assigning another attorney, named Gail Baez, to it. Baez wanted to go to Chicago with a delegation of Minneapolis police to view Madson's Jeep and all the potential evidence for the homicide case. Comparing notes might be a helpful enterprise. Tichich thought it would be a waste of money and time and said so.

He argued that in the absence of evidence to rule out Madson, Cunanan could try to pin the murder on him. Not necessarily, says Baez. "We had people who could testify to the nature of the relationships." In the end Baez won out, but the Minneapolis delegation did not receive a warm welcome in Chicago. By then the official Chicago police spokesman was refusing even to confirm that the victim murdered in the garage was Lee Miglin! "Chicago preferred not to deal with anybody, basically," says Minneapolis Police Lieutenant Dale Barsness.

When the Minnesotans arrived in Chicago, Pete Jackson says, they got a condescending lecture from Commander Joe Griffin "about the Chicago Police Department and the release of information." They were then taken to see the Jeep at the Illinois state police crime lab, but could pick up little in the way of new knowledge or evidence. Chicago had had such a hard time getting any fingerprints of Andrew's, that they were now searching for his dental records in order to compare them with the bites taken out of the ham found in Lee Miglin's den. The need for dental records was part of the reason law enforcement finally got a search warrant to go through Andrew's Hillcrest apartment on May 9, the day of Reese's murder.

Although Chisago Sheriff Schwegman participated in the search of Andrew's San Diego apartment—a search in part to facilitate the Chicago investigation—Chisago felt shut out by the big city. When Chisago officials asked Chicago for help, says Rivard, they were told

" 'Sorry.' They would tell us little information and send nothing. The only report I had was an inventory of what was in the red Jeep; that's all I have, period. These guys were between a rock and a hard place. They said, 'We're really sorry, but we have this captain guy who's above us; we are under strict orders, blah blah blah.' "

"We shared our records with [Chisago] which turned out to haunt us," says Commander Griffin, speaking of the later decision made by Chisago to release all the paperwork it had on the Cunanan case. "They had no right to decide to do that. We weren't sharing? That's a lie! That's ridiculous! That's my statement on that."

Asked if it is his conclusion that the murder of Lee Miglin was a random killing, Joe Griffin pauses for at least ten seconds before answering, "I just told you, I don't care to talk about it."

After explaining that Chicago police did not find evidence of Lee Miglin being gay or knowing Andrew Cunanan, Chicago Superintendent Rodriguez concedes that he can't rule out the possibility of Lee Miglin being bisexual. "That could be," he says. "I could not say anything with certitude with regard to sexual preference."

A few days before Pete Jackson, Gail Baez, and Sergeant Gregory Gordon went to Chicago, Bob Tichich called Monique Salvetti in to make a formal statement. She hadn't seen him since she had identified Andrew's duffel bag a week and a half earlier. As she recalls, "Sergeant Wagner starts to go back to all the information I'd given previously, and then after about ten minutes he says, 'Oh, I should note it's Wednesday, May 14, 1900 hours. Present are—'

"I said, 'Wait a minute. Is this being taped? I didn't realize that.'

" 'Oh, have we started the formal interview?' Tichich asked. 'I didn't realize that either. Did you turn on the recorder?'

" 'No, I thought you did,' Wagner replied.

" 'No, I thought you turned on the recorder.' "

Salvetti sums up, "It's hidden mikes, everything."

Meanwhile, in Chisago, a new development threw the investigation of the first two murders way off course. Jean Rosen, the owner of the Full Moon Cafe, a funky beer-and-burgers bar about eight miles from the site where David Madson was killed at East Rush Lake, told a Minneapolis BCA agent that she was convinced Andrew and David, driving a red Jeep, had come into her place on Friday afternoon, May 2. They had ordered two California cheeseburger baskets, drunk two bottles of Grain Belt beer, and left about forty-five minutes later. Her friend Michelle, who tended bar at J.J.'s Bowl and Lounge, a bowling alley a few miles away, had been there that day and could confirm it.

"I made a comment to Jean," Michelle says, " 'I bet they're gay.' Just the way they carried themselves and looked at each other. What a waste. I thought the blonde was very good-looking." Although there was no evidence of recently eaten food or alcohol in David's stomach at the time of his autopsy, Jean Rosen's sighting bolstered the coroner's resolve that David had been murdered on Friday; Todd Rivard agreed, despite the discovery of the Chicago parking stub showing that Andrew had parked David's car there the Wednesday before Lee Miglin was killed, which Chisago authorities interpreted as evidence that Andrew and David had gone to Chicago together before driving back to East Rush Lake where David was killed. Nobody listened when Ralph Madson griped that David would never drink Grain Belt beer, and nobody seemed to pay attention to the fact that the clothes the women described David wearing did not match the jeans he was found in. Rivard maintains, "That lady at the Full Moon was very good. That was a good sighting."

In the meantime, San Diego police reopened the investigation into Lincoln Aston's murder to make sure they had the right man. They concluded that Andrew had had nothing to do with it. The *San Diego Union-Tribune* ran wire copy on the story in the metro section, even reporting that some of Andrew's friends in Hillcrest were going into hiding, but again didn't bother to file a story quoting local sources. One of the many unforeseen consequences of Andrew's rampage was its effect on his friends. A young bartender at Flicks, for example, got recognized by his father on *Hard Copy* in a group photo of Andrew's friends. The father, who did not know his son was gay, cut him off.

Robbins Thompson was ripped out of the closet when his heterosexual roommate saw Andrew's face on television as part of the "gay love triangle" murders and recognized him. "He was kind of blown away," Robbins says. The roommate asked him to move out. Then Robbins was dropped by his partner in a construction business to rehab houses. "My worst fears are realized," Robbins says his partner told him. "You're gay."

"It ruined my life. When my business partner left me, he basically cleaned out our accounts, took everything." Robbins says he had to declare bankruptcy and start over from scratch. He went to live in Mexico, where he worked different jobs on the *Titanic* set, unsure what to do next, since his credit was wrecked.

Robbins could not shake the story. He went into a construction supply house, and the man behind the counter recognized him as "the guy who came out." "I am pretty well known surfing," Robbins admits. "I go to the beach and people are looking at me, and I don't know what they're thinking. I don't know if they're thinking anything. It is just the fact that they know all this stuff about you, and you don't know about them." It has been even harder with straight friends, whom he has resisted talking to about what happened. "It's a fuzziness between you and them, because your friendship is not the same anymore."

Yet despite the havoc Andrew was wreaking, he still had a certain amount of support. A number of people he knew proved less than willing to cooperate with authorities. When Michael Williams, Jeff Trail's friend, attempted to get clear photos of Andrew for the police, he was turned down more than once. People who had supposedly been close friends of Jeff's wouldn't even attend the San Diego memorial service Williams organized for him, either out of fear "Andrew would show up and take everybody out," or fear of being outed themselves. "I called a lot of people in the navy. Some had very good careers," Williams recounts. " 'Would you mind getting up and saying a couple of words about Jeff?' A number of them said no." Those who braved going entered a back door guarded by police so as not to be seen by the press. Others flatly refused to believe that Andrew would murder anyone, even though they had also known Jeff and might have been expected to have some sympathy for him.

"Right after the New Jersey cemetery guy, an FBI agent asked me,

'Has he had any direct contact with you?' " recalls Dominick Andreacchio, Andrew's former frequent dinner companion. " 'Would you give him any money, and would you tell us?' And I was, like, 'I don't know. I can't answer that, because at this point it just seems like my friend is being framed.' "

Although the San Diego police department was cooperating with Minneapolis's requests, Hennepin County prosecutor Gail Baez wanted Tichich and two other detectives to go to San Diego to see what they could learn. Once again, her request precipitated a confrontation. Tichich thought she was meddling in his case just because it was receiving national publicity. "I think what really irritated her was that I said, 'Tell me why this case isn't fatally flawed. Tell me why it isn't. Based on the fact we have two sets of footprints in blood and the fact that Madson was dead and we didn't have a videotape. We just have two people present in that apartment and witnesses who say they are both, as far as they could see, moving about freely. One wasn't coercing or threatening the other one. Tell me, how are we ever going to make this case in the absence of clear motive or somebody who provides some really concrete information as to why this happened?' "

"I don't think any case is fatally flawed," counters Baez. "You never know what's going to turn up during the investigation. There's always the possibility someone will confess. There's always a possibility the person who did the crime could talk to someone else. There are many reasons you really shouldn't rule out any case."

Over Memorial Day weekend, three Minneapolis police detectives went to San Diego. They talked to Robbins, who invited them to Mexico, but Tichich, though he was impressed by Robbins's ability to surf, wouldn't cross the border without car insurance for Mexico. The Minneapolis cops were also scheduled to talk to Erik Greenman at Flicks, but they had to reschedule because Tichich didn't want to go inside. They talked to agents at the San Diego FBI, to Andrew's friends David Gallo and Ken Higgins, and to Jeff's close friend Jon Wainwright. Greenman showed them a picture of Liz Coté, whom Andrew had often represented as his ex-wife. The tiniest glimpse of a license plate on a white truck in the margin of the photo got the officers' undivided attention. Maybe it was Andrew's truck, they thought, but it turned out to be a dealer truck from Bud Coté. Their interviews didn't get them any closer to solving the case, "but we just learned a ton," says Tichich's boss, Dale Barsness. They also considered new theories.

According to Barsness, "He [Andrew] wanted a long term relationship with David Madson, but Madson doesn't really know him—he'll talk to Jeff Trail, and what will Trail say? He'll have nothing good to say about Cunanan—he's not very complimentary. Jeff Trail always said that Cunanan had a 'very dark side' to him. The point is this—it's a love story. We see it all the time with heterosexuals: If I can't have you, nobody will. So Andrew tells his roommate, Erik, 'I'm going on one more run to Minneapolis to win Madson back.' Then I think Andrew took Jeff Trail's gun and Jeff saw his gun was missing. He'd check for it. What would be the most valuable thing in the house? If you think he's shady, the last thing you want is somebody with your gun. So Jeff comes home and checks—his gun is gone!

"We're theorizing he's looking for his gun, he's going to be pissed off. He'll go directly over to David Madson's. He storms up so Andrew Cunanan can't take off with his gun. Jeff Trail confronted him about his gun. If Cunanan picks up the hammer, is it Madson who says, 'Get the fuck out of here'? I have never worked a case in twenty-nine years with so many unanswered questions."

Months after the killings, many of his questions remained unanswered. Barsness felt sure about one thing, however, concerning the Full Moon Cafe sighting that had helped determine David's time of death. "I don't believe it for a minute. I also don't believe the medical examiner's time of death for David Madson."

The case was closed, Madson's official time of death unchanged, when Barsness told me of his lingering doubts. But he didn't need to convince me of his position. The day before we spoke, I had discovered proof that the sighting was bogus.

26

Cross Purposes

THE SUNDAY AFTER Bill Reese's murder, I personally became aware of Andrew Cunanan for the first time. The New York *Daily News* had run an interesting story about a "fun-loving social butterfly" voted "Least Likely to Be Forgotten" in high school who was wanted in a series of murders. It was not until the fourth paragraph that the story mentioned that Cunanan had spent much of his adult life "dating and living with rich, older men." I immediately sensed that this was not an ordinary criminal; even his victims all appeared to be outstanding individuals. The story might be worth exploring for *Vanity Fair,* for which I was a special correspondent.

Within a week the editor gave me the go-ahead to begin reporting, and over the next few weeks I set out to learn as much as I could. By then each investigation had at least three law-enforcement entities on the case—not to mention the various prosecutorial offices in each state involved—although William Reese's murder brought a fundamental change in strategy. Local authorities in both Minnesota and Illinois had ceded the search for Cunanan to the FBI, figuring that he was never going to return to their jurisdictions. It didn't take long to figure out, however, that throughout the investigation unfortunate errors had already been committed that would continue to complicate the cases and would at times set the families of David Madson and Lee Miglin at cross purposes, if not at odds, with the authorities investigating their murders.

In Minnesota, for example, police had shifted their focus to concentrate on working out a motive so that their prosecutors could present the strongest possible case when Cunanan was caught. Although Andrew was still at large, the police were finished with David's loft as a crime scene. When the Madson family and Rich Bonnin went to the loft one day in late June to remove personal items, they discovered in the bathroom two dop kits that had been overlooked, one belonging to Andrew, the other to David. Andrew's may well have contained DNA evidence such as beard stubble to match the stubble found in Miglin's washbasin in Chicago. Even more important, in a pile of clothes near the bed was a pair of blood-splattered Levi's, size 36. David Madson wore size 32. By then every shred of evidence was crucial, because the police had not been able to match any of the fingerprints taken from the various crime scenes and vehicles.

"The pants were overlooked," admits Tichich. "And the tag on the luggage was embarrassing also. But the shaving kit is something that I don't think we should take criticism for, because how do you tell whose shaving kit it is?" I ask why they didn't test both. "You can't take everything in the apartment and bring it back here," Tichich declares. "You just can't do that."

To his credit, Tichich tried to work with a renowned fiber expert to see if there was any way to find "fiber transfer," that is, show if any fiber from the bloody Banana Republic T-shirt found in the plastic bag in David's loft was also on the blood-splattered jeans. Since the Levi's were size 36, and David was size 32, says Tichich, "that's pretty good evidence that it was Cunanan who was wearing both garments with blood splatter on them. But even then the question becomes, Could Cunanan have been standing in close enough that he could have gotten blood splatter on him by watching *Madson* bludgeon this guy to death? So even that, though it sounded more promising, fell short of proving anything conclusively, really. So my point stands: What do we need? We need a video camera."

This lack of incontrovertible proof was infuriating to the Madsons, who knew that David was incapable of murder. They set out on a campaign to clear David's name and to repudiate what they considered the rush to judgment of the police, which they believed had colored the media coverage of the case. The family claims that they made up to a hundred unanswered telephone calls to the Chisago police, trying to get them to do tests that might clarify the time of David's death and in the coming months I would find myself a factor in their effort, learning through my reporting of procedures what they could use to help them in their quest.

At my suggestion they asked if the Chisago medical examiner, Dr. Lindsey Thomas, had done the test for vitreous humor—the eyeball fluid measuring potassium—which can be used as an indicator of time of death. She hadn't—and once the doctor complied with their request to do so, the test results showed that the potassium levels in David's fluid were high, which suggested that he had been dead longer than was first estimated. The vitreous-humor results boosted the Madsons' confidence, but a much surer test would be to measure the age of the blowfly larvae found in David's mouth at the time his body was discovered. Their development is temperature dependent, so comparing their age with climatic conditions at the lake would give a fairly accurate estimation of time of death. By now, months had passed since David's death, and trying to have that test done would become an arduous tug of war between the Madsons and Chisago County. The county did not want to spend the money on a closed case, particularly if it meant admitting that their officials had been wrong. Even the Madsons' pleas to allow them to pay for the test went unanswered.

Later, on my first visit to the Full Moon Cafe, I found another flaw in the argument that David had lived for days after Jeff Trail's murder. Jean Rosen had been interviewed by both the police and the media numerous times by the time she told me her story. She also told me where to find Michelle, the confirming witness who had also been there that day at the Full Moon Cafe. Rosen remembered some details that didn't correspond with other evidence, such as Andrew's having slicked-back dark hair (Andrew's hair was shaved at that point), and both Andrew and David's wearing Dockers or khakis (David, we know, was wearing jeans at his death). But the most significant revelation came from Michelle, who recalled after a little prodding that she had written a check to Jean Rosen for thirty dollars on the day she saw the two men she thought were Andrew and David enter the Full Moon. I asked her to go home and look at the date on the canceled check. When I called her to verify the date, she told me the check was written Sunday, April 27, the day Jeff Trail was murdered, not Friday, May 2, the official time of David Madson's death. Neither the Minnesota BCA nor the Chisago police nor anyone in the media had bothered to question her about that.

The coroner's estimate was falling apart, but it died hard. According to Captain Stephen Strehlow, the officer in charge of the special investigations division and Tichich and Wagner's boss, the Full Moon sighting "set up a chain of circumstances that weren't valid, and we were trying to make them valid. It just throws you way off." Therefore the charges, Strehlow says, "were never publicly disproven, and because of that other things happened. If you're the coroner, for instance, and you're asked to come up with time of death, and then you hear, unofficially or officially, that it looks like they were alive on this day [Friday] for sure—if you could call it either way, you go the way you think you have some support." It would be over a year before the Madsons saw the official record change and their son exonerated.

The Chicago police didn't think Andrew was coming back there either. They focused on trying to obtain matching fingerprints and on getting the Lexus back. Most of all, by the time I got involved, they wanted to keep the lid on the case. Later, as in Minnesota, I was able to learn things that challenged the police's position, though their course had been set and never wavered. "The powers that be protect their own here," Sugar Rautbord warned me. "Woe to them that mess with the powers that be."

Doubts remained about the possibility of an association between the Miglin father and son and Andrew Cunanan. To help Duke's image, Sugar had hoped to stage an impromptu walk down the street by Duke

Miglin and a girlfriend that could be captured by the press. A model the gentlemanly Duke had dated in Los Angeles had come to Chicago to visit. But the idea was nixed as being too contrived. Although the two had gone out for a year, they had never been intimate.

Lee Miglin remained the most perplexing of all of Cunanan's victims. Certainly Duke Miglin, who had reportedly been in San Diego the day before his father was murdered, was someone Andrew would have liked to brag about knowing. He was Andrew's type—rich, blond, handsome—and he drove a fast car and flew airplanes. But what about his father? It certainly would be easier all around if the police were never to find out.

Paul Beitler is convinced that Lee would never have known Andrew Cunanan or questioned his son about his friendships. "Lee and Marilyn were not people who would jump into their son's life enough to ask, 'Are you having a relationship with a girl?' But you know, Lee never walked around either and said, 'Here's a picture of my son. Isn't he good-looking? With this girl?' " Beitler, however, can't understand why a very wealthy, attractive young man would live on the beach with a male roommate. "One, he didn't need it for the money. And two, it certainly doesn't help your heterosexual advantage." Beitler feels sure that Lee did not lead a double life. "Lee was not gay. I can tell you he was effeminate, but he was not gay." In fact, Beitler says, "Lee used to run around and make gay jokes here in the office all the time—clumsy, stupid jokes. He'd tell a joke that was bashing a gay."

Beitler was distraught for months after Lee's murder. He couldn't sleep at night for thinking about what therapists he had contacted said: "You can't believe this is a random event." Yet the family had a great stake in protecting its reputation, and they had a lot of help in doing it. Marilyn Miglin cherished and publicized the call she had gotten shortly after Lee's murder from Michael Jordan's mother, who had endured widespread doubt about the official position that her own husband's murder was motivated simply by car theft. "My husband was killed by a random murderer too," she told Marilyn. In Chicago, with the exception of the Virgin Mary, what mother had more clout? It's quite understandable that Marilyn Miglin would cling to her beliefs and make them known in the face of such a shocking tragedy.

Professionals who study the psyches of serial killers had grave doubts that Lee Miglin's killing was random. "Totally unnecessary overkill" is the way William Hagmire, head of the Child Abduction and Serial Killer Unit of the FBI—the behavioral-science-and-profiling unit—describes the more than forty facial contusions, the slit throat, and the broken ribs that Andrew inflicted on Lee Miglin. "There was a tremendous amount of overkill. Those are the kinds of things you see sometimes in homosexual murders—this tremendous stabbing over and over. . . . If Miglin is a total stranger, then Miglin reminds him of somebody else that he had a tremendous amount of anger towards. Or maybe Miglin isn't a total stranger," Hagmire theorizes. "For somebody to spend that kind of time, to put that kind of effort into this, there's usually something much more personal there."

"With a city the size of Chicago, the chances of him just happening to go down that alley behind Miglin's town house and then seeing him in the garage—how remote is that?" asks special agent Steve Kives, the FBI agent in charge of Cunanan's case for the profiling unit. Kives speculates that there was "some type of prior knowledge somehow of Miglin. . . . The chances of Andrew just blowing into Chicago and finding Miglin are pretty damned remote." Kives adds, "There was an allegation also that maybe Andrew did know the son and had a liaison with him. It may only be an allegation. But if that were the case, he may have gone to Miglin's looking for the son."

Hagmire speculates that the brutality could have been triggered by "alcohol or drugs," or "maybe he just saw a particularly masochistic or sadistic movie," which could have been an immediate triggering event, as opposed to a longer, thought-out motive. "This could be like living out a fantasy from some movie or book that he's read. Ted Bundy used to do that with his victims. He'd dye their hair, he'd cut their hair different ways, he put different clothes on them, because he was reenacting covers of detective magazines."

The fact that Andrew repeatedly struck the faces of both Jeff Trail and Lee Miglin indicates to experts that the Miglin crime was also personal, not random. "Given the facial battery," says Hagmire, "usually there's more likelihood the person was known to him. Everybody has hands and feet, but what angers you most is the mouth. That's

where the venom comes from. Usually people who are angry with people, it's because of something they said, particularly if there was any
kind of passion or romance involved. They try to disfigure the face
because, 'This is the face that laughed at me. This is the mouth that
made me feel bad.' "

Chicago boasts one of the first members of a metropolitan police
force to have graduated in profiling from the FBI's Behavioral Science
Unit in Quantico, Virginia. Captain Tom Cronin, who has since been
promoted to Commander, head of the Forensics Services Division and in
charge of all Chicago crime scenes, did not work on the Miglin investigation, but he is considered the force's expert on serial killers. Months
after the murder, as we walk around the block on which the Miglins'
town house stands and make several forays into the alley to look at the
garage where Andrew murdered Lee Miglin, Cronin explains how a
profiler might assess the scene.

"We try to understand victimology—knowing about the victims
helps you learn about the killer," Cronin tells me. "How did the killer
get the victim into this vulnerable position? How does he not know Mr.
Miglin, working in his garage, is not carrying a .357 Magnum? When
killers target people, they target people they can overpower. This is *not*
Mr. Stranger Danger. If he doesn't know Lee Miglin, how does he know
he doesn't carry a gun in his garage? Look at this neighborhood—iron
fences, hedges, all put up to keep people out. You don't see too many
people who live here walking around. At night you can hear a pin drop
here. Two blocks away, it's crazy."

What struck Cronin first was the considerable distance of Miglin's
garage from his house. In fact, the garage really belongs to the Byers'
duplex. It is located diagonally across the alley, about thirty yards from
the Miglins' backyard. There are three parking spaces on an apron just
outside the Miglins' iron gate, which would seem to be the logical place
for their cars to be parked. "How does one know I park my car in that
garage if I live right behind a place with three parking spaces? I'm a
mad serial killer and I find this garage open. Now how do I know he
lives diagonally across the alley? I'm about to kill you. You're gonna
die, and you give all the information?"

Cronin says that the way Miglin was killed combined with the fact that Andrew then felt comfortable at the scene "suggests more than a casual knowledge of the household. Do you get that kind of intimate knowledge when you are torturing someone? Does it suggest prior knowledge? It certainly makes a reasonable person believe the information he got was not so off the cuff."

"Maybe he had a gun pointing at him," I say, even though Lee Miglin was not killed with a gun. But how could Andrew have tied Miglin's ankles with a double knot while holding a gun on him? Did he have Miglin tie himself? Questions pile upon questions.

"One of the things that strikes me," says Cronin, "is that he purposely leaves a trail—connect the dots, find me. It's his ego saying, 'I don't want to not get credit.' Serial killers do that, usually in a much more subtle way. Keeping a picture of your friend in one car and leaving the Jeep around the corner, for example. He probably would have loved to put the Jeep closer, but that was the closest he could find a parking space, and they almost didn't get it—it took four tickets." Cronin concludes, "He wants credit—he's playing a game to see if someone can connect the dots, to see if someone can put this puzzle together. He can't be sure of the intelligence of those putting the puzzle together: 'Put the connection together, folks, when you find this rich guy dead in Chicago.'

"He thinks he has to be more obvious when he wants you to connect the dots. He says 'real-estate tycoon' to one guy, and 'going to Chicago on business' to another. He's thinking, if you put Chicago and rich real-estate tycoon together, and then I'll put my Jeep nearby, hopefully they'll connect to: Oh! It's got to be the same guy!'"

Hagmire agrees. "He didn't have to leave those vehicles behind. He could have burned them; he could have stashed them. He knew they were going to be found—he was just buying time." Hagmire explains that, even if a killer begins with a motivation of anger or jealousy, it often becomes something else. "As most serial murderers materialize and accelerate, the motivation changes from a personal crime to more of a power thing. In other words, 'I can play God with anyone I want and I want everyone to know that.'"

"These guys are very cunning predators," says Gregg McCrary, the former supervisory special agent of the Behavioral Science Unit. "They have the ability to cut a victim out of a herd—much like those nature documentaries you see on TV, where the tiger picks one zebra to hunt. They have this innate ability to sense who's vulnerable."

At the end of our walk, Cronin tells me, "I never believe in 'random' with a guy who is leading us all along, leading us with his behavior. He wants us to make a connection between Minneapolis, Chicago, New Jersey. Why would he do something random now?"

Officially, Andrew Cunanan's killing of Lee Miglin was declared random, and it stayed that way. "According to our investigation, we have no concrete evidence to indicate it was anything but a random crime," says now former Police Superintendent Matt Rodriguez. "We know Cunanan committed it—we are certain beyond a reasonable doubt. Yet we have no motive, no explanation for it based on our investigation."

As I began piecing together the story, the Miglin motive remained a closed issue to the Chicago police. "I don't have anything to discuss. I don't think it's necessary to discuss this case," says Commander Joe Griffin, who led the investigative unit. "We did as much as we could to find a motive. I'll leave it at that." Even a year later, Chicago detectives who worked on the Lee Miglin murder are reluctant to talk about the possibility of a prior association between Andrew Cunanan and Duke or Lee Miglin (or both). "Mrs. Daley showed up there with flowers at the time of the death. The governor's wife came. The outpouring of political people was overwhelming. She's a very political person, and she's got a lot of money," a ranking Chicago police officer tells me. "All you have to do is upset Mrs. Miglin and we could wind up garden fish out at Wolf Lake."

A very high city official puts it even more plainly: "The case is closed. There's nothing in the file. His employees loved him. The church loved him. His wife loved him. The case is closed."

The case has never been closed in my mind. When I first started crossing the country after the murder of William Reese, I began talking to many of the same people the FBI were also interviewing, as well as many people they missed. It didn't take long to find out about the association that would soon emerge as being tragically significant—an association that the FBI was reportedly told about as well.

For as his friends had already chronicled to me, Andrew had repeatedly mentioned knowing one of the most famous and successful openly gay celebrities in the world: Gianni Versace. After he assumed his new identity as a serial killer, that presumed association apparently weighed heavily on Andrew's mind.

PART

THREE

27

Escape

ANDREW SHOT DOWN I-95 in Bill Reese's stolen vehicle without being spotted. In Florence, South Carolina, he stopped to steal a license tag— SKW 263—in a Wal-Mart parking lot near an intersection of I-95 and South Carolina State Highway 20. The owner of the license plate never even reported it missing—he thought he had lost it. By May 11, Andrew had arrived undetected in Miami Beach, having covered 1,100 miles in two days. His first order of business was to find a place to stay.

The pink-and-red-trimmed Normandy Plaza Hotel, a mostly single-occupancy place on Collins Avenue and Sixty-ninth Street, was a few miles north of South Beach. With its framed pictures of Marilyn Monroe, who supposedly once stayed there, its stuffed alligator head, and its peeling linoleum floor, the Normandy Plaza was on the other side of the moon from the paradise-on-steroids that "SoBe" has become to gay travelers, but it did front on the ocean and was within walking distance of a gay nude beach. Andrew pulled up and parked Bill Reese's red pickup right in front of the hotel, and it stayed there for several weeks. He had found his escape.

On May 12, three magazine articles of particular interest to Andrew hit the newsstands. Both *Time* and *Newsweek* featured him as the suspect in four murders; *Time* called him a "gay socialite" and *Newsweek* an "upbeat party boy." The third article was in *Vanity Fair,* which Andrew read religiously every month. The June issue carried an article by Cathy Horyn that spotlighted Donatella Versace, the sister of Gianni, and showed off their voluptuous South Beach villa, Casa Casuarina. It included a vignette of a family picnic at the gay beach across the street from the mansion served by staff who had to wheel everything over in carts. For the Versaces, munching their sandwiches for a reporter to observe, the idea that such displays might make them a target probably didn't occur to them. They were merely feeding the ever ravenous publicity beast.

The beast, however, was a Frankenstein that had created not only them but also South Beach itself. South Beach has become the gay pleasure capital of the western world, where the crumbling Art Deco decay is juxtaposed with the gleaming facades of the terminally hip, meticulously restored hotels, some of which have no clocks, no chairs, or desks, nothing to remind visitors of mundane existence. The whole economy bobs on a sea of international drug money, and out on the street pensioners on walkers mix it up with nouveau riche Latinos, German and Russian Mafia, and crews of international fashion shoots. On Ocean Drive, where Gianni Versace's ostentatious villa is the only private residence, fifties Via Veneto meets Bourbon Street. Here, in season, which is November through April, hundreds of models flood the outdoor cafés and restaurants, and perfect physical specimens are as common as the tropical downpours that send the Speedos streaking off the beach. Certain gyms are regularly trolled for newcomers to audition for gay porn movies. Indeed, many poor, beautiful boys, north and south, no longer aspire to Hollywood, but choose to come to South Beach in hopes of being discovered and put into a homoerotic ad campaign.

With forbidden, seething Havana waiting to open up nearby, South Beach is a riot of loose luxe and easy sleazy, where dancing the night away amid hundreds of tanned, undulating bodies is a standard prelude to hot, anonymous sex. In the wee hours of a typical night at Warsaw, the first big gay nightclub in South Beach, the scene is dominated by buffed bodies that don't seem real; they look pumped up, airbrushed, and retouched. Woe to the also-rans in these places. "Versace used to go out to clubs all the time, in the early days," says Tom Austin, the acute chronicler of the SoBe scene, first for the *Miami Herald* and now for the glossy *Ocean Drive* magazine. "It was at another gay club, Paragon, that one night Versace spotted a go-go boy dressed as an angel and began to beckon to him. At first the go-go dancer said, 'Get away, old man.' Then Versace pointed to his chest and mouthed, 'Versace.' The boy hopped down from the stage."

Versace even used to employ a doorman from Warsaw, Jaime Cardona, to be his procurer. Cardona would take boys to the back door of Casa Casuarina to be auditioned. "Versace is central to the mythification of this place," says Professor Ralph Heyndels, a gay Belgian who teaches French history and literature at the University of Miami and lives in South Beach. "All these models look Latin. That was his preferred type—Cuban boys. South Beach is the Latin gay capital of the world. So many boys from all over South America are dreaming to get to the U.S.A. So they jump on a plane and all of a sudden one Versace or another will adopt them, and in that sense it is much more than Hollywood. For young boys it is much more alluring than Hollywood." Tom Austin says, "The whole point of South Beach is sex. Never has there been such an accumulation of sex and money, or sex for free, in history." One's priorities, says Heyndels, are based on desire. "Desire renders you more vulnerable. This country, the U.S., is always about organizing around your work. Here gay culture is driven by desire in the immediate sense." Dana Keith, former Versace fitting model, now concierge at Hotel Astor favored by the hip and Hollywood, explains the scene by saying, "What is the vibe of the room? What is the level of the drugs? How many cute guys are there? It's a pretty mixed-up sense of priorities."

"The cycle of the dominant South Beach culture is this: (a) go to the gym, (b) go to the beach and plan for the evening, (c) go to the clubs, and (d) trip on Ecstasy with friends who have successfully completed (a), (b), and (c), thereby establishing oneself in an untouchable circle of gods," *Ocean Drive* magazine editor Glenn Albin wrote in 1995 in *Out* magazine. "These circles are then broken into further categories of professionals, waiters, and those doing steroids—though on the dance floor,

Ecstasy clusters (groups of three to five shirtless men joined like an enzyme) often blur the distinctions the later it gets."

"We have the most intense night life in the country," says "Queen of the Night" Tara Solomon, who writes a column for the *Miami Herald.* "People take night life very seriously. People dress to go out. There are more genetically blessed people in South Beach than in all the world. That's never more apparent than in the clubs."

"We are the top. There is no place with better-looking people. You can be totally numbed to it," says Brian Antoni, a lawyer and novelist who grew up in the Bahamas and now divides his time between New York and South Beach. "It was Versace's 'look.' He loved the Cuban boys. I've been with people who are beautiful, and someone would come over and say, 'Versace is interested in you.' We all become like weird concierges, because we love the community, and everyone who comes down here thinks they deserve anything they want and you're supposed to get it for them. You get twisted on reflected fame or glory.

"The town is almost like a border town. It can supply almost anything you want; it's why it developed so fast. It's like the Wild West—anything goes. First there were the slums. Then the models came—they were the parsley that attracted the Eurotrash and the rich, dirty old men and then the celebrities. It's like a big Pac-Man game. Now little drag queens from the Midwest come with their little shoes and think they can be discovered here. It's an alternative to Beverly Hills and becoming a movie star."

For Andrew, Miami Beach was both familiar and sheltering. His dark looks were so commonplace that he could fit in anywhere, and the large, transient tourist population guaranteed anonymity. If one allowed for all the layers of splash and flash in Miami, there were remarkable similarities between South Beach and Hillcrest, in San Diego. Both places were warm and near the water, with miles of beaches to walk and hustle on. Both had large gay populations with comforting infrastructures; the two communities had been gentrified largely by gays. And both communities were easily covered on foot and full of bars, bookstores, porn supermarkets, restaurants, and newsstands—all the pausing points of Andrew's universe.

It hadn't always been this way. Built between 1923 and 1943,

Miami Beach's Deco district had fallen into disrepair and poverty by the 1970's and was inhabited mostly by elderly Jewish retirees. In the early eighties, thanks to Fidel Castro, the Mariel boat lift dumped thousands of Cubans in Miami Beach, a number of them criminals and undesirables. The dilapidated, boarded-up buildings rapidly became crack houses; crime soared 30 percent. But in 1984 the hit TV series *Miami Vice* began showcasing the pastel palette and striking backdrops of "the beach," as it is called by natives. The beachfront property was cheap, so a few developers and gays began to rehab the neighborhood. As *Miami Vice* broadcast images of hip, cool South Beach throughout Europe—where the series still plays today—German catalogs began featuring their models in the creamy golden light and exotic flora of favorite local haunts. Gloria Estefan and her husband, Emilio, contributed the hot, hot, hot beat of the Miami Sound Machine. By the mid-nineties, Sylvester Stallone and Madonna, not to mention Versace, had bought mansions in SoBe.

For Versace, South Beach was a strategically located relaxation zone, which he had captured in a 1993 coffee table book, *South Beach Stories*. In recent years Miami has become the northern capital of the Latin American market, and potential banking possibilities are attractive. Many feel that Versace gave the community a certain validation. "Versace infused a huge dose of glamour," says Tara Solomon. "Every new young city needs a mentor. Versace was that to us." Versace first came to South Beach on his way to vacation in Cuba during the Christmas holiday in 1991. By then many members of Euro fashion and café society were spending holidays in South Beach. The tiny Century Hotel threw a famous New Year's Eve party that attracted Paloma Picasso and Egon von Furstenberg. "In those days Claudia Schiffer Rollerbladed down Ocean Drive," says Louis Canales, a walking Rolodex known as Mr. South Beach. At that time Canales was organizing the party to reopen the Versace boutique in nearby Bal Harbour on December 28, 1991, and the party blew Gianni's mind. "It was *le tout le monde*," says Canales. "Andre Leon Tally, Thierry Mugler, Claudia Schiffer—anyone who was anybody in town was there. Gianni said, 'What's it all about? It's about South Beach!' "

One of the attractions for celebrities—apart from the wall-to-wall beauties of both sexes—was that no one there would tattle to the tabloids. "We have very short memories, so people under scrutiny all the time could come to South Beach and be themselves in a lush, happening environment," says Canales. "It's like being a bird-watcher and seeing a very, very rare bird and not scaring it away. Privacy was assured." Tom Austin recalls, "When I first started covering celebrities coming here they thought they were in Nicaragua." But then in January 1992, *New York* magazine ran an attention-getting cover that called South Beach "SoHo in the Sun." *"New York* magazine came out, and it brought every Tom, Dick, and Harry, hustler, charlatan," says Canales. "Grifters, hustlers, con artists had a deal. That started changing the scene." Previously, Canales says, "the social scene was always as flat as the topography. All of a sudden there were newcomers who wanted a pecking order: who's in, who's out. Gianni didn't create South Beach, but he understood South Beach, as he understood the value of publicity."

The two were a fabulous fit. To Gianni Versace, South Beach "was like his fashions come to life," says Tom Austin. "It's the only place you can sunbathe wearing Versace. Where else could you, except L.A.?"

"Gianni Versace—he knew to be in the right place at the right time," Louis Canales maintains. "People like Versace, Demi, Oprah, Madonna, Bruce Willis, they don't take risks; they go to a guaranteed place. They don't lend their names to places unless something is starting to happen. When it happens and you hitch your name to it—it's safe."

Yet many of the town's realized fantasies, from architecture to personal reinvention, hide a chilling reality: the number of people who have come to South Beach to die. Like Ratzo Rizzo in *Midnight Cowboy,* who bused himself down to Miami because he wanted to die in the sun, South Beach has become home to thousands of HIV-positive men. Many are living off of funds gained by leveraging their illness, having cashed in their insurance policies for less than their full value by selling them to investors who have gambled that the original policy holders will die soon. (As drugs to combat AIDS have improved, these "viatical" settlements, as they are called, have lost appeal to investors and become less common; one group of investors even ghoulishly filed a class action suit claiming companies underestimated life expectancy.)

Meanwhile, a number of those who are ill rarely mention their condition. They may have come to die, but with their illness held in check by new medications, plenty of time to sunbathe and work out in the gym, plus steroids to reverse or forestall the effects of wasting, they no longer even look that sick. Then, blending in to the tanned and muscled vacationers keeping the clubs busy, they perpetuate the SoBe spirit of reckless joie de vivre.

The party never stops. After dancing at Warsaw on Fridays and Salvation on Saturdays comes the Sunday Tea Dance at Amnesia, where hundreds of Speedo-clad men form in conga lines while barrels of iridescent foam are poured onto the dance floor; for the thirsty off to the side are tubs filled with iced bottled water, also the preferred drink of the Ecstasy clusters. Once the foam reaches waist level, the scene becomes group grope in the suds of a giant bubble bath. Then Mondays it's Fat Black Pussycat party at Liquid with "gender illusionist" Kitty Meow. On Tuesdays there's Twist, where you can sip Sex on the Beach. Wednesdays are Amateur Strip Night at Warsaw, Thursdays are free choice, etc. November brings the hautest of all the circuit parties, the White Party, an AIDS benefit, where many pay scant attention to behavior that can lead to contracting the disease. But who would spoil the party? The gay tourist industry is worth many, many millions annually to the economy of South Beach, and Miami, says gay columnist Eugene Patron, "has always been a city of escape."

Versace's residence, the Casa Casuarina (named after the only tree on the property) at 1116 Ocean Drive, not only saved the oceanfront from becoming another Bourbon Street, but also stood as a testament to another form of gay abandon. In 1992 Versace bought the old Amsterdam Palace, a run-down apartment building that had once been a grand Mediterranean villa. It had been built in 1930 to resemble the house in the Dominican Republic of Christopher Columbus's son, Diego, for the grandson of the treasurer of Standard Oil, Alden Freeman. Versace paid $2.9 million for the property, which came with its own copper-domed observatory, and then scandalized the historic preservationists the following year by paying $3.7 million for the decrepit Revere Hotel next door and leveling it to build a patio and pool. However, the natives were impressed enough with their rich new neighbor that Versace managed to win over one of the leaders of the historic-preservation movement who helped him run interference at city hall. After Versace spent more than a million for restoration, and another princely sum on furnishings, the fabulous Casa Casuarina emerged—a 20,000-square-foot, sixteen-bedroom paean to pagan excess which has been variously called "a flagrantly visible Xanadu," "a high-camp tropical-fever dream," and "a palazzo in drag" decorated in "gay baroque."

Versace preserved the busts of Christopher Columbus, Pocahontas, Confucius, and Mussolini found in the courtyard; covered every available inch with Byzantine mosaics, Moorish tiles, Versace fabrics, Medusa heads (his logo), Picassos, and Dufys; and threw in hand-painted ceilings and a few murals. The effect is rather like the Sultan of Brunei meeting Louis XIV, if they both were drag queens stranded in Sicily.

In his ceaseless pursuit of celebrity and commerce, Gianni Versace made his embarrassment-of-riches lifestyle his greatest marketing tool, a braiding of living and selling. The family, the palatial houses, the artwork, the parties, the famous friends such as Elton John and Sting who came to sit frontside at his high-voltage shows, where he blasted their music and stacked his runway with supermodels guaranteed to attract the press—all were fodder for his branding. In fact, the multi-talented Versace, impresario as well as designer, shamelessly manipulated the media and gained a reputation for fusing fashion with a rock 'n' roll sensibility, making it more immediate but somehow rougher. "Now you talk about Versace you copy my style," rapped the late "gangsta" Tupac Shakur.

Versace freely admitted that his clothes were inspired by antiquity and sadomasochism, and that the woman who inspired him most was the streetwalker. "I don't know how many people who believe that story have actually been to southern Italy and seen the whores," British fashion historian Colin McDowell said in an interview, "but they're no more magnificent or exciting than their sad sisters anywhere else." Despite his *nostalgie de la boue,* Gianni Versace worshiped wealth and fame and art and coveted status as much as Andrew Cunanan did. His label, launched in 1978, metamorphosed into a global empire that sold not only expensive and flashy clothes that offered security to the up-from-the-street nouveau riche (epitomized by actress Elizabeth Berkley's, Las Vegas lap dancer, bragging in the camp classic *Showgirls* that she was wearing a "Versayce") but also three hundred other products ranging from jeans to books to baby fragrances.

After awhile, the garish blend of Versace high life and sales appeared to spew out automatically, like a personal twenty-four-hour news service, or a never-ending video fashion reel with a familiar cast of characters: his steely younger sister, Donatella, creative director of the company, the alter-ego muse with the platinum shank of hair out discoing night after night; her American husband, Paul Beck, in charge of Versace advertising and rumored to have once been Gianni's lover (an allegation denied by the Versaces in *Vanity Fair*), at home with their young children, Allegra and Daniel; their brother, Santo, the company's CEO, a former accountant who hovered in the background and whose 1997 conviction for bribing tax officials was overturned on appeal; Versace's attractive and long-standing companion, Antonio D'Amico; the dressmaker mother and father who sold small kitchen appliances in interviews that gilded the designer's humble childhood in Reggio di Calabria, at the very tip of the Italian boot. His takeoff at age twenty-five in Milan led, in quick succession, to the flamboyant shows that melded rock and fashion, the nonstop acquisition of antiquities and priceless Etruscan art, the over-the-top residences, and the exploitation of key relationships for mutual benefit. "By the time of his death," wrote Holly Brubach of Versace in the *New York Times,* "he was more famous for the company he kept than for the clothes he designed."

The model Janice Dickinson, former girlfriend of Sylvester Stallone, described in a British TV documentary how Versace courted the actor. "When I was at Stallone's house, Versace sent out cases of china and sent over rooms of cushions and fabrics for the furniture, and trunkloads of clothes and wardrobe. I mean thousands and thousands of dollars' worth of clothes for Sylvester—he courted Sly like you read about." Stallone subsequently posed with supermodel Claudia Schiffer, on the cover of a German magazine to launch Versace housewares. The two were nude except for Versace plates covering their private parts. "For reciprocity's sake," Dickinson continued, "Sly did pose naked for him with Claudia Schiffer in one ad, so I suppose Sly's daily fee for taking his clothes off would be trunkloads of clothes and just pantries full of china. I mean, he courted him big-time."

In a move widely noted in the fashion industry, in Europe, where he could get away with it, Versace provided and paid for top photographers to shoot pictures of him, his sister, and his clothes for magazine stories—editorial coverage given in exchange for ad pages. Somehow, the reasoning went, if he was seen on a glossy's pages hanging out with Elton or Sting, designing for Elizabeth Hurley the famous black dress held together with safety pins, or making over Courtney Love's image and upgrading her from the dregs of cheesiness, other aspiring nouveaus around the world would also snatch up anything with the name Versace on it.

"The average Joe walking down the street didn't recognize the Gianni Versace the fashion crowd knew," says Louis Canales. "The power of Versace was in his advertising money—the amount he spent guaranteed him editorial coverage and at the same time, to expand it, he'd multiply it by having Elton John or Sting around, so that at the same time the press was covering Versace, these stars are getting publicity and press they wouldn't be getting otherwise. At the same time [they're helping] open up new markets for buying his clothes. Latin America and the Far East are filled with spanking-new money. The Arab emirates are supposed to love his stuff. Like any fashion corporation, the lion's share of the profits comes from fragrances and housewares. Versace needed the publicity so people felt they could afford the sunglasses." Not one to miss an opportunity, Versace painted "Miami" on silk shirts and sold them for $1,200; his T-shirts sold for $200. His appetite for acquisition, like his appetite for publicity, appeared insatiable. He spent like a pasha, and sometimes he apparently overreached. At the time of his death, the Italian government was investigating how Versace had acquired some of his priceless collection of Etruscan art and ancient statues; if they were deemed part of the archaeological or cultural patrimony of Italy, the state maintained, they would belong in a museum.

Shortly before his death, Versace was further embarrassed when his greatest celebrity conquest, Princess Diana, abruptly pulled out of a charity benefit of Elton John's that was to serve as the launch for Versace's latest book, *Rock and Royalty*. Without any evident irony, Versace had cheekily posed himself and his siblings opposite a Snowdon portrait of Princess Diana and her two sons, as if to suggest that they were on a par and equal. "The ultimate impression left by the book," wrote Andrea Lee in the *New Yorker,* "is the opposite of the stylish, irreverent romp that is intended: it conveys a diehard infatuation with rank and power and a tremendous yearning for status that was, it seems, a motivating factor in Versace's success."

That success was built on clothes that sought to turn upside down conventional notions of status and good taste. "[Versace] legitimized vulgarity," the fashion critic Holly Brubach wrote. "The brazen colors and the baroque prints, the hodgepodge of motifs appropriated from antiquity, all smacked of 'new money,' and he reveled in them, flaunted them, threw them in the face of those who preached understatement. Until Versace came along, new money aspired to the conditions of old money; he reversed the flow."

To someone as consumed with a similar heated yearning as Andrew Cunanan, such a life would be enraging. The level of vulgarity would be an affront to his own narcissistic grandiosity; he would take umbrage at the forms of Versace's ostentatious materialism.

What's more, they were both southern Italians; Versace was Calabrese, Andrew was half Sicilian. They both came from port cities and deeply Catholic environments. They both started out at roughly the same economic place, although Versace did not have the privileges of a Bishop's education. Yet here was Versace with a family he was proud of, from whom he never had to hide his gayness; a loving, longtime partner; and the riches of the world at his feet, including palazzos with views, which could be filled at will with beautiful boys. Except for the boys, Versace's life sounded a lot like the life Andrew had wished for at age thirteen when he wrote down his definition of success in his application to Bishop's. It was as if Versace had discovered the buried gold bullion that Andrew's father was dreaming of excavating.

Hiding in his seedy hotel room, eating take-out, and venturing forth only after dark, Andrew would have had plenty of time to fume. From following Versace and reading about his opulent lifestyle in South Beach, Andrew knew that given the right day, he could probably reach out and touch him. In the *Vanity Fair* article about life at Casa Casuarina, one of the headlines read, "The Versace lifestyle is almost mind boggling in its grasp of the consumption ethic. The message: absolute freedom." But everywhere Andrew turned, he was trapped.

28

Underbelly

"Andrew was a hustler. I knew that from the moment I saw him. He was on the take. I set him up. He was very, very generous." Ronnie is a sky-blue-eyed, forty-three-year-old Normandy Plaza resident with long, stringy blond hair, usually barefoot, who is gay, HIV positive, and living on disability. He saw Andrew almost daily while Andrew was hiding out in Miami Beach. Ronnie is outgoing and knows the street life around the hotel well. In 1997 he was sharing his room with a lesbian and generally stayed outside while she slept. He couldn't help but notice the red truck with the South Carolina license plate parked out in front day after day; he'd first see it when he'd be sipping his tea on the porch of the hotel at 5 or 5:30 A.M. He often saw Andrew too. "This guy comes out every day in his baseball cap and sunglasses, at all hours. I would always speak: 'Hey, how are you?' He finally came up and said, 'Where can I get some rock [crack cocaine]?'

" 'C'mon. I'll show you.' "

When Andrew arrived, he gave Miriam Hernandez, the manager, a French passport and a driver's license stating that he was Kurt Matthew DeMars, age twenty-seven. The real Kurt DeMars was a friend of Andrew's who lived near San Francisco and worked in advertising for *Out* magazine. Andrew had spent a lot of time with DeMars in April, in San Francisco, shortly before his killing spree began.

Miriam Hernandez is a kindly Cuban woman in her sixties who spends long hours behind the Normandy Plaza's front desk. On May 12, about 8 P.M., Andrew walked in wearing the same outfit he would wear for the next two months: shorts, a tank top, flip-flop sandals, and a backpack. He told Miriam he was a tourist, and paid her for room 116—$29.99 plus tax. Miriam is very sweet but also very firm about getting her room rent. The hotel accepts only cash. "The next morning I call at ten A.M. 'Good morning. How are you?' At ten-thirty he paid another day. At eight P.M., I saw him come out for something to eat. Next morning, same process. Andrew said, 'I'll pay you one day more.'" Again Andrew went out at night, but just for a few minutes, and returned carrying take-out. But the third night Andrew went out, Miriam didn't see him come back. On the fourth day he asked about weekly rates. "I've come here looking for an apartment," he told Miriam, "and I don't see anything I like."

She offered him a better room. He moved to a room on the second floor near Ronnie that cost $32.50 a night plus tax. He declined phone service. Then he started coming down at 8 or 8:30 every night to buy food. He would eat and go out at 10 or 10:30. "I never see him come back. We open the gate to the beach at nine P.M.," Miriam explains. "You can go out without coming round here. One night he asked me for the laundry facility. 'You have laundry powder?' I get the chills. I never seen such a beautiful smile. The teeth were perfect." In all Andrew's time there, Miriam had never seen him smile. She thought of him as "very lonesome. He never brought any company in or talked to another guest." Miriam, however, had no idea about Andrew's secret life with Ronnie.

Andrew regularly bought crack cocaine from Lyle, a dealer who sold him $10, $40, or $100 rocks (the last weighing a little over two grams). "He definitely liked his dope," Lyle says. "I had a couple of girls working for me who sold to him. I met him personally a dozen times. He'd come three or four times a week. He was low key, always looking over his shoulder." Andrew spent several hundred dollars a week on crack, but nobody asked any personal questions. "I was dealing with thirty or forty people per week," Lyle says. "He was just one of them. It didn't make any difference to me who he was. All I wanted was his money." For Lyle, "Andrew just blended into the scenery. He was a loner." Ronnie adds, "For people who are straight, the gay world is like any other. What the gay world is, is if you take care of me, I'll take care of you. In the gay community we are all a close-knit people. We don't reveal."

Andrew slipped into a netherworld of prostitutes, pimps, and drug dealers who frequented the neighborhood—the underbelly of the glittery world of Versace a few miles to the south. Lyle would walk past the red truck every day until Andrew transferred it on June 12 to the Thirteenth Street Municipal Parking garage a few blocks from Versace's villa. Meanwhile, Andrew would contact Lyle on his beeper and often send Ronnie to pick up the dope at the McDonald's two blocks from the hotel or at the nearby Denny's. Andrew smoked the dope in his room or in Ronnie's room. He also made a daily habit of going across the street to a liquor store and buying a pint of cheap McCormick vodka, which he sometimes downed all at once in front of the annoyed owner. When high, he'd disappear into the bathroom. "I had no idea what he was doing," says Ronnie, who maintains that they never had sex. Ronnie was merely Andrew's facilitator; he took umbrage whenever people at the hotel referred to him as Andrew's "bitch." "I'd go and cop and he'd give me twenty bucks, which is great. He never said anything as to why he was here. I copped for him. There's other people who went out and copped for him. I knew what he was doing. He was hiding. I didn't know it was for killing people.

"What happened was, I was sitting out back one day. He walks by and I'm looking at him, scoping him.

" 'You see something you like?' Andrew asks.

" 'Yeah,' I said. 'You've got a cute ass. I could make some money off you.'

" 'How could you make money?'

" 'You hustle?'

" 'I've done that before,' Andrew said.

"I asked him how big he was, and he told me. I brought him up here and he showed me. I picked up the phone. That's how it got started."

He told Ronnie his name was Andy, and Ronnie helped him become a hotel-back-gate man. "He never said where he was from. I set him up with a few old men, old rich guys around here. They would use my room. I got money that way." Ronnie claimed he knew a "sir," knighted by the Queen, "older than God, worth ninety-three million," whom he had met while working at a chic church in nearby Bal Harbour. "Wealthiest people in the world live there. . . . Saks and Neiman and Gucci all have stores. Bob Dole and Sir are members of the same church." Sir was Ronnie's first fix-up for Andrew. According to Ronnie, Andrew also made his own pickups, on the gay cruising beach, which was five blocks away, or at the hotel next door catering to German tourists. "One day this guy he brought in had a Cartier bracelet," Ronnie says. "When he came in, he was wearing the Cartier. When he left the building, he didn't have it on."

After a while, Andrew's cash started to run low, and Lyle sensed he might be losing a good customer. So he decided to intervene. "Two times I set him up with a couple of guys—male prostitutes." Soon Andrew and the others were stealing jewelry. According to Lyle, "He was a male prostitute, but he was also doing burglaries, doing whatever he could to get money. He'd stay in the hotel all day long and he'd go out at night—sneak out the back and go in the back. Nobody knew his business." The thefts were mostly jewelry—"stuff," Lyle says, "he could fit into his backpack." Lyle is very proud of the signet ring Andrew traded him for crack. "He took the ring right off his finger. He gave it to me and I handed him a twenty-dollar rock for it." Andrew also traded a Walkman and a gold razor for drugs.

On June 26, Robin Avery's wallet was stolen from her grocery cart at a supermarket two blocks from the Normandy Plaza. Avery had noticed someone who looked like Andrew in the store just before the theft occurred. Later, a person matching Andrew's description used one of Avery's credit cards to purchase some items at the neighborhood Radio Shop.

Roger Falin, the owner of the Normandy Plaza, does not venture above the lobby level. "I've made it a point never to go upstairs because of liability problems. I just don't go upstairs except with a police officer." Nobody but Ronnie paid any attention at all to Andrew, and the world he inhabited was petty and bleak. After two weeks of renting by the week, he came down to Miriam one night and said, "Miriam, I can't find the apartment I'm looking for. I want to pay you for a month." She gave him the key to room 322, which faced the beach and made him a deal for rent—$650 for the month. Andrew had told her, "I love it."

Room 322 is entered through a narrow hallway with a closet on the left. A floral-printed polyester bedspread in kelly green with pink, peach, and blue flowers covers a double bed. The furniture is painted different colors, and the rug is green. The curtain rod is bent, a TV is stuck in one corner, and a tiny, rusted stove, sink, and refrigerator sit off to one side. There may be a view, but the windows are filthy. The tiny bathroom with a tub shower is tiled. The hotel hallways are clean and smell of ammonia, but the crystal chandeliers are broken and most of the bulbs are burned out.

Inside his small, dingy room, which he rarely let the maids in to clean, Andrew surrounded himself with books detailing the worlds he preferred to inhabit, and into which he could further escape. By the dim light of his shabby hideout he read mostly about the famous rich—Sally Bedell Smith's biography of William Paley, *In All His Glory;* Caroline Sedbohm's biography of Condé Nast, *The Man Who Was Vogue;* Slim Keith's memoir *Slim,* written with Annette Tapert. There was one best-seller, *How the Irish Saved Civilization,* and two books by Robert Graves on the emperor Claudius—a favorite subject of Andrew's since his days at Bishop's. In addition he was reading about the arts and crafts movement in John Updike's essays on art, *Just Looking,* and Kenneth Clark's *The Romantic Rebellion,* plus a half-dozen other books on art and architecture and one on the contemporary artist Francis Bacon, who was known to pick up rough trade. For his supper Andrew would get a slice of pizza at nearby Cozzoli's or a tuna melt at the sub shop before disappearing out the back metal gate attached to the Cyclone fence and into the humid night.

Andrew also apparently frequented some of South Beach's better-known areas. Books & Books is a popular bookstore on Lincoln Road, the upscale pedestrian walkway lined with restaurants, boutiques, and galleries. In May, Andrew must have purchased some books there, because a flier about the store's book club sent to him under the name Andrew DeSilva was returned to the store for having the wrong address. Three employees at the Pleasure Emporium, a large porn store laid out like a supermarket on Alton Road, about a mile from Books & Books, also remember Andrew as a regular customer who purchased gay porn magazines. "He bought *Jock* and *Inches* magazines and was very polite and reserved," says Marcia Suarez. "He was one of our regulars. He always paid cash. He'd say hello and smile, but if I tried to make conversation, he wouldn't talk. He stayed quiet." She adds, "He blended in with everybody on the street."

On July 7, it was nearly two weeks since Andrew had last visited Lyle. Andrew was getting desperate. He walked around the block near the hotel to the Cash on the Beach pawnshop owned by Vivian Olivia and showed her a gold coin that he had stolen from Lee Miglin. Olivia weighed the gold and told him she'd give him $190. Andrew was upset. "Why are you paying me so little if I paid so much more for it?" he whined. "I explained to him how the pawnshop worked," Olivia recalls. "So I ask him for his I.D., and he gave me his U.S. passport, which said Andrew P. Cunanan. I asked him his address. Andrew answered, "6979 Collins Avenue, Room 205." Instead of his own room, 322, he had given Ronnie's. Olivia remembers that he had a two-day growth of beard. His skin was pale, and he was wearing a baseball cap and round glasses. He signed the papers "Andrew Cunanan." "It's nineteen dollars a month," Olivia explained. "You miss three months, you lose it." Andrew assured her, "I'll be back before three months."

As required by law, Olivia immediately turned over the paperwork, including a copy of Andrew's signed application stating he was residing at the Normandy Plaza, to the Miami Beach Police Department. There it languished.

Whether Andrew sought other ways to make money on the run is subject to question. Jack Campbell, a politically prominent, wealthy gay bathhouse owner in Miami Beach who hires models for videos and spends part of the year in San Diego, claims Andrew first applied for a job with him in San Diego. Andrew kept his business card and in May looked Campbell up at his house in Coconut Grove. Two Venezuelan employees who are no longer around to verify the story apparently gave Andrew directions in Spanish on how to get to Campbell's house by Metrorail. Campbell is under the impression that the person he dealt with was bilingual—Andrew was not. When he showed up, Campbell says, he didn't recognize him. "I must have given him my business card and said, 'If you're ever in South Beach . . .' I do that to a lot of young men." Campbell, who advertises in several gay publications, says, "I just assume he was looking through and saw my name and recognized my name."

Campbell recalls that Andrew, who was wearing a baseball cap and carrying a black backpack, was much too unattractive to be a model. He balked at taking his shirt off to be photographed and would remove only his shorts. He wouldn't give an address, saying, "I live in South Beach. I'm moving, so I'll let you know." Campbell told him, "To be a model you have to have a tan. You're so pasty-faced. You're fleshy. I don't know what kind of model you think you'd be."

On June 21, the day before Campbell left on a trip to Europe, he claims, Andrew showed up looking for work again at his health club, Club Body Center. "He was pasty as can be and fatter than ever. I said, 'Don't bother. I don't want anyone looking like you working here. He had a growth of beard, his cap on backwards, with glasses and that big bag. I was sort of nasty to him." Andrew was nasty right back: "I don't give a fuck whether you hire me or not!"

Considering the pains Andrew was taking to hide himself at the Normandy Plaza, the best explanation for his interest in model work— if indeed he sought it—is that it might have been a more upscale way to hustle. The only bar in Miami Beach that Andrew is known to have frequented—at least until a few days before he shot Versace—was a gay hustler bar called the Boardwalk in North Beach. A pickup place for older men, it features go-go boys who semi-strip on the "block," a wooden platform in the front, and then go around pressing themselves up against the patrons, who shove tips into their underwear. Mickey, one of the bartenders, says Andrew's "was a face we remember seeing a lot of" in May and early June. As for South Beach, Bobby Guilmartin, vice president of the Florida Hotel Network, who knows the scene well, says he doesn't think that someone like Andrew, in search of older men, would spend much time trolling there. "South Beach is about being Venezuelan, twenty-one, and having designer pubic hair."

One place he did drop in was the popular 11th Street Diner on Washington and Eleventh. Andrew was definitely remembered there, and the location carries a special irony. The diner is located right across the street from the Miami Beach Police Department, and the chief and his minions eat there on a regular basis.

29

What's Gay Got
to Do with It?

IN EVERY JURISDICTION where Andrew had previously murdered, law enforcement was convinced that he was gone and never coming back. "We knew he was headed east; we thought he was headed south," says Kevin Rickett, the Minneapolis-based head of the FBI's Cunanan investigation. "We didn't see him backtracking. He wasn't staying around to make friends where he was." But where would Andrew go?

William Hagmire, the head of the FBI profiling unit, who had taken Ted Bundy's final confessions, remembers that in a meeting in late May he speculated, "This guy's making a Bundy run; he's going to hit Florida next." Bundy, after crossing the country from the Northwest, killed in Milwaukee and Chicago before going through New Jersey and Washington and Atlanta and ending up in Florida. "It was a wild guess, because at that point we didn't know where his contacts and where his holes might be. But then, Bundy had none in Florida either. He just decided to head south because it was cold." Hagmire's hunch was on target, but he was not really listened to. The profiling unit had not been invited to join the case until after William Reese's murder. Moreover, according to FBI records of May 20, the unit had not received copies of pertinent interviews about Andrew or investigative reports or copies of crime-scene and autopsy photos, which the Child Abduction and Serial Killer Unit (CASKU) considered "important to fully develop offender characteristics." (In another CASKU report, dated July 16, the day after Versace's murder, the profiling unit would again state that it "does not have the necessary information . . . to assist in providing an assessment of Cunanan.")

The FBI was following its policy of not paying close attention to character traits in a fugitive investigation, and Kevin Rickett, a thirty-one-year-old, fresh-faced, analytical type who looks more like a grad student than an FBI honcho, didn't think he needed any profiling help. "We already knew who Cunanan was" Rickett said dismissively. "We interviewed hundreds and hundreds of his associates. We don't need the profiling unit to tell us he's going to hang out in gay bars."

On May 13, Philip Merrill called the FBI in Chicago to volunteer his and Liz Coté's help in finding Andrew, whom he characterized as "a delicate butterfly who constantly fantasized about being rich." Later he spoke to an FBI agent in the Los Angeles office. Merrill says, "When the FBI asked, 'Where do you think he'll go and who do you think he'll get in touch with?' I said 'Florida' and I said 'Versace.' There is no question I said this to the guy, the local FBI agent." Merrill is adamant. "When the FBI asked who would he hook up with, I said, 'Gianni Versace and Harry de Wildt should be identified. And think of Florida and nice places. Plus he'd have an easier time concealing himself there.' I told that to the first local agent." (The FBI agent in Los Angeles did not file a report on the conversation, and refuses to comment.)

Merrill says he told the FBI, "Think places you'd see on Robin Leach [host of *Life-styles of the Rich and Famous*]. He's not going to go to Newark." In Merrill's FBI report, filed from Chicago and obtained with his permission under the Freedom of Information Act, Florida and Versace are not mentioned. Merrill is merely quoted as saying "he lived 'the lifestyles of the rich and famous' by hanging on and pretending" and "if and when the authorities caught up to Cunanan he would probably be found in some exclusive country club or expensive restaurant."

"I'd do all this analysis, and talk about him to the FBI, and they'd say, 'What we're really interested in is who he'd get in touch with and where he'd go.' I said, 'There are only two coasts that stay warm. And warn the owners of 7-Eleven's if anyone's buying Fritos and milk. . . .

He'd go a day and a half without any real meals—just Fritos and milk, and then he'd have a sub.' "

In early June, Norman Blachford also told the FBI that Andrew might be in Miami, particularly the South Beach area. Blachford had no specific information to that effect—it was strictly a hunch—but Andrew had told him that he had visited the area, and Blachford felt that it would be a logical place for Andrew to blend in. Blachford's suggestion does not appear in FBI files either.

In retrospect, the manhunt for Andrew Cunanan appears to have been riddled with missed opportunities. Although Merrill, Doug Stubblefield, and Eli Gould all say that they had mentioned to the FBI Andrew's knowing Versace before Versace's death, Versace's name simply does not appear in any FBI file prior to his murder. Even more curious is the idea that just as they professed not to be interested in learning about Andrew's character for their fugitive investigation, some of the top FBI officials involved in the Cunanan manhunt maintained that his sexual orientation didn't really count either. "The media keeps linking his sexual preferences with his actions. We don't care," said Paul Philip, the tall, elegant African-American head of the Miami FBI during the Cunanan investigation. "You can't take the issue of sex and say it's the basis of the investigation. Being gay was not emphasized. It's not all that clear being gay had anything to do with it."

Philip argues, "The interest in Cunanan and the grave digger has nothing to do with sex. In Minnesota they found him using a .40 millimeter gun—that's the weapon. The weapon has nothing to do with sex. The car has nothing to do with sex. You can't base a fugitive investigation on sexual orientation." Rather, he says, "if you focused on his sex or what he's done in the past, you'd be focusing on those places. Bank robbers don't rob banks where they ultimately hide. I'm saying down here we didn't see evidence of the same actions you'd see in San Diego. He wasn't doing whatever he was doing in San Diego down here."

One of the reasons Philip believes Andrew's behavior had changed was that law enforcement never really had a clue as to the extent of Andrew's drug use and drug dealing in San Diego; there was never any emphasis placed on how habitual use of crystal meth and cocaine, particularly in combination, can contribute to psychosis. Yet Peter Ahearn, the number two in the San Diego FBI, says, "We have the third-largest number of bank robbers in the nation, just over three hundred last year, and half of the people are tweakers. They were users of crystal meth, robbing to feed their habit." Greg Jones, the Miami FBI agent in charge of the Cunanan investigation, says, "I never heard of him being a petty drug dealer." Kevin Rickett stated flatly, "That serves no purpose for us."

Perhaps the FBI's reluctance to admit that being gay was integral to Andrew's killing spree, not to mention whom he targeted, is due to a general unease that is currently being addressed but that still persists when law enforcement has to deal with homosexuals. "We used to call them 'fagicides,' " a Florida investigator told me. Not surprisingly, there is prejudice on both sides. Constance Potter, coordinator of the Minneapolis branch of the Gay and Lesbian Anti-Violence Project, says, "Seventy-five percent of gays would not call law enforcement [regarding crimes]. They may not be out. They may feel shame or guilt. . . . There's also a lot of distrust and a history of slow movement and failure to respond." Traditionally, a pattern of us versus them has existed between police and gays. "We talked to people who told us, even after Cunanan killed four people, 'I'll give him any safe haven he needs,' " says Peter Ahearn of the San Diego FBI.

"This is a lifestyle issue within the gay community," states Darryl Cooper, the former chairman of Gay Men and Lesbians Opposing Violence. "A lot of us are capable of moving through the mainstream, but there are segments of the community who aren't. Some of them have had bad experiences with straight people and don't want to be involved with them. Some have grown up in small towns where being gay is considered a huge stigma, so the only way to have contact with other gays is to have illicit sex in bars, in parks, in the dark, so they learn that's the only way to be gay." Cops who bust such areas are not natural allies. Cooper says, "It's always been a fear in gay communities when gay people are murdered that police do not do a good job. A lot of times they ignore the murder or do not pursue the murderer."

To prevent prejudice and foster awareness, a coalition of gay and lesbian antiviolence groups began monitoring Andrew's case early on. "When Cunanan broke, we started having weekly conference calls among fifteen cities," Cooper explains. "Cunanan didn't come to the nation's attention until Chicago, which triggered a nationwide alert." Even though all major cities on both coasts and places such as Detroit and El Paso were involved in the calls, Jacksonville was the only city in Florida to participate. Miami, for example, was not sufficiently organized. "How do we create a community," asks Eugene Patron, formerly a gay issues columnist with the *Miami Herald,* "when everything you see is geared to the visitor who comes down here to get his rocks off?"

On June 12, Andrew became the 449th person to make the FBI's Ten Most Wanted List. In large part this was due to the efforts of the *America's Most Wanted* TV program, which has become a highly effective tool for the capture of FBI fugitives. *A.M.W.* continued to feature Andrew's case and nudged the FBI into action. "We really had to push. He became a special addition to the Ten Most Wanted," says Bob Long, the media spokesman of the Chicago FBI office who often works with the show. "I think he made number eleven."

For the FBI to move with this speed was a break from its usual practice. "We did everything to get him on the Top Ten, and that happened very quickly," says FBI Deputy Assistant Director Roger Wheeler, who adds that it typically takes at least six weeks "to get somebody on the Top Ten who isn't a Tim McVeigh or Terry Nichols or someone like that." FBI headquarters in Washington felt that it had scored a publicity coup. "When Cunanan became part of the Top Ten list, it was a major event," says FBI Fugitive Publicity Unit spokesman Ed Cogswell. The FBI's former number two, William Esposito, says, "If you're on the Top Ten, it means you're a very dangerous person, and you're known not only to the FBI but to all of law enforcement. Your picture is plastered all over the place." He adds, "Any leads in the Bureau involving Top Ten people are supposed to be covered within the hour."

Down in the trenches, however, the same gung ho enthusiasm is not always felt. Furthermore, the FBI guards its territory, often discouraging cooperation with local law enforcement. "Prior to Versace, all we got were two crappy pictures like faxes," says Christine Quinn, who directs the New York Gay and Lesbian Anti-Violence Project. "The FBI certainly wasn't working with the New York Police Department. I had to get the FBI to give the NYPD Ten Most Wanted pictures. I had asked the FBI for pictures because we had posted a ten thousand dollar reward for Cunanan's capture. First we started using pictures from the newspaper and the Internet. Then they finally got a series of pictures which were improved. They were very resistant giving those photos to NYPD."

I was interviewing Bob Tichich in the Minneapolis homicide bureau when the newly minted Ten Most Wanted poster was dropped on his desk. "What does this mean exactly?" I asked. "It means, according to the guys over in the task force, a lot more paperwork," Tichich answered. "Well, who is in charge of the investigation?" I wanted to know. "That's a good question," Tichich answered.

Nearer to headquarters in Washington, D.C., however, the FBI was a model of cooperation with the gay community. "It was very reassuring to the gay population here in D.C. We had access to the FBI," says Darryl Cooper. "Local agent Daniel Mingione was completely accessible. He came by and gave us posters of Cunanan before he was on the FBI's Ten Most Wanted List. He even offered to help us put them up."

Yet the twisted tale of what happened to Cunanan fliers in the Miami FBI office is one of the most interesting hot potatoes of the entire manhunt. The Miami FBI office is one of the busiest in the country, since Miami is at the hub of the drug wars. Drug money is so ubiquitous there that the Catholic Archdiocese of Miami was found to be unknowingly laundering Colombian cartel money through a housing-loan program. Furthermore, corruption is so rife that in 1997 the Miami mayor's election was annulled. Therefore, the announcement of a "gay serial killer" on the FBI's Top Ten list was hardly front-page news. "The *Miami Herald* did a story, and nobody paid attention," says Paul Philip defensively.

"To paint a picture solely on Cunanan without understanding the enormity of what we do is unfair," charges Deputy Special Agent Paul

Mallett, the number two of the Miami FBI. "Our number-one priority is organized crime and drugs. We have ten squads with a hundred agents and it's hopelessly inadequate. Number two is white-collar crime—medicare, health care, fraud by wire, mail fraud, bribery, and embezzlement. Number three is violent crimes, which Cunanan fell into. Number four is national security—intelligence and terrorism." At any given time the Bureau is working on 2,500 cases, and Mallett says between four hundred and five hundred new leads open up every month. "Cunanan was one of those. Typically, what happens, because of the notoriety of the guy's actions, is that leads go out to all offices— shotgun leads. There's a vague chance you might hit on something: 'Contact all possible sources.'

"No one knew where he was, so [the lead] goes to all fifty-six offices. No one knew he was coming here," Mallett continues. "What we were doing, we were out contacting people in case he shows up." Mallett's view differs from that of Paul Philip, who in some interviews, including to me, has stated that the FBI had thought Andrew was in South Florida since May. Either way, the Cunanan investigation in Miami was hardly considered high priority. Accordingly, it was assigned to Keith Evans, a rookie with thirteen months experience. "They give Top Ten cases to rookies," says a Miami U.S. attorney, "because you never find them, or they turn themselves in."

Evans is a clean-shaven and stocky thirty-one-year-old, a former local cop from Plantation, Florida. During the third week in May, Philip says, the Miami office received a tip that Cunanan might be in West Palm Beach, seventy-five miles away. A construction site where some-one resembling Andrew had worked was staked out, and a suspect was taken in for questioning and released—"washed out" of the lineup in FBI lingo. Evans, who worked with a female partner, Talarah Gruber, decided that Fort Lauderdale was the best place to look for Andrew, because the FBI had gotten a tip that there would be a Gamma Mu fly-in there, and the Bureau knew Andrew had ties to the group. Fort Lauderdale also had a large gay population, but it tended to be older and more conservative than that of South Beach. According to *Ocean Drive* magazine editor Glenn Albin, "Fort Lauderdale is based on an

Anglo, All-American, very white-bread mentality. They have S&M and leather. Any older established [gay] community has that. Their gay community grew up in a much more closeted society."

In May, Keith Evans made an obligatory visit to the Miami Beach police about Andrew. He had one flier with a photo of Andrew on it with him, and spoke to Sergeant Lori Wieder, an openly gay police officer, one of two on the Miami Beach force then. He asked her help in contacting local gay groups for an undercover operation to infiltrate gay clubs in the area. "He was very unfamiliar with the gay community in general," says Wieder. "I supplied him with information—gay newspapers and lists of clubs. He had one flier. I made a copy." Wieder's instinct was to get the fliers out to gay media and clubs so that they could see what Andrew looked like. But Evans said no. "He didn't want me to distribute fliers," Wieder says.

Getting the word out immediately was also the first idea that came to homicide detective Paul Scrimshaw when he was introduced to Evans. Ironically, two months later, Scrimshaw, a thoughtful ex-schoolteacher on his way to retirement, was put in charge of the Versace case. But Evans also made it clear to Scrimshaw that he didn't want publicity about Andrew, that he preferred to keep the investigation low key. Scrimshaw, both sardonic and laconic, is given to wearing leather vests and brushing his longish hair straight back. He projects the classic cop attitude of having seen it all and thinks much of it is foolish. "The FBI came here, and talked to us, and we said, 'Let's get this out.' But the FBI said, 'No, no, we want to soft-pedal this,'" Scrimshaw says. "If you come to the police station and say, 'We want this guy,' and we say, 'OK, let's put the fliers out,' and he says, 'No, no, no, we got leads,' I take it he's saying that because he wants the glory of it—he's thinking, I want to do the grab." By May 16, Scrimshaw remembers, "the Cunanan flier was on the homicide bureau's bulletin board. It was just one more flier." One more flier that nobody looked at for two entire months.

According to Lieutenant Carlos Noriega, the Miami Beach supervisor of the Versace murder investigation, "Keith wanted to speak to the gay community to further follow up and to infiltrate a 'secret society' and gay underworld escort services." Lori Wieder put Evans in touch with gay city official Dennis Leyva in South Beach, who could facilitate an introduction to the clubs. He was also referred to the Broward County sheriff's office and met gay activist Dilia Loe in Fort Lauderdale.

Leyva is an ebullient and well-connected music-and-entertainment coordinator for the city of Miami. He had already read about Cunanan in the national media. "Three FBI agents took me into a room, and they explained to me the whole gig on the murders. They suspected Cunanan was here because of that fly-in party that Gamma Mu does." The FBI showed Leyva a Gamma Mu newsletter. "They asked me about the club scene, what was happening in South Beach. I said I didn't think anyone looking to hit on older men would be here—it's a very young gay scene. Fort Lauderdale is older and more closeted, with piano bars. I explained the bars here and said, 'Either it's Twist or the Boardwalk, if that's what he was into—meeting older men.' Discos were hard places to strike up a conversation. They then asked if I would take them around town as a cover. I did tell them I could facilitate a meeting with all local gay and lesbian organizations. In the back of my mind, though, I was thinking I didn't want to start hysteria. [But] they said they were here to case the place out, be low key. They never followed up with me."

In May, Keith Evans also called Dilia Loe, who runs the Gay and Lesbian Community Center in Fort Lauderdale. "They wanted to set up a time to meet, and were trying to decide how to approach the gay community. They wanted names of leaders and how to get in touch with certain people," she says. The meeting finally took place in mid-June with Evans and his partner, Talarah Gruber. Loe gave them a list of bars, gay publications, people they should contact. Evans said he would give Loe a flier to put in her newsletter.

"He was very specific about who they wanted to talk to," says Loe. "He asked about Gamma Mu, also affluent gay men and leather clubs." The FBI told her they had found a Gamma Mu letterhead with a Fort Lauderdale address in one of Cunanan's vehicles. Loe says, "They said that was the only lead they had to South Florida." At the time Loe had never heard of Gamma Mu, but she later verified that it did exist and gave them the phone number of the founder, Cliff Pettit, who lives in Fort Lauderdale. Again Keith Evans promised to supply Loe with fliers. A week later Loe talked to Deputy Barbara Stewart of the Broward

County Sheriff's Department, which was working with the FBI. She too said they were distributing fliers, but Loe never got any. On yet another occasion, Talarah Gruber promised Loe that she'd get fliers, but it didn't happen until two days after Versace died. Finally, Loe created her own flier and began to contact gay publications about the FBI's visit so that they could warn the community.

Yet there was only one mention of Andrew Cunanan in Miami, in the local Miami gay press, and no fliers were distributed to gay establishments until after Versace's murder. "There were no fliers. They were not on Lincoln Road, they were not on Washington Avenue. They were not in clubs," says Dennis Leyva. "I do go out a lot, and I live here. It happened after the fact of Versace's murder. The FBI was here undercover and wanted to see if they could catch him." Donna Cyrus, a manager of Club Body Tech, one of South Beach's most popular gyms, says, "We were never warned by the police or the FBI. I personally had to go down to the police station and get wanted pictures two days after [the Versace murder] happened. Here of all places. Versace lives one block away. Yet there were no signs in storefronts."

It wasn't until July 2, 1997, when *Scoop* magazine, a weekly gay entertainment guide in South Florida, published a story under the headline: Wanted by the FBI! Accused Killer Has Many Faces that the gay media in South Florida ran anything at all about Andrew. *Scoop* issued a full-page warning by Dan Pryor, a local radio reporter, who got his information from the Internet and decided to write the piece because of "the high concentration of affluent gays in South Florida." There were no other warnings.

Had the FBI made the decision to work more openly with the gay community in South Beach, rather than taking its cue from Paul Philip's opinion that Andrew's sexual preference was not relevant to their investigation, it could have benefited from the unusual insight of the Miami Beach Police Department, which has an ongoing outreach program to the gay community. Gary Knight, an arts executive and father of two sons, who relocated to South Beach from Miami in 1989 when he came out, helped shape a program begun by Police Chief Richard Barreto and led by two gay psychologists to give each Miami Beach police officer four hours of sensitivity and diversity training.

Knight worked to get more cops on the streets, especially on weekend nights, and to sponsor ride-alongs for any gays who wished to accompany the police on midnight patrols. Over a hundred gays accepted the offer. "Everybody comes back with an enormous respect for what the police have to do," Knight says. "South Beach is really Iowa City with a New York City nightlife—a little village that becomes Manhattan at night. This really is a very tough street scene here."

While it may make South Beach a rougher place, its nightlife could have provided the perfect venue in which to spread the word on Cunanan. But to date South Beach lacks the gay political structure to make that happen. "It's easy to get them into bed, but try to get them out of bed on election day," quips Andrew Delaplane, editor of the Miami Beach newspaper *Wired.* "What kills me is, if we had put a poster up—it's really a small town here, it gets talked about," says *Ocean Drive* editor Glenn Albin, who had seen numerous posters during a trip to New York in May. "This guy would have been found in a second."

In talking to dozens of the leading movers and shakers of South Beach—the mayor, the police chief, politicians, journalists, and club, bar, and business owners—I did not find a single one who had ever gotten a flier of Andrew Cunanan from the FBI. Yet South Beach has one of the highest concentration of gays in the country. The mayor of Miami Beach then, Seymour Gelber, told me, "Previous to Versace, I don't think they [the FBI] did anything. I think the FBI did what they did in the cities where the crimes were committed, rather than anticipating him. Our police were certainly not aware of Cunanan. The fact he was on the Most Wanted list never entered into the domain of the police. The police have their own Top Ten list for the city." Miami Beach Police Chief Richard Barreto agrees. "I get a hundred Top Ten lists across my desk. I was not aware he was on the FBI's."

The one exception I found was in Fort Lauderdale, where Wade Gibson, owner of the Moby Dick, a gay bar with go-go boys and an older crowd, actually got a flier from Keith Evans. Gibson said that the FBI visited the bar five times, particularly after Gibson thought he had spotted Andrew in the bar one night, all dressed up and playing pool with an older man. The FBI responded immediately and staked out the parking lot, not wanting, Gibson says, "to disturb business." But the two had already left. "The FBI said his MO was to go to clubs, try to spot exotic autos in the parking lot, go into the clubs to try to find out who the owners of the cars were, and then warm them up," relates Gibson who praises the FBI for their quick response to him. Still, when the FBI spoke to Gibson, after Andrew had committed four murders and gained extensive national media attention, they persisted in playing it very close to the vest. "The FBI came in here and said Cunanan was wanted for some very serious things—they didn't say murder."

Despite widespread charges to the contrary, the FBI insisted long after Versace's murder that thousands of fliers of Andrew had been distributed in the Miami area. "The implication that the FBI did not pull its weight in Miami is unsubstantiated completely," says Kevin Rickett. "Regardless of whether you saw posters or not, I can tell you that they were mailed down. I can tell you agents went out and delivered them, because I personally talked to the agents that did that." Anne Figueiras, the FBI spokeswoman, repeating what she had said to the media many times before, reiterated, "We gave out over two thousand fliers between the fifteenth and twentieth of May." Her boss, Paul Mallett, who was made the interim head of the Miami bureau after Paul Philip left in December 1997, said, "If someone in this office is responsible for sending out three thousand fliers and didn't, I'm going to kick his ass."

To prove his point, Mallett, in his Miami office, got Keith Evans—whom I was not allowed to speak to directly—on the phone at his work station in the basement. He asked Evans, specifically for my benefit, about the fliers. Mallett then told me, "Keith says we initially received about ten fliers."

"When?" I asked.

"Timing is critical here," Mallett relayed to Evans on the phone. Evans then admitted to Mallett that the ten fliers didn't really arrive "until the end of June" and then Evans called for more.

"Approximately three thousand is accurate," Mallett told me. "Sometime a week or so later, around the first of July, three thousand came in. They were distributed throughout the community. The focus was on the gay establishment. They were given to various state and local authorities."

"That was done after Versace died," I countered, not saying that there really is no organized gay establishment in Miami Beach. Certainly the members of the South Beach Business Guild never received fliers.

Then Mallett blew his stack. "I can tell you Keith Evans was not passing them out after Versace was dead! It wasn't dismissed by us that Cunanan was probably in this area. And the distribution of fliers in this area—it was done." Mallett got up out of his chair and pointed his finger at me. "I am telling you categorically and positively there was no indication of suspicion Cunanan was headed to South Florida from San Diego. There was never any indication, solid or nebulous, that he was heading to South Florida. There was no anticipation that he was traveling in a southeasterly direction."

"The reality," says Dilia Loe, "is if the FBI had followed through, Cunanan would have been caught a lot earlier. They should have been more responsible about getting the fliers out." She cites the example of a convicted murderer of a gay man, who escaped from Dade County three months after the Versace murder. This time the Miami Beach police did not have to yield to the FBI. They immediately distributed fliers to gay bars locally and nationally. They caught the man three weeks later in New Orleans, where a bartender in a gay establishment recognized him and called the police. In Cunanan's case, Loe does not see the FBI's behavior as being prejudicial regarding gays. "It's more neglect than overtly anti-gay. They were too casual. The FBI didn't take the lead they had seriously enough."

30

The Secret

In July 1997, at the age of fifty, Gianni Versace was on the verge of making a great leap forward in business. After years of careful preparation, he wanted nothing more than to be the first Italian designer to have his name listed on both the Milan Bourse and the New York Stock Exchange: Gianni Versace SpA. This trip to America—first to New York and then to South Beach—was extremely important. Versace had come to sign the preliminary papers to have Morgan Stanley, one of the leading Wall Street investment banking firms, manage the U.S. portion of the initial public offering.

In 1996 the Versace Group, as it's known in English, had reported total revenue of about $500 million (853 billion lire) and a net profit of $42.8 million. (Although some press reports often gave the misleading impression that the company was a $900 million or even a billion-dollar enterprise, their figures were based on estimates of the retail sales of Versace brand merchandise, which is not equivalent to revenues earned by the Versace Group itself.) An even higher estimation of the company's value came from the *Financial Times* of London, which reported in October 1997 that the placement value of the Versace stock would be "estimated at a whopping $1.4 billion"—more than thirty times annual profit. But those bullish estimates preceded a sharp drop in profits reported at the end of the year—down to a net profit of about

$33 million on revenue of about $560 million for the Versace Group in 1997. And even the $33 million figure was swollen, since it included a one-time payment of about $20 million for a "keyman" life-insurance policy the Versace Group had with Lloyds of London that was payable on Gianni Versace's death.

Versace signed with Morgan Stanley on Thursday, July 10. In recent months Gianni's brother, Santo, the company's brainy CEO, had tried to rein in his brother's wild spending and had taken his credit cards away. To prepare for the stock offering, the family had also spun off their own personal holdings into a limited company called Ordersystem, consisting of their houses and art and acquisitions, the value of which was estimated to be between $80 and $100 million. Since so much of the company's promotion was also personal and fueled by a small army of publicists and photographers, the $70 million annual promotion budget, which included the freebies to the stars and parties paid out of corporate funds, gave some idea of the level of extravagance to which Gianni had become accustomed. Later, the family would try to justify the excess to the numbers crunchers by saying, "This is what it takes to get people into our shows."

From now on, Gianni would have to temper his whims. Nevertheless, the stock offering represented the culmination of everything Gianni, Santo, and Donatella had worked so tirelessly to realize. To have arrived at this juncture, both Gianni and his business had had to overcome great odds. There had always been rumors that the Versaces, who came from Reggio in southern Italy, a town "in the grip of organized crime," were somehow beholden to the Mafia. How else, the international fashion community wanted to know, could they have managed to come from nowhere, spend so lavishly, and keep open so many "empty" boutiques?

Their private company was tightly held and secretive. Despite the fact that Italian law required Versace's financial statements to be publicly filed and audited by the Italian unit of KPMG, one of the world's largest accounting firms, the rumors persisted. But whenever those rumors got into print, the Versaces were quick to move against the paper that had published them, particularly in Britain where the burden of proof in a libel action rests with the publication—the exact opposite of

U.S. libel law. In 1994, for example, the *Independent on Sunday* newspaper in London questioned the finances of the Versaces—"How much does he really sell? . . . . There is confusion about how the numbers add up"—and was forced to apologize and pay damages.

As the stock offering neared, those tiresome questions were becoming moot. Even old-line firms like Morgan Stanley had loosened their requirements considerably in the go-go eighties as competition got stiffer. Still, in order to pass muster with a major investment house, the Versaces would be subjected to a due-diligence investigation to see whether anyone was cooking the books or whether any other irregularities were in evidence. Just two months before, in May 1997, for example, Santo Versace had been convicted of bribing Italian tax officials in 1990 and 1991, and had received a suspended sentence of one year and two months. (In 1998 the conviction would be overturned on appeal when the judge accepted Santo's claim that he had been the victim of extortion, forced to hand over the money or face prolonged tax inspections that would have prevented the company from meeting orders.)

Despite that minor setback, plans had gone forward. Banca Comerciale Italiana on the Milan end was to conduct the due diligence. Sid Rutberg, who covered the fashion industry's financial market for *Woman's Wear Daily* for many years, says due-diligence investigations these days are not particularly rigorous. "If any officers were arrested or charged, that would have to be disclosed, as would a guilty plea or a settlement." Beyond that, he says, "How they could have gotten their money years ago is not pertinent at this point. It's pertinent how their business has done—the rest, unless it's something blatantly outrageous, is not a problem if they can show where the sales are coming from and where they do their manufacturing. Say they got their money from an unsavory source at the time of the start-up. Who cares? So forget it."

Still, nagging questions persisted about the Versace Group's finances. Did the figures really make sense? The company claimed that only 15 percent of its income was generated in the United States, the country with the world's largest economy. "If you don't sell here, you don't sell anywhere!" a leading journalist covering fashion told me. "Everybody else who has a big company, there's visual evidence they're doing business." In various reports the Versace Group also claimed that its Asian market was similarly a mere 13 to 25 percent of total sales. Were there sufficient Versace sales in Europe, the Middle East, Africa, Latin America, and Canada to account for the lion's share of Versace's sales? The responsibility for conducting the due-diligence investigation before the company could go public would fall to the managers of the proposed public offering, Morgan Stanley in New York and Banca Comerciale Italiana in Milan.

As part of that process, the investment bankers would be reviewing the audited financial statements of the Versace Group prepared by the Italian unit of KPMG. According to a source familiar with the due-diligence investigation, "They did a pretty thorough audit of inventory and sales." However, the investment bankers thought, according to the source, that "the profitability of the company should be much higher—one of the things they found was that it's a hit-or-miss business. . . . What doesn't sell so much is haute couture. What does sell are the jeans, perfume, bags. The reason the haute couture doesn't sell is that the market is pitifully small and the prices are too high. They view the haute couture as a marketing tool to put the Versace name in the fashion capitals of the world."

Banca Comerciale Italiana had the primary responsibility for conducting the investigation, and Morgan Stanley, according to the knowledgeable source, was depending on its Italian co-underwriter to review allegations of Mafia involvement and money laundering. Morgan Stanley did not hire private investigators itself but had received "repeated assurances. They were informed that Gianni may have known some cruddy people but that the company itself was not mobbed up." The dependent American bankers were told, "There was no evidence these friends had any role in the company."

After signing the papers with Morgan Stanley, Gianni flew directly to South Beach. He always claimed he went to South Beach to relax, but whether he could ever really let go was a matter of conjecture. He carried the twin burdens of having to be constantly creative and always responsible for so many and so much. After all, he was Versace; his army of young designers, his worldwide sales personnel, his family all depended on him, and in the end they all yielded to his ideas and fanta-sies. "No other major fashion house in the world," remarked *Business Week,* "is so closely identified with the life-style of its marquee name designer." Now Gianni Versace was about to go public and realize ever greater wealth and enter more and more world markets. He wanted to pioneer for all Italian designers once and for all what it meant to be an instantly recognizable global trademark, like Coke, and he was deter-mined to achieve that goal. Amazingly, he persevered despite guarding the greatest secret of his life: What no one in the fashion or business world was ever supposed to know was that Gianni Versace had con-tracted HIV, the virus that causes AIDS.

The news would be shocking if it leaked now, and the consequences to his business would be incalculable. Certainly the public offering would be jeopardized. Was it nerve, greed, or folly that made Versace push so hard to go global with the help of outside shareholders when he knew his health was in jeopardy? When I asked a financial analyst whether Versace's being HIV positive would have an impact on the stock offering, his answer was an emphatic yes. "Can you imagine say-ing, 'Please buy stock in Disney, but oh, by the way, Walt has a disease he will eventually die from?' " Would such a public offering have mis-led investors? "It's an interesting question never tested in court."

Perhaps in no other business is the image of one person so crucial as it is in the world of fashion and design. "When an entire multimillion-dollar business is dependent on the creative abilities of a single individ-ual, constant good health—and good cheer—is an absolute imperative," wrote the *Irish Times* after Versace's death, presciently speculating about Versace's health at the time of his murder and citing the example of Italian designer Franco Moschino, who had died of an AIDS-related illness in 1994 but whose condition was not made public until after he died. The American designer Perry Ellis had also died of AIDS, in 1986, but had been very ill before the public was ever told, and when designer Willi Smith died in 1987, his lawyer claimed that he had been tested for AIDS only shortly before his demise. "Too much is at stake to risk offering the consumer anything other than an endless diet of selec-tive information," said the *Irish Times*. "Gianni Versace knew this to be the case and throughout his career he was careful to offer outside observers only a carefully airbrushed image."

If the Versace business was dependent on the creativity and mystique of Versace himself, and his health was integral to his business, what an irony it was that Versace's physical and financial health was tied to his sex life: the man who dressed women as hookers and urged the world to "flaunt it," who created his empire by selling sex, had to buy sex for himself furtively and keep his behavior utterly secret. To the world, Gianni and Antonio were a deeply devoted, monogamous couple—an image that would be used to repudiate the idea that Versace could ever have met or been involved with someone like Andrew Cunanan. Yet in the early and mid nineties, Jaime Cardona, the handsome Colombian who was once a doorman at Warsaw, was regularly asked to procure for Versace and Antonio D'Amico. Sometimes candidates in nearby clubs would be lined up for Versace to choose from, sometimes Jaime would choose the hustler and send him over, but always secretly and to the back door of the mansion.

A male escort named Alex says that he was first selected by Jaime out of a crowd at the Palace Bar and Grill, a popular gathering spot just down the street from the Casa Casuarina. Jaime took him to the rear door of the Versace mansion "with instructions to go directly up the rear staircase leading to Gianni and Antonio's bedroom." They "had a brief conversation and proceeded to have sex." Alex says he felt "the whole scenario was more for Mr. D'Amico's needs than for Mr. Versace's." He subsequently returned to sell his sexual favors half a dozen times.

For over a year between March 1994 and July 1995, Versace did not travel much and rarely visited South Beach. When he did appear in Europe to take bows on the catwalk after his shows, people noticed that he had lost weight and looked weak and emaciated. The news finally emerged that he was suffering from a rare, inner-ear cancer and undergoing chemotherapy. Nevertheless, the publicity juggernaut steamed on; Versace continued to publish books and stage shows. When he did return to South Beach toward the end of 1995, people who hadn't seen him in the interim were shocked. One says, "He could barely walk a

half a block, and needed to be supported by Antonio the whole time."
Another frequent visitor to Casa Casuarina says he would see Versace
eating breakfast with an array of prescription medicines in front of his
plate. "Gianni was like someone had pulled the plug, and all the energy
had been drawn out."

The once ebullient maestro became depressed, reclusive, and world-
weary. "In the last four years of his life, Gianni was utterly contemptu-
ous of everybody else in his life," the source continues. "He was bitter;
he only had nasty things to say about people. He only had energy to
bitch and groan." Gianni, like one of those ancient Roman emperors,
had reached a point of material saturation that seemed to bring only
malaise. "Gianni Versace, in the last year or two, could have cared less if
he had gotten laid one more time," the observer confides. "He was so
bored, jaded, and tired. The first few years it was titillating. Then he
was bored by how empty it all was. Gianni wouldn't make the slightest
effort to get boys in his bed. It was really down to a small trickle." He
concludes, "Being a diva, it does something to you—you lose perspec-
tive."

In 1996, Gianni was felled again—this time reportedly for a cancer-
ous bone tumor in his cheek—and Donatella, who supposedly since
1993 had been groomed by Gianni to take over, emerged much more
forcefully as a design entity in her own right, responsible for the lower-
priced Versus line. They both acknowledged friction during the winter
and spring of 1996, when Gianni disagreed with her choices for an
advertising campaign and she seemed to overstep her bounds. However,
as Gianni's health improved in the last six months before his death—at
a time when many people with HIV were experiencing similar results
with new, life-saving medications—the family once again began to pursue vigorously their longtime dream of a public stock offering.

Had Andrew Cunanan not crossed his path, Gianni Versace might
have lived on for years, his secret intact.

31

Most Wanted

WHEN ANDREW'S MONTH at the Normandy Plaza was up in the second week of July, he told Miriam Hernandez that he would be staying only three more days.

"I found an apartment. By the weekend I'll be gone."

"I enjoyed your stay," Miriam told him kindly. "You're a very nice guy; I'm sorry to see you go."

"Thank you," Andrew said, obviously pleased. "You're a very nice lady. You're a sweetheart."

Andrew paid Miriam the daily rate on Tuesday, Wednesday, and Thursday. On Friday morning she called. "Kurt, are you leaving us today?"

"No, tomorrow," Andrew answered.

"Your rent is due today."

"Can I pay you in the morning when I check out? I'm very, very tired. I don't want to come down."

Miriam told him that would be fine. After all, she says, "The guy had been here almost two months." She didn't see Andrew Friday, and when she left she told her brother, Alberto, the night clerk, "Three-two-two is checking out." Roberto was to get the last night's rent in the morning.

Friday night about 9:00 P.M., Andrew went out for his usual fast food, crossing Collins Avenue to Miami Subs and ordering the "Sixer Tuna Combo" for $2.99. Kenny Benjamin, who waited on him, thought he recognized him from *America's Most Wanted* and immediately called the police. He told them there was a guy in the shop who resembled someone he'd seen on *A.M.W.* but he couldn't remember which program or what the person's name was. He added, "Man, this is no joke."

"OK, where is he at now?"

"He's walking down the street, and he was just in here ordering food, but I think he just walked down the street now."

"Is he a white male or a black male?"

"You know the guy—the guy, they profiled him on *America's Most Wanted*." Kenny had told the 911 operator, "It was the guy who killed his homosexual lover and a couple of other people, like, four people." But there was no indication the police had any idea who he was talking about.

Unfortunately, Kenny himself was standing in front of the store's video camera, so all it showed was him talking on the phone. (Roberto Fabrizzi, the daytime manager, later said Andrew was a regular, but he never made conversation when he came in and he did not linger.) Kenny made the call at an extremely busy time at headquarters. Twenty-four 911 calls were backed up. Nevertheless, the police were at Miami Subs in minutes, but by then Andrew had disappeared.

On Friday night, Versace, Antonio, and a friend had a pizza at Bang, a restaurant on Washington Avenue owned by an Italian whom Versace liked. They were relaxed and left early. Versace was still decompressing from the fall fashion shows he had staged in Paris to rave reviews shortly before arriving in New York. A few blocks down the street, Andrew was sighted at Twist, the club where Dennis Leyva had told the FBI to look for him. Andrew danced one dance with a hairdresser named Brad from West Palm Beach, identifying himself as Andy from California. On the dance floor, Brad said, Andrew had his hands all over him, grabbing and rubbing him. When Brad asked him what he did for a living, Andrew blithely said, "I'm a serial killer." He laughed and said to Brad that he was really in investment banking. Then he disappeared into the crowd.

That night Andrew was dressed rather preppily, in long pants and a long-sleeved shirt. Twist manager Frank Scottolini, three bartenders, and one of the regulars were all convinced they saw Andrew several times over the weekend. Andrew told one bartender, Gary Mantos, that he lived in São Paulo, Brazil, but that he was originally from San Diego, California, and that Miami reminded him of "Los Angeles in the eighties." He sat at the bar and talked to an older man. "He didn't know anybody," says Mantos. "He was trying to act fabulous."

Jimmy Nickerson, another bartender, who also saw Andrew on Friday from his station on the second level near the dance floor, figured from the way Andrew was dressed that he'd order Chivas Regal. Instead, Andrew asked for a glass of water and bummed a cigarette from Carlos Vidal, a regular customer. To Nickerson, those were telltale signs: "He was acting like a hustler."

Vidal is a news junkie. Not only had he followed the Cunanan case in the media but also he had seen the poster of Andrew in *Scoop*. Sitting right next to him, however, he did not recognize him. He recalls only, "The guy looked slightly familiar." They exchanged a few words. Andrew said, "I'm down here on vacation." Vidal also got the pickup vibes. He joked to Michael Lewis, a friend, "I'm sorry for who he picks up tonight."

"He made me uneasy," Vidal says, "because I had [the serial-killer idea] in the back of my mind." Vidal got up and went downstairs to the bathroom, where notices are posted, to see if there was a poster of Andrew. There was not. On his way downstairs, Vidal saw Andrew go out. "I thought there should be a poster up," he says. Frank Scottolini, the manager, had never been contacted by the authorities. "To my knowledge the FBI never contacted anyone in the bar," Scottolini says, despite the fact that the Bureau had been told that Twist was a most likely hangout for someone like Andrew. Back upstairs at the bar, Vidal recalls he laughed and said to Lewis, " 'That's probably the serial killer.' I'd seen him on network news. You say it, and you don't believe it's real."

Nevertheless, Vidal was uncomfortable and decided to leave. On his way out around midnight, he told Scottolini, standing at the door, "I think you had a serial killer in there. That guy I saw was the serial killer." Scottolini had also seen Andrew, but he didn't pay any attention. The next night Andrew showed up again, wearing a white baseball cap, glasses, shorts, and a backpack. The security camera was on at the door, and as Andrew walked in and out quickly, Scottolini was on the street talking to his assistant manager. Scottolini recognized Andrew and remembered what Vidal had told him. He was momentarily overwhelmed by a sickening feeling in his stomach. He turned to some friends, he remembers, and said, " 'There goes the gay serial killer.' Then I dismissed it like it couldn't be true."

When Alberto, the night clerk, called Andrew at ten o'clock on Saturday morning, he said he'd be down in ten minutes to pay the rent. At ten-thirty, Alberto realized that Andrew had skipped—gone out the back gate, leaving the key to 322 on the bureau. In the room, Alberto found a box for hair clippers. Andrew had apparently shaved his head. There was also a box for a lady's girdle.

Sunday night Versace went to see the movie *Contact* with Antonio and a friend. He stayed in Monday night, when Andrew was supposedly seen at Liquid, at the Fat Black Pussycat party, pretending he lived in one of the most luxurious buildings on the beach. Earlier he had tried to borrow a dollar at Cozzoli's Pizza, down the street from the Normandy Plaza, one of his fast-food hangouts.

Tuesday morning Andrew was up bright and early. So was Versace, who walked three blocks south to the News Cafe and bought five magazines. Dressed in his trademark gray and black, Gianni Versace walked back to his villa at about 8:40. Andrew was across the street wearing shorts, a tank top over a baggy T-shirt, and a black baseball cap pulled down over his eyes. Carrying his backpack on his right shoulder, he crossed quickly and sidled past Mersiha Colakovic, who had just dropped her daughter off at school. Then, ignoring Colakovic, Andrew walked rapidly up the first few steps in front of Versace's mansion. Versace was bent over, fitting his key into the lock of the black wrought-iron gate. Colakovic, who had walked past the two, glanced back to take another look at Versace, whom she had recognized. Appearing completely relaxed, he had smiled at her. Now she became an eyewitness to his murder.

32

Broad Daylight

Versace lost consciousness instantly, his brain dead, although his heart continued to flutter and was kept beating by the paramedics who rushed him to Jackson Memorial Hospital in Miami. Andrew had come up from behind, holding Jeff Trail's .40 caliber Taurus semiautomatic straight out in front of him, pointing the long barrel at Versace's neck, right behind his left ear and cheek. The first bullet cracked the base of Versace's brain, fracturing his skull and tearing the upper part of his spinal cord and neck. Andrew was so close to his target that the bullet produced a stippling effect—a tattoo of burned gunpowder the size of a half-dollar—on Versace's neck. (When the high-performance Golden Saber bullet left the barrel of the gun, the force expanded the top of the slug so when it hit Versace, the entry wound was far larger than a normal bullet would have made.) The bullet flew out of Versace's neck and hit one of the metal railings of the gate. The bullet then broke apart, and flying metal particles hit a mourning dove in the eye. The bird died instantly and was found lying on its back in front of the mansion.

After the first shot, Versace's head turned slightly, his eyes open. He received the second bullet through the right side of his face next to his nose. Shot from even closer range, that bullet lodged in his head and cracked the top of his skull. Versace immediately slumped to the steps in a pool of blood. Mersiha Colakovic stood on the sidewalk frozen in horror—she had seen the whole thing from less than thirty feet away. Andrew, displaying utter sangfroid, walked calmly away down Ocean Drive. Colakovic remembered that he walked oddly, like Donald Duck, with his feet turned out. Almost instantly, the front door of Casa Casuarina flew open. Antonio was the first to reach Versace. "No! No!" he cried. Lazaro Quintana, who lived nearby and had come over to play tennis with Antonio, saw Colakovic in front of the house. "What happened?" he demanded. She simply pointed to Andrew, now halfway down the block, going toward Twelfth Street. Quintana gave pursuit.

Running down Ocean, Quintana shouted, "You bastard!" Andrew did not even seem fazed. He turned left onto Twelfth Street and then right into an alley—Ocean Court—that led directly to the Thirteenth Street Garage, where William Reese's red pickup had been parked for nearly five weeks. Three sanitation men at Twelfth and Ocean Court saw Quintana chasing Andrew. Quintana warned them that Andrew had a gun, just as Andrew lifted the gun and pointed it at him. Quintana then gave up the chase, and the garbage men knew better than to follow an armed man up an alley. They ran to Twelfth and Collins, one street over, hoping to see Andrew emerge at Thirteenth and Collins, which was across the street from the garage entrance. But all they saw was a police car with its overhead lights on in the middle of the street.

The police were responding to a rear-ender that had occurred on Thirteenth between Ocean and Collins, and Andrew slipped right by them. The person who had been rear-ended, coincidentally, was Gary Knight, the gay activist, who suffered knee injuries. Knight cannot be sure, but he thinks he saw someone matching Andrew's description hail a cab going south on Collins through the intersection at Thirteenth. After the person threw a bag into the backseat and hopped in, the cab drove away.

Across the street and down from the Casa Casuarina, Victor Montenegro, a city employee who was fixing a parking meter between Tenth and Eleventh, heard the first gunshot. He looked up in time to see Andrew fire the second shot into Versace's face and then coolly walk away on Ocean Drive. Montenegro radioed police and ran toward Versace. Meanwhile, inside the mansion, Charles Podesta, Versace's cook, called 911 at 8:44 A.M. "A man's been shot. Please, immediately, please!" Cops on bikes showed up in two minutes to find Versace sprawled on the steps. Officer Calvin Lincoln, the first to check, found no vital signs. Hotel Astor employee David Rodriguez was on his way to work when he heard a shot and then, a few minutes later, saw Versace's body on the steps, with people slowly gathering round. Versace's sandals were left behind, and his sunglasses had tumbled down the steps. Rodriguez says, "I looked all around for a camera, it seemed so set up." When he arrived at the Astor, he told Laura Sheridan, the manager, "They're shooting a movie at Versace's house." If the scene itself seemed unreal, the aftermath was even more so.

For the Miami Beach Police Department, July 15 was another terrible Tuesday. "Everything major happens on Tuesday," says Detective Paul Marcus. "Most homicides, big fires. You get up in the morning, and it's Tuesday and you think, Oh, jeez." Marcus was the acting sergeant in homicide when the first call about the murder at 1116 Ocean Drive came in. Sergeant George Navarro, who was usually in charge, had the day off. Detective Paul Scrimshaw, who had been investigating homicides for eleven and a half years and was the most senior detective in the bureau, was out the door immediately. He arrived on the scene by 8:55. The beat cop asked, "Do you know who this is?"

"No," Scrimshaw answered, in a way that signified, Why would I care?

"It's Gianni Versace."

"Oh, shit."

Marcus arrived two minutes later. "I didn't think anything but that it was a normal, everyday South Beach shooting," he says. "I looked at the scene in the middle of Ocean Drive. I saw the blood in the shoes. I didn't even see Versace's house. I just thought, Another shooting, but on the steps of the Versace mansion."

When Marcus pulled up, Scrimshaw told him, "You're not gonna believe this—it's Gianni Versace." Marcus reacted swiftly. "I'm on the phone with the lieutenant, the captain." Soon the police have visitors. "Then we are descended upon by the media," Marcus continues. "All of a sudden, they are dropping out of the sky. On the grass across the street, it grew and grew and grew. It got to a point that it was overwhelming there." At that particular moment South Beach was also saturated with cops. The night shift was still out, and the day shift had been on for an hour and a half. Because the garbage men had seen Andrew running down the alley toward the parking garage, the cops on patrol checked the garage at 8:56 A.M. More cops were already out front for the fender-bender. A half-dozen police covered the garage, including exits and the alley. At 9:12 a pile of clothes was found on the third level, outside the passenger door of a red Chevy pickup: a black tank top underneath a gray T-shirt and a pair of boxer shorts. The T-shirt appeared to be damp with perspiration. Inside the truck under the brake pedal was a black backpack. A license check was run on the South Carolina tag, but it yielded nothing, since the plate had not been reported stolen.

At 9:17 the patrol officer in the alley radioed that he saw someone on the roof wearing a red shirt and glasses. "He might be part of the parking crew. He just peered over the edge. He's just walking around. Dark skin, Latin male. He looks like security for the building, wearing one of those kinds of shirts." Whoever it was went from one corner of the garage roof to the other, peering over, but when the police made it up to the roof five to ten minutes later, he was gone. (That afternoon, when a bloodhound named Emily was taken to the garage to follow Andrew's scent, she went straight to all four corners of the roof level.)

At first the crime looked very much like a "murder-for-hire type of hit," Scrimshaw says. The dead bird, a traditional Mafia symbol, was duly noted. As a result the FBI was notified early, and four agents from the murder-for-hire squad were dispatched. Two .40 caliber brass jacket casings were recovered right away, one on the street and one on the steps. (The bird was between them.) Many people didn't know who Versace was, including the Italian vice-consul in Miami, who asked, "Is he the guy who makes the jeans?" At FBI headquarters in Washington, few recognized the name. "I thought he was a singer," says Roy Tuber-gen, the head of violent crimes. Versace was hardly a household name, but he would soon become one.

At 9:21 A.M., at the Ryder Trauma Center at Jackson Memorial

Hospital, Gianni Versace was pronounced dead. Detective Gus Sanchez, assigned to hospital duty, retrieved Versace's personal effects— $1,173.63 in cash and a small religious picture of the Virgin of Medjugorje. (In interviews, Gianni had pooh-poohed organized religion.) The family had requested that a priest administer last rites. Sanchez entered with the priest and found that "Versace's T-shirt was gone from the room—disappeared." Later there were "unconfirmed rumors," Sanchez says, that Versace's X rays also vanished. Were grisly profiteers already at work? A nurse told Sanchez that the T-shirt had probably been left in the emergency room and thrown away.

In that crucial first hour after the murder, when all the forces were alerted and stood the best chance of apprehending the killer, an unfortunate diversion over another suspect drew many officers away from the original area of pursuit near the parking garage. The first calls describing Versace's shooter were unclear as to whether he was black or white or brown. A rookie cop spotted a dark-skinned male he had tussled with before. The man, who had just been released on probation, had dope in his pocket and started to run down Espanola Way, drawing the police several blocks from the garage location. The rookie radioed for help, and police converged on him. The suspect was caught and then released without being charged when it became apparent that he had had nothing to do with Versace's murder. While the chase was on, however, Paul Scrimshaw says, "Andrew could have walked up Collins Avenue and nobody would have looked at him."

By now investigators were tripping all over each other at the mansion. Versace's celebrity was drawing a crowd of law-enforcement officials. The state's attorneys, who rarely show up at crime scenes were photographed for the papers peering at the site. Was it a hit or was it random? No one had a clue, but most of the police thought it had to be a hit. The Florida Department of Law Enforcement (FDLE) began to process the scene and do the forensic work. More FBI officers arrived, "to the point where there was getting to be too many investigators there walking around, and trying to get information without a specific function," says Marcus. "There were agents walking Ocean Drive, walking the alleyway. We probably hit a peak locally of fifty investigators."

In the first hours, the dining room at the front of the mansion became police central. That was disconcerting to members of the household, who were numb with shock and grief. Marcus says, "Mr. D'Amico didn't want the house turning into the command post. He was devastated. They were on the phone and wanted to leave to go to the hospital. By then the information was relayed to us that Versace had died." Marcus told Antonio, "Listen, there's nothing you can do at the hospital. You're much more vital to the investigation." But Antonio, not to be deterred, insisted on going there. "We had to remove police cars and tapes to let him go."

A few blocks away in Chief of Police Richard Barreto's office, a high-level meeting began at ten o'clock with the city manager, members of the city government, and the state's attorney's office. Also in attendance was Michael Aller, tourism and convention coordinator for the city of Miami Beach. It may have been only an hour or so since Versace had been shot, but already the powers that be were deep into spin control, guarding the city's image as a carefree, escapist visitors' attraction. When two German tourists were robbed and murdered in Miami in 1993, the city's reputation had suffered a severe blow. Now Carnival Cruise was scheduled to run its first gay press junket the following weekend. A reputation for random violence in SoBe would be ruinous. Assistant State Attorney Rose Marie Antonacci-Pollock, who was present at the meeting, says, "All the spin doctors were up there basically figuring out what face to put on this. This wasn't productive in advancing the case. The city manager and the chief of police wanted to make sure it had nothing to do with South Florida tourism."

While the suits were spinning, a phalanx of uniformed officers were trying to identify the owner of the red pickup. When the South Carolina license tag didn't pan out, the police tried to check the red truck from the VIN—vehicle identification number. Miami Beach police dispatcher Gerry Zabrowski doggedly kept on running the number different ways until he got the Super Computer hit with the FBI advisory that the red pickup was not only a stolen vehicle but also had been part of another crime. By this time Sergeant George Navarro, who would supervise the investigation, had arrived. A fast-rising thirty-seven-year-old originally from the Internal Affairs Unit, Navarro was playing golf on his day off when he got the call to report immediately. His boss, Lieutenant Carlos Noriega, named the force's best cop in 1986, was already there. The hierarchy of the Miami Beach police investigation was thus established: Noriega, Navarro, and Scrimshaw as lead detective.

A little before noon, Keith Evans, Miami's FBI fugitive stalker, also joined the group at the mansion, because the description of the shooter sounded like Andrew Cunanan. "By the time Evans arrived, we had information it might be Cunanan," says Scrimshaw. "We had derived that much. As we told Evans, his face lit up—he got visibly excited." Evans had brought his Cunanan file with him. Scrimshaw and Marcus were getting information from the garage via radio as the pickup's VIN was being processed from there. "I'm relaying the info to Keith and Navarro," says Scrimshaw. "Keith says, 'Red? What type?' "

"Chevy 1500."

Evans asked for the VIN number and compared it with that of the truck stolen in New Jersey. "Oh, my God! This is William Reese's pickup truck! That's the pickup taken in the New Jersey murder we think Andrew Cunanan is responsible for."

"At that moment," says Scrimshaw, "Cunanan is linked to this investigation."

"Hot damn! It's Cunanan!" Keith Evans said.

"It was so exciting being there when everything fell together with the truck," Marcus relates. "It's not a whodunit anymore. A whodunit of this proportion is a lot more fun."

In a little more than two hours, a major piece of the crime had been solved. Sighs of relief emanated from the spin controllers. Now the challenge was to find Cunanan. Despite the fact that he was one of America's Ten Most Wanted and his picture had been hanging on the homicide bureau's bulletin board for two months, nobody in the Miami Beach Police Department except for Scrimshaw, Marcus, and Lori Wieder had any idea who Andrew Cunanan was. "What does he look like?" Navarro and Noriega asked Keith Evans. After a police press conference around one o'clock, at which no information on Cunanan was released—the beginning of a sorry pattern—Evans walked Noriega and Navarro to his car. There on the backseat Noriega and Navarro saw the answer to their question—boxes filled with fliers showing Andrew Cunanan's face. How many fliers? "I don't want to turn on Keith," Navarro demurs. According to Navarro, "He had a *lot* of fliers." Another mystery was solved.

33

King Kong

In less than twenty-four hours the murder of Versace became the number-one story in the country, and I found myself in the middle of it. From the gitgo, however, the story was made very difficult for the press to cover. In the language of the beach police, Versace was an "APE case"—acute political emergency. In fact, says Detective Paul Scrimshaw, "Versace was the King Kong of all APE cases." Within minutes of the shooting, the first media trucks rolled up to the Versace mansion. The first profiteer had already raced home for his Polaroid camera upon seeing Versace's body laid out on the Casa Casuarina steps, and was only able to make it back in time to get a shot of the designer's bare feet sticking out of the ambulance. Nevertheless, within forty-eight hours the huckster was trying to get $30,000 for his Polaroid. The "money shot"—the term was borrowed from pornography and signified ejaculation—went to the local ABC cameraman, who abandoned the story of a little girl who needed a kidney transplant at Jackson Memorial Hospital to run over and shoot the body on a gurney being raced into the trauma center. Hot damn again! It was Versace! Meanwhile, there were ten unauthorized hits on the hospital's computer system in the first few hours after the murder—people were trying to read Versace's medical records.

Law enforcement was quickly overwhelmed. Miami Beach has a population of 100,000 and a police force of 300. The department, like that of many smaller cities, is not computerized for many functions. The department's idea of the time it takes for the police to do their job thoroughly, clashed hopelessly with the voracious needs of a twenty-four-hour, nonstop global news cycle. It was as if the two entities existed in different time zones; there was no sense that the press could actually help in a criminal investigation. The first instinct of the local authorities was to protect the city's image and preserve their evidence for court—much as the Minneapolis authorities had responded to Jeffrey Trail's murder. The Miami Beach police were muzzled.

The state attorney's office, fearing—perhaps even secretly wishing—they had another O.J. on their hands, took every precaution and would not allow the police to give out even basic facts. "Jurors have a different view of the criminal justice system, of prosecution, of police work, because of O.J.," says then Chief Assistant State Attorney Michael Band, who supervised the investigation for the state attorney's office. Band feels that jurors have became more skeptical. "And they should be skeptical—not just about police but about everything that's presented to them." The Los Angeles district attorney's office's stunning loss in the Simpson case had made a deep impression on Band, who had sat down with the Dade County medical examiner's office, the commander of the homicide unit of the Metro-Dade police department, and several others to make sure nothing like that ever happened to the Eleventh Judicial Circuit of Florida. Band wanted no screwups, but he got them anyway.

Al Boza, the veteran detective who handled the Miami Beach Police public information office, felt strongly that there should be two official press briefings a day, but that never happened. "Just to say, 'Folks, this is what happened today—we are moving forward, we have received X number of tips, we have investigators working all night.' We didn't do that, and I do believe we paid dearly for it." From the beginning, everything Boza did was criticized from above. His first press release, for example, announcing Versace's murder, had to be rewritten, he says, "untold times." Boza originally wrote, he recalls, "As Mr. Versace approached the iron gate of the entrance of his residence,' and somebody says, 'I don't feel comfortable with the word "iron gate." It gives the sense of a fortress.' So you will never see the word 'iron gate' in any report that I put out about Gianni Versace."

Police relations with the media went sour the first day and got worse. Gail Bright, a local ABC-TV reporter in the supercompetitive Miami TV market, knew that the red pickup had probably been traced to Andrew. The local NBC and ABC affiliates both had cameramen who were able to get into the garage early and get the truck's license plate, which they then checked on their own. They could also hear the VIN being read on the police radio and a non–Miami Beach police source told Bright that the truck belonged "to a guy wanted all over." Bright asked Miami Beach Police Chief Richard Barreto at a 4:30 P.M. press conference on the day Versace was shot if the suspect was "the guy the Bureau's looking for." Barreto, who is six feet three with a thatch of silver hair and looks dashing in his uniform, refused to confirm even the existence of the red pickup, let alone the identity of the suspected killer. Just as the Chief was declining to answer Bright's question, the TV cameras caught the truck being towed right past the police station. That set a tone that kept each side from cutting the other any slack.

To Michael Band, who was present at the press conference, Bright's question meant one thing: They're already leaking this stuff. "The idea that a reporter knew enough to ask that specific a question told me that there was a leak." The police were strongly cautioned that any leaks would bring down severe consequences. Paul Scrimshaw thought that policy was wrong. "Used properly, the media can help solve your case and move people forward. The problem usually is, you can't get their attention." A few months before, Scrimshaw had handled the homicide of Paul Sigler, a gay man who worked for American Airlines. "We begged the media to publicize it," he says, yet the police got nowhere. Says Detective Paul Marcus, "Our attempts to get coverage for Sigler's murder went unnoticed because the Miss Universe pageant was going on. In that case, we needed the media to put his face in the public eye, but we didn't get any." In the Versace case, says Scrimshaw, "all of us believed that in the first few hours we should have given the media substantive information."

But when police brass could have been broadcasting an all-points bulletin for Andrew, in the hours they had their best chance of finding him, they chose to keep silent. Instead, their priority was to get a photo line-up "professionally prepared." Lieutenant Carlos Noriega recalls, "Once we established Cunanan, we had to relocate witnesses [who had been released] for a photo line-up." Had these witnesses seen Andrew's picture in the media, the line-up would be tainted. There were other technical difficulties as well, which could haunt the authorities later in court. The "wanted" picture of Andrew was too large to fit with the photos of Andrew look-alikes the police had. According to Noriega, "By law the pictures have to be identical in size. Otherwise the defense attorney can argue a defendant sticks out." It took police until early evening to prepare the line-up. The principal witness, Mersiha Colakovic, had given police a false name—Liliane De Feo—and disappeared; Andrew's looks were so common locally that a Miami Beach cop in the line-up had to be taken out—he was too similar to Andrew. As it turned out, the line-up was a wash: nobody could positively identify Andrew Cunanan.

Even so, Paul Scrimshaw wanted to charge Andrew with the murder of Gianni Versace. Reese's truck, like Lee Miglin's Lexus before it, yielded dozens of items of incriminating evidence, from Cunanan's driver's license and passport to Lee Miglin's Lexus insurance certificate to William Reese's Social Security card. The .40 caliber casings recovered at the scene of Versace's murder were from the same type of gun that had killed Madson and Reese. That afternoon arrangements were made to deliver the recovered casings and projectile by hand to the FBI lab in Washington in order to compare them with the others Andrew had used, and by the next day the match had been made; the gun used to kill Versace was the same gun that had been used to kill David Madson and William Reese. Scrimshaw felt the circumstantial evidence was strong, but soon learned that it wasn't strong enough for the state's attorney's office. "Michael Band, when we asked him for a warrant on circumstantial evidence ten or twelve hours after the murder, said, 'I won't give you a warrant, nor will I prosecute without the gun or a confession.' "

"I did not want an arrest warrant issued. I did not have a case," Band says. "I did not have the gun—I had a projectile that matched up to that gun. How do I know that gun wasn't picked up by somebody else?" Scrimshaw was infuriated, feeling that his investigation was being thwarted because the Versace case was about celebrity and wealth and the state attorneys were stalling on everything. "It added a great deal of pressure to things, because of their presence and the way they wanted it to go." He wasn't used to being second-guessed, but just as the police and the media were on two different clocks, the investigators and the state attorneys saw two different realities.

Florida law has two provisions that work in favor of defendants: the right to a speedy trial within 180 days and one of the most liberal discovery statutes in the country. If Florida were to charge and arrest Andrew, he could demand a speedy trial and might have to be tried in Florida before any other states. Moreover, prosecutors would be barred from introducing his prior crimes (although there might be a slight crossover because he had used the same firearm), and jurors would be instructed to consider the fact that he had no prior convictions when weighing the death penalty. Furthermore, his Florida attorneys would have the right to depose all other witnesses and have access to police reports in the other jurisdictions where he was charged. His lawyers could thereby learn what the other states' prosecutors were going to use against him, thus exposing their cases in advance. "Early on I made a shot call," says Band's colleague, State Attorney Rose Marie Antonacci-Pollock, who spent much of her time at the police station during the investigation. "We wouldn't be the first ones to trial."

Late Tuesday afternoon a second press release was issued, explaining that a photo line-up of possible suspects was in preparation, and asking for media "discretion when releasing information that may later adversely affect the outcome of this investigation." There was little chance of that. As Sergeant George Navarro says, "The media was cut-throat; they never cared about the case." They cared only about the story. Finally, at 8:30 P.M., a third press release admitted what had been known for almost ten hours: The police were looking for Andrew Cunanan, "27-year-old white male, 5′9″, 5′10″, brown hair and brown eyes. Cunanan's known to be a male prostitute servicing affluent clientele. Cunanan is well educated, dresses well and is very articulate. Cunanan should be considered armed and extremely dangerous."

I first heard that Versace had been shot from my husband, who called from the NBC News Washington bureau. I waited at home in Washington D.C. throughout the day hoping to hear whether a .40 caliber gun had been used. *Vanity Fair* was doing the final fact-check on a 10,000-word piece I had completed about Andrew and his first four murders, and when the news broke that Versace had been killed at point-blank range by someone wearing a baseball cap and carrying a backpack, I knew it could be Andrew. Moreover, my piece contained—originally in a little throwaway anecdote—the fact that Andrew had met Versace in 1990, at events surrounding a San Francisco Opera production of Richard Strauss's *Capriccio,* for which Versace did the costumes. I made the point that Versace was the one big name Andrew, the celebrity hound, actually had met.

By late afternoon, still having heard no news about Andrew from Miami, I called New York and said they should send me to Miami anyway—just in case. I was told that the story would be mine if Cunanan was really the suspect. But if it turned out someone else had shot Versace, then the story would go to Cathy Horyn, who had just written the *Vanity Fair* article about Donatella Versace in South Beach. We both made plans to go.

Before the final police announcement on Tuesday night, Kerry Sanders of CNBC mentioned that the killer had used a .40 caliber gun. That was it for me; I knew Andrew had struck again. By Wednesday morning, the opening shot of the *Today Show* was live from Miami Beach in front of Versace's mansion, signifying that Versace's murder would be the number-one news story of the day. On my way to the airport, I broke the news on the *Today Show* that Cunanan and Versace had at least met before, which the Versace family immediately denied. With the official announcement that Andrew Cunanan was the suspect, the story now was on two tracks: the bottled-up investigation and the

killer's personality. Who was Andrew Cunanan? Few knew, and luckily
I had just spent two months trying to find out.

By the time I got to the Raleigh Hotel in South Beach, the tsunami
had hit. I had about two dozen requests for interviews, including all
three TV networks and newspapers throughout the country and the
BBC. They continued to pour in all day. Out by the Raleigh's pool,
crews lined up to do interviews with me. I had a choice—to keep
accepting interview requests in order to publicize my piece and the
magazine, or to try to report the story myself. After appearing on all
three network newscasts, I bailed out of *Larry King Live* early to meet
Cathy Horyn, have a drink with two great sources, and hit the Boardwalk, the hustler bar where witnesses had seen Andrew. When one of
the male go-go dancers rubbed himself up against me so that I could
feel his protrusion—the usual manner of asking for a tip to be put in
the top of his briefs—I had no idea what he was doing and recoiled.

I was amazed at how much South Beach resembled Hillcrest, and
how easily Andrew would have fitted in there. The next morning at
6:30, Cathy and I walked on Ocean over to the Casa Casuarina. The
bloodstains were still on the front steps, which had become an ad hoc
shrine to Versace. Even at that hour, women in skin-tight leotards and
shorts were pretending to stroll by the mansion, hoping to be caught by
the cameras of at least a dozen TV crews set up on the lawn across the
street. For the next ten days along Ocean Drive, Andrew's face would be
on every TV in the bars of the outdoor cafés and restaurants. The reports
about Andrew and Versace, in English and Spanish, would drone as
relentlessly as the tides on the beach across the street. The News Cafe,
where Versace had bought magazines just before his murder, was
mobbed day and night with foreign TV crews.

Another video camp was set up on the plaza in front of the police
station, much to the consternation of the homeless who considered it
their turf. When a CNN producer complained about a one-eyed, alcoholic, homeless lady trying to get into his shots, Al Boza defended her,
saying, "This is her backyard. She hasn't made a complaint about you
people, so we learn to behave with each other."

One unnerving individual, a neighborhood fixture, invested himself with full authority. "All of a sudden he began to realize that this was the greatest thing that ever happened to him," Boza says. He walked up to a very pregnant female reporter during a live feed to her Miami TV station, and interrupted her in the middle of her stand-up, saying, "I got important information. Are you live on the air?" The woman was so startled that she let out a bloodcurdling scream right on the air and then ran for the safety of her satellite truck. She later filed a harassment complaint against the man with police, and he sued her in return. The media circus was on.

34

The Family

Versace's body was autopsied in the early evening of the day he was shot. Florida law demands that any body involved in a homicide remain intact in the state for at least forty-eight hours. Since the Florida autopsy would test for AIDS, the HIV secret Versace had so fiercely concealed would be revealed. The family did not want to wait forty-eight hours; they wished to rush the cremation and get the ashes out of the country as soon as possible. Furthermore, they didn't want to stay around to talk to police. "They did want it to move quick," says Chief Assistant State Attorney Michael Band. "And they came to me. I told them, 'Absolutely not.'"

The autopsy was performed by Dr. Emma Lew, a slim, attractive Chinese woman with a ponytail and purple bee-sting lips, and arresting eyebrows shaped like pagodas. In her office she had a paper tiara that said, "Scene Queen." Dr. Lew also performed the equivalent of a bird autopsy, a pecopsy—her first—on the dead bird found next to Versace. "It was a cute little thing. The only area of damage, of course, was the left side of the head," Dr. Lew says. "The eyeball was hanging out of the socket, just clinging to the left side of the head. When I X-rayed, I found tiny radial paint fragments, which means there were tiny fragments of metal in that eye. Which is even more supportive evidence that this bird was knocked by this ricocheting projectile."

Versace's autopsy was straightforward—simple but instantly destructive head wounds from two bullets fired at close range. "We knew that this was a very high profile case," says Dr. Lew, "and we took extra care to ensure that everything was done properly." She says there were small traces of prescription drugs in Versace's body. Dr. Lee Hearn, the Dade County toxicologist who would later perform toxicology tests on Andrew, told me that drugs taken for HIV are normally so water-soluble that they do not show up in testing. In any case, Florida laws concerning confidentiality are very strict about releasing any information about infectious diseases such as HIV.

"Did Versace appear to be in good health?" I inquired of Dr. Lew. She answered elliptically. "He had no natural disease that would have caused his death at that time." The usual procedure in a homicide investigation is for the police and the medical examiners to obtain a medical history of the victim from the family and to pool information. The police, says Dr. Lew, "compile what we call the pump sheet, a summary of the case." According to Scrimshaw, "That procedure wasn't done because the information was not available to us."

Versace's body was kept overnight at the morgue and released on Wednesday morning to the Riverside Gordon Funeral Home in North Miami, a Jewish funeral home chosen because it was out of the way, but the paparazzi discovered it anyway.

Santo and Donatella Versace, stoic and withdrawn, had arrived with a bodyguard by private jet Tuesday night. They proceeded to distance themselves, literally and figuratively, as quickly as possible from Andrew Cunanan and the crime. They and their publicists and lawyers, who had gathered at the Casa Casuarina, were emphatic that Gianni had not known Andrew Cunanan and that they did not want to talk to police before Thursday. At one point they had thought of offering a reward for Andrew's capture, but the idea was nixed. "We said, 'Wait and see what happens,' " says Lieutenant Noriega. "We had ten thousand dollars [already offered]. We didn't want it to appear that we couldn't catch him."

Scrimshaw and Navarro, as well as the FBI, were eager to talk to the family before Thursday, but it was made clear that they would not be allowed to. The state attorney for Dade County, Kathy Fernandez Rundle, and her deputy, Rose Marie Antonacci-Pollock, would be the go-betweens. "They claimed they were trying to make it easy for us," says Navarro. The family would not talk unless their lawyer from Italy was present. They also hired a Miami lawyer.

Police had questioned the household staff on Tuesday. Antonio had told one detective about his and Versace's use of male escorts, but he said they'd done this only in New York, never Miami, and not in the past two to three years. (Jaime Cardona's memory was prodded by means of a subpoena, and he later admitted to police that he had procured for Versace and D'Amico.) Scrimshaw, meanwhile, had developed four theories for why Versace was murdered: (1) It was a Mafia hit; (2) the motive was a robbery; (3) Versace had given the murderer AIDS; (4) it was a completely random act of violence. He also wondered whether there was a substantial insurance policy on Versace, and for how much. "Was he worth more dead or alive?" Scrimshaw wondered. "I don't find it strange to ask that question. You always look close to home first with murders. It's not just theory to kick around, but de rigueur in the initial stages of an investigation."

Scrimshaw never got the opportunity to ask, and he suspected that the two state attorneys were bowled over by celebrity. "There was a verbal agreement with Kathy Rundle over at the house with the family," Scrimshaw charges. "We tried to get in for a couple of days—we were pissed we weren't privileged to get in. I'm bitter because in the first few days the state's attorney's office absolutely impeded the investigation by shielding the family and taking part in decision-making they should have taken no part in."

"We may have made an arrangement to meet with them on Thursday," says Antonacci-Pollock carefully. "I never got the idea that this family was stonewalling us. I know the police did." With the state's attorneys in charge, the customary "next-of-kin conference" never took place in the usual sense, and no probing questions were ever put to the family. "We never had a sit-down with Donatella or Santo," Navarro says, calling the experience "odd." He and Keith Evans talked only to the family lawyers while Donatella and Santo were in other parts of the house, and "[The family's lawyers] denied having anything to do with the Mob or anything bad." Neither Antonacci-Pollock nor Fernandez

Rundle brought up such unpleasant subjects as a Mafia hit or who might have wanted to get rid of Gianni. "We didn't go into a lot of detail with them like that," says Antonacci-Pollock. Rather, her major concern was from a "victim's rights" point of view. "I didn't want the family going back to Italy, if [Cunanan] had been caught and not charged, thinking, Why not? That's why we spent so much time with the family, frankly, and they were gracious and understood." Moreover, Antonacci-Pollock says, "It kind of bothers me, being Italian, that everything that has Italians involved—[people assume] it's the Mob."

On Wednesday, the FBI's liaison from the Italian government in Washington called Scrimshaw to offer his assistance as a go-between to get answers to questions about Versace and his business from the Italian authorities. Scrimshaw was interested in finding out if there were any ongoing investigations in Italy. Only two months previously, in May 1997, Santo had been convicted on a bribery charge later overturned. But Scrimshaw was never told that.

Also on Wednesday, the Versaces used all their clout in an effort to get the body out of the United States before the required forty-eight hours were up. While the body was being embalmed—it had been released to the funeral home from the morgue at 8:50 A.M. on Wednesday—a donnybrook ensued between the Versace lawyers and handlers and the lawyers for the funeral home, who insisted that the law could not be subverted. The argument went on for hours. "The Mayor stuck his nose in," says Band. At one point things got so heated that Florida Governor Lawton Chiles was reportedly appealed to directly on the phone to query the law—hoping that Versace's remains could be removed. The request was denied.

In the early afternoon before the cremation took place there was a viewing of the body for the family. Israel Sands, the Versaces' florist in South Beach, had created five elaborate arrangements to place around the coffin, each representing a member of the family—white for Donatella, blue for Santo, bright yellow for Gianni, pink for Gianni's niece, Allegra, and blue for her brother, Daniel.

After the viewing, the body was transported to a crematorium in Pompano Beach in hopes that it could be cremated immediately. It was never left alone. First it was in the care of one of the Versace publicists.

When it became impossible for the body to be cremated before the forty-eight hours had elapsed, Charles Podesta, the family cook, was sent to spend the night with the corpse. Gianni Versace was finally cremated on Thursday morning.

Early Thursday afternoon, Donatella, who was scheduled to talk to the authorities but never did, called Israel Sands and asked him to decorate the 20-by-14-inch gold Versace neoclassical box that would carry Gianni's ashes back to Italy with flowers. When Sands arrived about 4 P.M., Antonio was being interviewed by the police, and he was far more candid about his and Gianni's use of male prostitutes in Miami Beach than he had been on Tuesday. The interview was cut short, however, by the family's request that he be able to assist with the ashes.

Israel Sands, meanwhile, was taken to a room in the cellar with white walls and a big table in it. When Charles Podesta came in with the Italian consul and the box containing the ashes, Sands was asked to move to the library. "Charles said, 'I want you to work upstairs. I don't want to take Mr. Versace into the cellar.' " The box with the remains was then placed in a larger wooden box with official seals all over it. Finally, the box was wrapped with wire tape in the presence of the consul.

Donatella had asked to have lots of white orchids on top of the box. Sands remembers thinking, "If I have to tie it, I'll do the whole work as a gift wrapping. I did two garlands to be able to encircle the box in both directions with dentrobium orchids and weeping podo carpus branches." Observed the whole time by a member of the household staff, he worked fast because the Versaces "were in a big hurry." Sands left at 7:30 P.M. "Twenty minutes later Donatella was in a car on the way to the airport." She has never returned to South Beach.

35

Miami Mishaps

THE MURDER OF VERSACE and the massive amount of coverage it engendered jolted both the FBI and local authorities. "Absolutely, the press drove it," says San Diego FBI's Peter Ahearn of the ensuing investigation. Andrew Cunanan suddenly became the subject of one of the largest manhunts, if not *the* largest manhunt, in FBI history, comparable to the hunt for Martin Luther King assassin James Earl Ray or in its day the Bureau's successful pursuit of John Dillinger. The evidence discovered in Reese's pickup led both Chicago and New Jersey to issue warrants for his arrest for first-degree murder. Both charges carried the death penalty—New Jersey's in federal court, Chicago's in the state of Illinois.

If, in the first hours after Versace's death, the Miami Police Department had to make do with shoe leather and few computers, within a day the force was inundated with the most up-to-date technology available—analysts and computers from the Florida Department of Law Enforcement and the FBI and all of the FBI's resources, from its top guns at headquarters in Washington to its agents in fifty-six field offices across the country.

"With the Versace killing," says the FBI's former number-two deputy director, William Esposito, "I called the people who were supposed to be in charge of this investigation and I said, 'Look, we have got to find this guy. I want the command center activated. I want two conference calls a day with all the offices involved.' But I want it at lower levels—usually I don't want the agents in charge. I want the super case agents on the supervisory level." He ticks off all the offices on the hunt: San Diego, Los Angeles, San Francisco, Chicago, Minneapolis, Philadelphia, New York, Miami. "I want twice-a-day phone calls out of our command center to find out what's going on and what they're going to do in the next twenty-four hours." Moreover, Esposito told FBI special agent in charge in Miami, Paul Philip, "I don't care if you have to put all four hundred agents on the street. I want you to do it. I want you to leave no stone unturned."

While the FDLE created a time line of Andrew's crimes and whereabouts and monitored the media from a newly constituted command center inside the Miami Beach Police Department conference room, fliers of Andrew were finally going up all over South Beach. Paul Philip turned his office into a mini TV studio, "to keep the heat off the troops," he explains somewhat disingenuously. "We'd start with the *Today Show* live shots at six A.M." His first interview of the day, Philip says was "with *Good Morning America* or *Today,* depending on who won the fist fight, and I'd close with *Nightline.* You just can't keep this up." The only real news to report, however, did not make law enforcement or local government shine. How could it be, people asked, that Reese's red pickup could have stayed at the municipal parking garage for such a long time without being tagged by police? A parking attendant I spoke to explained that cars started to be checked only after about the fourth or fifth week. It was not unusual for people to stash cars there for weeks in the off season.

On Wednesday morning, Vivian Olivia of the Cash on the Beach pawnshop called Lieutenant Noriega about the pawnshop transaction form she had submitted with Andrew's information six days before, on July 10. At the police department, pawnshop forms were not computerized but hand-filed. Because Andrew's concerned a coin, it was passed along to property detectives, who were asked if anyone had reported stolen coins. They said no. The detective in charge of the pawn receipts then took three days off. When he got back, the day Versace was killed, he was pulled from the pawnshop detail to help with the Cunanan investigation. Meanwhile, the form languished on his desk until it was discovered the next day, after Olivia called in. As if the police weren't embarrassed enough, the *Miami Herald* reported—incorrectly—that the pawnshop ticket had been found in Reese's truck.

The *Herald,* the hometown paper, never quite got up to speed. For the first crucial days, it allowed the biggest story in the country to be covered by reporters from its "Neighbors" section of local news, while its top crime reporter wasn't anywhere near the beach. The competing *Sun-Sentinel,* however, deployed a full team and blanketed the area. In an unfortunate coincidence, the *Herald* had started, the previous Sunday, a well-researched, multi-part exposé of a Miami Beach Police Department overtime scam under the headline Collars for Dollars, which said the scam had been "tolerated by police brass and prosecutors for years." Now editors at the paper felt—mistakenly, the police argue—it was payback time from the MBPD. According to one state attorney, "I received a call from an editor over there who was desperate for information, and the quote essentially was 'We're getting our ass kicked in our own backyard.' "

Olivia told police that Cunanan might return to her shop, because she had felt that the coin Andrew pawned had special meaning to him. The police began to stakeout the pawnshop, but by Friday the news had leaked. Both *America's Most Wanted* and the *New York Post* sent reporters. Olivia recounts, "I said, 'I say nothing,' because I was sure the Cunanan guy would come back." By Saturday, however, she says, "I was feeling like Bill Clinton. I had to run like Madonna with sunglasses to the store."

The information Andrew gave on the pawnshop form led the authorities to the Normandy Plaza, where early Wednesday evening thirty cops showed up to swarm the hotel and search for him. "Within a couple of minutes they had five guys on the roof across the street," says Normandy Plaza owner Roger Falin. "They had blocked off the street. Within minutes after that they had fifty or sixty people here." Ronnie claims to have been harassed by the authorities because Andrew had listed his room number on the pawnshop form. "I had to hire a lawyer. The SWAT team did break the door. I threatened to sue," he says, flopping on his bed to demonstrate how he was held. "I had the SWAT team in here spread-eagled over me." Ronnie, however, claimed not to recognize Andrew's picture. In fact, when the police first searched the Normandy Plaza, nobody at the Normandy Plaza claimed to recognize Andrew. Paul Philip says, "Unfortunately for us, when we were there, they hadn't yet had that 'moment of clarity.' "

"First we search the rooms and come up empty," says Rose Marie Antonacci-Pollock. But that soon changed, she continues. "Overnight, Miriam is able to describe him down to his well-manicured toes and well-developed calf muscles." Miriam Hernandez defends her momentary lapse of memory: "I thought to myself, I know this face—I can't place it. Maybe I was afraid. They made me so nervous when they said he was a killer—that he had already killed five people. I could not place him—he changed three different rooms. . . . They said, 'Andrew Cunanan.' I said, 'That name? No.' " All day Thursday she thought about it. "My head pounded all night; I couldn't sleep. I came that morning, and you know when that light flashes in your brain? I went right to where I had his registry—I pulled it and called my brother and said, 'This is the guy.' " Miriam claims that she called the FBI but that the agent was not at his desk. She later called the FDLE, which relayed a message to the Miami Beach police about 4 P.M. to check out room 322. The room had not been previously searched because the search warrants applied only to occupied rooms, and 322 was empty. But before the police got there Friday, Miriam recalls, "then comes everybody from every newspaper. That jerk was first."

She is referring to Chuck Goudie, a veteran crime reporter who was covering Cunanan for WLS-TV, the ABC-owned and -operated station in Chicago. Back in May, Goudie had done the first interview in San Diego with Erik Greenman, Andrew's roommate, and had also covered Lee Miglin's murder. According to Rad Berky, a longtime respected correspondent for WPLG, the ABC affiliate in Miami, Goudie was "in town doing a story on leads followed up on. He knew [police] had gone to the Normandy Plaza. He went there just to do a stand-up. While he's out front, somebody from the hotel says, 'I now remember him [Cunanan]. He's been here. Come on in—his room is still here.' " Goudie knew immediately that police had not searched the room. "At the head of the tape the manager explains the police had not been in the room," says Tom Doerr, then news director of WPLG. That minor detail, however, did not deter Goudie. Sensing a scoop of major proportions, Goudie not only entered the room—but also picked up and displayed for the camera all sorts of items that Andrew had left behind, from a hair-clippers box to porn magazines, thereby tainting it all as evidence.

When the police showed up a short time later, they had no idea that Goudie had been allowed inside, and they proceeded to dust the room for prints. When Goudie's piece appeared on the six o'clock news that night, the authorities were enraged. "If we would have been prosecuting the case, everything in that room would have been challenged and thrown out," says Carlos Noriega. "God forbid we found the gun in there." Rad Berky says of his ABC colleague, "It is one of the most egregious acts I've ever seen a reporter commit. He's supposed to be one of the better reporters in this business. It's symptomatic of this type of story. There's this incredible urge to be first—I got what nobody else had."

"We always have to remind ourselves that no story is larger than the public safety and no story is worth a human life," Tom Doerr stated on a piece that WPLG felt compelled to air in the wake of what Goudie had done. "We used the video from his report; we didn't know he'd gone in before the cops," says Doerr. "It's kind of strange, but everyone is so hungry to get the exclusive, you don't think."

Rather than apologize, Goudie made no comment. His news director, Phyllis Schwartz, issued a statement and suggested to Miami colleagues that it made no difference that he had entered before the police, because hotel personnel had told him that they had already cleaned the room. Doerr says, "Goudie insists he called police to tip them *after* he'd done the piece. But they blew him off." Phyllis Schwartz said in her statement, "WLS-TV maintains that its news gathering and reporting activities are legal, ethical and appropriate in this ongoing investigation." Just in case, WLS hired a prominent Miami law firm to represent Goudie, who later received an Edward R. Murrow Award from the Radio-Television News Directors Association for "his continuing coverage of the Cunanan manhunt."

Lieutenant Noriega was so angry with Goudie that he ordered Al

Boza to issue a scathing warning to the media not to tamper with the case. "We were very upset," Noriega says. "I called Boza and said, 'You do a press release saying we expect [the press] to exhibit proper conduct. This is a homicide, and it's ethically wrong.'" The release was never sent. "To make a long story short," Boza explains, "that news release received about four or five revisions before a very, very mild copy went out." The release that did go out did not mention Goudie or tampering with evidence, but focused on the use of anonymous sources. It was nevertheless deeply resented by some news organizations, which interpreted it as an incursion on First Amendment rights.

Although police remain profoundly skeptical, the personnel at the Normandy Plaza are adamant that they took no money for showing room 322 to Goudie. However, a hotel resident told police that he had seen one hotel employee accept at least twenty dollars from a local NBC news producer trying to gain entry. The police were then told that approximately nine camera crews had been in the room.

For Miami media, the Cunanan manhunt was equivalent to covering a war. Ramon Escobar, an assistant news director at NBC's WTVJ who is openly gay, was elevated to field marshal for the station. As the resident expert, he knew where to deploy his troops to look for Cunanan. He was also able to answer embarrassing questions such as, What is a bubble butt? Escobar received anonymous calls from a fellow escort of Andrew's in New Jersey named Steve, who claimed (incorrectly) that Andrew had been to Clinton's first inaugural. He also said that he had received e-mail from Andrew, though no one remembered Andrew ever using a computer. Acting on a tip from Steve that Andrew might be using the computer at the local library, Escobar, who lived near the Normandy Plaza, visited the nearest branch of the Miami Beach library and found that the FBI had been there before him. Andrew had indeed been using the facilities, but it could not be established that he had used the computer.

The locals watched the big networks roll in with astounding resources. Satellite trucks maintained with a twenty-four-hour crew—at a cost of $10,000 a day—became a common sight. Sometimes the media veered dangerously close to being out of control. On Thursday, for example, the naked, bloody corpse of a Cuban doctor was found hogtied in his bed S&M style in nearby Miami Springs. The suspect was a young man he had taken home, who robbed him. The doctor, who had a wife and children in Cuba, was not known to be gay, but because the description of the suspect resembled Cunanan, his murder got tangled up in the manhunt frenzy and he was outed live on TV.

One of the great made-for-the-media, performance-art pieces surrounding Versace's murder was the first of his two memorial services. On Friday at 11:00 A.M., the Mass of Resurrection for Gianni Versace was celebrated at Miami's St. Patrick's Catholic Church by a number of priests, including two bishops. It was officially organized by the Archdiocese of Miami, which sent out a press release announcing it. The Casa Casaurina sent over floral arrangements. "Even people paying their respects barely knew who Gianni Versace was," says Jim DeFede, a reporter with the *New Times*. "Every bozo and loser in South Beach was there," adds Tom Austin. "The entire city commission, all the mayors and city managers. They didn't let cameras inside." But outside, the drenched-in-black congregation preened for the cameras in their shades and their $200 Versace T-shirts while police and the FBI infiltrated the crowd, lest Andrew attempt to return for a final blaze of glory in the spotlight. "The service was very strange," says Israel Sands. "The priest was bending over backwards to be up to the level of trendiness. He quoted Madonna and sang in the pulpit from *Evita*—'Where Do We Go from Here?' " Tara Solomon says, "We stopped whimpering and had our jaws politely drop." Sands adds, "The priest did a very nice sermon, and he alluded to Joseph's coat of many colors—a Versace coat. This priest left no stone unturned in the family of Christ. He got away with it. Well done."

Not everyone appreciated basking in the media glow. "In this case the media got in our way," says Miami Beach Police Sergeant Richard Pelosi. "We couldn't use our radios." Detective Paul Marcus adds, "We had to talk on land lines because of the media. The *Herald* and the TV stations could monitor the radio. We had to be very careful—we couldn't even use cell phones." Pelosi recalls, "One day, all of a sudden, a camera and boom mike are outside our window of the third-floor detective bureau. The boom mike was from a local channel. We made them move it." Navarro would play Noriega messages on his answering machine from female reporters begging for the slightest crumb of information. "It sounded like they were offering their bodies—'anything you want, anything you need.' I couldn't answer my phone for the first month," Navarro says. One reporter even broadcast a story about not getting anything but the answering machine!

Scrimshaw grew more and more disgusted. "The state attorney's office wanted to completely close communication with the press, because they were thinking O.J. And what the press wanted to know was innocuous. The whole factor in this is the case took over from us."

Scrimshaw continues, "We were forced into the position of running down leads instead of conducting the kind of investigation we needed to conduct." The FBI wasn't sharing information either. "We depended on the FBI for certain things, and if they did them, they didn't tell us. We were told that the FBI was not going to give us written reports." As a result, the practical outcome of all Deputy Director Esposito's directives to the Bureau nationwide was reduced—at least for the lead investigator for the Miami Beach police—to word-of-mouth reports passed on by rookie agent, Keith Evans.

One of the most frustrating parts of the investigation for Scrimshaw was that he could not get any feedback from Europe about Versace or his business. "At first the Italian [liaison] told me he'd give me whatever help he could," Scrimshaw relates. "When I called back the second time, he said, 'I have to get clearance from my supervisor.' I thought I heard a hesitation when I asked about organized crime. I said, 'I need to know if there is an investigation.' That's when the communication stopped. He never returned my calls, and he disappeared off the face of the earth."

Meanwhile, useless leads poured in from all over the world. A Swiss psychic swinging a pendulum said Andrew would be leaving Ottawa for Montreal. Others claimed to have spotted him in Brazil and Mexico. The only lead of any consequence came from a sailboat owner, Guillermo Volpe, who returned Wednesday, the sixteenth, after four days away, to find that someone had broken into the twenty-four-foot sailboat he anchored in a slip off Collins Avenue on Indian Creek, about fifteen blocks south of the Normandy Plaza. He found old pita bread and newspapers opened to stories of the Versace killing, including Versace's hometown paper, Milan's *Corriere Della Sera*. He also saw a man resembling Cunanan sitting on a bench nearby reading a navigational book that he later realized had been taken from his boat. Police were never able to find any forensic evidence on the boat, but they did find a red polo shirt, which could have been the red shirt on the person seen by a police officer on the roof of the Thirteenth Street parking garage right after the Versace murder, where the dog picked up on Andrew's scent.

Since the FBI had not begun the process of profiling Andrew, the Miami Beach police decided to profile him on their own. They were aided by Steve Nauck of San Diego who was in training in Miami for PanAm World Airways and who told the police he was like a "baby brother" to Andrew. Nauck filled them in with a long list of Andrew's likes and dislikes—that Chicago and Minneapolis were among his favorite U.S. cities, and that Milan was among his favorite European cities, for example. Nauck told police a favorite fantasy of Andrew's "involves bondage and 'fucking someone to death.'" Nauck believed that Andrew would disguise himself either as a surfer or as a transvestite. And thus another stereotype, that of the drag queen, which gays so objected to when citing law-enforcement and media reports about Andrew, came from one of his gay friends.

By Sunday, the fifth day after Versace's murder, there was still no sign of Andrew, and the investigation started to stall. The FBI had already pulled out of the Miami Beach Police Department and gone back to their own headquarters building in Miami. Some saw this as a sign that the FBI was dismayed by the pawnshop blunder and other police mishaps and had decided to withdraw. Paul Mallett insists that the FBI withdrew strictly in order to not to impede "a homicide investigation."

On Sunday a sighting of Andrew came in from the Miami Airport Hilton Hotel. Rose Marie Antonacci-Pollack, who accompanied the police there, says, "Enough weapons were assembled to run a small war." A squad of FBI commando types donned Velcro flack vests that rolled down to reveal the letters "FBI." Agents found two trembling maids who thought they had seen Cunanan. As a result, the register was scanned for "hot rooms"—those inhabited by walk-ins with no reservation, individuals who paid in cash, and single men. The FBI agents were allowed to search only after knocking on the door and announcing who they were. In one room in which they heard no response, says Antonacci-Pollock, "they broke in on a family who was sound asleep and never woke up."

All in vain. Andrew was not found at the Hilton either.

36

Show Me
the Money

Gay Killer and Tom Cruise
Exposed!
Shocking
Truth Behind
Murder Spree

Gay serial killer Andrew Cunanan is madly in love with Tom
Cruise! The sick monster talked openly of killing the superstar's
beautiful wife, Nicole Kidman, so he could have Tom all to
himself—to tie up, torture and humiliate for pleasure.
—*National Enquirer*, August 5, 1997

Inside Gay Serial Killer's Sick Mind
I'll Be More Famous than Liberace or Rock Hudson
I am leaving to take care of business . . . I'm going to make
these people suffer for what they did to me. I will be the night-
mare from which they will never wake up.
—*Globe*, August 5, 1997

Kiss of Death
Behind the Killer's Smiling Mask: The Shocking
Untold Story.
Secret Wife and Child
Stream of Rich Lovers
His Cruel Killing—At Age 8
Lover Who Escaped
—*Star*, August 5, 1997

THE STAR'S "LOVER WHO ESCAPED," Tim Schwager, the assistant manager of a San Francisco Denny's who spent one night with Andrew and woke up with three hickeys, was transformed for the tabloids after Versace's death. After first "writing" his story for a special box in *Newsweek*, he next appeared in *Star* as a "restaurant manager." In the even more downmarket British tabloid *News of the World*, Schwager became a "Hollywood restaurateur" who "woke up with strange, Vampire like markings all over his body."

The tabloids landed on Andrew Cunanan as the next O. J. Simpson or JonBenet Ramsey. While the manhunt went on, the story of "Who Is Andrew Cunanan?" centered on Hillcrest, where only a handful of close friends abstained from giving interviews. A number of former friends of Andrew attempted to cash in. The coverage went from the false and lurid in the *Enquirer* to the trivial and trumped-up in *Star*, which, for an interview and an old backpack of Andrew's filled with condoms and Nair hair-removal lotion that Shane O'Brien had lying around, reportedly paid O'Brien five figures. The tab breathlessly reported, "We handed the backpack to the FBI, who were thrilled with the latest piece of the Cunanan jigsaw puzzle. 'This is an important piece of evidence,' says a high ranking agent. 'Our thanks go out to *Star* for going out of its way to help.' " According to an unnamed neighbor whom nobody at the tabloid could remember interviewing, Andrew "strangled a cat at age eight," and Gamma Mu was "a sordid homosexual society whose millionaire members spared no expense indulging their kinky passion for sleazy, jet-setting sex."

Even more outrageous, for those *Enquire*-ing minds who wanted to know, Andrew "described bizarre sexual fantasies about dressing Tom in full leather bondage outfits and dominating and humiliating him." Despite the fact that Erik Greenman, Andrew's last roommate had barely mentioned Tom Cruise in previous interviews—then only in passing as a favorite movie star—Greenman's story changed radically after he got paid $85,000 by the tabloid.

The frenzy over the Cunanan story surprised even a tested tabloid veteran like *Hard Copy*'s Santina Leuci. "You're writing checks for more than your paycheck in a *year*." Erik Greenman, for example, was hotly pursued because the people who knew Andrew best avoided the press. Robbins Thompson went underground to Mexico after being outed, and Norman Blachford didn't need the money or the publicity. Nevertheless, Diane Sawyer sent Blachford a personal letter hoping for an interview for *Prime Time Live.* Cunanan's brother and sisters were favored with bouquets from "concerned" network producers who could not pay outright for interviews but who could offer all-expenses-paid trips to New York including limo service. Some network magazine shows were reportedly willing to pay for still photos in hopes of getting an interview that way.

"The secondary people who kind of knew Andrew Cunanan were the biggest sleazebags I ever dealt with," says Santina Leuci. "Here's a guy who's supposed to be their friend, who killed five people, and here they are negotiating with TV shows. They weren't even being helpful to the police or the local press." San Diego FBI Deputy Supervisor Peter Ahearn confirms this: "The lengths people would go to avoid talking to us in order to make money—it's mind boggling." Santina Leuci didn't even have to do her usual pitch: "You're not going to get paid by *Dateline* or *PrimeTime Live.* I can pay you this. It takes persistence, and you don't let them have too long." In the aftermath, however, even the police wanted to cash in. Lee Urness, who as head of the Minnesota Fugitive Task Force was at the forefront of the investigation, signed on as a consultant for an aborted ABC-TV movie of the week on Andrew. He then made himself scarce for interviews.

Even some of Andrew's affluent friends had their palms outstretched. Two classmates from Bishop's, one of them an Ivy League graduate, were willing to talk, but only if they would be paid. When I turned them down, they countered by offering to sell me Andrew's inscriptions to them in their yearbooks as an alternative to a fee for their interviews. The La Jolla mother of one Bishop's girl acted as her agent. "How much are you willing to pay my daughter?" she demanded. "I don't pay, I can't," I answered. "Then my daughter has nothing to say to you."

MaryAnn Cunanan, under heavy medication, was guarded by the FBI. "The media was practically living at Cunanan's mother's residence," says San Diego FBI spokesman Carl Chandler, "shining lights in her windows, pounding at her door." Reporters finally got so intrusive that the Bureau decided to move Andrew's mother out late at night and put her on a plane to San Francisco, where they hid her under a program to protect witnesses. "They came up with this elaborate plan to block the media with our cars," explains Peter Ahearn. "I said no." Instead Ahearn suggested moving in when the media left, about 11 P.M., after the last news shows. "They drove right up—she was scared to death. These agents cared about her. She's the classic example of 'you can choose your friends but you can't choose your relatives.' "

Andrew's stunned father was informed of the Versace murder by a local politician in the Philippines, who showed up with a TV crew and never tried to talk to him alone. Pete Cunanan quickly disavowed that his son was homosexual or remotely capable of committing such a crime. Once again he contradicted his wife to the Associated Press. "She was lying. My son is not like that. He is not a high-class male prostitute. He had a Catholic upbringing. He was an altar boy." Pete Cunanan claims that when he would be out driving in his car, "the TV crews didn't even let me mourn my son. They tried to ambush me."

Since reporters were not able to interview Cunanan family members, who would not start accepting money until after Andrew's death, Erik Greenman was the big "get." Poor, untutored Erik was originally going to settle for a mere $40,000 from the *Globe* for his story, but then he called that wise old queen, Nicole Ramirez-Murray, who barked, "Get in your car, and come over to my house. Forty thousand? You're nuts!" Erik was nervous and uncertain but not Nicole, who called the *Globe* to say that the new price was $80,000. The *Globe* insisted on first seeing what kind of pictures the two had to offer. Fine, said Nicole. The fee for the viewing would be $5,000 nonrefundable, up front. The *Globe* acceded and sent a check, which Nicole kept as a negotiating fee. Then Nicole called the *National Enquirer,* which offered $85,000. Erik had no stomach for more. He told Nicole to accept the $85,000, saying, "I want to get out of town." Nicole was deeply disappointed. "I'm a wheeler-dealer. Erik got scared. He could have gotten a lot more than that. But Erik started getting paranoid." Even Nicole was surprised at the resulting articles. "Some information he gave was B.S. I said, 'What's this Tom Cruise stuff?' He said, 'They told me to spice it up, to make it more interesting. I thought it was stupid too.' "

Anthony White, the caterer who worked for California Cuisine and knew Andrew only slightly, was contacted by a self-appointed agent who told him he could make him thousands of dollars if White would go on TV and say that he was one of Andrew's best friends. When White demurred, the agent told him, "Don't be ridiculous. I got a guy who left the Heaven's Gate cult seven years ago, and he's a senior consultant in Hollywood right now on a made-for-TV movie." (Before the week was out, White got $4,000 from *Hard Copy,* but he didn't say he was a close friend of Andrew's.)

Even before Versace was killed, Steven Gomer, Andrew's longtime friend in San Francisco, had told the *San Francisco Chronicle* that Andrew had spoken to him about bondage and latex masks and his keen interest in sadomasochistic sex. After Versace's murder Gomer was inundated: *"Larry King, Entertainment Tonight, Inside Edition, Good Morning America,* the *Today Show*—and *Hard Copy* called a million times." Before appearing anywhere, Gomer tested the market with a *Hard Copy* producer. "She had said five thousand dollars, and I said fifty thousand and she said, 'Well, maybe we can do something in the middle—fifteen to twenty-five thousand.'" Gomer was told that if he chose to go on the show with his face darkened in silhouette, he'd get only fifteen thousand dollars, but if he was willing to show his face to the camera, he might get twenty-five. That price was not considered high. "If this was during sweeps," says one tabloid producer, "checkbooks would have opened a lot more."

In the middle of negotiating with *Hard Copy,* Gomer got a message from another tabloid show producer. She told him, "I know you're friends with Andrew. I just wanted to talk to you. I'm on my cell phone, calling from my car. I'm on the way to my shrink's appointment. I'm going into couples therapy. I'm meeting my boyfriend, and it's an hour appointment. We're doing group therapy. Let me give a call as soon as I get out."

"That was a mouthful," Gomer says. "She told me more than I would tell someone I had known for three years." When the producer called back, Gomer thought he heard the noise of small children in the background. "'Oh, I'm sorry, that's my boyfriend's rats,'" she said. "So

I started giving her a little bit of this information, and she starts foaming at the mouth." Gomer received a total of 175 requests from the press and television. Speaking for any number of Andrew's friends, he said, "As upset as I am on one side for my friend, and truly feel for what is happening, you can't help but feel some excitement over the fact that people actually care about what you have to say." In his own small world, Gomer was all of a sudden a celebrity. His friends were dying to know which offers he'd choose. He ended up turning all of them down because his bosses took a dim view of the proceedings. "The only thing I would do," Gomer asserts, "would be *The Capital Gang* [CNN's inside-the-beltway political show from Washington]." Gomer's friends were mystified. "They said, 'Who is Capital Gang?'"

Others had few scruples. Philip Horne, though he had met Andrew only once, with Steven Gomer at the Midnight Sun, when Andrew lied to him about becoming his roommate, thought going on TV and doing interviews would help his law practice. He appeared dozens of times in print and on the air, paid and unpaid, as a Cunanan friend. Eric Gruenwald, to whom Andrew had allegedly told the Coco Chanel line after meeting Versace, was also seen many times. But Karen Lapinski, a pal of Lisa Kudrow's and college friend of David Madson's, and her fiancé, Evan Wallit, who works for the Federal Reserve in San Francisco, were in a class by themselves. They may have collected the most money of all—reputedly six figures—for the "World Exclusive Photos" they sold to *Star* of Andrew and David Madson hugging on a sofa—pictures in which Andrew looked drugged. Lapinski and Wallit, who professed a close friendship with David and were also privy to the intimacy of his relationship with Andrew, later also put on the market from the same roll of film an obscene picture of a smirking Andrew brandishing his penis for the camera.

In the beginning Wallit looked into a book deal for Lapinski, though she had never written professionally. When the couple offered their pictures for ever-escalating sums, David Madson's family asked them not to. The Madsons said that seeing such pictures of David and his killer would be extremely painful for them. But Lapinski and Wallit were determined, having turned down all interviews. "I can't control what other people feel," Wallit says. "I think it's unfortunate, but that's all I'm going to say." Lapinski, who once thought her wedding reception was going to be paid for by Andrew—after David walked her down the aisle—sent Mrs. Madson an orchid plant for Mother's Day in 1997. After Lapinski and Wallit's pictures of Andrew and David appeared in *Star,* Carol Madson sent the orchid plant back, dead.

37

The Rainbow

ANDREW'S FORMER ACQUAINTANCES weren't the only ones in overdrive in California. The San Diego FBI had snapped to attention as soon as it heard that the brass in Washington wanted twice-a-day conference calls. Richard Sibley, the agent who had organized security for the Republican National Convention in San Diego in 1996, was in charge of setting up the local command post. "I told Sibley, 'After Versace got whacked, the shit's hit the fan on this,'" says San Diego FBI Deputy Director Peter Ahearn. "'Let's be ready. It's gonna get out of hand.' And it *did* get out of hand."

San Diego opened up a command center with extra staff and computer support, ready for the first conference call at 7:30 every morning. The pressure was on. Suddenly the Bureau, which had previously had no interest in the fugitive's personality traits, was all over town, trying to find out every little thing about Andrew. Keith Evans's counterpart in San Diego was thirty-two-year-old, hip-looking John Hause, who wore jeans and carried his gun in a black backpack slung over his shoulder. "We began a command post automated seven days a week," says Hause. "We put in long hours every day. Things needed to be done immediately; results needed to be communicated immediately. It involved a lot more people—the activity level was just way up. So was the stress."

One of the priorities was to step up efforts to get in touch with people who hadn't been contacted or recontact old friends. But from FBI records there is no indication that tips from friends such as Shane O'Brien, who told the FBI that Andrew had mentioned having dinner with Versace at least once a year from 1991 on, were passed on. If the FBI agents who received this information felt that they had missed anything with regard to Versace, they didn't reveal it in the files. Kevin Rickett, in charge of the Cunanan investigation, told me that he too had heard that Andrew had met Versace, then asked me, "Have you been able to substantiate it? I heard all kinds of stories." A few minutes later he told me he wasn't sure when he'd first heard it—before or after Versace was shot. "I'm going to say afterwards."

When high-profile gays and VIPs were mentioned as names that had been thrown around by Andrew, they were warned by the FBI, especially on the West Coast. In San Diego, the FBI alerted cop-turned-novelist Joseph Wambaugh, who disavowed ever having known Andrew despite several people who claimed otherwise. His defense to the press was a strong blast of hypermachismo: "I got a new 357 Magnum, and I'm just dying to try it out. . . . Apparently he's a name dropper and a fan of my books. I only hope he gets to buy a few more before the cops dust him."

In San Francisco, the FBI visited socialites Gordon Getty and Harry de Wildt, both for the first time. "It seems Gordon Getty and I were two people who they felt should be warned," Harry de Wildt told the *San Francisco Chronicle*. "It seems that Gordon and I are two of his biggest idols here in San Francisco. Apparently he admired our lifestyles much like he admired Gianni Versace for his success." Harry de Wildt appeared quite cool. "So there's a lunatic somewhere in the world—I'm not nervous." According to de Wildt, he was not asked if he knew Andrew.

David Geffen also tended to brush off the notion that Andrew posed any threat when the FBI warned him, but not Steven Spielberg, who called his Dreamworks partner and begged him to hire a bodyguard. Geffen says he refused, and continued to live at his Malibu beach house without security. "I've lived on a public beach for twenty-four years; I've never had security. That's not to say someone couldn't kill me or you. If they can get Reagan, they can get me." Yet his friends kept after him, and they had an effect. "People were frightened for me, so much so it got scary for me," Geffen continues. "I live my life quietly, comfortably, thinking everything will be OK. A lot of people are terrified of living their lives. That's not me."

The FBI maintains that only with the killing of Versace did it understand that celebrities might be victims of Cunanan. "I got into a live interview," says Ahearn, "and the guy said, 'The public has a right to know who, in this community, is being targeted by Andrew Cunanan. We hear there's a hit list.' Because they're immediately making the assumption, right away, if Cunanan talked about them, then they're gay." Ahearn says that assumption is unfair. "What is our responsibility to these people? To tell them, 'This guy talked about you, you should be aware. That became a hit list. These names emerged after Versace. There was no reason to ask about famous people *before*. His MO was that he would hang out with the rich. Versace brings in the famous."

To relieve the growing panic, the FBI in San Francisco, for example, denied to the *Chronicle* my story in *Vanity Fair* that Andrew had met Versace at the time the opera *Capriccio* was presented there, in 1990. When I phoned the FBI office in San Francisco to protest, my call was not returned. Months later, however, George Grotz, the FBI's spokesman in San Francisco who refused to be interviewed, implied he had denied what I reported "because people thought there was a hit list" and the Bureau needed to calm them down.

The most controversial part of the Cunanan coverage in San Diego had nothing to do with hit lists, however. The *Union-Tribune,* which had downplayed the Cunanan story for months, suddenly appeared on Saturday, July 19, with a page-one banner headline: Cunanan Vowed Revenge Over HIV, Hillcrest Counselor Says Killing Suspect Was Confused, Angry. The paper quoted Mike Dudley, a volunteer counselor with David's Place, a nonprofit agency and coffeehouse in Hillcrest, who maintained that in February 1997, two months before the murders, Andrew had gone to him fearing that he had the AIDS virus. The *Union-Tribune* explained, "Dudley kept quiet for months but then told police of his encounter with Cunanan Thursday night after deciding his obligation to protect society from Cunanan was more important than Cunanan's confidentiality." Dudley described a nervous, partied-out Cunanan kicking the wall and saying, "If I find out who did this to me, I'm going to get them."

All hell broke loose. Nicole Ramirez-Murray branded Dudley a liar and saw the story as a plot. "The more demented they could make Andrew sound, if he was caught and implicated anyone prominent, then he could be dismissed," raged Nicole. "My crusade was this HIV gay male thing. To educate people that Michael Dudley was false. There was no proof." David's Place also disavowed Dudley, charging that he had spoken to a reporter-neighbor who referred him to the paper, and had told his story to the press before going to the police. Dudley says he did call police first, but they didn't care.

Dudley considered Andrew a classic tweaker worried about not using condoms. "I've dealt with hundreds and hundreds of them, and his reactions were typical—including the violent outbursts—except he acted like a scared kid." He says that he knew Andrew from earlier visits. "He came in frequently enough. I recognized his face." Dudley claims that he keeps audio diaries of everything he does. Nicole Ramirez-Murray, however, scoffed at the story—as did many in Hillcrest—and was flown to New York to appear on the *Today Show.* Brandishing the *Union-Tribune,* Nicole condemned the story.

Kelly Thornton, who reported Dudley's story, says that she believed him and that she also interviewed the owner of her paper David Copley, who maintained that he did not know Andrew, even though Nicole charged otherwise. Thornton, who was assigned to cover Cunanan on June 12, the day he made the FBI's Ten Most Wanted list, says nobody told her not to interview Copley, but adds, "I'm not going to pose titillating questions—he is my employer."

Nicole created a furor even though many in Hillcrest thought that Nicole was being, at the very least, opportunistic. The media, however, were desperate for any angle on the story. "I've never been in more limos in two weeks, and I've been in limos," Nicole relates. *"G.M.A.* and the *Today Show* fought over me and tried to make me swear I wouldn't go to the other one."

Dudley, meanwhile, was banned from the premises of David's Place.

But while Nicole was on *Today,* Dudley showed up in New York on *Good Morning America.* Dudley made the FBI agents in San Diego, who wanted to question him, do so before 4 A.M., "because we had to get on a morning plane for *G.M.A.*"

By the time Nicole returned to Hillcrest, "the limos were lined up out there in the street. They would take me to one thing, and then another one would show up. At an independent TV show, they knew if I wanted two lumps of sugar." Nicole eschewed drag on national television, and appeared in tweeds and pinstripes. "People noticed. They said, 'We never saw you in the same thing twice.'"

The media hysteria soon created its own form of community hysteria in Hillcrest. The annual Gay Pride celebration was scheduled for the following weekend, and people were petrified that Andrew Cunanan would return. Although the FBI said nothing publicly, the Bureau and police in Seattle were interviewing a man named Aaron who described himself as a friend of Andrew's from Los Angeles and a fellow queen. He claimed he had communicated with Andrew recently via e-mail, and that Andrew was headed toward California. He told the authorities that Andrew had purchased a Canadian passport for $3,200. According to FBI records, Aaron "did not ask him probing questions but did ask him once why he was doing what he was doing. Cunanan replied that he was tired of being used. . . . It is obvious to interviewers [Aaron] was not completely cooperative. This could be out of a desire for attention by police, loyalty or attraction to Andrew, a concern that his identity will become the focus of media attention, or, more than likely, a concern as to his own status on unspecified things he may have done to help or harbor Cunanan."

Esposito also says that Andrew had contacted the mother of a Bishop's classmate living on the East Coast to inquire about obtaining a passport. These old friends whom he contacted, however, did not come forward voluntarily. The FBI learned about them in the course of interviewing other people who knew Andrew. The FBI needed more people who were willing to open up, and yet it did not know where to reach out to find them. In San Diego the situation became so desperate that Ahearn was willing to meet with a former FBI agent who had been dismissed from the San Diego office in 1990, after twenty-one years, for lying about his sexual orientation: Frank Buttino, who had already written a book about his experiences, *A Special Agent: Gay and Inside the FBI*. According to Buttino, "So here we are Monday [after Versace's murder] and the FBI never came to me, the most prominent gay FBI guy in the country. I know gay FBI people all over the country. You'd think they'd contact me." A female agent who was not assigned to the Cunanan case finally asked Buttino if anyone had. When Buttino told her no, she arranged for him to have coffee with Ahearn. "To me it's an eye-opener, sitting there having coffee and walking on eggshells," Ahearn relates. "I said 'homosexual community,' and Buttino says, 'You know, we prefer to be called gay.' "

Buttino had already told the female agent, "This is a very difficult one for the FBI, because they have no sources, and the gay community distrusts them. It's not like the black community, where they've built up sources over the years. A lot are closeted, so how do you reach them?" Buttino now told Ahearn, "I'm going to do this very publicly with the gay community, especially with Gay Pride Week." They struck a deal: Buttino would become a paid consultant with a phone and a desk at office headquarters. He would teach, as he says, "Gay 101. They need to know the gay and lesbian community and how much the people have to lose talking to you." Buttino suggested, "Why not team me up with a gay person who knows Cunanan, and we could hit the bar scene in Miami—put a wire on or whatever."

Robbins Thompson, in fact, had already suggested just that to the FBI, but they had never gotten back to him. (Steve Nauck had already gone out wired hitting South Beach gay bars one night with Miami Beach police to no avail.) "I offered to fly to Miami. I'd go to a bar—I'd find the guy in one day. I'd sift through leads. I'd say, 'Give me these tips,' and I could go through them in twenty minutes." Robbins felt he was getting the brush-off. "I thought it was a bit of a gay issue," he says. "They wanted to play by the book in case they got into trouble." Ahearn counters, "Give me a reason and I'll send him there, other than 'I'll hang out on a street corner.' It wasn't cost-effective." Both Robbins and Norman Blachford thought that Andrew would go next to New Orleans, where weather reports were predicting Hurricane Danny. Blachford had even volunteered to go to New Orleans to help. He felt that he knew where Andrew would most likely hang out, and he was sure he could speedily identify him. The FBI simply had no clue *where* Andrew was. Homicide Inspector Joseph Toomey of the San Francisco Police Department listened in on the conference calls in the FBI's office there during the manhunt. He says, "I didn't have any sense they knew he was in Florida."

In Hillcrest, where people were freaked out, the FBI was undercover all over the neighborhood. "The FBI was a girl who pulled me aside and gave me her number," says Matthew Roman, manager of Hamburger Marys. "She told me if I knew information or felt something was up, don't worry—everybody was being protected in the whole community."

Erik Greenman was being tailed everywhere, most solicitously. "We had the FBI outside our bar I don't know how many times," says Joe Letzkus, part owner of Flicks, who is active at the Gay and Lesbian Center, "because Erik would continue to come in." When the FBI needed to talk to Erik, however, it had to schedule talks around his media appearances. "You get disappointed when people would rather talk to the media than us," says Ahearn. "For example: 'I'm not going to talk to you, but I'll fly to New York, and if you get me at five-thirty A.M., on my way to the airport, fine.' [Greenman] knew we were busting our ass to talk to him."

When the police and the FBI showed up on Tuesday at the Gay and Lesbian Center to discuss with the community their concerns for Gay Pride observation the following weekend, there were more media than attendees. "They had every station in the country and thirty satellite dishes," Letzkus relates. Ahearn was amazed by the meeting, which the San Diego police had organized. "I was humbled by the gay community's treatment of us, and the leadership there. We went up to this conference. We expected it to be accusations: *You're not doing enough.* It was information-sharing, preparation for the parade." Recalling his wonder, Ahearn asks, "Did you hear about the rainbow? I'm standing to one side. All of a sudden, everybody said, 'Look at the sky.' There was a big circular rainbow over the meeting."

38

Profile and Prosecute

A week into the Miami manhunt, three months after Jeff Trail's murder, police and prosecutors were still struggling to understand Andrew Cunanan and assess his motives. The Child Abduction and Serial Killer Unit of the FBI—the profiling unit—was eventually put on alert to profile Andrew. The process was to begin on Wednesday, July 23, when investigators from all the places in the country where Andrew had killed people would meet at the unit's headquarters in Quantico, Virginia. Tichich was expected; so were Rivard and Scrimshaw. The investigators and the profilers hoped to pool their knowledge of Andrew. Each jurisdiction would give a presentation of the evidence it had accrued and show pictures of the crime scenes. This gathering would serve as a prelude to another scheduled meeting for prosecutors who were planning to assemble at 11 A.M. on Friday, July 25, in Miami. Chief Assistant State Attorney Michael Band had called the meeting so that if and when Andrew was caught, they'd be ready with a plan to bring him to swift justice—preferably with the death penalty.

Band recalls, "The first time that prosecutors spoke [with one another] was when I literally picked up the phone, after I essentially said to myself, 'You know, I've talked to the public, but have you talked to the other agents?' " When he found the same held true for the others, he told them, "Whether or not he's found with a bullet in his head, or the cops catch him, we need to get ourselves together, to organize how are we going to handle the prosecution of this case." Band had already decided not to prosecute first, if Andrew were captured in Florida, in order to protect the other jurisdictions because of Florida's liberal discovery laws. He also realized that the media would question any obvious strategy. "We professionals would make a decision here, but it would go back to my boss, [and to] their bosses who are political," Band says. "I don't know that one wanted to say, 'Hey, I want to go first.' I wanted professionals to make a reasoned decision on *who* should go first."

So far, there had been little sharing. New Jersey still had Miglin's Lexus. Minneapolis had done no DNA testing of the bloodstained jeans or the dop kits to see if there were matches with the beard stubble in Chicago or the clothes left behind in Florida. The blood in the trunk of the Lexus, in New Jersey, hadn't been tested by Chicago. Band had insisted that Scrimshaw bypass the Florida Department of Law Enforcement lab and instead bring the clothes found outside the red pickup to a qualified Ph.D. for blood testing. Scrimshaw says he ended up at the Dade County crime lab, where he was informed, "We don't do blood testing unless we can see the blood."

In the end, the thumbprint on the pawnshop form matched Andrew's thumbprint on his California driver's license, which had been found in the red truck. On Monday the FBI finally learned from Duke Miglin that gold coins were missing from Lee Miglin's safe. The coins—tokens of appreciation that Miglin had routinely given out to employees—had not been reported stolen previously. Their identification brought up the whole question of how Andrew could have gotten into Miglin's safe if he had just happened upon him in his garage. Did Andrew manage to get Lee Miglin to give him his safe combination while Andrew found a pencil and wrote it down in the middle of murder? Or were they in the house together?

Such questions plagued investigators. Minneapolis had not charged Andrew in Jeff Trail's death because it still did not have a level of proof necessary to bring him to trial. Chisago, according to Rivard, had made a deal with the FBI to yield to a death-penalty state if the FBI came into the case. Whether Chisago investigators realized it at the time or not, they were wrong about the time of David Madson's death, a mistake that would have jeopardized their case. So far no other jurisdiction had been able to match a single print besides the license/pawnshop-form match. The most conclusive evidence that Andrew was guilty of the murders was the match-up of bullets from Jeff Trail's .40 caliber gun. But investigators did not have the gun, so the case thus far was anything but slam-dunk.

Scrimshaw was trying to figure out a way either to prove or disprove one of his theories about the motive for Versace's murder—that the designer had given Andrew AIDS. He could do this only if he could test Versace's and Andrew's clothes for viral DNA. Although Florida authorities knew Versace's HIV status from the autopsy, the laws of confidentiality regarding DNA makeup of the virus are so strict in Florida that not even Scrimshaw was allowed to know those results, even in investigating a homicide of this magnitude. Yet, the medical examiner at a public meeting did say that Andrew was HIV negative.

The FBI did not have the same constraints regarding viral DNA. "Since we couldn't get official results and 'he dead,' we were going to go for DNA on the clothes in the beginning, before we caught Andrew," Scrimshaw explains. "If both had the same viral DNA, then the case is closed. You could tell if one gave the other HIV—a viral DNA study shows where the two strains come from; if both have the same DNA strain, you can assume both came from the same source." Scrimshaw did not want to embark on this complicated notion if there was no hope that it would prove correct, however. "I had to know whether Gianni Versace was HIV positive or not, and I was able to find out from autopsy results that he had tested positive for HIV."

Knowing that, Scrimshaw could now see why the Versace family had been so determined to cremate early and leave the country. Furthermore, nobody was getting back to him with his questions about the Versace business in Italy, and he thought that he should be getting a lot more cooperation all around. Versace's murder investigation dominated the airwaves and the Cunanan manhunt held the whole country in its thrall, but the investigative effort was not in the least coordinated. "We needed background information on Versace. We needed to understand what we were looking at here," Scrimshaw says. "We needed information on Cunanan, and we talked to one lousy person [Steve Nauck]. And we weren't getting any information back from the FBI, even though we were asking for it. Once the focus changed—by Friday with the Normandy Plaza information—it was a full-throttle manhunt. Marcus and I were still making inquiries, talking to Chicago—it was real one-way. Chicago was very interested in what *we* found in the truck. I'm getting *some* information back, but not much. And I'm getting next to nothing on Reese, because it's an FBI investigation."

George Navarro did not share Scrimshaw's negative views; he thought that the FBI *was* cooperating. But Navarro did not have to run down leads the way Scrimshaw did, and did not face the frustrations of that process. For the Quantico meeting, for example, all participants were asked to bring crime-scene photographs. But under Michael Band's policy of no leaking and his fear that they might end up humiliated like the O.J. prosecution, Scrimshaw was forbidden to take the Versace crime scene photos. "Band says, 'No, because we don't know what will happen to them.' I say, 'You are talking [about showing them] in front of the FBI. Are you telling me the state attorney doesn't trust the FBI?' " Scrimshaw took the photos anyway. "We *certainly* wanted the profile."

Tichich and Scrimshaw arrived at the meeting well prepared. Chicago's representatives dressed down in jeans and T-shirts and were less impressive. "The Chicago people were very uncommunicative, but they had far more evidence than anybody else," Scrimshaw says. "They had latent fingerprints from the scene but nothing to compare them to. Chicago had [Cunanan's] teeth marks from the ham. They only brought four-by-five snapshots." What caught everyone's attention was Chicago's deliberately downplayed report of a male prostitute who had come forward on July 18, three days after Versace's murder, to claim that he had provided sex to Lee Miglin and Andrew together on two occasions. "They didn't think it was much," recalls Tichich, "but we were looking at each other and saying, 'This sounds pretty good.' "

According to FBI records, a "rent boy" who goes by the name of Daniel and pays his way through college with his earnings was solicited for sex by two men, one older than the other, who answered an ad he had placed in a gay magazine. The younger, who called himself "Tadd, Todd, or Tom," was driving when he and the older man picked Daniel up in a car—possibly a Cadillac or an Oldsmobile. They took him to a second-floor apartment of a doorman building (the exact locations have been redacted in FBI files). They had a drink and sex, and after a "fifty-minute hour" he was paid $140 plus money for a cab. The older man was introduced to him as "Lee."

"Approximately one to two weeks later, he received a second call on his voice mail from either 'Lee' or 'Todd.' " He was told to come to the same building. On the second occasion, which was more friendly, " 'Lee' spoke of the fact that [redacted] was involved some way with the 'Home Shopping Network.' " "Todd" told him that he too was a rent boy and placed ads in a magazine, the *Advocate Classified.* "Daniel" saw Todd once more, at a gay bar about a month later. Todd did not speak to him but bought him a drink. He saw Lee once again in a store with another couple.

The physical descriptions Daniel gives are fairly close, but he remembers Lee as having short, stubby fingers and a pinkie ring, and Paul Beitler says Lee didn't have stubby fingers and he never wore a pinkie ring. Daniel told police and the FBI that he did not recognize Andrew as the person he had met until he saw a photograph dated April 1997, in which Andrew was heavier and his face fuller. Then he realized "that this individual was in fact the person with Miglin when they had sex."

He told the authorities, "It is common knowledge in the 'gay community' that Lee Miglin is gay." Daniel, who later reportedly supplied police with the exact address of the building to which he had been taken, told them "that he was not providing this information to 'dirty Miglin's name,' but was attempting to assist in the investigation. He explained that whatever Miglin's sexual preference was, it was no reason for him to have been murdered."

By now the FBI had completely reversed itself. From purporting to be disinterested in Andrew's personality profile and to be pursuing him solely as a fugitive, the Bureau now tried twice-a-day post-Versace conference calls to dissect Andrew's innermost psyche. The calls dealt with "historic information, pre-Minnesota, his lifestyle," says Gregory Jones, the Miami FBI supervising agent of the Cunanan case. "It began to paint a picture to us—where to send the next lead off to. We were particularly interested in these subtle nuances—he liked to do this and that, his general lifestyle, his haunts at bars." Suddenly Andrew being gay was also germane. "It was important from the standpoint of the homicide," Jones asserts. "From the fugitive standpoint it wasn't that important."

Jones says the briefings revealed a "cold-blooded person. We heard he had a high IQ. I don't remember anything being discussed about porn or S&M." Profiling chief William Hagmire says, "We were trying to learn everything we could to see what his soft spots were and who might be able to talk him out—if it was possible. We were trying continuously to put pressure on him obviously, to try to look like we could back him into a hole."

The profilers felt that Andrew's old friend and housemate Liz Coté should make the appeal, because she would appear to be more independent and less controlled by the FBI than Andrew's family. According to Philip Merrill, Liz Coté suggested on Sunday that she make a plea to Andrew via TV. On Monday she gave the agents a draft she and Merrill had written. The FBI edited it, and on Tuesday John Hoos of the Los Angeles FBI arranged for Coté to be taken to the local ABC-TV studio, where she recorded the plea for general release on Wednesday. She was also available for interviews that other networks would have prized.

At that point, Merrill says, as his and Lizzie's close relationship to Andrew became known to the media, even his corner grocer was being offered interviews, "just because he was my corner grocer." Once the media realized that Liz Coté was the woman whose photo Andrew had shown around while pretending she was his former wife, and that she and Phil Merrill had lived with Andrew during his years in Berkeley, they were both besieged. "Lizzie's sister-in-law was offered $16,000 from the *Globe* for an article and picture," says Merrill.

John Hoos, who acts as the media spokesperson in the FBI's Los Angeles field office, told Coté she should get an agent. Merrill recalls, "He said, 'You're going to need somebody who will take care for you, and who will field some of this stuff down the line, and the movie of the week or something—that's just going to get made anyway.'" Merrill says that Hoos, "based on his good relationship with the local ABC affiliate," also facilitated things for ABC to put Liz Coté on *Good Morning America* and *Nightline*. When she was later offered an exclusive consulting deal for a movie of the week (that never got made), Coté called Hoos, who told her, according to Merrill, " 'Yeah, sure [do it].' She kind of felt she had his blessing to do that and called him before she signed the papers and stuff." John Hoos will not comment. "I have no desire to have my name associated with Mr. Cunanan in a book."

The plea was carefully thought out. Liz Coté talked affectionately to Andrew in a code language filled with nicknames for her children. "Since he was a creature of style and great vanity," says Merrill, "it would be more likely to work against his remaining at large if he were treated politely."

Liz Coté, much blonder and fuller-faced than she appeared in the photo Andrew carried, was shot in close-up. She said, "The Andrew Cunanan I know is not a violent person. The Andrew Cunanan who is the godfather to my children is not a thief. . . . Please stop doing what you're doing. I know that the most important thing to you in the world is what others think of you. You still have a chance to show the entire world the side of you that I and your godchildren know. The time has come for this to end peacefully. . . . D.D. loves you, Schmoo. I bring with me a special message from our papoose. Grimmy says she loves her Uncle Monkey and hopes that you'll remember her always. Your birthday will soon be here, and someone else who loves you will be five years old." Coté ended with a Latin phrase that Andrew would remember from his days as an altar boy: *"Dominus vobiscum"* (The Lord be with you).

Trying to use the media to lure Andrew, however, might be playing right into his hands. Before Andrew killed Versace, Captain Tom Cronin, the Chicago policeman and Quantico graduate, had told me, "Down deep inside, the publicity is more sexual to him than anything else. Right after one or two of these homicides, he probably goes to a gay bar in the afternoon when the news comes on, and his face is on TV and he's sitting there drinking a beer and loving it. You hide in plain view."

Hagmire says that as such murders "accelerate, the motivation changes from a personal crime to more of a power thing: 'I can play God with anyone I want, and I want everybody to know that.' " Hagmire explains that many serial killers leave something behind so they can become nicknamed and notorious: "The 'Son of Sam,' he wrote notes. Or he uses the same gun—'the .44 caliber killer.' 'The Atlanta Strangler.' " Andrew, however, was obviously aware that law enforcement knew who he was. As a result, "when he's traveling around the country, he's got to leave something of his signature behind," Hagmire concludes. "And maybe that's stealing the vehicles and leaving them where they can be found."

These vehicles, Hagmire feels, were left almost like business cards. "He wants it to be picked up in the national media, because this reinforces his strength, his power and control over other people, including not just his victims but law enforcement and the media. It becomes like a chess game. We in law enforcement have to react to [the killer's] moves, but the chessboard is the media. And when they make a move and it's reported, and then we respond to it, the way we react and what we say in the media sometimes dictates their next move."

The profilers wanted to keep the pressure on Andrew so that he would stay in Miami. At the same time they needed to understand how he had killed. They went over and over the scenes of his crimes, trying to figure out what he might do next. As Hagmire says, "He'd used a .40 caliber more than once. He kept the same gun. That's significant, because the real sophisticated ones get rid of the guns right away. And a lot of serial killers don't use guns." Hagmire adds, "It's not uncommon for a serial killer to use his hands the first time, because the first crime is usually a representative victim, symbolic victim, or somebody they personally want to destroy, and they take more pleasure in doing it with their hands than a gun."

Hagmire calls Versace's murder "a *hit*. It's a high-risk crime; people are going to be there, he wants people to know who did it." Whether or not Versace is "personally symbolic," he's "the wealthy, high-profile homosexual success story that Andrew Cunanan was never going to be," Hagmire says. "The only way he's going to get famous is the same way John Hinckley got famous. So he gets a lot of ink out of Lee Miglin.

Reese he gets some ink out of, but it's really not good for his ego. He basically needs the truck, and that's why he whacks this Reese guy, as far as I know.

"Then maybe he does somebody else, and we don't know about it. Versace appears to me to be that he wants everybody to know he's doing it. He's deteriorating, but he's got these ego needs, and it's, like, Is this gonna be Little Big Horn or not? The question is, What's he do after Versace if he doesn't get caught? He's going to kill for one or two reasons: He's going to kill out of necessity again, because he needs another vehicle, or he takes a step above Versace."

For Andrew, a step above Versace would be someone like Elton John. "Maybe we'd never hear that song about the princess," Hagmire speculates. The other possibility the FBI had to consider was a gay political assassination—Harvey Milk revisited. Someone like that "brings you a lot of ink. He represents, if not wealth, then certainly power." And who might someone be? Barney Frank?

Scrimshaw considered the meeting at Quantico a valuable experience. "I don't think I learned that much about Andrew until I went to Washington," he says. "And that's the day he was captured. We're always the last to know. It happens a lot. This investigation drove *us*— we didn't drive *it*."

Because it was only possible to leave Miami Beach on land by crossing a causeway, and the airport was on full alert, law enforcement hoped that Andrew was still in Florida. It had been nine days since he killed Versace, and the last time anyone had seen him was in the alley a few minutes after the murder. News reports on Wednesday had a store owner in New Hampshire swearing that she had seen him going north in a Mercedes. One of Hagmire's old friends at the Bureau called him from Miami to say he thought Andrew was in Central America. Hagmire hoped Andrew would stay put. "I said if he's still in Miami, he plans on dying in Miami."

39

The Last Night
of Carnival

FERNANDO CARREIRA, a Portuguese immigrant, has lived in Florida for twenty years. Before that he lived in New York, where he owned a carnival and a cigar business and was proud to be the founder of a merchants' association on Manhattan's Lower East Side that worked with police to combat neighborhood crime. He earned a special New York City police badge. Carreira wears a lot of gold jewelry, including a gold identification bracelet with the name "Richard" studded in diamonds. He says he bought the bracelet in a pawnshop, and it would have cost too much to rearrange the diamonds to spell Fernando. At the time of the Cunanan manhunt, Carreira was seventy-one, his wife was forty-nine. They had a fifteen-year-old son. Carreira made his living looking after properties, and one of these was a baby-blue houseboat at 5250 Collins Avenue, berthed on Indian Creek, not far from the landmark Eden Roc and Fontainebleau hotels.

The houseboat, which was trimmed with white filigree and colored lights, had a three-tiered white plaster fountain in front and a small white awning over the front door. It was owned by Torsten Reineck, a flamboyant German with a salt-and-pepper ponytail who was living in Las Vegas, where he managed a gay bathhouse called the Apollo. Normandy Plaza residents such as Ronnie and his friend Lyle, the drug dealer, knew the houseboat well and later remarked how they had often seen ExCalibers, Rolls-Royces and Bentleys parked out front. The houseboat had a colorful history. It had once served as part of the set of an old TV series, and, according to Jack Campbell, it had at times been a trysting place for rich gay men who did not wish to take the hustlers they had picked up in Flamingo Park home to their villas across Indian Creek.

On Saturday, July 19, Carreira says, Reineck called from Las Vegas to ask if he had checked on the houseboat. Carreira had, and told him all was well. On Wednesday, July 23, about 3:45 P.M., Carreira and his wife stopped by again. Right away Carreira noticed that the top lock on the front door was stuck or broken, but it had given him trouble before. When he fitted his key into the bottom lock, however, he was shocked to find that it was unlatched. He pushed the door open. "I told my wife, 'Somebody was here. Maybe somebody here now.' " His suspicions mounted as he and his wife entered, because all the lights were on and the drapes, which were always open, were drawn. "So I walk all the way down to the living room," which faced the water, and there Carreira found more surprises: The cushions had been pulled off the sofa and made into a bed on the floor with a blanket, and a chair had been turned over as if to form a barricade. Fernando Carreira crossed to the sofa. "I looked to the left side, and there were two sandals. When I see the sandals I tell my wife, 'Somebody sleeps here. Somebody is here right now.' "

Carreira keeps a handgun tucked in his waistband. As he pulled it out to conduct a search, a loud shot rang out in the second-floor master bedroom. "It was a very big noise, and I have to run out," he recalls. Carreira thought someone had fired at him and missed. He and his terrified wife ran outside and hid in the bushes. Carreira was convinced that whoever was inside had seen him from the second floor.

He tried to dial 911 on his cell phone, but he was too nervous. He phoned his son instead and told him to call. Crouching in the bushes, he watched the front door and told his wife to watch the back—someone could dive from the rear deck into the creek and escape. The police were there within four minutes and told Carreira to move back. The first officer radioed the dispatcher at headquarters that he had reached the houseboat and was "hiding behind some concrete in front of it."

"What color is it?"

"It's the blue one."

A few minutes later, the dispatcher radioed the marine patrol. "Check out the blue houseboat. . . . If there's a victim, he's inside."

The officer and the Carreiras walked to another houseboat anchored not far away. Carreira remembers, "The policeman says, 'It's better we go up there, because maybe someone can see you from the window. It may be someone dangerous.' When police tell me 'someone dangerous,' I know what he mean. Only at that time I can figure out it maybe was Cunanan."

The police were taking no chances. An order quickly crackled across the police radio: *"Shut down traffic on Collins Avenue."*

The first call from the houseboat to the police came in as "occupied burglary—possible shots fired inside." Al Boza, the Miami Beach Police public-information officer, recalls that he was relieved. "Thank God, I'm going to have a break. The press is going to run somewhere else. This is some idiot who broke into a place and expected to sit there on vacation at a nice location." Since the call had nothing to do with Cunanan, and there had been no major sightings that day, Boza figured he could catch up with scores of phone calls. After all, he had seen this scenario unfold before. "We dress in black, and we march with shields and helmets, and we bang doors down, and they are long gone." He sent his deputy, Officer Bobby Hernandez, to cover for him.

By Wednesday, says NBC's WTVJ station manager Don Browne, the Cunanan story, so hot the previous week, had "cooled off. There was a real sense he'd moved on, gotten out of here." But minutes after Carreira called in, Detective Gus Sanchez, monitoring his police radio and remembering the Volpe sailboat sighting, alerted his superiors: "FYI, the subject we're looking for was on a boat a few days prior, so keep that in mind." Sanchez says, "We had information that Cunanan was possibly hiding on a boat near the area of the call. [So] I notified

them, 'heads up. Begin treating it as the subject we're looking for.' "
The houseboat was quickly surrounded.

Someone on the radio warned, *"Lieutenant Noriega, or George Navarro, reference this call up here. I don't want to put too much out over the radio here, but you have a good idea for what it is, right?"* Sanchez declares, "From the very onset, police believed it could be Cunanan on the houseboat." And they acted accordingly.

"We're going to try to get a chopper here—a little air support," the police radio beamed, "and do an entry with either the county or Miami SWAT team."

A few minutes later, another officer radioed, "I'm on the roof of that building across from the houseboat. The houseboat has no access to the roof—no access to its roof—and the front door is still open."

Noriega assigned the interior of the houseboat to Navarro, and another officer was put in charge of the exterior perimeter. "I didn't want this to turn into a circus," Noriega says. But the media was already gathering for what would become, for that day at least, the greatest show on earth. However, the reporters and cameramen were once again frustrated. They were kept several blocks away from the houseboat to the north and to the south on Collins Avenue as heavy traffic was detoured.

"We've got the media here at 5101 Seacoast Towers," an officer radioed from a few blocks away. *"Would you advise on media? He's trying to get through here."*

"He needs to stay outside the perimeter. He's not to pass that point."

"You want me to hold him here? He's advised me he has a right to go through."

Over the next two hours, the chaos increased. "Residents can't drive home. People are parking on both sides of side streets. People got pissed," says Officer Bobby Hernandez. "They start walking through the beach to get home. We had to deal with a very angry public."

"I have three media here—they're getting a little hostile," an officer radioed. *"But I'm keeping them back. . . . They're really getting hostile. They're telling me I don't know the law."*

Even people living in the area posed a risk. Residents of the luxury high rises and hotels lining Collins Avenue hung out over their balconies, straining to see the action. Across Indian Creek, "police were going into backyards, trying to clear reporters out of the line of fire," recalls Jim DeFede, of the *New Times.* "There were helicopters overhead and people hanging out of balconies—it was definitely an event," says Detective Gus Sanchez.

At 4:30 P.M., the first inkling that the houseboat might not be a random location was introduced when the Miami Beach police lieutenant who was the liaison with the Drug Enforcement Administration in Miami informed Navarro of a "possible connection" between the houseboat owner, Torsten Reineck, and Gianni Versace. Wow. How interesting. But there was so much going on right then that no one followed up on the lead.

At police headquarters, Chief Richard Barreto was in his office being interviewed by John Walsh of *America's Most Wanted* for another *A.M.W.* show on Andrew Cunanan to be broadcast the following Saturday. "I'm in Barreto's office all set up, and a phone call comes in they've surrounded a houseboat," Walsh relates. "The timing was incredible." Walsh had already earned the resentment of other reporters, who objected to the privileged access he was getting. "They're going, 'Why is John Walsh inside talking to Barreto, etc. etc.?' Tough *shit,* that's my response. Tough *shit.* O.K.?" He adds, "Every reporter wants to get wounded and be on the cover of *Time* magazine for getting shot and getting Cunanan's story."

Barreto told Walsh, "We had to call the Metro-Dade SWAT team to come across the causeway. They're coming across. We've got boats there. . . . Can we end the interview?"

The local Miami Beach Police SWAT had recently been disbanded in a dispute over whether they should be paid for their physical-training time. Now they reported to the houseboat as the reconstituted "Warrants Search Team." Much to their chagrin, they were relieved by Metro-Dade's Special Response Team (SRT). This meant that Barreto was briefly ceding jurisdiction for the houseboat interior to another law-enforcement entity. The Metro-Dade SRT was fully equipped, but confusion would ensue because no provisions were made for any direct communication to occur between them and the Miami Beach Police Department, which was controlling the area outside.

"All this took time to set up the team, and attempts to negotiate were made," says Detective Paul Marcus, who was part of the Miami Beach police team. "There was an attempt to put a phone in. The phone inside was disconnected." Finally, "we ended up throwing a hard-line phone into the houseboat." Numerous efforts followed to get whoever was inside to answer. "We were verbalizing through the bullhorn, 'Pick up the phone, pick up the phone.'"

By then the poles and dishes on satellite trucks, like so many giant lollipops, dotted the sky. The local TV stations were broadcasting the houseboat scene live in English and Spanish, and police had turned the firehouse across the street from the houseboat into a command center. "This place looked like a movie," Marcus recalls. "The FBI moved in with computers." Meanwhile, TV helicopters were sending live shots from overhead, chronicling the movements of the Metro-Dade SRT team and interfering with their work.

"Inside the war room they're saying, 'Can we cut the power to the boat?'" recounts John Walsh, who was allowed to listen. They wanted to prevent anyone in the houseboat from watching TV—which was capturing every move of the siege from the news helicopters above. Officer Bobby Hernandez says, "As an officer, it's a safety issue—there's a huge amount of vulnerability. The media would not back off."

"At the time we had our helicopters in the air—like flies we were there," says Tom Doerr of WPLG Channel 10. "I'm sorry to say that all of us were guilty at that moment of overzealousness." Al Boza started calling TV stations, saying, "Folks, you're giving tactical information, because whoever that is inside is delighted to see we have got three people in the front, two people on the side." The SRT team and many others were in potential danger. "What if he has automatic weapons and he's firing across the street and he hits somebody who's standing on the sidewalk in front of the Fontainebleau, some German tourist or something?" asks John Walsh. "He could have opened up a round with an AK-47 that would have gone right across Collins Avenue and hit fifteen people."

The helicopters finally heeded and did not return until the power was cut off. The media had been given no information whatsoever to indicate that the police suspected Cunanan might be inside, and since no one really *knew* if he was or not, the regular business of getting the story out continued apace. The *Vanity Fair* issue in which my story would appear, for example, was officially closed. Any changes at that point would have to be made on final proofs—an expensive process—not to mention that the article had *already* been rewritten once, after Versace was killed. I watched MSNBC cable at home in Washington—desperate to learn if Andrew was on that houseboat—until it was time to leave for the Washington premier of *Air Force One,* which starred Harrison Ford as the President and in which Duke Miglin had a walk-on part as a pilot.

That week, the Rifat family in San Diego had dug up a number of old photographs of Andrew—Rachel Rifat had even unearthed her high school diary, in which she recorded that Andrew had confessed to her that he was gay—and decided to see what their material could fetch in the still white-hot media marketplace. They were offering Halloween photos of Andrew and Rachel dressed as a nun and a priest, plus interviews on background. By Wednesday, *People* magazine had already called.

"Let's open at twenty-five thousand dollars," Anne Rifat recalls them offering. The *National Enquirer* was also interested. The tabloid's Los Angeles office had telephoned on Wednesday morning, asking, "What do you want?" Rifat wasn't sure: "What are you prepared to offer?" Could they make a deal on the whole package—pictures and diary? The *Enquirer* promised to get back late in the day with a specific amount. Then *Hard Copy* called, Rifat says, and made a preemptive bid: "We'll give you forty-five thousand dollars." Anne Rifat told *Hard Copy* she needed to hear back from the *Enquirer.* By then the houseboat was surrounded and the *Enquirer* did not call back that day. Whether Andrew was on the houseboat or not would determine bidding prices.

By the time the evening news went on, the houseboat scene was alternating with pictures of Gianni Versace's elaborate funeral, which had taken place Tuesday in Milan's historic Duomo. Princess Diana and Elton John were there, seated next to each other. Perhaps remembering that the princess had backed out not long before from his AIDS benefit, which was supposed to launch Versace's book *Rock and Royalty,* Elton John did not appear overeager to acknowledge Diana's attempts to comfort him. (All that would change in a matter of months, with Diana's death.) Knowledgeable sources in the Italian government whispered that the Versaces had donated one billion lira, or $750,000, to the church for the honor of having Gianni's funeral in the cathedral.

At 8 P.M. the Metro-Dade SRT began to shoot pepper and CS gas into the houseboat. "Again we tried to establish communication, but no response," says Officer Bobby Hernandez. He had called his boss, Al Boza, around seven, telling him that he ought to come to the scene. "Honestly, Bobby, I'm swamped with calls," Boza told him. Hernandez, wary of being overheard by the press, then told Boza in Spanish, *"Creo que tenemos nuestro socio"* (I think we have our pal). Boza says, "That was my first indication this may be Cunanan." He left for the houseboat. Michael Band had also just been called by Navarro: "Michael, this may be it." Band caught a ride with Boza, but they did not discuss the case. Band says, "Most of the media who had half a brain are figuring something is up if I'm at the scene."

A few minutes after eight, Chief Barreto arrived. Much to the chagrin of the assembled reporters, who were cordoned off from the scene, John Walsh was once again in tow. "The local news people were really angry," Tom Doerr says. "They were kept out, and John Walsh was allowed to walk around with police up to the houseboat. It irks me to see local law enforcement buddy-buddy with national figures."

At 8:20, the Metro-Dade SRT entered the houseboat for the first time. They searched the first floor, with negative results. On the second floor, however, they found a body in the master bedroom, "with a gunshot to his head and a handgun in his hand." In the dry language of their police report, "The subject was cold to the touch and had no pulse. The subject appeared to have been deceased for several hours."

But was it Andrew Cunanan? And was there anyone else on the boat? The SRT continued to search the bilges, "with negative results." Then a serious error occurred. Al Boza was told that the "primary search was negative," meaning that there was no *live* body aboard. Boza misunderstood and thought "negative on the primary search" meant that *no* body had been found. "At one point a call came: 'It's all clear,'" Boza says. "A sergeant asks, 'Can we move traffic? It's all clear.' I asked him to go to a command channel, and I said, 'I heard that it's all clear.' He says, 'Yes, apparently it is clear. They're doing a more thorough search, and we'll keep you informed.'"

"SRT members reenter the houseboat a short time later," according to a report prepared subsequently for the Miami Beach city manager's office. "Miami Beach police officers interpret this activity: No arrest and no resistance met, as an indication that the 'primary search' is negative, 'starting secondary now.'" (Secondary means looking for someone hiding in the bilges.) The report concludes: "This is an incorrect assumption made by MBPD officers on the scene, based on their observation and assessment of activity."

Wanting to be helpful, Boza, without confirmation, began putting the word out to the media that Andrew Cunanan's body was not on the houseboat. That fact was immediately broadcast over the airwaves, and nobody who knew differently bothered to correct it. (The *Washington Post* and the *Miami Herald* had page-one headlines in their early editions blaring that the houseboat was another false alarm.) Once the search was complete, the scene was returned to the authority of the Miami Beach police. "I didn't know till quite a bit later they had announced no body found," says Metro-Dade police spokeswoman Lieutenant Linda O'Brien. By that time, she says, "it was not our case."

"What was amazing was that everybody was looking at the story [on the houseboat] as the climax," says NBC Channel 6's Don Browne. "Then Boza says *nada*." Browne and Channel 10 decided to keep all their crews at the site anyway, but the *Miami Herald* and the other channels left, including the popular, intensely competitive Fox Channel 7, whose tabloid style made it the favorite channel of South Beach drag queens who told me they "Loved the drama." "I'm not sure whether he's there or not," Browne continues. "I made a decision to stay because, one, Miami Beach is paralyzed; you couldn't get in or out. My point is this: If Cunanan is *not* in there, why take this incredible risk screwing up the community? They claimed it was routine."

In Washington, I was too nervous to sit through the movie. Duke Miglin, shown for brief seconds, could hardly be recognized in pilot's gear. There was no way of telling if he really was Andrew's "type." In the middle of an exciting action sequence, I edged past twenty people in my row and ran out to a pay phone. "Have they found Cunanan's body?" I asked a colleague. "No," the answer came back. "Relax, he's not on the boat." I breathed a sigh of relief, but still it was hard to believe, particularly because all along the police had been so close-mouthed and so misleading. Few working on the story believed anything they said; I basically ignored them.

Scrimshaw got home to Miami from Quantico at 9 P.M. He called his partner Marcus, at home, and was told by his wife, "He's at the beach." Scrimshaw recalls, "I turned on the TV and saw Marcus standing there, on live TV, with the commentators saying there is no body on the houseboat, nothing's going on. I'm thinking, What a boondoggle this is—all these guys there scarfing up overtime on one more false lead. Then the phone rings and Pelosi says, 'Get in here, because we got him.'

"I say, 'Who?'

" 'Cunanan.'

" 'Where is he?'

" 'He's on the houseboat.'

" 'I'm looking at the TV. You're kidding me.'

" 'He capped himself,' Richie said. It's a police term for suicide.

"I said, 'The TV says there's nobody in there.'

" 'We lied.'

" 'I'll be there.' "

At the houseboat, excitement was running high. "We had to go back and forth and see it on TV in the firehouse. And then I'd go back to the houseboat," Marcus says. TV, he continues, was presenting "the magnitude of it, and then I'd go back outside and see the real thing. It's like you're watching history being made. You definitely felt the importance of doing it well." Sanchez, the rookie detective, says, "I was honored I got picked to go into the houseboat. It feels good when your supervisor says, 'I want you to handle this.' You're being asked to do it because they think you can."

It was essential to identify the body. Even after fans were brought in to clear the air, the amount of tear gas inside the houseboat precluded entry without gas masks. Sergeant Navarro and Keith Evans, both in masks, went in first and opened windows and doors. When they entered the bedroom area about 9:30 P.M., they turned to each other instantly and cried in unison, "It's him!" Andrew, eyes open, with several days' growth of beard, was lying in a pool of blood on a pillow propped on another pillow. He had shot himself through the mouth. Blood from his ears, nose, and mouth had caked, and the pillow was also soaked in blood. Jeff Trail's gun was still in his hand, resting on his stomach, and a single spent bullet casing was lying next to the sliding glass window. "We immediately high-fived each other," says Navarro. But at the same moment George Navarro suddenly experienced an overwhelming "adrenaline down. This guy created so much work, and so much energy spent. He's sitting in front of us—he looks like a typical Miami Beach yuppie, nothing unique at all. He could look Oriental or Hispanic; he could fit in anywhere."

By 10 P.M., all of the top brass knew: The manhunt for Andrew Cunanan was over.

Forensic experts swung into action, videotaping and photographing the scene. There were oddities throughout. The front-door lock, for example, was found in the refrigerator's butter compartment. Most of the kitchen cabinets were open, and a pair of binoculars lay on the counter. There were fast food wrappers in the bathtub and a plate of nut shells two inches high on the living room coffee table. Andrew was found to have an abscessed wound the size of a pencil eraser on his abdomen below the naval. On a cluttered table in the living room were rubbing alcohol, gauze bandages, a bloody bandage, and an empty Tylenol bottle. There was also a bottle of prescription medicine with "Reineck" typed on the label. A stack of magazines indicated that right up to the very end, while the unprecedented manhunt raged on, Andrew was still reading *Vogue*.

Finding Cunanan turned things upside down. "The joke afterwards," says Michael Band, "was that the first thing I did when I saw Cunanan was I gave him CPR. Because I said, 'You're ruining my book deal! Marcia Clark got a book deal—you can't do this to me!' " While Band made jokes, the media and the public still knew nothing—but the media race was on.

"I remember leaving, thinking, man, what fools are we," says Tom Doerr, recalling the mood after the announcement that Cunanan's body had not been on the houseboat. "We're going to suspect Cunanan under every rock. Like headless freaks, we get into this pack mentality and see Cunanan everywhere, and make people nuts, and not do ourselves any favors." While Channel 10 had dropped the story at 9:15, and Doerr was driving to Coral Gables to get away, the crew for the competition, WTVJ Channel 6, stayed at the houseboat and got word by 9:25 that in fact Cunanan's body may have been found. Reporter Robin Kish had a source who told her yes to all three of the big questions: Is there a body? Is it self-inflicted? Did it appear to be Cunanan? But the story needed further confirmation. Reporter Mike Williams asked a source of his the same three questions, and was told, "You've really been doing a good job, Michael." It was 9:45 when he hung up. "That's not a confirmation," said Assistant News Director Ramon Escobar.

At 10:19, NBC network newsman Pete Williams (no relation), in Washington with federal sources, reported on both CNBC and MSNBC that "a body was found on the houseboat." When Mike Williams got back to his local source, he got a direct confirmation, and the source also told him, "Remember the gun." He meant that cops on the scene could see that Andrew had shot himself with the same gun that had killed Gianni Versace. At 10:24, WTVJ was the first to announce that a body presumed to be Andrew Cunanan's—pending final fingerprint identification—had been found, and that he appeared to have committed suicide.

The news was out, but the Miami Beach authorities wanted to convene the media in front of the houseboat to confirm the finding. The FBI's Paul Philip arrived in black tie—he had been called to the scene from a dinner for the National Organization of Black Law Enforcement Officers. The ambitious mayor of Dade County, Alex Penelas, flew to the crime scene in his helicopter. Seymour Gelber, Miami Beach mayor at that time, remained at home, where he took several calls from the press. About 9 P.M., the former mayor says, "I was told by the city manager that it was Cunanan. When I was called by media people who said they had deadlines, I said I was fairly certain it was Cunanan." Miami TV later cut between the mumblings of the police chief, who did not disclose at an 11 P.M. press conference that the body they had found was Andrew Cunanan's, and the irrepressible Gelber, who contradicted him. "So I told reporters I was fairly certain and I would go with it. TV, I did the same thing. So I'm responsible for identifying Cunanan," says Gelber. Officially, however, there was no word.

The houseboat siege, like the O.J. white Bronco chase, was broadcast live across the country. Unable to resist the moment, Torsten Reineck popped up on TV in Las Vegas to claim ownership of the houseboat. He was seen by the German authorities in Miami, who had been looking for him in order to charge him with tax fraud. They meant business. The Miami Beach police had been notified in the afternoon that there might be a connection between Reineck and Versace, and that night a German confidential informant who went by the name Galleto, appeared at police headquarters, accompanied by Agent Dieter, a German narcotics officer assigned to the DEA.

Detective Dale Twist was already there, waiting to interview Fernando Carreira and his wife to see if their story held. Agent Dieter, it turned out, had actually tried previously to interest the police in a group of rich, shady Germans living in Miami Beach, but had gotten nowhere. Reineck was linked to them. Now Galleto told Twist that one of Reineck's associates had been friendly with Versace, and had bragged that Versace gave him a watch. Twist recalls, "Dieter comes and says, 'Hey, this guy is the one I've been telling you all about.' He's been trying to tell everyone about it, but nobody has taken the case of this little German clique that's into money laundering and whatever else they're into."

Dale Twist listened briefly and assumed that the FBI would follow through. He then went to interview Carreira, who said that Reineck was definitely the houseboat owner and that he had called on Tuesday, the day before, to check on things.

According to Galleto, Carreira was having a rough time at the station: "His wife was close to a heart attack. The police brought in the son. Carreira said that Reineck always called *him,* and he had no number for Reineck. Then the police asked the kid, and the kid said, 'Dad is always calling him—why is he lying about that?' His wife cried and screamed. The police lady tried to calm her down." Galleto contends that the police came close to arresting Carreira that night. "Then he's on TV, the big hero." Twist says Carreira was not in danger of arrest. "He stuck to his statement and was pretty clear on most everything." Nevertheless, Dale Twist in his gut did not trust him. "I didn't like Carreira. There was something about him I wasn't comfortable with," Twist says. "I wasn't comfortable with him and his contact with the Germans." Twist admits the police could never get to the bottom of their suspicions, however. "We've never been able to prove otherwise; every time we even come close, it ends up in a dead end."

In order for the forensic identification of Andrew to be made in the middle of the night, the Metro-Dade police, once again in charge, had to move in the Metro-Dade Roadside Command Post Bus, which would serve as the mobile command post. Their technicians, who had never worked at a crime site before, would make the identification matches of Andrew's fingerprints. Around 1 A.M. Navarro and Evans approached Andrew's body again, this time to remove the gun from his hand. First Navarro scribbled the gun's serial number down on his own hand. It came back a match to Jeff Trail's gun. "I removed the firearm from Cunanan's hand and handed it to Keith, and the gun cocked, so a bullet could shoot. We had to be very careful. Keith made it safe—I held it while he uncocked it." Earlier, forensic experts had come in to swab the gunpowder burns between Andrew's fingers in order to certify that it was Andrew who had pulled the trigger and killed himself. The number of bullets Andrew had killed his victims and himself with matched the number of bullets missing from the gun magazine. According to Navarro, "We can account for every missing round."

At 3 A.M., Navarro held Andrew's hands to take the swabs for positive fingerprint identification. "It was extremely difficult, because he was as stiff as a board." Inside the hot, humid command module, two nervous fingerprint technicians were supposed to match the corpse's thumbprint to Andrew's thumbprint on the pawnshop form and his driver's license. The original driver's license was at the FBI lab in Washington, which made their job even more difficult. They had to work off a copy while the bosses in charge paced in the background, breathing down their necks.

The VIP's would not go home. They all seemed determined to lend their presence to this high-profile event—the chief and assistant chief of the Miami Beach police, the mayor of Dade County, the city manager and assistant city manager of Miami Beach, the FBI's Paul Philip, the FDLE head of Dade County, Michael Band and Rose Marie Antonacci-Pollock, and the medical examiner.

As Navarro recalls the moment, "The chief is waiting. Everyone's gawking. Ties are loosening." To complicate matters, Chief Barreto's teenage daughter had recently been struck by a car and was scheduled for surgery in the morning, and he wanted to be with her. Nevertheless, Navarro took his time. He needed to be thorough, to document the scene thoroughly, "as found. It might be important, especially if conspiracy theories pop up." The fingerprint technicians, dubbed by the cops as the nutty professors, hunched over their magnifying glasses and scrutinized the loops and whorls of Andrew's right thumb, but could not agree on a positive ID. At 3:45 Navarro was sent out again to take more swabs. The wait was excruciating, but the alternative was worse. "My god, what if we're wrong? What if it's his evil twin?" says U.S. attorney Wilfredo Fernandez, who was on the scene. "You don't want to make a mistake." Finally, at 5:10 A.M., the technicians put down their magnifying glasses: The match was made. Andrew Phillip Cunanan was officially dead. At the press conference called at 5:15 A.M. to announce that Cunanan had been officially identified, Chief Barreto was still pronouncing his name incorrectly, with the accent on the first syllable.

Gregory Jones, the FBI supervising agent in charge of the Cunanan case, stayed for the press conference. Then, having been up almost two days straight, he headed for home. As soon as he walked through his front door, the enormity of the effort that he and everyone else had made searching for Andrew Cunanan overwhelmed him. He took two steps and threw up.

Looking at Andrew's corpse, Wilfredo Fernandez, who was one of the attorneys supervising the searches of the houseboat, did not think Andrew particularly good-looking. "I don't know that I'd recognize him. He looked very Filipino. I expected white preppy." Rookie detective Gus Sanchez disagrees. "I wouldn't describe him as Oriental, but even dead he was interesting-looking. He had interesting eyes. Even dead I could see a certain magnetism to him." As the cameras continued to whir, Andrew's body was removed from the houseboat to be autopsied at 6:45 A.M., Thursday, July 24. "Hey, kid, do you want to come out on national TV?" a veteran cop asked Sanchez. "Stand next to the body."

PART

FOUR

40

Dead Is Dead

NOBODY IN THE MIAMI BEACH POLICE close to the case thinks Andrew was on the houseboat by chance:

"My gut feeling is that Cunanan knew of this houseboat," Chief Barreto said the following day.

"I think Andrew had been there and knew of that place, and they helped him hide," says Sergeant Navarro.

"I'm sure there's a connection between Gianni and Andrew. Why that houseboat?" asks Gary Schiaffo, lead detective at the houseboat scene. "There aren't that many houseboats in the water. This particular one is vacant. Why there?"

Andrew's death came as such an overpowering relief to law enforcement that nearly all the investigating agencies concerned, especially the FBI, rushed to close the case. "Dead is dead and done is done," said Scrimshaw cynically. "I feel Cunanan might have been used—I do. There is nothing in our report to back it up. If I can't back up, it doesn't go in." Scrimshaw was most unhappy that the MBPD closed down its investigation before he thought he was finished. "Certain glaring areas needed to be examined." Along with Sergeant Navarro and Detective Dale Twist, Scrimshaw had hoped for some answers from the FBI, which assumed authority to follow through on the houseboat owners and the international aspects of the case. Instead, says Twist, "they never asked for any input and we never got any output. I can't figure it out."

"But why didn't the Miami Beach police pursue the case on its own?" I ask. "They told us in so many words, 'We're shutting it down, we don't have the resources,'" Scrimshaw explains. "'Let the FBI do it, let the State Department do it.' There was no one story." Scrimshaw, who says he dislikes conspiracy theories, speculates anyway that Andrew was on the houseboat because "he expected to be rewarded and taken to never-never land, but then he was taken as the fall guy. It's risky letting someone unprofessional do it, but if he fails, he's a nut case."

One reason Scrimshaw may be unable to rule out such a scenario is that he was not allowed to prepare the "psychological autopsy" that he usually compiles for suicides. "For my sake and for the family's sake, we try to interview everyone to eliminate the possibility this was something other than a suicide. Maybe that's what the FBI was doing, but I don't know whether they ever did that."

It appears not. From the very beginning, the houseboat posed intriguing mysteries, beginning with its caretaker, Carreira. According to Gary Schiaffo, the first detective on the scene, for example, Carreira did not initially mention to police that he carried a gun—that came out only in the retelling. Schiaffo also doubts that Carreira was too nervous to call in law enforcement. "How hard is it to dial 911?" After a night of interrogation, in which Carreira maintains he was never told that Andrew's body had been found, the police told Carreira not to talk to the media. Yet he went to Fox Channel 7, which kept him for hours and got an exclusive interview while the rest of the media pack waited for him outside. The police were suspicious enough about Carreira that the Florida authorities were in no hurry for him to collect the $45,000 reward he claimed from them.

Still, Schiaffo believes Carreira's claim that he had been in danger. "If Cunanan had wanted, he could have taken him out," he says. "Then [Cunanan] would have had a gun and keys to a car and been gone. But I think there were a lot of cops out on the street that day—Andrew was looking out the window and seeing cops. Carreira was pounding at the door. Andrew's thinking, 'This is it. Finally they got me.'" He adds,

"He doesn't want to be taken—he's too vain—and he only had four bullets left."

Inside the houseboat, police found .22 caliber bullets under the bed, some "white powder in a clear plastic bag," which was not tested, and a fake passport and driver's license in the name of Matthias Ruehl, the same alias that Torsten Reineck used—Matthias "Doc" Ruehl—as the operator of a gay bathhouse in Las Vegas. The passport and license were from the unrecognized principality of Sealand—a piece of rock about the size of a football field six miles off the British coast. "Sealand" was also the vanity license plate of the big Rolls-Royce Reineck drove around Miami.

The Miami Beach police saw Reineck in Las Vegas declaring himself owner of the houseboat on TV, and they interviewed Carreira extensively about his contacts with the owner. Everything on the boat, including prescription bottles, were in Reineck's name. Understandably, then, Miami Beach police were excited to get a call from the firehouse command post across the street from the houseboat on July 30, saying the owner of the houseboat was there to claim it. "So we're hauling butt up there because we figure it's going to be Reineck," says Dale Twist. "But it wasn't Reineck—it's this guy Ruehl."

If there was any confusion among police between Reineck and Ruehl, it was soon compounded when both disappeared. Reineck had gone voluntarily to the Las Vegas FBI with a lawyer the day following the discovery of Andrew's body. The FBI already knew he was wanted since 1992 in Germany for tax fraud (although Germany had not yet asked for his extradition) and also found out he had overstayed his visa. "He had serious [legal] exposure as to whether he could stay or not," says Las Vegas FBI Special Agent in Charge Bobby Siller. Despite what he had said on TV, Reineck told the Las Vegas FBI that he had sold the houseboat on June 5 to Ruehl. He claimed to be a big fan of Versace's and said he had met Versace's press secretary once, but he claimed that he did not know Andrew Cunanan and agreed to take a polygraph test the next day "on the Cunanan matter only." The Miami Beach police learned all of this secondhand, through verbal updates from Keith Evans. By then police knew that Reineck had a series of shell corporations listed with the houseboat address, but they were not given the chance to shape the investigation with the information they had gathered. "I would have asked different questions," says Twist. "How did they know what to ask? I don't know how they went into that interview."

The question was soon moot: Reineck never showed up for his polygraph. According to Siller, the FBI in Las Vegas didn't even start looking for him again until a week later. "I know we had trouble locating him around the thirty-first," Siller says. By then it had come out in the press that Reineck had briefly declared bankruptcy on the bathhouse in Las Vegas and owed people money there. As it turned out, July 31 was a big day for the houseboat. Under Florida law, a houseboat is like a motorcycle—a bill of sale is all that's required to change ownership. Ruehl had first shown up with a bill of sale to claim the property from the Miami Beach police on the thirtieth. He said he had flown in from Germany via Las Vegas, where he said he had tried unsuccessfully to find Reineck. In order to buy time, the leery Miami Beach police told him that they would have to check the records at the courthouse, and that he should come back in the morning. They drove him to his hotel—and never saw him in person again. Instead, the perplexed police saw Ruehl on the Fox Channel 7 news on the night of the thirty-first; he was shown at the Miami airport, boarding a plane to leave the country. "That day we all looked at each other," Navarro says. "Something's going on here, because only four of us knew this, and all of a sudden Channel 7 knows? We were all pissed."

Meanwhile, yet another German had already entered the mix that day, when Schiaffo was contacted by Siegfried Axtmann, who lived on exclusive Williams Island in North Miami Beach. Axtmann told Schiaffo that he was a friend of Ruehl—who had been "instructed to return to Germany immediately"—and that he, Axtmann, "would be in charge of the houseboat from now on."

The police had heard of Mr. Axtmann. He was one of the Germans whom Agents Dieter and Galleto were investigating, for all kinds of nefarious activities, including "big frauds with a soccer club in Leipzig," Galleto says. Axtmann was a large part of the reason Dieter and Galleto had originally sought to warn American authorities of a connection between Versace's murder and Andrew being on that particular houseboat. Galleto believed that Axtmann—allegedly an owner of one of Munich's biggest whorehouses, which is a legitimate business in Germany—was a partner in the Vegas bathhouse with Friedrich Ewald, a 250-pound high roller who bragged about knowing Versace. According to Galleto, who was acquainted with Axtmann and Ewald, Ewald had shown him a Versace watch he was wearing, boasting that it was "the first one made, and that Versace had given it to him personally."

Meanwhile, the police heard nothing from the FBI. The houseboat remained in police custody until early August; to the chagrin of the city, it quickly became a tourist attraction.

On August 4, the ownership of the houseboat came into question once again. A Miami Beach attorney named Paul Steinberg called Navarro to say that his client Enrico Forti was "the new owner of the houseboat as of June eighth." Navarro says, "I told him I needed proof." Two days later Steinberg called to set up a meeting between Twist, Axtmann, and Enrico "Kico" Forti, a nervous fast-talker who speaks in broken English and who represents himself as an Italian film producer. (He has produced sports documentaries for ESPN.) "He's an artsy-fartsy Ocean Drive film guy," Twist says. "They all seem the same to me." Steinberg counters, "Mr. Forti is a world-class athlete and film producer. He has competed in international tournaments in windsurfing." When I asked if Forti knew the Versaces, Steinberg said "I believe he knows members of the Versace family."

The meeting with Twist took place on August 6, and Axtmann and Forti, who lived in adjoining luxury condominium buildings on Williams Island, showed up together. Axtmann represented himself as a friend of Ruehl and an engineer. He denied he was Reineck's silent partner in the gay bathhouse, but said that he had visited him there twice "to check construction." Steinberg told Twist that Forti—who was planning to sell the rights to access the houseboat—was the one who had tipped off Channel 7 about Ruehl leaving town. Forti had big plans to write a book and make a documentary—*The Medusa*—on the "real" Versace, claiming he had spoken to Donatella Versace about it. With no word about any of these characters forthcoming from the FBI, Twist took the papers to the city attorney, and on August 8 Navarro released the houseboat to Enrico "Kico" Forti in the presence of Steinberg. (When I attempted to contact Axtmann, I got yet a different story from a woman who answered his home phone. She said that Mr. Forti did not own the houseboat, and was merely selling the houseboat rights for Mr. Ruehl. She told me that Mr. Axtmann was unavailable.)

Reineck, who had not been seen since July 24, remained missing until August 11, when he showed up in Frankfurt and turned himself in to the German police, having previously worked out a deal. Leipzig public prosecutor Norbert Röger says, "In my opinion, it was his realization that there was no way out that made Mr. Reineck return to Germany." Scrimshaw thought Reineck had probably been "ordered out of the U.S." by Ewald and Axtmann, who had confided to Twist that Reineck had embarrassed German authorities by going on TV. "Why would a guy go running back to jail?" asks Scrimshaw, acknowledging that again he had nothing concrete to back up his thinking. Reineck, once known as the "beer king of Leipzig," was sentenced to three years in prison for "intentionally delaying bankruptcy proceedings, 152 cases of fraud, breach of trust in two cases, bankruptcy, joint tax evasion and another misdemeanor for fraud." Still, he claims he doesn't know how Andrew ended up on his houseboat—not that anyone official has asked. Even attorney Paul Steinberg says, "something doesn't add up with Reineck and Cunanan." When I ask Steinberg if either Axtmann or Ruehl knew Gianni Versace, he says, "I never asked the question."

Galleto, like Scrimshaw, was disillusioned. He did not believe that Reineck was not acquainted with Andrew Cunanan. At six feet five, with deep sunken eyes and the manner of a middle-aged jock, he had roamed the world as a major narcotics agent for the Germans and at times had been hunted himself. Now he cannot understand why the FBI did not hold Reineck when they had him. "They should take his passport and say, 'Stay until we finish investigating.' The FBI let Reineck go, and the Miami Beach police let Ruehl go." Galleto cannot forget Reineck telling him one day that the burglar alarm on his houseboat was "so good not even a mouse can come in, my alarm is so perfect." Galleto adds, "Carreira: He said the alarm never worked. The owner said, 'not even a mouse.' "

One day Galleto took me on a tour of his Miami in a big beige

Mercedes convertible. We began driving up Collins Avenue with the top down, past the Normandy Plaza toward Williams Island, a gated community once heavily promoted by Sophia Loren. Along the way Galleto pointed out certain high-rises. "This one is half German Mafia, that one is Russian." He knows Miami as a haven for big-time international con men and fraudsters and whoremeisters who are trying to set up clubs there. He said he could not believe the local authorities were letting it happen.

Galleto said that the pimps loved to dress their whores in Versace and claimed that he had seen Ewald, who had bragged of knowing Versace, driving a dark green Rolls-Royce with a vanity license plate that read "Versace." When Dale Twist ran a check on the car, sure enough, the Versace plate was found to be registered "to a bankrupt German" who Galleto said ran with that pack.

While we were driving, Galleto, who keeps a rectangular electronic calendar on his lap, dialed Germany on his car phone. He yelled into the phone, "*Ja, ja.*" The only comprehensible words to me were "Versace" and "license plate." "The mechanic on the car is a friend of mine," he said. "The mechanic used to live in Miami. He worked on Ewald's cars and made the plate for Ewald. He doesn't know why he wanted it."

Galleto is convinced that "Cunanan must have connections to Las Vegas, to the gay bathhouse, and that's why he's on Reineck's houseboat." When I asked Galleto why, if he's so intent on investigating them, they are still so successful in Germany, he answered, "The problem is the German guys know the Russians are coming. So they say to the authorities, 'If you don't give us peace, we'll sell the business to the Russians, who are much worse.' "

When I talk to Bobby Siller, head of the Las Vegas FBI, I ask him whether he knew, via the Miami FBI, that the two undercover narcotics officers had gone to the Miami Beach police and told them all about Reineck and the other Germans. "You have me. I don't know anything about the DEA and those individuals," Siller says. "I'm not denying it—I have no knowledge. I'm not aware of it at all." In FBI records I subsequently obtained, the Las Vegas field office speaks of a number of individuals who identify Cunanan as being in the Las Vegas area shortly before he began his murder spree. One of them even states that he used the alias Andrew DeSilva. The report says, "The Las Vegas office is not prepared to dismiss a possible association between [Reineck] and Cunanan." There is even a heavily redacted report that could be from Dieter and Galleto.

On August 4, after Reineck skipped out on the lie detector test, the Las Vegas field office reported to the Miami FBI, "Leads regarding the [Cunanan investigation] are being left to the discretion of the receiving offices," meaning that if Miami wanted Las Vegas to continue investigating, they should say so. In its final report, issued August 7, regarding who might have known Andrew in the Las Vegas area, the Las Vegas FBI describes the possible associate whose name is redacted as an individual who "closely matches the profile of wealthy gay males targeted by Cunanan to prostitute himself." And in another section, the report appears to come to the conclusion that Reineck and Andrew did know each other. "It is therefore unlikely that Cunanan, who supposedly frequented Las Vegas, would not be familiar with [redacted]." Who would that be? Reineck, the wealthy gay bathhouse owner? After August 7, according to the FBI records I was able to obtain, the Las Vegas office makes no more references to Reineck or Cunanan.

"I'm surprised at the FBI," Scrimshaw says. "They've got this guy— he kills an international celebrity and a rich person. There are all these ramifications. That's it? He's dead—we quit? Why? Because it wasn't their case originally. Because all they were doing was fugitive work. If it's something where they are not the primary investigative agency, they're unconcerned, and they drop it."

After meeting with Galleto, I pose the question of what happened to Paul Mallett, the interim special agent in charge of the Miami FBI at that time, replacing Paul Philip, who took a job with Mayor Penelas's office soon after the Cunanan investigation. "You've seen the nature of our responsibilities here," says Mallett. "Once we solve a crime, unless we need to continue to maintain an aggressive posture, that case is closed."

When I ask about the Germans, Mallett dismisses the "rumors" about the German connection to Andrew Cunanan as "probably unfounded." Then he gives me an answer that is a bit poetic and condescending. "We're talking about a den of iniquity among thieves and con men who lie at the drop of a hat and tell you anything. I don't think you're going to understand it. You're trying to put a leash on a zephyr of wind out there."

Less than a month later, Anthony Pike, the son of a rich hotelier on the Spanish gay island playground Ibiza, arrived in Miami from Australia. He was in town to try to sort out what happened to $65,000 that had been embezzled from his father's account in London. He never found out. He was murdered within hours of being picked up at the Miami airport—shot twice in the head. In what authorities thought was supposed to look like a gay murder, his nude body turned up on an isolated beach on a key near Miami favored by windsurfers. Says a prosecutor, "How many people would know that beach is there?"

The man Pike was meeting at the airport, who was later charged with fraud, perjury, related charges, and suspected of murder, was none other than Kico Forti, the Italian producer who claimed to have bought the houseboat and who wanted to do a book and film on Versace. Forti, the former windsurfing champion, immediately pointed the finger at a German tennis pro, Thomas Knott, who lives in the same building as Forti on Williams Island; Knott in turn implicated Forti, who sold one of his Williams Island condos to make the nearly half million dollar bail.

Knott, who Galleto says is a close friend of Axtmann, has a series of fraud convictions in Germany, where he was jailed. He also was charged with fraud in the Pike case, and in the wake of Pike's murder, had pleaded guilty to one of two federal gun violations. In addition, police found Internet material in Knott's apartment on how to make fake passports. At the end of 1998, both men are suspected of murder, and both are awaiting trial for fraud.

41

Echoes

FIVE MONTHS AFTER Andrew Cunanan died, the "Houseboat of Horrors," as the *Miami Herald* dubbed it, was still making headlines. First Fernando Carreira, who continued to take care of the houseboat, made some headlines of his own. Carreira collected a total of $55,000 in reward money from various entities—the FBI, the Gay and Lesbian Anti-Violence Project and finally the Miami Beach police, FDLE, Dade County, and the Greater Miami Convention and Visitors Bureau—but not without a series of well-publicized struggles.

Within a day of finding Andrew, Carreira had acquired an aggressive lawyer who accompanied him on an all-expense-paid victory lap to New York City for his numerous media appearances. The New York media started a campaign on Carreira's behalf after New York Mayor Rudolph Giuliani refused to give Carreira the $10,000 reward New York had offered because he hadn't called the New York tip line. But when Giuliani wouldn't budge on handing the caretaker his Big Apple reward—which stung Carreira, who had brought along his honorary New York Police Department badge—Miami was shamed into giving him the Florida reward money. "Both Miami Beach and the Feds didn't feel he deserved it," says Dale Twist. "They felt forced by New York—it was political pressure at that point: 'Poor guy, you said you'd give a reward, and you didn't come through.'"

Naturally Carreira disagreed. "Because of me they found him. There were more than a thousand agents, the FBI, the policemen, a thousand a day working around the clock, twenty-four hours a day looking for him. You know how much money I saved the government, the taxpayers?" Carreira, who appeared on *Geraldo* and *Larry King Live* and flew back to his native Portugal for the first time in more than forty years, started wheeling and dealing almost immediately. He was a celebrity now and he even started wearing a knock-off silk Versace shirt. Still, as he disavowed his fifteen minutes, he pithily summed up our tabloid age. "The cameras and the reporters—not the kind of thing I want to be involved in," Carreira says. "But since I started, no way to avoid. So, since no way to avoid, keep going. That's it."

Carreira was also given power of attorney over the houseboat by Ruehl, and he and Forti clashed over who could give access to the media to film the houseboat interior. Forti had already collected a hefty fee from *American Journal* when Carreira gave the go-ahead to the *Today Show* for free, as compensation for his having appeared first on *Good Morning America,* ruining Forti's upcoming deal with Geraldo. Then, just as Forti concluded another deal that would give him possession of the houseboat on December 31, 1997, the houseboat started to sink. By December 23 it was tilting at about a thirty-degree angle. Carreira and Steinberg both claim the sinking was sabotage pure and simple, saying that a diver they hired found a wooden plank wedged strategically between the sea wall and the houseboat to jam the hull.

The city did not bother to investigate—they wanted the houseboat destroyed. But Steinberg raced to court to save the notorious structure, arguing that it was a historic landmark. "Any bathroom, any commode Mr. Cunanan used is not a historical site," Robert Dixon, Miami Beach deputy city attorney told the *Miami Herald.* "This is not a good attraction; this is an infamous attraction." He added, "The owner is just seeking the right to do this B-grade movie on Cunanan."

Before the final disposition of the houseboat was decided, however, Carreira and Ruehl, who had come over from Germany, tried to salvage it. The boat had to be lightened before it could be raised, and a spontaneous sale began when passersby started asking if they could buy items being taken out of it. "So the people start to ask, 'Do you want to sell?' " Carreira relates. "And so I ask Doctor Ruehl and he say 'For sale.' " Drinking glasses and pillowcases that Andrew might have used started going, and soon TV camera crews appeared. "They found out before me," Carreira quipped, but the city was not amused. Carreira got slapped with a fifty-dollar fine for holding the yard sale without a permit.

On January 8, 1998, the city seized the houseboat. The contractor who was awarded the demolition did not have proper insurance, and so the vessel stayed tipped in the inland waterway until January 28. About then, Carreira and two partners started marketing the CareTaker Quick Draw concealment holster, to be worn inside the waistband so that one would not have to fumble as Carreira had when he was confronted with the presence of the serial killer. The nylon holster cost $24.95, and Lonnie Wood, one of Carreira's partners, assured me that a number of Venezuelan generals were interested in buying it.

In early February 1998, a second houseboat owned by Torsten Reineck was destroyed by El Niño.

The Normandy Plaza Hotel changed all of its room numbers lest guests felt creepy staying in the same room as had Andrew.

Turmoil continued to surround the Cunanan case. Although Andrew's autopsy showed that he did not have any drugs in his body, no hair test was done so previous drug use could not be ruled out. "If there is no direct importance at the moment of suicide," says toxicologist Dr. Lee Hearn of the Dade County Medical Examiners Office, "it is of no concern to us." Andrew's corpse became an attraction unto itself at the "teaching autopsy" room off to the side of the morgue, with a parade of law enforcement and city VIPs wanting a peek, some reportedly posing with the body, while others snapped Polaroids. Finally a hand-lettered sign went up. No admittance. One day Scrimshaw got a call complaining that someone at the crematorium where Andrew's body was awaiting incineration was trying to sell the toe tag off his corpse. The body was not shipped home immediately either, because his parents were in a bitter dispute over who should claim them. Andrew's father originally wanted his body to be buried in the Philippines, but his cremains eventually landed in California.

About the only thing Andrew's mother and father agreed on was that their son had been set up by the Mafia to kill Versace. This idea grew out of comments made by Frank Monte, a heat-seeking private investigator in New York who insisted that Gianni Versace, shortly before his death, had hired him to investigate the murder of a friend and to find out whether money was being laundered through Versace's company. Monte's most audacious media moment came when he charged that Andrew had not committed suicide but had been killed before Versace and frozen, then later taken secretly to the houseboat. The Versace family angrily denied that Gianni Versace had ever even met Monte. Nevertheless, Monte's wild assertions spurred many—especially in Europe—to subscribe to the still unproved belief that Versace's murder had been a mob hit.

Clinging to this Mafia conspiracy theory, Andrew's parents sought to cash in on the tragedy. The family started to negotiate with TV producer Larry Garrison, who specializes in signing up the "life rights" of individuals involved in tragic and sensational dramas. Garrison delivers interviews to tabloids such as *Extra* and also attempts to set up movie and book deals. Garrison says he quickly gave up on the Cunanans, however, because there was too much dissension among them. "The father came in from the Philippines and convoluted everything. Then the mother started doing shows like *Hard Copy,*" Garrison says. "The sister Gina didn't want to do anything, so there was strife within the family." They could not agree on "what they wanted to do and didn't want to do."

Except for appearances on *Larry King Live* and *Prime Time Live,* Cunanan's older brother and sister refused to speak to the media if they were not paid. Their mother, though technically bound to do the same, was hard to muzzle. After being burned the first time by *Hard Copy,* which she asserted had tricked her into answering her door for its crew, she appeared on the tabloid show a second time and apparently used her earnings for Andrew's funeral expenses. In October she made another suicide attempt, but in December she surfaced again, on *Larry King*

Live. The producers carefully edited her footage so that she would not appear excessively irrational. Her estranged husband, Pete Cunanan, just in from the Philippines, appeared on the same program but he was taped separately. He reputedly received $10,000 for an appearance on *Inside Edition* but he went on *Hard Copy* for free in exchange for all the Associated Press clippings about the case.

MaryAnn Cunanan's smoky rasp became familiar to the police in the places where Andrew had murdered. She would call to protest an exploitation movie about Versace's murder being filmed in Miami and ask the police to stop it. By fall she was also making impromptu visits to California Cuisine, where the startled staff remarked on the eerie similarity between her cackling laugh and her son's.

The only member of the Cunanan family to eschew making a buck off the tragedy was Andrew's sister Gina, who was overwrought by the publicity the case brought to her just when she had gotten engaged and was planning to start a new life. She also kept an eye on her mother and tried to help her out. Gina Cunanan was married in the fall of 1998.

The tabloidization of events and the resulting money frenzy altered relationships among its beneficiaries. Erik Greenman became a pariah in Hillcrest for accepting $85,000 from the *National Enquirer* to tell stories about Andrew's obsession with Tom Cruise, which people acquainted with Andrew knew to be patently ridiculous. Erik cried all the way to the bank. He bought a flashy convertible and stayed out of sight for months. Nicole Ramirez-Murray had no such qualms about her transactions with the media. The gay activist and drag queen used the $5,000 she had received from the *Globe* for delivering photos of Andrew to get a face-lift—her eighth foray into plastic surgery.

Robbins Thompson regretted having fled to Mexico in the wake of his close friend's crimes. After Andrew's death, he figured he should be remunerated for being so unceremoniously blasted out of the closet. He made the rounds of tabloid TV, getting $5,000 for an appearance on *Hard Copy* and a few thousand more from Sally Jessy Raphael. But Robbins missed the big bucks money by waiting too long. Nevertheless, he ended up with a nice spread about him in the gay journal, *The Advocate.*

Anne and Rachel Rifat were contacted again by the *National Enquirer* the day after Andrew's death and told that the price for their material would be lower now. *The Enquirer,* no longer willing to foot a big fee, put them in touch with the Gamma Liaison photo agency, which paid them $20,000 up front plus 60 percent of the proceeds from their photos worldwide. The pictures appeared in the *Enquirer* and *Newsweek.* Matthew Rifat, Rachel's twin, sold pictures he had taken of Andrew at Bishop's for less than $10,000; he also participated in an A&E documentary on Andrew, with the stipulation, he says, that it was for one-time use only. When A&E made a videocassette to sell in stores, he sued parent company CBS for $7 million for breach of contract and fraud.

The Trails and the Madsons avoided the media, but they were hardly allowed to mourn in solitude. Both couples set up scholarships in the names of their sons. The Trails were struck by tragedy again early in 1998, when Ann's oldest son, Mike Davis, died of a heart attack at age forty-nine. They began to attend church regularly, and they also entered a daunting bureaucratic maze in an effort to retrieve Jeff's gun from the authorities. The Trails wanted to destroy the gun publicly as a symbol of the horror that Andrew had rained upon them and the other victims.

Lisa Stravinskas, Jeff's sister, spoke for all the victims' families after Andrew died when she told the AP, "What we really wanted was for the killing to end, because every time a killing was linked to [Cunanan], it was like Jeff had been killed all over again, and the nightmares and sleepless nights would start again."

In December 1998, Lisa organized in Jeff's memory a gun turn-in program in her hometown of Elgin, Illinois. On December 19, thirty guns and thirteen hundred rounds of ammunition were brought to the police; the program will continue twice yearly.

The Madson family worked tirelessly to convince the public that David Madson had had nothing to do with Jeffrey Trail's murder. They maintained that David had been held against his will by Andrew, and that he had died earlier than the official time of death, several days after Jeff's murder.

On June 16, 1998, more than a year after David's death, the Minneapolis Police Department called a press conference to say that there was "no evidence which would implicate David Madson in the murder of Jeffrey Trail." Without stating it directly, the department was trying to accommodate the Madsons and their attorneys. At the press conference, a formal "declination" of the original request to charge David with Jeff Trail's murder, which had been filed by Tichich more than a year before, was issued by the county attorney's office. It contained some sloppy errors. *Cunanan* was spelled incorrectly throughout the document, for instance, and the day of the week when Andrew and David were sighted walking Prints after Jeff Trail's murder was wrong.

As a result of the Madsons' experience, Captain Strehlow announced that the Minneapolis Police Department was planning to institute a program on how to deal with victims' families. A similar program is in existence in St. Paul, and Howard Madson sent an article about it to the captain with a note suggesting that Sergeant Tichich be the first to enroll. Strehlow concludes, "Something very valuable has come out of this."

The Madsons were heartened, but they are still far from being over David's death. "We realize Christmas will never be the same, but our life goes on," David's mother, Carol, wrote in December 1998. "Losing a son and compounded by death in such a horrendous manner is hard to accept. God gives us strength to cope each day, whatever comes our way."

The Miglin family continued to insist that Lee's murder was a random act. Duke had put his acting career aside for a time in order to help his mother with the real-estate empire. By Thanksgiving 1997, he was also helping her sell her products on the Home Shopping Network.

In April 1998, to the profound regret of Paul Beitler, Marilyn Miglin forced a sale of Miglin-Beitler, breaking up the successful partnership and forcing Beitler to acquire a new partner, Howard Milstein from New York, who in early 1999 bought the Washington Redskins football team. Beitler says that if he had not agreed to an auction, Marilyn would have forced the sale through court action. "This nightmare will come to an end once Miglin's name is off the door," he said. It came off in October 1998.

Yet Beitler has never really gotten over his partner's death either. He was instrumental in having a street named for Lee Miglin, and has attempted to have a chapel built at O'Hare Airport in Lee's name. "Lee was like my father. I lost my father at a very young age—he didn't die, he abandoned me. I lost my mother this year. Lee was like a father to me. It hurt me. A lot of people's lives were destroyed."

In November 1998, Marilyn Miglin, who had suffered mostly in silence, announced her engagement to a suave Egyptian widower via an item in Irv Kupcinet's gossip column in the *Chicago Sun-Times*: "It was a romantic candlelight dinner at the Ritz Carlton Club the other night when Naguib Mankarious presented his love, Marilyn Miglin, with a multicarat diamond ring, especially made in his native Egypt. As a true romanticist, Mankarious had the ring 'served' in the dessert, which caused a howl of delight from the bride-to-be."

There was no hint that it had ever crossed the mind of a single law enforcement official in Chicago that Lee Miglin's murder by Andrew Cunanan could be ruled anything but a senseless, wanton, spur-of-the-moment killing. Weeks after Andrew's suicide, there was finally tangible proof he had been driving the Miglins' Lexus. New Jersey State Police were able to match Andrew's fingerprint with one found on the inside of a back door handle on the Lexus. No Chicago police report was ever issued.

Rebecca Reese, William Reese's widow, went into seclusion after her husband's death. She appeared on camera only once—on *Dateline,* while Andrew was still at large—mostly, she said, because she did not want people to think her husband was gay.

In June 1997, the members of William Reese's 14th Brooklyn New York State Militia staged the first of a series of memorial services for Reese, one of their original founders. The services began in Laurel Lawn Cemetery in Upper Deerfield, New Jersey, and then spread to sister organizations in Gettysburg, Pennsylvania; Manassas, Virginia; and Fort Green Park, New York. At each service reenacters in full Civil War regalia played taps and eulogized their friend. "I don't know if he would have liked it," says his friend Bob Shaw. "He was pretty humble."

Now at the reenactment that draws 30,000 participants to Gettysburg each summer, the hundred or so stalwarts of the 14th Brooklyn hear all about Bill Reese. According to Shaw, "They give a little talk, and Bill's always brought up as a founding father of the regiment. His memory lives on. He's not forgotten, because people want to remember who put it together and did a lot of the work."

Interviewed shortly after Andrew's death, Craig Platania, Reese's brother-in-law, gave an apt description of the effect Cunanan had on the family and those around Finn's Point National Cemetery. "This thing was like a tornado coming over a hill—it's not heard, it's not felt, and all of a sudden this thing appears on your doorstep. Now we can see the tornado way off in the distance, and the clouds starting to clear, and everything that was in its place is now in another place."

The Versaces never acknowledged Andrew Cunanan. "I am sure my brother never met him," Donatella Versace said. In the first weeks after Versace's death, the family did not inquire further of the police investigation. Ironically, the company's sales soared. The tragedy achieved for Versace what he had so craved in his lifetime: the status of having an instantly recognizable name. In a *Dateline* interview with Katie Couric in December 1998, Donatella said she was "angry with people who didn't make sure [Andrew Cunanan] was in prison" before Gianni died. She also said Gianni had been "cured" of his inoperable ear cancer six months before his death.

Gianni Versace's will provided that his eleven-year-old niece, Allegra, would inherit his 45 percent share of Versace SpA, and that her brother, Daniel, would receive his art collection. Both Donatella and Santo already had substantial shares in the company. Antonio D'Amico was given approximately $30,000 dollars a month, "inflation-proof," for life, and the privilege of living in any of Versace's houses around the world. Antonio, however, told a Canadian newspaper, "I'll never set foot again [in those homes] because it would only be fruitless suffering." In a further distancing, Donatella and Santo struck a deal with Antonio to take his monthly payments in one lump sum. He returned to his native Florence to launch his own design company.

The Versaces were intent on managing their own version of the story to create a specially crafted image of continuity and triumph for Donatella, the new designer of Casa Versace. In order to enhance Gianni Versace's image and standing as a "major historical figure of twentieth-century fashion design," they poured significant sums into a major retrospective of his work at the Costume Institute of the Metropolitan Museum of Art in New York, sponsored in part by *Vogue* Magazine, and inaugurated with a gala opening in December 1997 that drew Madonna, Sting, Cher, and Elton John. On December 10, the New York *Daily News* ran a short item about the gala: "Madonna, wearing a Versace sari-esque creation, raised eyebrows when she mentioned in a speech that Donatella 'drops diamonds in her pockets' when she visits. Friendship or marketing? You decide." Ironically, the poster for the Met show was a picture of a sweeping black and white "behomoth eighteenth-century dress" for the San Francisco Opera production of *Capriccio.* Wags gossiped that the Met was quaking during the mounting of the show for fear that some unsavory item from Versace's past would surface to embarrass the august institution. The Versaces, meanwhile, responded to any suggestion of Mob ties to their company with an aggressive legal strategy to punish errant journalists. In England they won two libel actions after Gianni's death.

Initially, the Versaces were determined that nothing would deter their longtime goal of going public with shares of Versace SpA on the New York and Milan stock exchanges. In July 1998, however, they announced that for the time being they would shelve these plans, owing to complications brought on by the estate laws in Italy, which mandated that an outside trustee oversee Allegra's shares. As for Donatella's designs for the House of Versace, after a first wave of sympathy heralded them, they began to receive mixed reviews.

The Casa Casuarina soon became a must for tourists in South Beach. One day I observed a young European woman standing on tiptoe in her miniskirt and clogs and leaning over the chain barrier to finger Versace's junk mail, which had not been pushed completely through the mail slot.

Soon after the Cunanan manhunt ended, the FBI called representatives of a group of gay organizations to Washington for a meeting with the Bureau's then number two, William Esposito. He says he told them, "We need to foster a better relationship, because if you're being preyed upon by killers or victimized, we need to help."

"Esposito began by saying, 'Yes, mistakes were made,' " says Sharen Shaw Johnson, then executive director of Gay Men and Lesbians Opposing Violence. "There was a clear and immediate and unprompted admission on their part that while cooperation was OK in some areas, it was abysmal in others. My sense coming out of that meeting is that they knew very well they were quite vulnerable."

"They started the meeting by emphasizing that in order to solve these crimes the FBI needed to find out more about the community they were in," relates Darryl Cooper, former Chair of Gay Men and Lesbians Opposing Violence. He remembers the meeting slightly differently. "They didn't admit mistakes per se but that they had given wrong impressions—i.e., they weren't doing anything. We tried to explain to them how the gay community is always wary of working with police agencies."

Cooper says that at times he "wanted to ring the FBI's neck—like the times they said [Andrew] shaved his whole body and was wandering around in a dress." However, he adds, "One rumor I heard is that he used crystal meth. I heard it from other Anti-Violence people, but they didn't want to reveal it because it would make the community look bad. Gays want it both ways. I guess because we've been portrayed in such a negative way for so many years there are a lot of people in the gay community who want America to see us as we really are. But I think there is some censorship."

The Cunanan case prompted an outpouring in the gay press about the way gay crime is reported. The well-known Miami crime writer Edna Buchanan felt compelled to go underground after making remarks on TV which were interpreted to mean that the community of South Beach had brought the crime on itself by its campaign to attract gays to party there. Tom Brokaw was roundly criticized for introducing a segment on *NBC Nightly News* by characterizing Andrew as a "homicidal homosexual." Also in the wake of Andrew, GLAAD, the Gay and Lesbian Alliance Against Defamation, issued a glossary for the media to use when describing the gay lifestyle.

The Miami Beach Police Department's handling of the Cunanan investigation, much maligned in the immediate aftermath, was the subject of a report issued by City Manager Jose Garcia-Pedrosa. The report delved into what really happened regarding the sub shop 911 call, the pawnshop form, the parking garage, the closing of Collins Avenue, the role of the warrant service team at the Normandy Plaza, the shutting down of the Public Information Office during the weekend of the manhunt, and the misinformation conveyed to the media concerning the body on the houseboat.

The report said that "the investigation itself was on the whole very well handled by our Police Department. Not only did we 'catch our man' (whose suicide followed an intensive and ultimately successful manhunt), but we did so under relentless media scrutiny and pressure, and in unusual and difficult circumstances." The report chided the Public Information Office for shutting down "in the midst of an international story" and admitted that, "to make things worse for the media, we provided little or no information, deferring to the legitimate though different needs of prosecutors, whose concerns in retrospect, we probably took too literally." The report concluded, "Whatever the weakness in our protocols our Police Department cannot be faulted for not finding Andrew Cunanan before July 15th, especially when one considers that in the past we have not received copies of the FBI's 10 Most Wanted List." (Apparently this reference is to the FBI fliers on Andrew that did not get distributed.)

In order that such mistakes would not be repeated, changes were instituted. The pawnshop detail is now computerized—there is a direct link between the police and every pawnshop in the city, providing instant access to all transactions. The garage is under new management, and tickets must be purchased each day for every vehicle. The police and the *Miami Herald,* which were often hostile to each other during the investigation, in essence kissed and made up.

Inevitably, much of the blame came down on the head of Al Boza, the veteran public information officer. The city manager's office wanted a civilian to take over his position, but at the end of 1998 he was still in his job.

It was not until the last days of 1997 that the Miami Beach Police Department issued its final report on the Cunanan investigation—seven hundred pages in three plastic binders with more than one thousand photos. That fall I met Sergeant Navarro, who still had not been given any information by the FBI to say that Cunanan and Versace had ever crossed paths. I later gave the police the names of two of my sources in San Francisco who told Navarro that, based on their eyewitness accounts, Andrew and Versace had certainly met.

Shortly after Andrew's death, the medical examiner in a public meeting did admit—in a slip—that Andrew had not been HIV-positive. That eliminated one of Scrimshaw's putative motives. At the press conference announcing the final report, Chief Barreto said that the police could not come to any conclusion as to why Andrew had acted as he did. "The real answer to that went down with the ship, so to speak, when Andrew Cunanan committed suicide."

Paul Scrimshaw could not accept that conclusion. Disillusioned, he retired from the force after twenty years in July 1998 and left Miami Beach to live on the side of a mountain in an isolated part of New Mexico. He is still haunted by the biggest case of his career, which he feels he was prevented from pursuing. He cannot get over the fact that the bullet with which Andrew Cunanan shot himself traveled almost the same path inside his skull as the path of the bullet Andrew Cunanan had shot inside Versace's brain. Somehow, in his final desperate act, Andrew Cunanan was creating a parity between himself and Versace, someone whose wealth and fame he had felt should be his as well. Sadly, the only way that Andrew Cunanan could ever achieve any measure of recognition, however, was with bullets, blood, and evil.

Shortly before Andrew's body was found, Robbins Thompson went sailing on Dr. William Crawford's boat with Norman Blachford, keeping a sunset vigil for what they both realized would be Andrew's inevitable fate. Robbins says, "The more and more I think about this, I think he went on a suicide run. He could have gone back to Norman—he was unwilling to do it. It's almost like he wanted the glory to go out with a bang, like a rock star: Live fast, die young, stay pretty."

In an effort to avoid the humiliation of his own failed life, Andrew Cunanan, who had wasted his gifts and lived resolutely on the surface, struck back. Fueled by drugs and filled with rage, his unmitigated ruin also drove him to destroy others, including the only person he had probably ever loved. With the exception of William Reese, each one of Andrew Cunanan's victims—Jeff Trail, David Madson, Lee Miglin, and Gianni Versace—was like a piece of himself. In the end, Andrew Cunanan was a sad testament to vulgar, unrealized aspiration. The little boy who wanted a big house with an ocean view died hunted on the water with a gun for his last companion.

Acknowledgments

It took more than a village to write this book! Hundreds of people helped me: Throughout America scores of men and women gave me their time or searched their files, and I am grateful to every one of them quoted in these pages. My largest debt of gratitude goes to members of the Trail, Madson, and Reese families, stalwart, upstanding people who had no wish to relive the horror of what happened to them, yet were kind enough to endure my interviews and share their stories. I want also to thank the close friends of their sons—Jeff Trail's friends: Jerry Davis, Jon Hackett, Louis Feuchtbaum, Jon Wainwright, Daniel O'Toole, Mike Williams, Chris Gamache, and Judy Fleissner; his teachers, navy buddies, and coworkers. David Madson's friends: Rich Bonnin, Monique Salvetti, Doug and Wendy Peterson, Rob Davis, Cedric Rucker, the members of John Ryan, Co. In Chicago, Lee Miglin's partner, Paul Beitler, was enormously helpful, as was Miglin-Beitler spokesman Mark Jarasek, and Sugar Rautbord. In New Jersey, Linda and David Shaw were pivotal.

I am indebted to the FBI for the exemplary cooperation they offered. The FBI culture is not naturally open to journalists, but thanks to Director Louis Freeh, Chief of Staff Robert Bucknam, who was especially accommodating, and assistant director of the Office of Public and Congressional Affairs John Collingwood—all of whom went to bat for me. I was able to gain access to many helpful individuals in Washington—Roger Wheeler, Stephen Wiley, Roy Tubergen—and various field offices—thanks to Pete Ahearn, Kevin Rickett, Bobby Siller, Paul Philip, Gregory Jones, Paul Mallett, Steve Kives, John Hause, Carl Chandler, Linda Vizi, Ed Cogswell, Tron Brecke. Having access to some records through the Freedom of Information Act helped untangle a very complex chronology and scenario—thanks especially to Mike Shaver and Linda Kloss. A few days before he retired, FBI Deputy Director William Esposito graciously made time to speak with me. William Hagmire, head of the Child Abduction and Serial Killer Unit, gave me valuable insights. Retired head of the profiling unit Gregg McCrary was similarly superb.

To those important few who wished to remain anonymous but who were gracious about participating nonetheless, thank you. There are three names I changed to protect the guilty or the embarrassed.

Across the country many members of law enforcement kindly cooperated and they have my gratitude. In Miami Beach, Chief Richard Barreto, Assistant Chief James Scarberry, Lieutenant Carlos Noriega, and especially Sergeant George Navarro, who went out of his way, allowed me to relive through their eyes the tumultuous time of the Versace murder and aftermath. Retired detective Paul Scrimshaw shared with me the accumulated knowledge of his many years of homicide work without which I would not have been able to put all the pieces of this far-flung investigation together. I am deeply grateful for his patience, intelligence, and perseverance. I am indebted to Miami Beach detective Dale Twist, who generously gave me his time and brought me the incomparable Galleto, also to Paul Marcus and Gus Sanchez, Gary Schiaffo and Richard Pelosi, to Al Boza, Bobby Hernandez, and Lori Wieder. The savvy former chief assistant state attorney Michael Band, State Attorney Rose Marie Antonacci-Pollock, and U.S. Attorney Wilfredo Fernandez all helped me to more easily understand the law. In the medical examiner's office I want to thank Drs. Emma Lew and Lee Hearn for their interesting explanations of forensic medicine. Former Mayor Seymour Gelber was a fresh breeze of candor. I am indebted also to Lieutenant Linda O'Brien of the Metro Dade Police Department and Paige Patterson of the Florida Department of Law Enforcement.

South Beach is an exciting place to explore, filled with amazing characters and enough material to fill volumes of novels. So many people there made my work easier and more fun. My friends at the Hotel Astor, Dana Keith and Laura Sheridan, could not have been more ready to help, as was my friend Zachary Selig. Special thanks. For their general fabulousness and keen insight into their community, thank you to Israel Sands and Bobby Guilmartin, Tom Austin, Brian Antoni, Dennis Leyva, Frank Scottolini, Tara Solomon, Gary Knight, Dr. Ralph Heyndels, Louis Canales, Books & Books. In Fort Lauderdale, Billy Ruben and Howard Greenfield were courtly and charming—thanks to Wes Combs for introducing us, also Bob Wittek. A special thanks to Ian Gibson and Larry Chrysler and those who spoke from Gamma Mu.

In Coconut Grove, thanks to Jack Campbell. Thank you, Ronnie, for all your help, also Roger Falin and Miriam Hernandez and the Normandy Plaza personnel and Fernando Carreira and Vivian Olivia.

Members of the Miami media were especially generous with their time, and I admired their professionalism: Ramon Escobar and Don Browne at Channel 6; Tom Doerr, Rad Berky and Connie Hicks at Channel 10; Glenn Albin and Jacqueline Powers at *Ocean Drive Magazine;* Jim DeFede at *New Times;* Eugene Patron; Linda Robinson and Elise Ackerman at *U.S. News & World Report;* Andrew Delaplane at *Wired* and Dan Pryor at *Scoop.*

In San Diego dozens of people who knew Andrew Cunanan from the time he was an infant until he left Hillcrest have my gratitude. Childhood friends Lou "Jamie" Morris and Robert Arends were able to take me back to the old neighborhood and show me the grammar and middle schools Andrew attended. A special thanks to Delfin LaBao and Sister Dolores and Miss Bobbie Hatfield, who knew Andrew as a little boy, as well as his other teachers and classmates with whom I spoke and their families; at Bishop's, particularly Heidie Hamer and Stacy Lopez. The Rifat family, Anne, Rachel, and Matthew, were incredibly helpful and gracious to me—my warmest thanks for all their kindnesses. Thank you also to Pete Cunanan.

In Hillcrest, where Andrew's acquaintances ran into the hundreds, several people were key to my understanding: Robbins Brett Thompson has my most sincere appreciation, as does Tom Eads, who went out of his way to assist; a special word of thanks is also due to Dr. William Crawford, Franz vonRichter, Stan Hatley, Sheila Gard, Ronnie Mascarena, Michael Moore, J. Buchman, Joe Sullivan, Nathan Fry, Ron Williams, the staff at Flicks, Rick Rinaldi, and all the kind people of California Cuisine, Todd Kaufman, Hank Randolph, Buzz English, Jeffrey Keener.

Nicole Ramirez-Murray is in a class by him/herself.

Originally Anthony Dabiere was a source for my *Vanity Fair* article. After I interviewed him for the book he proved such a knowledgeable resource that I later asked him to be my Man Friday in San Diego. For his humor, his irrepressible spark, and his unfailing good nature while going down all the dark alleys I had him explore, he has my everlasting gratitude.

Thanks also to Billy Sorukas in the U.S. Marshals Service, Lieutenant Jim Collins at the San Diego Police Department, Frank Buttino, Kelly Thornton at the *San Diego Union-Tribune,* Ronald Johnston, and my first San Diego source, Vivian M. Warren.

To piece together Andrew's life in the San Francisco Bay Area, the outstandingly cooperative Philip Merrill and Elizabeth Oglesby were treasures of recall. Andrew's old friends and acquaintances from Berkeley and San Francisco made significant contributions: Doug Stubblefield, Eli Gould, John Semerau, Steven Gomer. Thanks to San Francisco Police officer Lee Militello for her friendly cooperation. To all the great San Francisco bartenders and bar owners who helped me at Lupann's, the Midnight Sun, Twin Peaks, Badlands, the Lyons Pub, and Alta Vista, I raise a glass. To Doug Conaway's sharp eye, I raise a glass.

Minneapolis was one of my first stops writing the article. I met Bob Tichich of the Minneapolis police then, and in the months that followed, throughout the reporting and writing of the book, he never failed to give me valuable cooperation and help for which I am grateful. In addition, Captain Stephen Strehlow, Lieutenant Dale Barsness, Sergeants Steve Wagner and Mark Lenzen, and Detective Pete Jackson were all generous about sharing their experiences on the Trail murder case with me, and I am indebted to them. Also to the efficient Penny Parrish in Public Affairs and Officer John Sullivan. Jennifer Wiberg, Perry Del Ghingaro, and the residents of Harmony Lofts, where David Madson lived, were extremely gracious and helpful, as was Rachel Gold of *Focus Point* in Minneapolis, Esme Murphy at WCCO-TV, Gail Plewacki at KSTP-TV, Dana Evans, Rick Allen, and Brian Wade Smith. Terrill Lamb, who helped the Madson family with media relations, was always a pleasure to work with. R.D. Zimmerman and Lars Peterson were unbelievably hospitable to a complete stranger.

Chisago County has the mythical friendliness and niceness of small-town America made real. Police Chief Randy Schwegman, Sergeant Todd Rivard, County Attorney Jim Reuter, Jeanette Olson, all went out of their way to be accommodating. I also appreciate the help of Dr. Lindsey Thomas of the Chisago County Coroner's Office, Jean Rosen of the Full Moon Cafe, and Michelle of J.J.'s Bowl and Lounge.

To Chicago Deputy Chief of Patrol Jim Maurer, a great guy, Commander Ettore De Vito of the Eighteenth District, and especially Commander Tom Cronin, who generously gave me his time and fascinating thoughts while walking the Miglin crime scene, thanks for trying to pry the lid. Former Chicago Police Superintendent Matt Rodriguez, Medical Examiner Dr. Edmund Donoghue, State's Attorney Nancy Donahoe, were all terrific pros—informative and interesting. Betsy Brazis and Stephen Byer have the potential to be outstanding on-scene reporters and were enormously helpful, as was Mike Fellner and Jim Ludwig of the Chicago Gay Alliance. "Bob," you were super. Thanks to Achy Obejas and Andrew Martin at the *Chicago Tribune;* to Steven Strahler of *Crain's Chicago Business;* and to the Boswell of the Gold Coast, Mark Weyerhauser.

In southern New Jersey and eastern Pennsylvania a great group of local reporters came through for me: Kelly Roncase, Clint Reilly, Eileen Bennet, Jennifer Farrell. My appreciation to the staff of Fort Mott State Park and to Pennsville, New Jersey, Police Lieutenant Patrick McCaffery, Detective Sergeant First Class Tom Cannavo of the New Jersey State Police, Ted Vengenock, Chief Investigator, Salem County, New Jersey, busy men, all who patiently took time for me.

At various points of my own reporting, my colleagues covering the story proved invaluable. I would like to give a special note of acknowledgment to Sue McHugh, working for *A&E Biography,* Wendy Walker Whitworth and Julie Mortz at *Larry King Live,* Santina Leuci of *Hard Copy,* Catherine Bailey of Pendragon Productions in London, all of whom generously aided me at critical moments. Thanks also to all those who were kind enough to provide cassettes and scripts. A big thanks to the hardworking gang at *America's Most Wanted.* To Darryl Cooper of Gay Men and Lesbians Opposing Violence, Christine Quinn, Sharen Shaw Johnson, et al of the Gay and Lesbian Anti-Violence Project, Cathy Renna of Gay and Lesbian Alliance Against Defamation, Dilia Loe, gay activists who provided context and enlightenment, my sincere appreciation.

For helping me to decipher inner workings and finance of high fashion and real estate I owe a large debt of gratitude to Larry Gurwin, whose impressive investigative skills and help I valued, and whose ability to read a balance sheet in both English and Italian made reams of unintelligible numbers comprehensible; Cathy Horyn, my *Vanity Fair* colleague and friend, now at *The New York Times,* was not only extremely helpful but a terrific companion my first days in Florida. Thank you also to Terry Agins, Susan Watters, and to ever-effervescent Christy Ferer.

Dr. Kathy Reback provided valuable assistance about the effects of crystal meth. Sam Schad was very helpful about gay pornography.

Along the way I've bumped into people I knew ages ago, such as Armistead Maupin and David Geffen, who generously cooperated and found old friends, the Zachers, and long-lost relatives, the Kleinbubs, who have all been great supports. So have my friends: Jill Abramson, who read the first half of the manuscript; fellow journalists Sally Bedell Smith and Jurate Kazickas; Laura Handman, a fine lawyer who gave me sage counsel; Kazuko Oshima for her magic; Blair Sabol for her humor; Lorana Sullivan and Suzanne Wright for their encouragement; Bill Carrick and Bee Gee Truesdale, who put me up; financial sleuth Kevin Frawley; his gracious sister, the Ambassador; and Al Kamikawa, my coconspirator.

Throughout the process of reporting and writing this book I have been blessed with topflight assistance. Researcher Catherine Berger provided an exhaustive detailed chronology. I appreciate her gameness in having to go into subjects she considered less than savory. Rebecca Carroll, now in the Peace Corps in China, was brilliant on the computer and brilliant in general, a great help and a real joy. The last third of this book was written in one frenetic month. This would not have been possible without the dedication and excellence of eight months duration of Bridget Bentz, who kept my myriad notebooks and hundreds of files in her head and at her fingertips. Her sunny disposition and kindness saw me through. Peter Griggs was a terrific transcriber and Barbara Oliver a digger nonpareil.

As an agent Amanda Urban is a wonder, and I am deeply appreciative to Susan Kauffman and Alicia Gordon of ICM, and to Cathy Wright-Isaacson, for their efforts. Thank you, Gerry Weintraub and John Tomko, for your faith in me and your patience.

Editor in chief Graydon Carter and managing editor Chris Garret at *Vanity Fair* were with me on this project at the beginning and have been more than understanding about giving me leave to write this book. I think I have one of the best jobs in journalism working for some of the best people, particularly my editor, Wayne Lawson, a living treasure of the magazine world, highly skilled, compassionate, and giving, who has my most heartfelt appreciation. The *Vanity Fair* research, publicity, and photo departments are also uniformly wonderful to work with, and I thank Robert Walsh and Pat Singer, David Hoffman and Susan White and Beth Kseniak and their staffs for the continuing teamwork. And, of course, I don't believe this book ever would have happened without the kind intervention of *Vanity Fair* deputy editor George Hodgman.

My editor at Dell, Tom Spain, has been unbelievably smart, available, and supportive and has given me the confidence to work at the end at breakneck speed. I appreciate the courtesy and dispatch of his trusty assistant, Mitch Hoffman. Thank you, too, to Carole Baron, Leslie Schnur, and everyone at Dell for making my first experience with book publishing so positive. I doubt I would have developed as a book writer at all if it weren't for the patience and kindness years ago of my old and dear friend Larry McMurtry. It took only a quarter of a century, Larry!

Finally, to my family and especially the two great guys in my life, Tim and Luke, who have had to share their space with me for almost two years with a cast of characters they never imagined. They have been incredibly accommodating and tolerant of my comings and goings and helpful in a thousand ways. Our mutual love sustains me.

Index